# Soviet/East European
## Survey, 1987–1988

# Soviet/East European Survey, 1987–1988

## Selected Research and Analysis from Radio Free Europe/Radio Liberty

EDITED BY

## Vojtech Mastny

**Westview Press**

BOULDER, SAN FRANCISCO, & LONDON

Published in 1989 in the United States of America by Westview Press, Inc., 5500 Central Avenue, Boulder, Colorado 80301, and in the United Kingdom by Westview Press, Inc., 13 Brunswick Centre, London WC1N 1AF, England

ISSN: 0887-0500
ISBN: 0-8133-7642-4
Library of Congress Catalog Card Number: 86-641367

Printed and bound in the United States of America.

The paper used in this publication meets the requirements of the American National Standard for Permanence of Paper for Printed Library Materials Z39.48-1984.

10    9    8    7    6    5    4    3    2    1

# CONTENTS

## V. THE ECONOMY ON THE ROAD FROM SOCIALISM

## VI. THE CASUALTIES OF REFORM

## VII. THE CHALLENGES OF NATIONALISM

## VIII. RELIGION CLAIMS RIGHTFUL PLACE

## IX. SPREADING DISCONTENT

# EDITOR'S ACKNOWLEDGMENTS

Preparing the fifth annual volume of *Soviet/East European Survey* was an experience at once heartening and sobering—in regard to both the overwhelming subject matter and the technicalities involved.

So much happened in the Soviet part of the world during the year that even the most inveterate of skeptics must regard as good; yet the fragility of the good was painfully evident. In the selection and interpretation of the major themes, the balance between hope and sobriety was difficult to strike. It was often agonizing to decide what, in a longer perspective, was most likely to prove important and lasting rather than dated and ephemeral—a particularly daunting task for an editor reared as a historian.

As far as the technical matters are concerned, the heartening novelty was the introduction of a state-of-the-art word processing and printing system, which eventually made the publication of the book much speedier without any sacrifice of its physical appearance. Yet the many defects and breakdowns that had to be overcome before the system was made to work with perfection served as sobering reminders of the fragility of the technology on which we are so unwisely inclined to depend.

In overcoming these difficulties while performing the crucial task of associate editor, Clodagh Devlin again deserves the greatest credit—the more so since the editor's presence in Munich, where the project took place, was more limited than before. Its progress, despite his other research and writing assignments as a fellow of the Bundesinstitut für ostwissenschaftliche und internationale Studien in Cologne, was greatly facilitated by the excellent working conditions provided by the Institute.

In Munich, the skill and dedication of Joan Shields, Cameron Hudson, Claude Spiese, and David Wakeman were crucial in making the computers work as they should. Clari Kovacs again provided her typing expertise at important times. Thanks are also due to Evan A. Raynes for preparing the index.

Vladimir Kusin, RFE's deputy director of research, was an infallible source of support. Kenneth Thompson, Director of Corporate Affairs, and Stephen Miller, Assistant Director of Corporate Affairs at the Washington office, proved invaluable for the timely completion of the project.

At Westview Press, its director Frederick A. Praeger and Susan L. McEachern gave the project their keen interest and expert attention.

Vojtech Mastny
Wassenaar, Netherlands

# INTRODUCTION

# THE WANING OF THE SOVIET SYSTEM

## Vojtech Mastny

In the time between the Soviet party plenum in June 1987 and the party conference a year later, changes took place that made the Soviet system of power, as it had been known for seventy years, seem increasingly a matter of the past. If its crucial hallmarks had been the arbitrary exercise of political and economic power, habitual mendacity, routine disregard of individual rights and external expansionism, General Secretary Mikhail Gorbachev's program of perestroika, glasnost, and democratization, complemented by "new thinking" in foreign policy, meant that the system was beginning to wane. The seemingly meager accomplishments in view of what needed to be accomplished must not be construed to deny the fundamental character of what was being attempted. The changes often created more problems than they solved and still provided no institutional guarantees against a reversal. Yet the program showed the political will necessary to proceed with changes substantive enough to make it irreversible. In ways never experienced before, the Soviet Union was becoming a better country to live in and live with.

Having inherited from his predecessors a system decisively shaped by Stalin, Gorbachev at last confronted unequivocally the tyrant's legacy—something that he had hesitated to do earlier. Stalin's misdeeds were condemned as the crimes they were, rather than being circumvented as errors or distortions. Most of his prominent victims, including Nikolai Bukharin and others who had for decades served as the rogues' gallery in the Soviet political mythology, were not only legally rehabilitated but also recognized as what they had been, namely, good Bolsheviks. The rehabilitation did not extend to one of the best of all, Lev Trotskii, whose revolutionary adventurism was not a legacy Gorbachev could comfortably invoke. Also, Stalin's foreign policy, which—unlike his domestic record—had been previously sacrosanct as having allegedly served the nation's interests well, was at last subjected to the criticism it deserved. In a critique suggestive of the new willingness to ask the right questions—the most appealing feature of glasnost—the unavoidable issue of Lenin's responsibility for the system that made Stalin possible was at least tentatively posed. So was the venerated founding father's role in frustrating pre-revolutionary Russia's promise of pluralism—the promise now back on the agenda as a desirable goal.

The words and deeds casting aspersions on the system to which the Soviet officialdom owed its power and privilege fueled unrest even in the highest places.

Political intrigue and an abrasive personality combined to doom Boris Eltsin, the vocal proponent of perestroika who was in charge of the Moscow party organization. The menacingly vague critique of his "errors," followed by his abject self-criticism during the Politburo meeting which sacked him in November 1987, raised fears of a relapse into Stalinist practices. The fears proved unjustified; although Eltsin was relegated to the shadows as an unreliable team-player, his demise did not translate into an ascendancy of perestroika's enemies. Within the leadership, the presumed conservative faction seemed to amount to an inchoate grouping within a large spectrum of more or less willing supporters of reform rather than to any organized group purposefully conspiring to reverse it.

Nevertheless, Gorbachev deemed it expedient to pre-empt attack by reaffirming his course against unnamed enemies of perestroika. Taking advantage of the new openness in the media, the conservatives then attempted to slow down reform in a characteristically underhanded fashion. The attempt took the form of publishing in the main Russian regional newspaper a scurrilous letter to the editor by a Leningrad school teacher, expressing alarm about the current trends and nostalgia for the Stalin days. Gorbachev, ever the master tactician, responded promptly by having a rebuttal printed in the national party daily. The outcome put in doubt the position of Egor Ligachev, known as Eltsin's adversary and the Politburo's leading conservative. Yet Ligachev kept his job as Gorbachev dismissed any speculation about discord within the leadership—under the circumstances a sign of the general secretary's strength rather than his weakness.

In May 1988, his successful summit meeting with President Ronald Reagan further bolstered Gorbachev's position. The summit heralded a new and better era in East-West relations. It put into effect the Soviet-American treaty banning medium-range nuclear missiles—a landmark agreement which, though concerning but a small portion of the superpowers' huge nuclear arsenals, nevertheless prepared the ground for further, more substantial reductions. The treaty incorporated the principles of reduction, verification, and asymmetry—all Western desiderata which Gorbachev's predecessors had rejected. Indeed, the change in the military relationship, which brought about the extraordinary sight of Soviet and American inspectors roaming through each other's innermost sanctums of secrecy to prepare for the scuttling of elaborate and expensive weaponry, was nothing short of breathtaking.

The progress in nuclear arms control rendered more topical the balance, or rather imbalance, of conventional forces. There the Soviet Union was widely believed to be superior, although its superiority was not easy to define, much less to exploit. The coming of a new era was evident in Moscow's indisputable interest in negotiating reductions, despite persisting Western skepticism that the Soviets could not possibly have the incentive to do so. Their acceptance of some of the key Western conditions caught NATO by surprise. As a result, the negotiating position of the pluralistic Western alliance matured but slowly.

The terms of reference of the new Conventional Stability Talks (CST), designed to be loosely associated with the Conference on Security and Cooperation in Europe (CSCE), were being negotiated in Vienna. They were delayed by their linkage with the overall concluding document of the CSCE follow-up conference, in which disagreements about human rights figured prominently. In blocking the necessary consensus, however, the obstacle was less the Soviet Union than the increasingly wily and self-centered Romania. Although the numerous factors involved in conventional arms control made predictions about its progress hazardous, the diminishing role of the military component in the East-West security equation was a significant new development.

While the Soviet Union could hardly be expected to have given up global ambitions, its foreign policy nevertheless took a turn toward accommodation. Rather than embarking upon new adventures in the Third World, Moscow signaled to its clients there that they must do more to fend for themselves. This exacerbated especially Nicaragua's severe economic problems, yet failed to make its Sandinista government any more willing to compromise with the stubborn domestic opposition. Nor did Cuba follow the Soviet example of perestroika in its internal policies. Politically motivated Soviet foreign aid did not diminish everywhere in the Third World, and in some countries, notably Angola, it increased. Yet the incipient disengagement made breakthroughs in some of the main regional trouble spots possible.

Most spectacularly, Afghanistan turned out to be the Soviet Vietnam after all. Discouraged and determined to cut its losses after seven years of inconclusive warfare, Moscow negotiated with the United States and Pakistan the agreement to withdraw its more than 100,000 invasion troops. More important, it proceeded to implement the agreement, despite the probable collapse of its client government in Kabul and the consequent loss of its huge political investment in the country. It also appeared to be successfully pressing its economically destitute Vietnamese allies to quit Cambodia, thus coming closer to the fulfillment of the second condition, besides the evacuation of Afghanistan, that China had set for the normalization of Sino-Soviet relations. The third condition—a substantial reduction of the Soviet forces along the Chinese border—was addressed by their partial withdrawal from Mongolia.

A reassuring interpretation of Moscow's new thinking on foreign policy could be drawn not so much from Soviet diplomacy alone as from the internal changes in a country where the *Primat der Innenpolitik* had always been paramount. Not only did domestic exigencies dictate a more accommodating external posture. More tolerance at home also translated into more tolerance abroad. How otherwise could one explain Moscow's more relaxed attitude toward Soviet émigrés, which enabled visiting Soviet cultural figures even to conduct interviews on the Munich premises of Radio Liberty, officially still the devil's den? The message conveyed there by one of the interviewees, the well-known poet Andrei Voznesenskii, was that a "revolution by culture" was underway in his country.

In view of Russia's distinctive political culture, this was a far-reaching proposition with profound implications for the functioning of the Soviet system. For even though the  nation might be lagging in other intellectual pursuits, there could be no doubt about an upsurge of its artistic creativity—traditionally an effective substitute for political discourse Western-style. The passionate literary battles between Stalinist and anti-Stalinist writers were therefore no mere esoteric skirmishes about novels and poems but closely followed public confrontations about the ideals and concepts that should guide the behavior of the body politic and its trustees. On the outcome of such battles depended not only the careers of the authors involved but sometimes also the directions in which perestroika might be moving.

Similarly crucial was the progressing reinterpretation of the past for a nation which, more than most others, tended to see its history not merely as a record to be known and understood for its own sake but also as a justification of the present and inspiration for the future. Far beyond giving posthumous justice to individuals whom Stalin had sought to permanently disgrace, at issue was nothing less than reclaiming the Soviet Union's European heritage. This could be sensed also in Gorbachev's otherwise controversial invocation of "our common European home." The quest continued with his régime's elaborate commemoration of the millennium of Russia's Christianization as a historic step in the achievement of the country's full-fledged membership in the community of European states. Above all, the urge to account for the Stalinist aberration and consign it to history was suggestive of hopeful stirrings in a nation of great culture for truth, rationality, and civility—stirrings that were as authentically Western as they were un-Soviet.  In opening up to the outside world, both the people and their leaders evidently wished to judge and be judged according to higher standards of decency than those provided by the system to which they had been subjected so far—perhaps the surest sign that the system was on the wane.

For a régime which described itself as socialist, however, more critical was its incipient departure from the socialist economic model of the Soviet variety—a model whose failure after seventy  years of experimentation was painfully evident. Although the Kremlin leaders must not be suspected of any intent to restore capitalism, they nevertheless began to implement economic principles and practices previously ruled out as capitalistic. In doing so, they put the established verities of the Soviet system in doubt.

To encourage agricultural output, peasants received incentives calculated to appeal to their instinct for private property; the collectivized land was to be given to them for secure long-term use almost tantamount to ownership. To increase productivity, wages were being set in accordance with not only individual performance but also the competitiveness of enterprises—a prescription for unemployment. To improve services, genuine cooperatives were introduced and allowed to operate for profit, though heavily taxed. Even the arbitrary pricing system that had been the hallmark of Soviet economic mismanagement was under review to conform with the capitalist principle that prices should reflect relative scarcities. Western economic experts wondered whether these long-overdue reforms could work without conceding the private ownership of the means of production which, according to the Marxist writ, was the *pièce de résistance* of capitalism. Yet even without this crucial concession, worries that reform was already going too far were spreading in the Soviet Union—and not only among ideological diehards.

Unfortunately for Gorbachev, the reforms he rightly described as both necessary and revolutionary had failed as yet to produce tangible material gains while producing tangible problems and sometimes even losses. One problem was the credibility of the old institutions and their personnel in performing new tasks, even if their conversion to the new thinking was genuine; the role and image of the KGB, the nation's notorious security agency, was a case in point. The losses were not only those experienced by officials demoted because of incompetence or worse. The victims of reform included also those countless ordinary citizens who, having become accustomed to simply following orders, were now expected to take the initiative and assume responsibilities. Pressures brought to bear on them endangered the very foundation of the Soviet "social contract"—another hallmark of the system summed up in the quip "They pretend to pay us and we pretend to work." Already job security was being eroded by increased emphasis on performance and mobility. Poverty and homelessness, though far from unknown before, were on the rise.

The pitfalls of reform, noticeable in the relatively docile Soviet society, glared in the rebellious Poland, whose régime Gorbachev regarded as the most congenial. Although the Polish standard of living still exceeded the Soviet one, the country's economy was nearly bankrupt, not merely "stagnant." Its condition was beginning to resemble that of Third World debtor nations, and the necessary remedies were also the same: decentralization, end of price subsidies, wage controls even at the cost of a decline in the standard of living, incentives to private enterprise, and the uprooting of corruption. All this the government of General Wojciech Jaruzelski tried with presumably good intentions, though hardly with the best of expertise, yet the populace, loath to make the sacrifices demanded by a régime it despised, decisively rejected it. The economically sound price increases were thus thwarted for equally sound political reasons in a wave of strikes that rocked the country in the spring of 1988. As usual, the government compromised enough to preclude substantial economic improvement yet not enough to placate the people politically. Greatly though the specifics of Polish nationalism preconditioned the resulting stalemate, the handwriting on the wall was for Gorbachev too, should the Soviet economy further deteriorate.

The challenge to Gorbachev in economic matters was how to implement change; its prevention, or at least control, was at issue in his dealing with the upsurge of nationalism, which cast doubt on the viability of the Soviet Union's sham federalism. The upsurge of Russian nationalism abounded most in contradictions. On the one hand, there was a patriotic rejection of the destruction by the Soviet system of those traditional Russian values that make life richer and more humane. On the other hand, there was a reactionary appeal to the chauvinistic proclivities of the country's still largest, but demographically embattled, ethnic group. Supported in high places, assorted proponents of Russian supremacy posed sometimes as conservatives who branded reformers as unpatriotic, at other times as defenders of reform against its supposedly alien enemies, particularly Jews. Common to both groups were a quasi-Fascist appeal to irrationality as a means of political struggle and a backward-looking political philosophy—expressed either in the desire to uphold the Soviet system in its Stalinist form or in a nostalgia for the still more distant authoritarianism of the tsarist era. Ironically, the fragmentation of the society, which had been Stalinism's foremost accomplishment, inhibited the resurgent Russian nationalism from coalescing into a political force.

The same obstacle did not apply to nationalities whose exposure to the corrosive effects of Stalinism had been shorter—as in the Baltic republics—or to relatively small, compact ethnic groups whose common experience of a particularly fierce oppression fostered solidarity—as in the case of the Crimean Tatars and the Armenians. The ferment in the Baltic states resembled that in Eastern Europe by its blending of nationalist aspirations with demands for political and economic pluralism, which went the farthest in positing both a multi-party system and private enterprise. Yet neither the mass demonstrations against the vestiges of Stalinism nor the endorsement of the nationalist demands by the local party leaderships prompted Moscow to rebuff these fundamentally anti-Soviet trends. The régime chose not to discourage the organizers of quasi-political parties in support of perestroika, let alone those Lithuanian Catholic priests who urged the faithful to pray for the general secretary's continued well-being. With the success of special zones of capitalist enterprise in China before his eyes and perhaps also recalling the autonomy that tsarist Russia had granted to Finland with mutually beneficial results, Gorbachev anticipated the transformation of Estonia into a special economic zone, which would inevitably imply special political status as well.

A more immediate threat to the integrity of the state was posed by nationalist movements that were not inherently anti-Soviet but were directed against a rival nationality. The Crimean Tatars demanded the restoration of their homeland, from which they had been summarily expelled by Stalin but which had since become the home to a Russian majority. Moscow could no longer afford to ignore their grievances but was still able to reject and contain them because of the small numbers involved. No such solution could be readily applied to the Armenians, who took to the streets in their hundreds of thousands, supported by their party and government representatives. Demanding the annexation of the largely Armenian enclave of Nagorno-Karabakh, a formally autonomous territory within the neighboring republic of Azerbaijan, they made the obscure mountain land a household name around the world. The crisis offered a sobering reminder of how easily ancient ethnic feuds could flare up—especially under communism, whose theory and practice had not been conducive to imbuing people with the virtues of conciliation and tolerance.

Centered on an ethnic island regarded as a cradle of national culture in a region of exalted historical consciousness, the demand for the unification of Nagorno-Karabakh with the bulk of Armenia marked a new stage in the perennial quest for self-assertion by a people of an ancient Christian culture, who had been battered and scattered more than most by ferocious foreign enemies. At issue was not resentment of Soviet rule—which, after all, ensured the preservation of Armenian identity within a national homeland. Instead the ferment derived in a circuitous way from the recent upsurge of Islamic militancy in the wider region. Among the Armenians, this was bound to revive the traumatic memories of the genocide their ancestors had experienced during World War I at the hands of Moslem Turks—a people related by race and religion to the neighboring Azerbaijanis. Once the dispute about Nagorno-Karabakh erupted, the suspicion of the Azerbaijanis' bloody-mindedness seemed confirmed by the anti-Armenian pogroms they proceeded to perpetrate with appalling loss of life.

Gorbachev handled this imbroglio with patience and skill. He resisted the habitual Soviet impulse for a massive use of force, even when hundreds of thousands gathered spontaneously in the Armenian capital of Erevan, a general strike paralyzed Nagorno-Karabakh, and the Armenian legislature voted unanimously for its secession—an act which the Azerbaijani authorities promptly annulled with equal unanimity. In the deadlock, the central government was at pains to appear even-handed although it could not possibly satisfy the Armenians without creating a precedent liable to set off avalanches elsewhere in the multi-ethnic Soviet state. It ruled out the transfer of the enclave to Armenia but did not fully satisfy the Azerbaijanis either. Rather than sanction their supremacy, Moscow clipped it by installing in the district a plenipotentiary equipped with vast powers. This could provide better preparation for a genuine autonomy than would have the widely expected but more cumbersome alternative of Moscow's direct rule. To be sure, the viability of true autonomy, without precedent in Soviet practice, was for the future to prove.

Similarly unprecedented was Gorbachev's effective rejection of the notion that in a socialist society religion is condemned to extinction. Although the régime continued to endorse the Marxist dogma of the infallibility of atheism and to anticipate religion's eventual demise, it affirmed the compatibility of religious beliefs with loyalty to the state. Moreover, it improved institutional and material guarantees for the exercise of those beliefs by transferring some of the previously secularized property to the Church. While the Russian Orthodox Church proved to be the main beneficiary, other denominations also benefited from the new atmosphere of tolerance, even though an estimated several hundred people still imprisoned for their faith did not. In the demographically booming Central Asia, the activities of mullahs evading official supervision contributed to a rapid spread of Islam's religious practices. This posed more than a merely imaginary threat to public order in view of the inflammatory fundamentalist broadcasts emanating from neighboring Iran and of the approaching probable defeat of the pro-Soviet Afghanistan régime by Islamic guerrillas.

Religion was becoming a political force to be reckoned with also in those countries of Eastern Europe where it had not been such a force already. In Czechoslovakia, the struggle for religious freedom assumed larger proportions, particularly notable in the Czech lands, perhaps the most profanized part of the region. The aged Roman Catholic Primate of Prague, Cardinal František Tomášek, became a rallying point in the struggle which suffered a setback, but gained wide publicity, as a result of police brutality against demonstrators in the Slovak capital of Bratislava in March 1988. New repression was directed also against East German dissidents, many of whom enjoyed protection by the influential Protestant Church. Soliciting its cooperation, however, the régime allowed it greater freedom than in Czechoslovakia. This proved to be a mixed blessing whenever dissidents expected from the Church support liable to strain its relations with the authorities and reduce the limits of its freedom. The ensuing maneuvering for positions pertained more to future possibilities than to current accomplishments.

In 1987 and 1988, Soviet and East European dissent spilled into the streets as the once tightly controlled police states became the world's foremost stage for mass anti-governmental disturbances. Neither leniency nor brutality seemed to protect the governments against unrest, which stemmed ultimately from their common failure to live up to the political and economic standards that came to be expected in late twentieth century Europe. In Yugoslavia, the most open of Eastern Europe's one-party states, indignant workers hit near the very center of power by marching on the parliament in protest against incompetence and corruption within the privileged ruling class. But in the most rigidly repressive Romania as well, workers in the city of Brașov rioted in frustration about their miserable living conditions, destroying party buildings and other symbols of President Nicolae Ceaușescu's misrule.

The protest in the streets took a new twist with demonstrations against the same target in the capital of neighboring Hungary. Provoked by the oppression of Romania's Magyar minority in Transylvania, and particularly threatened by the Bucharest ruler's bizarre scheme to "systematize" villages by razing them and displacing their inhabitants into urban dwelling blocks, this was the first time that popular protest in one "fraternal" state turned against another—and with the connivance of local communist authorities. Significantly for the resurgence of old ethnic frictions and their ability to overrule other considerations, Communist Hungary offered asylum to growing numbers of refugees from Communist Romania—not only Magyars but also ethnic Romanians.  In contrast, Moscow's new respect for legality found a dubious expression in its policy of returning to Ceauşescu's tender mercies those few of his subjects who had become so desperate as to seek refuge on Soviet territory.

The ascendancy of both legality and spontaneity in the age of Gorbachev did not preclude setbacks of either, thus attesting to an uneven waning of the system. There was a rising awareness of the necessity of pluralism, yet doubts about the desirability of its institutionalization.  Facilitated by the new atmosphere of permissiveness, pluralism found a novel expression in the thousands of "informal groups" that proliferated not only in the main Soviet cities but also throughout the provinces. These were authentic voices of diversity within the society, distinct and independent from the party, diluting though not replacing its monopoly of power.  When representatives of several of the groups convened in Moscow in May 1988 to create a "Democratic Union," vaguely resembling a political party, the authorities disbanded them. Yet when a potentially more disruptive "Coordinating Committee of Non-Russian Nationalities" established itself a month later, it was allowed to exist, at least for the time being. Discussion about the merits of the multi-party system continued in public and private, commanding growing attention. Meanwhile, the Communist party's own willingness to divest itself of direct responsibility for everything amounted to a transition from totalitarianism to a sort of pluralism.  Its form, however, was certain to differ from the Eastern European varieties.

In Eastern Europe, where the ruling régimes were typically regarded as alien and Western-style democracy was widely considered a desirable substitute, independent pressure groups challenged the power holders more fundamentally. In Poland, pluralization had long advanced much further than in the Soviet Union. Even the GDR and Czechoslovakia, despite their resistance to reform, were in their own ways more pluralistic than the Soviet Union. Among East European innovations were plans for alternative national service for conscientious objectors, to be introduced in both orthodox East Germany and unorthodox Poland, as well as Hungary—the one country where pluralization within society proceeded with the régime's blessing, even encouragement.

Unlike in Poland, in Hungary the growth of a civil society tended to blur the rigid lines between the rulers and the ruled. Only there could a person in a high official position—the head of the Patriotic People's Front Imre Pozsgay—publicly condone the activities of an oppositional group posing as a rudimentary political party—the Democratic Forum. And only in Hungary was it possible—though not necessarily accurate—for the régime to maintain that a multi-party system would be compatible with the preservation of "socialism" and continued alignment with  Moscow.  What was not possible was to maintain with any certainty that the political opening up could suffice to resolve the nation's deepening economic and social crisis.

The crisis deteriorated despite attempts at reforming Hungary's previous reforms—by expanding rather than by rejecting them. Sympathetic on both economic and political grounds, the West helped by easing the repayment of Budapest's hard currency debt, the highest per capita in Eastern Europe, and by extending further credits. Yet the absence of a decisive turn for the better left unanswered the disturbing question of whether anything that the West could do would be enough to rescue even the most reform-minded Communist régime. The resulting pressures bearing on the  leadership of the aged, inflexible, and authoritarian János Kádár, led to his reluctant transfer of power to Premier Károly Grósz in May 1988.

The obsolescence of the politician who earlier had presided over making Hungary the most livable country of the Soviet bloc, attested less to his diminishing adaptability to change than to the magnitude of the change itself. Unlike in Prague—where the replacement in December 1987 of the similarly obsolete Gustáv Husák by a political clone, Miloš Jakeš, was mainly cosmetic—in Budapest the passing of the Old Guard was real. All the leading officials associated with Kádár's spent paternalism were replaced by men not similarly burdened. In the end, however, the reformability of the Hungarian reform depended on whether these men could muster enough courage, imagination, and credibility to avoid a relapse into kádárism without Kádár.

The capacity of any system originally modeled on the Soviet one to effectively reform itself could best be judged by what would happen in Yugoslavia—which had already gone  the farthest in repudiating the model, yet found itself in deep trouble all the same. Some of the main reforms attempted by Gorbachev had long before been implemented in Yugoslavia—and found wanting. Increasingly its problems came to resemble those of the Soviet bloc, regardless of its independence from the bloc. Its political system was still a one-party system, only aggravated by the diffusion of power into the largely self-governing constituent republics, and its economy was still a command economy, though its commands were no longer obeyed.

In the fall of 1987, the Agrokomerc scandal in Bosnia served as a catalyst of public indignation about the failings of the Yugoslav system. Managers of the company, in league with some of the nation's highest officials, succeeded in defrauding close to a billion dollars—a feat surpassing even the standards of corruption of Soviet Central Asia. However, the Yugoslav people, educated by their outspoken investigative press, had become sufficiently close to Western Europe to apply Western standards and expect them to be met. Less susceptible to the corrosive cynicism permeating the Soviet empire, they were more prepared to believe that what needed to be done could be done, and to insist that it must be done.

As a result, in Yugoslavia the ruling elite found itself under greater pressure to act than anywhere in the Soviet bloc; however, it proved too divided and absorbed in its own squabbles to rise up to the occasion. The national party conference in June 1988 acknowledged the magnitude of the country's crisis, but delivered no credible plan for its solution. The concessions to private enterprise were not sufficient in a country which already had more of it than any other that called itself communist yet still chafed under the stranglehold of the inefficient public sector.  Moreover, there were signs of a temptation to resort to strong-arm methods. In Slovenia, the most liberal and prosperous of the Yugoslav republics, muck-raking journalists disclosed plans for a crackdown by the armed forces.  Once on trial for divulging state secrets, however, they touched off a public uproar, and the relatively lenient sentences they received suggested that the time for using force to stem the irresistible course of events may have passed.

But what was the irresistible course of events in Yugoslavia and elsewhere in Eastern Europe? Alone except for the Soviet Union, the Yugoslavs did not need to worry about a foreign power that might prevent them from implementing any reforms they wished. Having already become in many ways a part of Western Europe, having grown accustomed to a significant measure of pluralism, and having demonstrated a vigorous spirit of private enterprise if given the opportunity, they were in the best position to complete their repudiation of the Soviet system by complementing their external independence with a functioning democracy and prosperous market economy. The course of reform in Yugoslavia was thus best suited to demonstrate what future, if any, socialism might have also in the Soviet Union and its allied countries. Meanwhile their relations were becoming "Yugoslavized" in the sense of Moscow's preferring to avoid interference and let the local régimes fend for themselves. This foreshadowed more, rather than less instability. Yet while Gorbachev certainly wished to keep the inevitable destabilization within limits, it was no longer clear, presumably not even to him, what the limits were.

As the Soviet system of power was thus waning also in matters of alliance management, opportunities for Western influence in Eastern Europe grew. But their exploitation depended on the interest and resources available, and in this regard only one country qualified in full—West Germany.  Heir to a nation whose historic involvement in the area had been even longer and deeper than

Russia's, it alone had the political conception and economic base necessary to provide the East Europeans with the assistance they so badly needed. At issue was not competing with Moscow for power and influence—something that most Germans loathed—but a redefinition of their historic role in the region to promote its pluralization.

In its diplomatic activism, Bonn had surpassed other Western nations. Besides its special relationship with the GDR, which was no negligible factor in the East German state's relative economic success, the Federal Republic established close rapport with Hungary. Its massive loan to Budapest was calculated to boost reformism. Also with Bulgaria, another historically Germanophile nation, the relations quietly flourished. In the fall of 1987, the West Germans established diplomatic ties with Albania, and proceeded to position themselves as its chief provider of modern technology. In the Polish political minefield, they cultivated the régime without alienating the opposition. There was even progress toward more normal relations with Czechoslovakia, a particularly difficult neighbor, during Chancellor Helmut Kohl's visit to Prague, where he met not only with his official hosts but also with their critics. For enough reasons, therefore, the Soviet Union took the Federal Republic ever more seriously.   Gone was the flogging of the dead horse of German "revanchism" as official and unofficial visits proliferated and the eastward flow of credits gained momentum. Voices were even heard from Moscow which wishful thinking could interpret as favorable to German reunification, but which were more likely merely indicative of the range of opinion now permissible there.

Uncertainties about where the Soviet Union might be moving were widely expected to be clarified at the special party conference convened in Moscow in June 1988. This was preceded by remarkably open debates conducted at countless party meetings and in the media. The conference itself, not designed to make binding decisions, failed to meet the highest expectations. But it added substance to the notion that the Soviet system was on the wane, albeit unevenly. On the one hand, there was a perceptible yearning to revitalize the real or imaginary merits of the system's original pristine state, attributed to the genius of Lenin. On the other hand, enough happened during the proceedings that was suggestive of a desire to repudiate wholesale, though not necessarily in so many words, much of what the system had stood for since its inception. The difference was more temperamental than substantive, for there was no question of either recreating the conditions that had once brought it into being, or of gainsaying the necessity of rejecting what it had become. Still, temperamental differences sufficed to ensure a genuine and lively discussion, which left no doubt that the repression and manipulation of opinion that had been the system's hallmark ever since Lenin were no longer taken for granted.

In his keynote speech, Gorbachev unexpectedly presented proposals for institutional change that would provide safeguards against arbitrary exercise of power. He envisaged a presidential form of government consisting of a powerful president of the Supreme Soviet who would be elected by and responsible to a new assembly chosen by popular vote. At the same time, the local soviets were to be transformed into more genuinely representative governmental bodies. The gist of these innovations was a rudimentary system of checks and balances and something more than a mere semblance of a government by the people. Allusions were made to the American rather than the European form of democracy.

There was still a long way from what Gorbachev insisted would remain a one party state to a genuine democracy. Yet his vision also marked a long way from what the Soviet system had been in not only its Stalinist but also its Leninist variety. The proposed presidency, for which he himself was the obvious candidate, was no attempt at crypto-Stalinism, for the goal was not solely to equip the incumbent with impressive powers but also to credibly limit them. As far as the new soviets were concerned, they were to resemble neither those that had enabled the Bolsheviks under Lenin to manipulate politically inarticulate masses nor the earlier, spontaneously created committees that had given the institution its name before the Revolution. Rather than manipulated or spontaneous, the reformed soviets were to provide an institutional expression of the new respect for the rule of law that Gorbachev deemed necessary for the functioning of a modern state.

If implemented, these institutional reforms promised to amount to a critical turning point in the waning of the Soviet system and the waxing of something else that was yet to take shape. Yet institutional change, while a precondition for deeper political, economic, and social change, does not alone guarantee it. Italian historians, when referring to that great exertion of mind and will known as the *Risorgimento*, which brought about the institutions of the Italian state in the nineteenth century, have coined the phrase *"rivoluzione mancata."* The allusion is to a turning point at which history failed to turn, in Italy's case superseding the previous "era of stagnation" but otherwise leaving the country much as it had been before, and postponing its push to modernity for another hundred years. This kind of specter Gorbachev did not succeed in banishing.

# I. GORBACHEV BETWEEN RIGHT AND LEFT

## 1
## GORBACHEV CONFRONTS STALIN'S LEGACY
Vera Tolz

The entire first part of the speech that Mikhail Gorbachev delivered to mark the seventieth anniversary of the October Revolution was devoted to the history of the USSR and, in particular, to the period of Stalin's rule.[1] As was expected in the West, Gorbachev laid down the official party line on the Soviet past at a time when sharp press debates over Stalin's legacy were taking place between Soviet writers, journalists, and historians.

Some Soviet intellectuals clearly entertained high hopes of the speech, expecting Gorbachev to give due credit to those of Lenin's associates who fell victim to Stalin's purges. Soviet playwright Mikhail Shatrov, whose works were concerned primarily with examining the historical alternatives to Stalin's rule and promoting the rehabilitation of the revolutionary Nikólai Bukharin, told Western journalists on October 14, 1987, that once Gorbachev's speech had been delivered, a previously published encyclopedia of the Great October Socialist Revolution would look "shameful."[2] The encyclopedia, while including separate entries on such of Stalin's victims as Trotskii, Bukharin, Zinovev, and Kamenev, claimed that there was no real alternative to Stalin, and that Stalin was absolutely right in crushing the opposition posed to him by Trotskii and Bukharin.[3]

Shatrov's forecast proved wrong. In evaluating the Soviet past, Gorbachev adopted a very cautious position, similar both to that outlined in the encyclopedia to which Shatrov referred, and to that spelled out by the more conservative Soviet historians, including ninety-one-year-old Academician Isaak Mints, who was once one of Stalin's top historians.[4]

In his assessment of Stalin's rule, Gorbachev also followed the line laid down in numerous speeches by chief ideologist Egor Ligachev, according to which although Stalin had often used the wrong methods, he nevertheless put the Soviet Union on the map as one of the world's leading industrial powers. Therefore, criticism of Stalin's mistakes should not be allowed to descend into criticism of the Socialist system as a whole.[5] The main message of Gorbachev's speech in regard to historical issues was that in the second part of the nineteen-twenties, after Lenin's death, there had been no real alternative to Stalin in the party, and that Stalin had been the best man to implement Lenin's ideas on the development of socialism in the USSR.

Contrary to the expectations of some Soviet intellectuals and Western observers, Gorbachev criticized the leaders of the anti-Stalin opposition in the party. Gorbachev said that at the end of the nineteen-twenties—the time of discussions within the leadership on the future of the Soviet state—some revolutionaries demonstrated their "petty-bourgeois nature" and put their own ambitions higher than the interests of the state. This, according to Gorbachev, applied above all to Leon Trotskii, whose arrogance and inconstancy had been criticized by Lenin. Trotskii did not believe in the possibility of building socialism in the USSR, Gorbachev said, and was supported in his wrong views by two other revolutionaries—Lev Kamenev and Grigorii Zinovev. They were rightly criticized by Stalin, and their opposition was rightly crushed, Gorbachev suggested. The fates of Trotskii, Kamenev, and Zinovev were not specified by Gorbachev.

Gorbachev's critical attitude toward these victims of Stalin was not surprising. In April 1987, *Sovetskaia Rossiia* published a lengthy article condemning Zinovev's and Kamenev's views,[6] and in September the same newspaper carried an article stating categorically that the rehabilitation of Trotskii was not on the agenda.[7]

Gorbachev's evaluation of the role of another of Stalin's opponents, Nikolai Bukharin, was disappointing. Since the beginning of 1987, Bukharin, who had opposed Stalin's policies of rapid industrialization and forced collectivization and supported the more gradual introduction of Socialist principles in agriculture and industry, was presented in a favorable light in articles in the press and literary works. Moreover, in July, *Literaturnaia gazeta* published a short play by political journalist Fedor Burlatskii that depicted Bukharin as both a viable and desirable alternative to Stalin.[8]

According to Gorbachev, Bukharin's theories were not applicable, since Bukharin had failed to take into account the importance of the time factor—the need for rapid development of the USSR—foreseen by Stalin. Gorbachev failed to clear Bukharin, Zinovev, and Kamenev of the absurd charges of being agents of foreign intelligence leveled against them by Stalin in the nineteen-thirties. The need to withdraw these charges had been stressed even by such conservative historians as Professor Iurii Poliakov, who discussed the issue at a press conference in Moscow at the beginning of October.[9]

According to Gorbachev, Stalin deserved criticism for the methods he used to implement his plans: they were too administrative and at times brutal. The main example cited by Gorbachev was the collectivization of agriculture. A more careful approach to the peasantry had been needed, Gorbachev said; but collectivization had been the only correct policy.[10]

With regard to the methods used by Stalin to implement his policies, Gorbachev criticized as false Stalin's theory that the class struggle would become more intense during the development of socialism in the USSR. This theory, Gorbachev said, had resulted in the unjust repression of thousands of innocent party members and ordinary people.

In speaking of Stalin's mass arrests, Gorbachev merely mentioned in passing that Stalin's violations of legality were a departure from socialism. Again, contrary to expectations, he failed to examine the causes and conditions that led to the emergence of the Stalin cult, regarded by many Soviet intellectuals as the most crucial issue of all. Gorbachev's cautious position was reflected in his evaluation of Stalin as a military leader. He failed to refer to the mistakes made by Stalin on the eve of World War II but insisted that the Soviet Union had no choice at the time but to sign the non-aggression pact with Nazi Germany in 1939.

The occasion on which the speech was delivered significantly limited the possibility of any really sharp criticism of the USSR's past. Traditionally, such anniversary speeches were concerned primarily with praising the country's achievements rather than criticizing its failures. Gorbachev seemed not to want to break this tradition. It remained  uncertain what effect Gorbachev's speech would have on the debates about Stalinism among Soviet intellectuals, debates which diverged greatly from the positions adopted in his speech.

## 2
## THE ELTSIN AFFAIR
### Alexander Rahr and Kevin Devlin*

*The Champion of Reform.* In the week leading up to the celebrations of the seventieth anniversary of the October Revolution, Moscow was swept by rumors about a serious leadership dispute. The clash occurred at the Central Committee plenum on October 21, 1987, when Boris Eltsin, candidate member of the ruling Politburo and first secretary of the Moscow City party Committee, criticized the unsatisfactory pace of perestroika.[1] Eltsin, who spoke directly after Gorbachev, reportedly referred to the creation of a personality cult around the general secretary and accused ideologist Egor Ligachev of being partly responsible for slowing down reforms. In response, Ligachev and the head of the KGB, Viktor Chebrikov, attacked Eltsin for his

---

*Author of the section on the *Corriere della Sera* article

own failures in running Moscow.

At a news conference on October 31, Central Committee Secretary Anatolii Lukianov confirmed these rumors.[2] Lukianov explained that Eltsin had not been supported by other members of the Central Committee and as a consequence had offered to resign.

Eltsin and Ligachev were regarded as representing opposite poles within the Gorbachev leadership. Since replacing Viktor Grishin as first secretary of the Moscow City party Committee in late 1985, Eltsin had acquired a reputation as being one of the most outspoken members of Gorbachev's leadership and the strongest supporter of the general secretary's campaign for glasnost. At the Twenty-Seventh Congress of the CPSU in 1986, he had delivered the most open criticism the public had heard for decades. Eltsin laid great emphasis on glasnost, declaring that no leader should be allowed to be above criticism, and attracted particular attention by calling for the abolition of special benefits for party officials.[3]

Later in the year, Eltsin attracted further attention with two other speeches at party meetings in Moscow. A samizdat account of an address in April in which he discussed the shortcomings of the Moscow City party apparatus caused a sensation when it reached the West. At a meeting in July, Eltsin lambasted the  main diplomatic training schools for their encouragement of privileges and corruption.[4]

During a visit to West Germany in May 1987, Eltsin discussed the Chernobyl nuclear accident with German politicians. He also impressed Western journalists by giving rare interviews to the newspaper *Die Zeit*[5] and the magazine *Stern*.[6] In October, the Yugoslav magazine *Nin* published an interview in which Eltsin discussed political change in the Soviet Union.[7]

*A Shift of Power in the Kremlin?* Some analysts have suggested that Gorbachev suffered a political setback late in the summer of 1987.[8] In June he had emerged triumphant from the Central Committee plenum, having succeeded in placing three of his allies—the CPSU Central Committee Secretaries Aleksandr Iakovlev, Nikolai Sliunkov, and Viktor Nikonov—in the Politburo. Senior officials in Washington judged that he had "finally turned the corner," and it was rumored in Moscow that his close adviser, Iakovlev, was being groomed to take over from Ligachev as chief ideologist.[9] The promotion of Iakovlev, who had been very outspoken on issues of democratization, was regarded as an important precondition for the success of the long-awaited liberalization process in the Soviet Union and raised hopes for further implementation of economic reforms. Furthermore, Gorbachev, during his tour of farms in Moscow Oblast on August 5, announced that a Central Committee plenum would soon be convoked to discuss agricultural reform.[10]

Only a few weeks later, however, Western diplomats discerned among the party leadership unexpected signs of growing opposition to Gorbachev's reforms. On August 7, Gorbachev dropped from public view, and he did not appear again in Moscow until September 29. During his absence, Kremlin politics were orchestrated by Ligachev, who seemed to consistently advocate a more cautious approach to reform, urging restraint in revisions of Socialist doctrine and   practice. His views placed him in alliance with Viktor Chebrikov, who, as head of the KGB, voiced concern over the increasing number of demonstrations in Moscow and the Baltic States.[11] It seems that, under Ligachev's guidance, the conservatives were able to strengthen their influence and reverse some of the trends Gorbachev's policy of democratization had set in motion.

Two of the most outspoken supporters of reform—Eltsin  and the chief editor of *Moscow News,* Egor Iakovlev—became the main targets of the conservatives' attack. Ligachev reportedly reprimanded Iakovlev at a jour- nalists' meeting on September 16 for having printed Viktor Nekrasov's obituary without permission. Iakovlev subsequently wrote to Gorbachev, who at that time was away from Moscow, and placed the chief editorship of his journal at the  disposal of higher authority; but the general secretary refused to accept Iakovlev's resignation and intervened in his behalf.[12]

*Eltsin and Ligachev.* Eltsin's discontent with Ligachev's management of the Central Committee Secretariat became evident in his speech to the Twenty-Seventh Congress of the CPSU in February, 1986.[13] The Moscow party chief again criticized the way things were run by the party secretariat at a Politburo meeting on the eve of the Central Committee plenum held in January, 1987.[14] Gorbachev later admitted that the plenum had had to be delayed three times owing to controversies among the Soviet leadership. It later became known that the Politburo then decided against Eltsin and in  favor of Ligachev.[15] This may perhaps be the reason why he never gained full membership of the Politburo.  On numerous occasions Eltsin complained about Ligachev's resistance to radical changes in the Moscow party organization. Ligachev seems to have used all his authority to prevent conser- vative party officials from losing their jobs. Apparently he was informed about all Eltsin's actions by the head of the city's cadres department, Vladimir Skitev, who said that he had bypassed Eltsin and sent secret reports "to the Central Committee"[16] (presumably, to Ligachev himself). Others tried to provoke Eltsin by accusing him of "Bonapartism."[17] (This term was used in an anonymous note to Eltsin at a Moscow party meeting in April, 1986.  In November 1987, the accusation was made openly at the plenum of the Moscow City party Committee that ousted Eltsin from his job.)

Three months after the January plenum, Eltsin, in an interview with *Mos- kovskaia pravda,*[18] made an indirect reference to his differences with Ligachev, saying that "there are diametrically opposed viewpoints, ranging from the radical—'eliminate,' 'abolish,' 'introduce tomorrow'—to the cautiously skeptical: 'aren't we going too fast?' and 'more haste, less speed.'" In view of the accusations that were to be made against Eltsin seven months later, the following passage in his interview acquires a certain irony:

> It is impossible to find our bearings unless we can chart a clear course between pernicious sluggishness and impermissible haste and bustle. We may also lose our political sense of touch. The person who over-dramatizes temporary setbacks and panics at the absence of instant benefits is just as politically immature as the person who underes-timates how little time there is and postpones matters, waiting for "the necessary conditions" to be created (by whom?).

In his speech on the seventieth anniversary of the October Revolution, Gorbachev criticized these positions as "avantgardism" and "conservatism" respectively.[19]

Tensions mounted during Gorbachev's summer absence. At a meeting on September 26, Eltsin reportedly asked Ligachev to give the Moscow City Committee "more autonomy" in the reshuffling of personnel,[20] but Ligachev, who had always emphasized that reforms should be conducted within the framework of scientific socialism and through the medium of party organs, could hardly agree with Eltsin's caustic complaints that despite frequent personnel changes he was unable to find people capable of carrying out reforms efficiently and intelligently. In consequence, Eltsin sent a letter of resignation to Gorbachev, who was still absent from Moscow. When he returned, he told Eltsin that the period just before the festivities marking the anniversary of the revolution was not an appropriate time to discuss such matters. Nonetheless, Eltsin raised this issue directly at the Central Committee plenum, bypassing the Politburo.

*The Clash in the Central Committee.* The account of the October plenum of the Central Committee was not published, but Gorbachev's speech to the plenum of the Moscow City party Committee in November[21] and the testimony of Moscow brigade leader Vladimir Zatvornitskii, which was printed in *Sovetskaia Rossiia*,[22] shed some light on what happened at the closed-door meeting.

In his speech at the plenum of the Moscow City party Committee, Gor-bachev pointed out that Eltsin had criticized not only the work of the Politburo and the Secretariat, but also "individual comrades." According to Gorbachev, Eltsin attempted to present the "atmosphere" in the Politburo, particularly as regards the principles of "collegiality," in a false light. Gorbachev's words gave the impression that Eltsin had named Ligachev (among others) as an obstacle to reform and that he may even have criticized the general secretary himself—as is suggested by some Western sources—for deviations from the principles of "collegiality" or of "collective leadership."23

Eltsin's remarks aroused a storm of debate, not only at the Central Committee plenum but in the days that followed. Describing the reactions of those present at the plenum to Eltsin's "outburst," party Secretary Anatolii Lukianov said that members of the Central Committee did not agree with him and that " *many* [emphasis added] felt that there were political mistakes in his statement."24 Lukianov added that he himself had been *"among those* [emphasis added] who had disagreed with Eltsin." Lukianov's remarks indicated that not all speakers at the plenum condemned Eltsin. Unofficial sources reported that at least three members of the Central Committee—Aleksandr Iakovlev, Gennadii Kolbin, and Georgii Arbatov—agreed with some of Eltsin's criticism.25

An analysis of all the available material shows that Eltsin's critics held widely differing opinions as to what was wrong with his work. KGB chief Viktor Chebrikov, for example, recalling Eltsin's acknowledgement to Western diplomats that the Soviet Union had the world's largest number of prisoners, accused him of "talking too much about matters outside of his field."26 The conservatives blamed Eltsin for having declared war on the party cadres. Zatvornitskii, on the other hand, in the above-mentioned article in *Sovetskaia Rossiia*, seemed to take a more moderate view of the affair, criticizing Eltsin primarily for his threat to resign:

> You can't just drop everything halfway and go off to the sidelines, so many promises were made, people believed them and became enthusiastic, and suddenly there is the capricious gesture.... Responsible people involved in serious work do not do that kind of thing.27

But the reformists also sharply criticized Eltsin for discrediting perestroika and thus serving the ends of the conservative opponents of reform. A prominent professor of economics, Gavriil Popov, later described Eltsin's position as "authoritarian conservative avantgardism" and even compared his "shake-out of personnel" with tactics promoted in the early nineteen-twenties by Leon Trotskii.28 Eltsin's desire to achieve perestroika at an unrealistically rapid pace was also criticized by his successor as Moscow party boss, Lev Zaikov, at a gathering in Warsaw.29

At the Central Committee plenum, Gorbachev smoothed over the row, saying that, in view of the approaching anniversary of the October Revolution, the Politburo should not fire Eltsin. The party leadership showed no compunction, however, in dropping First Deputy Premier Geidar Aliev from the Politburo at that time. The true reason why Gorbachev, as Zatvornitskii put it, "did his utmost" to keep Eltsin in his job[30] seems to have been that the general secretary regarded the fortunes of perestroika in Moscow as a kind of litmus test of the restructuring process in the country as a whole. Eltsin was not, in fact, any more radical than Gorbachev himself in replacing personnel; in two years, Eltsin had replaced 80 percent of the Moscow Raion first party secretaries and 40 percent of the chiefs of the city party committee departments. By way of comparison: on the all-Union level, there had been a turnover, since Gorbachev came to power of 70 percent of the heads of Central Committee departments, 60 percent of the USSR ministers, and 46 percent of the obkom and kraikom first secretaries.

Eltsin's boldness in speaking his mind without regard for the consequences also seems to have played a role in his downfall. In an address to those attending anniversary festivities held at the Bolshoi Theater on November 5—only two weeks after the latest Central Committee plenum, which had been presided over by Ligachev—Eltsin shocked his audience by saying that the reforms were getting bogged down and that, if the country's problems could not be dealt with at a rapid pace, the Soviet Union was heading toward a crisis.[31] Unofficial sources told Western journalists that Gorbachev had telephoned Eltsin the next day to ask him to reconsider his threat to resign, but that Eltsin had refused to do so unless Ligachev apologized for attacking him at the Central Committee plenum.[32]

According to one usually well-informed Western source, Eltsin suffered from an incurable disease,[33] and this may explain his impatience with the speed of reform. He was hospitalized before the plenum of the Moscow City party Committee and left the hospital only in order to attend the meeting.[34]

Western diplomats were shocked by the way local party officials attacked and humiliated their former boss at the Moscow party Committee plenum. In his article about that meeting, Zatvornitskii deplored the fact that only Eltsin's opponents—mainly the raion party secretaries—were allowed to speak.[35] This suggests that the events at the plenum were staged in advance—in the old Stalinist manner.

Eltsin's demotion provoked several demonstrations in Moscow and Sverdlovsk. It was the second time within a year that a decision of the leadership to replace a high party official had met with popular resistance: in December 1986, the replacement of Kazakh party chief Dinmukhamed Kunaev with the Russian Gennadii Kolbin had led to serious riots in Alma-Ata.

Despite the harsh criticism leveled against him, Eltsin was not totally banned from the leadership nor even expelled from the party—measures that might have been expected to be taken against a man who had been officially accused of "political mistakes." He found refuge under the aegis of USSR Deputy Prime Minister Iurii Batalin, who headed the State Committee for Construction from 1986.

After Eltsin's fall, Western observers detected signs of a slowdown in the process of reform.[36] Only a few days after Eltsin's ouster, *Pravda* published an article entitled "Democracy and Discipline," based on readers' letters.[37] The article warned that "playing at democracy might lead to catastrophe" and, by counterposing democracy to discipline, appeared to set limits on the process of democratization launched by Gorbachev. The views expressed in the article appeared to echo Ligachev's position.

*Soviet Journalist Explains Eltsin's Ouster.* On May 12, 1988, the Milan daily *Corriere della Sera* published a long and extraordinarily frank interview with Soviet journalist Mikhail Poltoranin, a strong supporter of perestroika who served as editor in chief of *Moskovskaia pravda* during the last ten months of Eltsin's tenure as Moscow party secretary.

Poltoranin described the struggle for perestroika against an entrenched network of vested interests in terms of dynamic reformers from Siberia tackling corruption and incompetence in the capital. Moscow posed special problems, Poltoranin said; with all the head offices located there, and all the ministers belonging to the Moscow party organization, "no one dared to ask too much of the city's enterprises."

When [Viktor] Grishin was Moscow party secretary, the officials only pretended to work; but things functioned, because bribes and corruption flourished everywhere.... Eltsin tried to bring order into this mess—to stop the feuds and intrigues and to cut through the network of mafia-like corruption. As a result, the whole apparatus went into opposition.

The Italian reporter remarked that, as he understood it, Eltsin's fall was due not only to resistance within the Moscow party apparatus, but also to the fact that he had "enemies higher up." Poltoranin agreed:

Certainly, there was the conflict with Ligachev. Their relationship reached a crisis point on the question of social justice. In Moscow, Eltsin had begun to close down the special stores for officials and to abolish other special privileges for the nomenklatura. He tried, for example, to reestablish order in the special schools reserved for the children of high officials. He had begun to do what the people wanted. Ligachev says that this is "social demagoguery." According to him, one should not touch existing privileges but should improve conditions for those who do not enjoy certain opportunities.

The conflict between Eltsin and Ligachev, Poltoranin continued, was further sharpened by the fact that the apparatus, seeing this division, hastened to send to higher levels distorted reports that were harmful to Eltsin. The result was that some ministries that should have helped to finance development projects in Moscow gradually cut off funds.

Another circumstance that contributed to Eltsin's frustration, Poltoranin said, was the fact that almost all the party officials in Moscow had a patron higher up. Toward September 1987, Poltoranin got the impression that Eltsin had "even been deprived of the possibility of replacing leaders of the various raion committees."

After painting this picture of impotent frustration on the part of a man who had mounted a spirited but ultimately vain campaign against the entrenched forces of bureaucratic inertia, privilege, and corruption, Poltoranin was asked about the circumstances of Eltsin's removal from office. At the Moscow party plenum at which Eltsin was ousted, Poltoranin said,

> his main accusers were those whom he had removed and, above all, those whom he had not succeeded in removing. On the other hand, we—those who had collaborated with him—had no right to speak, because we had arrived in Moscow after the city party congress, and so had not been elected to the Executive Committee.

Poltoranin went on to say that "Eltsin was on the ropes, and he knew it. I think that this difficult psychological situation influenced his speech at the plenum in October, which brought down on him the condemnation and disavowal of the Central Committee." When the interviewer mentioned that that speech had never been published, Poltoranin said he could not talk about it, because it was the business of the Central Committee. He added, however:

> Certainly the copies that one can buy at street stalls are a blatant falsification, put into circulation in order to harm him, to make him look stupid. But if one knows what went before, it is not difficult to imagine what he would have said at the plenum. Anyhow, even before the Central Committee plenum, in his interventions at the city party meetings, Eltsin had explained his thinking.

> As he saw it, the primary enemy of perestroika was the apparatus itself, and the need was to struggle against its omnipotence and its dictatorship, because, if it were up to the apparatus to decide on its own fate, it was only too clear what the outcome would be.

What was more, Poltoranin continued, when Eltsin spoke about the apparatus he was not referring only to lower- and middle-level officials but also to "[party] secretaries, ministers, and high-level leaders." There followed a significant passage linking Eltsin with Gorbachev:

> Basically, this is an analysis that Gorbachev, too, has made publicly several times. And Eltsin has never departed from Gorbachev's line. He is a faithful disciple.

This pointed claim elicited a fairly obvious question: Why, then, had the general secretary not intervened to save his "faithful disciple?" Poltoranin said he could not be completely certain about this,

> but I think that Eltsin never turned to Gorbachev to settle his conflict with Ligachev. He thought that the general secretary had more important things to do and that he ought not to be involved in internal disagreements. As I see it, Gorbachev did not want puppets in the Politburo but rather people with different, even conflicting, opinions.

At this the Italian interviewer observed that, in the West, Eltsin's ouster had been interpreted as also constituting an indirect blow at Gorbachev himself. It must be borne in mind, Poltoranin replied, that Eltsin was not a man of common qualities:

> He is faithful to perestroika to his last breath. He is ready to make any sacrifice [for it]. For the conservatives, he is an uncomfortable personality. Hence they had to try to strike at him in any way possible. In striking at him, however, they also in a certain sense left the general secretary open to attack, limiting his freedom of maneuver.

## 3
## GORBACHEV'S COUNTERATTACK
### Elizabeth Teague

On April 8, Mikhail Gorbachev told a meeting in Tashkent that his policies had sparked "a real struggle" in Soviet society. He said that perestroika (restructuring) was not to everybody's liking and that its opponents would not give up without a fight. Perestroika had, however, achieved one important victory: it had "set the whole mass of the people in motion."[1]

Gorbachev was in the Uzbek capital to meet Afghan President Najibullah and clear the last obstacles to an agreement under which the USSR would start withdrawing its troops from Afghanistan. Using the opportunity to address local party leaders, Gorbachev stated that perestroika had entered a decisive phase.

The first phase, Gorbachev said, had been devoted to discussing the country's problems and deciding on policies to put them right. "The situation," he said, "turned out to be much more serious and profound than it appeared on the surface.... We came to the conclusion that we must start a thorough restructuring of the whole of society." The second phase of perestroika had now begun, he said, as the reforms decided upon went into effect.

Gorbachev said the main achievement of perestroika so far had been that "people are changing.... They are emerging from a state of social apathy and indifference.... People are becoming concerned and they are feeling anxious." Indeed, Gorbachev seemed to suggest that this might be the only concrete success his policies had thus far provided. Sociologist Tatiana Zaslavskaia said in March that the extension of glasnost had contributed to a revival of popular activity. "Today," she said, "it is a completely different nation from what it was three years ago."[2]

The transition from words to action, however, provoked stubborn opposition. "Now everyone is involved ... [and] passions are flaring," said Gorbachev, who went on to say:

The scope and novelty of the new stage of perestroika have frightened some people. Quite a few have lost their bearings.... Some have screamed for help. It is only a short step from this to sounding the retreat for perestroika.

Gorbachev was clearly referring to a letter from a Leningrad teacher, Nina Andreeva, that appeared in the newspaper *Sovetskaia Rossiia* on March 13. The letter stridently defended Stalin and denounced the "leftist liberal" tendencies emerging under Gorbachev's leadership.[3] On April 5, *Pravda* rebuked its sister paper for publishing what it called "an ideological platform, a manifesto of the anti-perestroika forces." The *Pravda* editorial, which bore the hallmark of Central Committee Secretary Aleksandr Iakovlev, was in turn seen as both a resounding victory for the reformist camp and its counter-manifesto. Gorbachev himself joined the fray, telling former West German Chancellor Willy Brandt on April 5 that "acute clashes of opinion" were causing "panic" among the population. Some people, he said, "think that everything is collapsing" and "socialism is vanishing."[4] Citing the *Pravda* rejoinder with approval in Tashkent, Gorbachev told his audience "Disapproving voices can be heard saying: This is what your democracy has led to; this is where your perestroika has got you."

Gorbachev seemed unprepared for the ferocity of the opposition. He declared the greatest enemies of perestroika to be those who were "nostalgic for the [Stalinist] past," who "worshipped" the "command-and-administer system." There were, he added, "a great many people who view their factory, village, collective farm, raion, or city as their personal fief." What such leaders demonstrated, Gorbachev said, was contempt for and distrust of the population. They needed to be reminded that the party should be the servant of the people, not the other way round. Gorbachev said that proposals to be laid before the party conference in June 1988 would have the aim of making society and the party itself more democratic.

The period following the November 1987 Eltsin affair had seen a marked intensification of the polemics between spokesmen for conservatism and reform in the press. As preparations for the party conference got under way, there was a clear polarization of opinions. Abandoning the tactic of passive resistance, representatives of the conservative wing went onto the offensive and began to speak out openly. It was not clear whether they were becoming bolder and more self-confident or just more desperate; it was nevertheless obvious that the opponents of Gorbachev's reform program had realized, somewhat belatedly, that they too could use glasnost to propagate their ideas. Andreeva's open letter was only one of a number of items putting the conservative point of view across.[5]

Two different models of socialism were being pitted against each other. Commentator Fedor Burlatskii described them as the "War Communism" model and the "New Economic Policy (NEP)" model.[6] According to the reformers, Andreeva complained, "what we have built is supposedly not proper socialism." The kind of socialism Andreeva favored had indeed been derided by Burlatskii and others as "primitive" and "barracks-style."[7] In turn, Andreeva deplored what she called "left-wing liberal intellectual socialism," champions of which, she said, "eschew proletarian collectivism in favor of the notion of the 'intrinsic value of the individual.'" Current debates, she went on, boiled down to "whether or not to recognize the leading role of the party and the working class in Socialist construction and in perestroika."

Andreeva openly disapproved of the role played by the intelligentsia in the reforms. Warning of "a resurgence of the classes overthrown by the October Revolution," she portrayed the intelligentsia, as one commentator put it, "almost as a force hostile to socialism."[8] The central question, she asserted, "is which class or stratum of society is the leading and mobilizing force of perestroika?"

This was stepping on delicate ground. Reformist intellectuals such as Gavriil Popov and Boris Kurashvili had warned of the danger of an alliance that might be formed by the bureaucracy and disgruntled sections of the working class in opposition to Gorbachev's reforms.[9] Such an "alliance" could completely undermine Gorbachev's reform program, which aimed to put pressure on officialdom not only from above but also from the general public. It could revive the kind of arguments that led to the abandoning of the NEP in the USSR in the late nineteen-twenties, when it was claimed that the revival of private enterprise had favored such bogeymen as the "nepman, prosperous peasant, non-party specialist, and artist"[10] at the expense of the working class. Prominent reformers indeed acknowledged that perestroika was launched with the support of only a minority—that is, the intelligentsia, and the creative intelligentsia at that.[11] (In fact, Gorbachev's reforms failed to receive the support of all the members of even that relatively small group.) Gorbachev's strategy was doomed to fail if his reforms did not succeed in "activating the human factor" and gaining a wider base of support among the general public.

The mood of at least one group of workers was graphically conveyed in a issue of *Izvestiia*. Miners in the Donbass, forced to wait in line for hours for their pay packets, began to jeer: "And this is perestroika?!"[12] Meanwhile, many members of the older generation were appalled by the revelations about the Stalin era that were appearing in the press; they felt that the sacrifices they made in their youth were thereby devalued:

Some frontline soldiers recalled the many occasions on which they went into the attack shouting "For the Motherland, for Stalin!" On this basis, they demanded an end to the denigration of history—criticism of the great leader, they claimed, cast aspersions on those who went into battle with his name on their lips.[13]

It was all the harder for Gorbachev to counter the opposition of such people to glasnost and perestroika because they did not consider themselves to be acting selfishly; indeed, they were defending socialism as they knew it. But in fact, Andrei Nuikin argued, their opposition to economic and political reform served the interests only of the bureaucracy.[14] According to journalist Arkadii Vaksberg, "the real danger is the still very prevalent administrative-bureaucratic way of thinking, the desire for iron discipline,... the belief in the infallibility of the *nomenklatura*." Many people, he said, "believe that this is what socialism means, that this is the Soviet Union's greatest achievement."[15]

Gorbachev told his audience in Tashkent that three years of perestroika had shown that "the reshaping of people's mentalities is the hardest thing of all." *Pravda* acknowledged in its editorial of April 5 that "perestroika is often understood in different ways" and that "diametrically opposed approaches are being put forward."[16] For his part, Gorbachev showed no sign of backtracking on his reforms, and *Pravda*'s rebuke to *Sovetskaia Rossiia* was clearly a victory for the reform wing.

# 4
# LIGACHEV'S POSITION IN DOUBT
Elizabeth Teague

On the evening of April 22, 1988, all eyes were fixed on the line-up of Soviet leaders attending a Kremlin ceremony to mark the anniversary of Lenin's birth. The anniversary came at a time when the Moscow correspondents of leading Western newspapers were reporting that Egor Ligachev, the unofficial "second secretary" of the Central Committee, had emerged the loser from a struggle with Gorbachev over the pace and scope of the general secretary's political reforms. In connection with Ligachev's defeat, oversight of press and television had reportedly been transferred, at least temporarily, from Ligachev to Central Committee Secretary Aleksandr Iakovlev, generally believed to be Gorbachev's closest ally in the leadership. Ligachev was said to have received a reprimand from the Politburo and to have been packed off on an enforced "holiday."

Steadily denied by officials, these rumors were deflated—but not dispelled—when Ligachev joined Gorbachev and other Kremlin leaders on the dais on April 22. During the ceremony, Ligachev sat in his customary place at Gorbachev's right; the two men were seen to engage in apparently amiable conversation as Central Committee Secretary Georgii Razumovskii, an ally of Gorbachev, delivered a speech strongly supportive of the reform program.[1]

Analysts had long predicted a showdown between Gorbachev and his second-in-command.[2] Both men favored economic reform, but Ligachev was far more cautious than Gorbachev about how far and how fast it should go. While Ligachev had strong reservations about the introduction of "the Socialist market" and the extension of private enterprise, he was even less happy about the political reforms Gorbachev wished to introduce. He repeatedly warned that glasnost must not be allowed get out of control and that revelations about the horrors of the Stalin era could destroy the population's faith in their system of government.[3] Ligachev was clearly alarmed by outbursts of ethnic unrest, as was the head of the KGB, Viktor Chebrikov.

On March 13, the newspaper *Sovetskaia Rossiia* published an "open letter" in defense of Stalin.[4] Ostensibly written by a Leningrad schoolteacher, Nina Andreeva, the letter was reportedly published on Ligachev's initiative, and it appeared just when Gorbachev and Iakovlev were preparing to leave the country for Yugoslavia and Mongolia respectively. Unconfirmed rumors held that Ligachev's purpose was to put a brake on Gorbachev's policies of glasnost and *demokratizatsiia*.[5] After Gorbachev's return to Moscow, Andreeva's letter was discussed at two special sessions of the Politburo—on March 30 and April 4. On April 5, *Pravda* carried an authoritative statement, apparently written by Iakovlev, that denounced Andreeva's letter as an attempt to revise party policy "on the sly."

The extent of Ligachev's personal involvement in the publication of Andreeva's letter was not, perhaps, the main issue. Important was that Gorbachev seized the opportunity to discredit conservatives both in the leadership and in society at large. The way the events were handled bore the hallmark of Gorbachev the political operator, a tactician unrivaled at turning potential defeats to his own advantage. Gorbachev's use of the Andreeva letter to trounce his opponents was reminiscent of the way he used the Matthias Rust incident to purge the Soviet military and the Chernobyl disaster to enforce his policy of glasnost.[6]

Unlike his Western counterparts, the general secretary of the CPSU does not enjoy the right to appoint his own cabinet on being elected to office. Gorbachev had to work with a number of men who, like Ligachev, were originally promoted by his predecessor, Iurii Andropov. Throughout Gorbachev's first three years in power, Ligachev had acted as his deputy. Despite the existence of strong differences of opinion between the two men, Gorbachev had managed throughout that period to develop his reform program and gradually to promote his supporters to key positions. Why then should his relations with Ligachev now have degenerated into confrontation?

The catalyst was the party conference scheduled to begin on June 28, which was set to review the progress of perestroika. It was to adopt new measures aimed at "democratizing" the Communist party and delimiting its functions from those of state and government organs. The period prior to the conference saw an outburst in the press of radical reform proposals. These included the introduction of secret voting and multiple candidacy even for high-ranking posts; a limit on the number of terms an official could hold a particular office; a compulsory retirement age (which would affect the sixty-seven-year-old Ligachev a good deal sooner than the fifty-seven-year-old Gorbachev); curtailment of party privileges; and some reduction of the party's powers of appointment (the *nomenklatura* system).

These proposals had many opponents. The playwright Aleksandr Gelman warned that Gorbachev's opponents might attempt to use the conference to wreck the general secretary's reform program.[7] The battle was being fought—as such battles must be fought in the USSR—on the ideological front. At issue was the fundamental question of what kind of socialism should be built in the USSR. This could not be resolved without a prior examination of the existing system, which in many respects was identical to that built by Stalin. Reformers were now openly saying that the Stalinist system was not Socialist at all, the implication being that the present system was not Socialist either. Stalin's brand of "command-administrative" socialism, which Andreeva's letter defended, was mocked by reformists under such epithets as "barracks socialism," "bureaucratic socialism," "the socialism of War Communism."

The reformers argued that introduction of state monopoly ownership in the USSR in the late nineteen-twenties and early nineteen-thirties created a bureaucratic "caste" that staged a counterrevolution and expropriated the workers in whose name the 1917 revolution supposedly took place. The result was, in Marxist terminology, the alienation of the Soviet working class—a term in vogue among reformers. Property relations under socialism accordingly became the focus of intense debate.[8] Reformers were calling for a return to something reminiscent of the "New Economic Policy" of the nineteen-twenties—that is, a system that would recognize the role of cooperative as well as state property, allow some play to market forces, and permit the articulation of the various—and, it was recognized, often conflicting—interests of different sectors of society.[9]

The leading role of the party was not being questioned. Gorbachev spoke of "Socialist pluralism," but he and those close to him indicated that the possibility of a multi-party system was not on their agenda. Nonetheless, Fedor Burlatskii went so far as to call for "a new model of democratic Soviet socialism." Burlatskii argued that the traditional authority of the state should be subordinated to that of "civil society," creating what he referred to as "people's self-governing socialism."[10]

Stalin and the system he created—which Burlatskii dubbed "state socialism" and which was still in essential respects in operation in the USSR in 1988—were at the heart of these debates. The evidence suggests that, when he first came to power, Gorbachev believed the Stalin issue to be so divisive for society that it must be left aside until his economic reforms had been set in motion. Soon, however, he came to realize that, until political reforms were introduced, economic reforms could not be made to work. The Stalin issue had to be tackled.[11] It was, in effect, forced on Gorbachev from below—evidence of the emergence of at least an embryonic "civil society" in the Soviet Union.

Speaking privately to Western specialists, knowledgeable Soviet citizens asserted that opposition between conservatives and reformers reached to the top of the party leadership and that a full-blooded power struggle was under way in the Politburo. Other well-informed citizens saw the confrontation in less personal terms, arguing that opposition to reform came from the Stalinist system itself and was being expressed in an ad hoc alliance between the eighteen-million-strong bureaucracy and disgruntled members of the working class. Whatever the truth of the matter, the choice of Georgii Razumovskii to give the keynote speech on April 22 was a sign that, for the time being at least, the reform wing of the leadership had gained the upper hand. His speech followed the Gorbachev line closely.[12]  He spoke at length about the need for "democratization," saying that perestroika hinged on "a serious renovation of the party." He told his audience that perestroika did not require everybody to think alike. "Different viewpoints," he said, "quest and argument, do not hinder unity as long as there is agreement on fundamental issues." He said, too, that the party must "have the courage to rid itself of those notions of socialism that bear the imprint of certain conditions, particularly those developed during the period of the cult of personality." There are some people," Razumovskii went on, "who cannot master this. We are talking here about the resistance of conservative forces displeased with perestroika."

Of particular interest was the fact that Razumovskii spoke approvingly of the informal groups that had sprung up throughout the Soviet Union. Razumovskii was the highest-ranking member of the leadership to have discussed this phenomenon—another indication of the existence in embryonic form of "a civil society" in the USSR.

Gorbachev and the party's reform wing might have won a battle, but they had not yet won the war. The election of delegates for the party conference was delayed.  Originally, it was announced that this would take place—by secret ballot—in April and May.  Instead, an argument broke out as to how the delegates should be selected. The reformist economist Gavriil Popov suggested in *Sotsialisticheskaia industriia* on April 12, that two thirds of the delegates should be rank-and-file party members rather than officials.  Popov's proposal—which he said was meant to ensure that the conference was not restricted to "the apparatchik version of perestroika"—showed that the ground rules for the elections were still undecided. On April 19, *Sovetskaia kultura* published a letter from a party member in Voronezh who complained about the lack of preparations for elections in his region. He suspected that there might be no elections at all and that, "once again, delegates will be nominated by the oblast committee." The weekly *Argumenty i fakty* published a letter in which a reader from Sumy called for the election of "as many shopfloor workers, women, and representatives of the creative intelligentsia as possible" and proposed that "two or three candidates should be put forward for every place."[13] Even later, in an editorial published on May 7, *Pravda* called on Communists to choose conference delegates who are "dependable foremen of perestroika." There was a further indication that preparations were not going too smoothly in the middle of April, when Gorbachev held a series of three, almost entirely unpublicized, meetings with republican and regional party leaders.[14] (With hindsight it is clear that the meetings were held to enable Gorbachev to hammer out a compromise agreement with party leaders. Most probably, this included his later proposal, voiced for the first time at the conference, to make party first secretaries heads of local soviets.)

Further evidence of problems came from the way proposals for the conference agenda were being made. In the preceding winter, report and election conferences were held in party organizations at all levels and in all regions. This unusually comprehensive campaign had been proposed by Gorbachev at the Central Committee plenum held in June 1987. Its stated purpose was to review the progress of perestroika throughout the country. The underlying aim, in the opinion of Western analysts, was to exert rank-and-file pressure on middle-ranking members of the party bureaucracy, who were obliged to report to their local organizations on what they personally had done to further perestroika. Numerous proposals for party reform were submitted at these meetings for consideration at the party conference, but they were, almost without exception, bland and cosmetic.[15] They were markedly less radical than those made prior to the Twenty-Seventh Party Congress in 1986.[16]

Gorbachev's purpose in calling a party conference was to have a second try at changing the party rules and promoting his supporters to the Central Committee. He could hardly have been satisfied with the timid proposals that emerged from the report and election campaign in the winter of 1987-1988. Since February, fresh proposals had begun to appear in the press. Western analysts noted that, for the reasons stated, they were being made not by party organizations but by individual activists. This suggested that party reform did not enjoy wide support within the party's own ranks.

A reader writing to *Moscow News* suggested that a "Law on the Party" should be enacted,[17] and *Pravda* published a letter on May 8 that called for the disbanding of various sections and departments of party committees at all levels. There were also proposals for putting an end to the secrecy surrounding meetings of the party Central Committee and the Politburo.

A letter signed by a Ia. Borokhovich in *Sovetskaia kultura* pointed out that "the support of the party apparatus for our leader is by no means ubiquitous, unanimous, or always sincere." Borokhovich stated that the removal of Gorbachev from his post at a Central Committee plenum "is a real possibility" and went on to propose that, in that event, because the general secretary was in effect the leader of the whole country, a national referendum should be held to confirm him in office or to approve his removal from power by the Central Committee.[18]

Gorbachev's strategy was to form an alliance with the grass-roots party membership in order to put pressure—"from above and from below," as he said—on the middle ranks of the party bureaucracy. His aim was to make the party both more obedient to direction from Moscow and more responsive to local needs. It was not clear, though, how far rank-and-file party members would be prepared to cooperate with the general secretary. Mindful of the fate of Nikita Khrushchev, who was ousted after he tried to reduce the security of tenure of party officials, low-level party activists would be certain to think long and hard before deciding to jeopardize their relations with their own, middle-ranking superiors. The evidence cited here suggests that far from everything was going as the general secretary would have liked.

# II.  TOWARD DEMILITARIZATION OF EAST-WEST RIVALRY

## 5
## TOWARD THE WASHINGTON AND MOSCOW SUMMITS
Douglas Clarke

Whatever the merits of Gorbachev's "new political thinking," it stirred the Soviet Union out of its traditional intransigent approach to arms negotiations. As a result, in 1987 the USA and the USSR signed two arms-related agreements: the treaty on intermediate-range nuclear forces (INF) and an agreement to establish Nuclear Risk Reduction Centers in both countries. After a hiatus of some seven years, the two superpowers resumed formal negotiations on nuclear testing. The Soviets opened up several of their most secret military facilities in moves calculated to influence Western public opinion. If anything, there was too much, too fast in East-West arms control, as the USSR and its Warsaw Pact allies continued to bombard NATO with various disarmament proposals faster than the West could or would respond.

*The INF Treaty.* The treaty banning land-based intermediate- and shorter-range nuclear missiles, which was signed in Washington on December 8, 1987, was the arms control highlight of the year. Yet even this accord, the first arms control agreement between the superpowers in eight years, was more important for what it might presage than for what it delivered, since it was to do away with relatively few weapons. For the first time, however, a treaty reduced weapons rather than just limiting them. The treaty eliminated two entire classes of nuclear weapons: land-based missiles, both ballistic and cruise, with ranges of between 500 and 5,500 kilometers. It provided an unprecedented system of on-site inspection to prevent cheating.

Few could have predicted in January 1987 that a treaty would be signed before the year was out, for the two sides were far apart. At Reykjavik in October 1986, Gorbachev had linked these negotiations, as well as the ones on strategic weapons, to the talks on space defense, in which he wanted the Americans to give up President Ronald Reagan's Strategic Defense Initiative (SDI). At the end of February the Soviet leader said that it would be possible to have a separate INF agreement without solving the SDI problem; then he appeared to relink the two issues when Secretary of State George Shultz visited Moscow in October. Within days this was followed by another Soviet about-face, which cleared the way for the treaty.

Other issues were overcome, almost as if the Soviets were trying to see how much they could get from the Americans, and then giving in themselves when they sensed firm resistance. As the year began, the Soviets only wanted to talk about intermediate-range missiles, those with a range of between 1,000 and 5,500 kilometers, and only those that were in Europe. They wanted to keep a free hand in Asia. In April they presented a draft treaty in Geneva that would have allowed them to keep 100 SS-20 warheads in Asia. In May Gorbachev made a rather ludicrous offer to give up these 100 warheads if the Americans would remove all their nuclear weapons from Asia (they had no missiles) and drastically limit the areas where they would sail their aircraft carriers. In July he accepted the so-called "double zero" option, banning land-based intermediate- or shorter-range missiles everywhere.

The Soviets were not the only ones to make concessions, however. Reagan overruled his Defense Department and agreed not to build conventionally armed missiles to replace the banned nuclear ones. New technology promised to make such missiles a potent weapon against Soviet reinforcements. The Pershing I missiles owned by West Germany but armed with American nuclear warheads threatened to throw the negotiations off course until Chancellor Helmut Kohl agreed not only to give up these admittedly obsolete weapons, but also not to replace them.

*Strategic Weapons and Space.* The broad terms of a strategic arms treaty had been agreed on since the summit at Reykjavik. Although progress on the many unresolved secondary issues was made during the year in Geneva and at the summit in Washington, the two sides did not quite resolve the most serious sticking point: how to accommodate the American SDI program with the 1972 Anti-Ballistic Missile (ABM) Treaty. The Soviets maintained that they could not reduce strategic weapons if the USA planned to deploy a ballistic missile defense. In Washington, Reagan and Gorbachev "agreed to disagree" on this issue, while instructing their Geneva negotiators to solve it and all the other outstanding problems in time for a treaty to be signed in Moscow in the summer of 1988.

The Americans were not the only ones feeling the pressure posed by the ABM Treaty. The USA charged that a large radar under construction near Krasnoiarsk in Siberia was a violation of this treaty. In an effort to defuse this issue, the Soviets invited a US congressional delegation to visit the site; but the consensus in the West remained that this radar was illegal. In October Gorbachev said that the Soviets would stop work on the radar for one year, but the Americans insisted that it be torn down or modified. There were hints that the Soviets might give in to these demands, placing the blame for this embarrassing violation of international law on a convenient scapegoat, the late former Defense Minister Dmitrii Ustinov.

In his annual report to the Congress on Soviet compliance with arms control treaties, Reagan claimed that in 1987 the USSR had broken another part of the ABM Treaty by moving smaller ABM radars to locations not permitted by the 1972 pact. The Soviet Union's response was the same as in the case of the Krasnoiarsk radar; they invited the Americans to come and look for themselves. The Soviets claimed that the relocated structures in question, near Moscow and the Belorussian city of Gomel, were merely the external housings for older radars now being used for other industrial purposes.

*Nuclear Testing.* The announcement of the moratorium on Soviet nuclear testing, which was made four months after he came to power in March 1985, was Gorbachev's first major arms control initiative. It was not a very successful one. The Soviet leader abandoned it 19 months later, in February 1987; and thereafter the USSR set off 22 announced underground nuclear explosions—16 military tests and 6 said to be for peaceful purposes. The United States conducted 15 nuclear tests in 1987, all of them military-related.

The USA and the USSR did agree, during Soviet Foreign Minister Eduard Shevardnadze's visit to Washington in September, to resume formal negotiations on nuclear testing. These talks began in Geneva on December 1, and the first round resulted in an agreement to conduct what was called a Joint Verification Experiment at each other's nuclear test sites early in 1988. Although the Soviet goal was to negotiate a ban on all nuclear testing, the US successfully focused the talks on better ways to verify the unratified but respected treaties from the nineteen-seventies that allowed underground tests no larger than 150 kilotons.

*All the Pact Members Get Involved.* While the maverick Greek Prime Minister Andreas Papandreou was the only NATO partner to go his own way on arms control, virtually all the Soviet Union's Warsaw Pact allies pushed individual arms control initiatives of one type or another in 1987. Many of these proposals were older ideas repackaged, such as the nuclear-free zone in central Europe suggested by the leaders of the GDR and Czechoslovakia in April and the Romanian and Bulgarian advocacy of a nuclear- and chemical-weapons-free zone in the Balkans. Both of these concepts were quickly endorsed by the Soviet Union. On behalf of the Warsaw Pact, Romania proposed on April 9 that members of NATO and the Warsaw Pact freeze their military budgets for one or two years.

One East European proposal did interject a new idea into East-West arms control. One of the four points in Polish leader Wojciech Jaruzelski's May 8 proposals on reducing tension in Central Europe called for a fundamental change in the character of military doctrines, so that they would be recognized as being strictly defensive in nature. The other members of the Warsaw Pact picked up on this idea, and at a summit meeting in East Berlin at the end of May they issued a special document both outlining their military doctrine and calling for meetings with NATO to compare doctrines.

Many in the West saw this attempt to discuss military doctrines as a thinly camouflaged ploy to attack NATO's strategy of flexible response and particularly the alliance's declared willingness to be the first to resort to the use of nuclear weapons if necessary. Others felt, however, that such a public debate would give NATO a good opportunity both to justify its strategy and to highlight its concern about the offensive potential of the heavily armored Soviet and Warsaw Pact forces just across the West German border. While several Soviet spokesmen claimed that an agreement in principle was reached at Washington to discuss military doctrines, there was no mention of this subject in the joint statement summarizing the results of the summit.

*Controlling Conventional and Chemical Weapons.* With the signing of the INF Treaty, European arms control priorities shifted to nonnuclear weapons. In the multinational negotiations at the UN Conference on Disarmament in Geneva, where some 40 nations were trying to forge an international ban on chemical weapons, the Soviets dropped their objections to one of the key American ideas for verification. The USSR accepted inspections "anywhere, anytime" without the right of refusal—an idea that even some American allies found hard to swallow. The Soviets also made a dramatic offer for representatives from the conference to visit their main chemical weapons base, at Shikany in the Ukraine, where they displayed what they claimed were examples of all the different types of Soviet chemical munitions. Most of the extensive Soviet pronouncements on chemical disarmament seemed to be part of an unsuccessful attempt to persuade the US Congress to halt American production of so-called binary chemical weapons.

When US binary production began in December, the Soviets for the first time announced the size of their chemical-weapons holdings. They claimed to have no more than 50,000 tons of "poisoning substances," which equaled Soviet estimates of the American stockpile. They repeated earlier claims that all their chemical weapons were on Soviet territory. Western analysts were inclined to be skeptical on both counts.

The little progress that was made toward reducing conventional forces in Europe occurred in Vienna—not at the moribund Mutual and Balanced Force Reduction Talks, but rather in the informal meetings between NATO and Warsaw Pact representatives on the fringes of the Helsinki Review Conference. Their purpose had been to agree on a mandate for new negotiations that became known in the West as Conventional Stability Talks.

NATO leaders, who had long claimed that the Warsaw Pact had an overwhelming superiority in conventional arms, were heartened by Gorbachev's admission in April 1987 that there were "asymmetries" between the two sides' conventional forces. He did not mean, however, that the Warsaw Pact was superior to NATO in overall conventional power. Eastern spokesmen made it clear that they believed there was an overall balance, despite one side or the other having more of any one particular type of weapon. This boded ill for any future conventional arms control negotiations.

The prize for the arms control nonevent of the year went to the often-rumored-but-never-materialized Soviet withdrawal of some of its troops from Eastern Europe. Despite hints of an impending announcement before Gorbachev's visits to Prague in April and to Berlin in May and December, the Soviet leader was silent on this topic.

*Movement of Strategic Arms Accord.* While public attention was focused on the INF treaty, the Soviet and American arms control experts who met during Gorbachev's visit to Washington devoted most of their time to strategic weapons. With the veteran arms control negotiator Paul Nitze heading the American team and Marshal Sergei Akhromeev, the Chief of the Soviet General Staff, leading the Soviet side, the experts cleared up some—but not all—of the disagreements between the two countries on the terms of a strategic arms accord. It appears from the Joint Statement issued at the end the summit meeting that both sides made some concessions.

*Where Progress Was Made.* One controversy was settled when the two sides agreed that they should each have no more than 4,900 warheads on ballistic missiles, that is, on the land-based intercontinental ballistic missiles (or ICBMs) and the submarine-launched ballistic missiles (SLBMs). This was one of the so-called sub-limits that the Americans had been pushing for. Both sides had long agreed that their strategic arsenals should contain no more than 6,000 warheads, but they had not agreed as to how these might be divided among the three different classes of strategic weapons: ICBMs, SLBMs, and the bombs and cruise missiles loaded on heavy bombers. The USA had felt that the ballistic missiles were the most threatening, since they could reach their targets in a matter of minutes and could not be shot down on the way. The Americans, therefore, proposed that no more than 4,800 of the 6,000 permitted warheads be allowed on such missiles. After arguing that such a limit would force them to restructure their strategic forces—since the vast majority of the Soviet weapons were on ballistic missiles, particularly ICBMs—the Soviets countered with an informal suggestion that warheads for ballistic missiles be limited to 5,100.

The Joint Statement issued in Washington also listed the number of warheads that were assumed to be on each type of missile; and here there were a few surprises. These numbers were important because they made up some of the so-called counting rules that were used to figure out what each side held.

The Washington talks also resulted in some significant progress in the steps that would be taken to prevent cheating after a strategic arms treaty went into effect. These verification measures were built on, but went well beyond, the verification provisions in the INF treaty.

Most important, the Joint Statement included provisions for what were known as suspect-site inspections. Each side would be given the right to inspect any site where it suspected illegal activity might be taking place; the INF treaty, in contrast, restricted inspections to "declared facilities," that is, places that had at one time or another been associated with missile production or basing. The notion of suspect-site inspection was at one time included in the American INF proposals, but was dropped, reportedly because the American military and intelligence agencies did not relish the idea of Soviet inspectors dropping in on their most secret installations. They apparently would be willing to pay this price, however, in order to more accurately verify a strategic arms agreement.

The verification provisions also included a ban on the encryption (or scrambling) of the signals broadcast during missile tests. These signals, known as telemetry, used to be one of the most useful sources of US intelligence on Soviet missiles. However, the Soviets began to make more use of encryption to deny the Americans access to this data. The USA responded by pushing for, and gaining, a ban on all encryption.

*The Remaining Problems.* The principal stumbling block on the path to achieving a strategic arms treaty remained the problem of American compliance with the 1972 Anti-Ballistic Missile (ABM) Treaty. The Soviets maintained that this treaty banned most space testing of the anti-ballistic missile components of the American Strategic Defense Initiative (SDI), and they wanted a firm US commitment not to withdraw from the treaty. The two sides could not agree, however, on how long this commitment should last, although they did apparently agree that, not later than three years prior to the end of this as yet unspecified period, they would begin "intensive discussion on strategic stability." If after these three years of intensive discussion there were still no agreement on space defense, the two sides would go their own ways. This would mean that the Americans would be free to deploy an SDI system.

So far as the details of a strategic arms accord were concerned, the two sides made little progress on the question of Sea-Launched Cruise Missiles (SLCMs). The Joint Statement merely repeated an earlier agreement that there should be some limit on these weapons but that they should not count toward the various other agreed ceilings, such as the limit of 6,000 warheads. The Americans, maintaining that it was impossible to distinguish nuclear SLCMs from those with conventional warheads, said that they would be willing to discuss limits if the Soviets could suggest some means of verification. The Soviets proposed banning nuclear SLCMs on all surface ships and limiting those allowed on submarines to 400. Reportedly, they also suggested a way of distinguishing nuclear missiles from conventional ones through the use of tamper-proof seals on the warheads and "challenge inspections" of submarines while in port. Neither their verification proposal nor their SLCM limits showed up in the Joint Statement, however, which indicated that the Americans still had misgivings.

The Joint Statement also made no reference to mobile land-based ICBMs, indicating that the two sides were still at an impasse over this issue. The Americans wanted to ban all such weapons, while the Soviets—who were deploying two different types in this category—very much wanted them.

*Early Withdrawal of Soviet Missiles from the GDR and Czechoslovakia.* At a lunch in East Berlin on January 23, 1988, honoring visiting Greek Prime Minister Andreas Papandreou, the East German leader Erich Honecker stated that Soviet nuclear missiles stationed in his country would be dismantled "earlier than originally envisaged."[1] Besides the GDR, Czechoslovakia was the only other Soviet Warsaw Pact ally on whose territory INF missiles were stationed. Czechoslovak Prime Minister Lubomír Štrougal was reported to have told a group of West German journalists that the Soviet missiles would be removed from Czechoslovakia "in the not too distant future."[2] Pulling their SS-12s and -23s out of Eastern Europe even before the INF treaty was ratified was a step that had little or no military cost and could bring the Soviets some public relations returns.

*Slow START.* Following the signing of the INF Treaty at the Washington summit meeting in December 1987, the arms control focus shifted to the Strategic Arms Reduction Talks (START). However, hopes for signing an agreement to reduce the number of strategic missiles by half during this fourth meeting between Reagan and Gorbachev had evaporated long before the two leaders met in Moscow. While both American and Soviet spokesmen still raised the possibility of a strategic arms treaty in the autumn, it had become clear that the superpower negotiations on long-range nuclear weapons and space defense would slide over into the next American administration's term of office. The problems were complex and the stakes for both sides were too high; neither could afford to rush into a treaty.

The slow pace of the strategic talks reflected the USA's growing disillusionment with these negotiations. From the very beginning, the USA's aim had been not only to reduce the number of strategic weapons but, more important, to end up with a mix of weapons that would be more stabilizing than the existing strategic arsenals. During the six years since START began in June 1982, they had been unable to sell this goal to the Soviets.

The American quest for strategic nuclear stability rested on the idea that some types of nuclear weapons were more desirable than others. Powerful and highly accurate ballistic missiles loaded in land-based silos, for example, were more objectionable than similar missiles carried by submarines or by slow-flying cruise missiles and heavy bombers. The land-based missiles, which could knock out the other side's missiles of the same type, had to be used before being destroyed themselves. The submarine-based ballistic missiles and the cruise missiles were more clearly retaliatory forces. Since most of them could survive an enemy surprise attack, they served to deter such an attack by threatening a devastating response.

The problem, as the Americans saw it, was that the Soviets had concentrated too much of their strategic nuclear power in land-based Intercontinental Ballistic Missiles, or ICBMs. Roughly 60 percent of the more than 12,000 Soviet strategic warheads were in this category, while less than 20 percent of the American stockpile was silo-based.

During the course of the strategic negotiations, the American side made a number of proposals that they believed would lead to a more stabilizing strategic nuclear balance, such as a weighted counting rule that would govern the way each side replaced its older weapons, or so-called "sublimits," favoring submarine-launched ballistic missiles. The Soviets rejected both ideas.

The American negotiators, largely stymied in their more direct efforts to promote greater stability in future strategic forces, waged a consistent battle to protect US options to counter what was certain to be a continued Soviet emphasis on ICBMs. They saw heavy bombers, air-launched cruise missiles, and sea-launched cruise missiles as the way to preserve the USA's nuclear deterrent capability.

These American concerns lay at the heart of most of the unresolved START issues, particularly on how to treat air-launched and sea-launched cruise missiles. As far as the former was concerned, the USA wanted to encourage their deployment by having them count less toward each side's allowed ceiling of 6,000 warheads than ballistic missiles. While refusing to concede that one type of nuclear weapon could be less dangerous than another type, the Soviets tacitly admitted this when they agreed with the Americans that nuclear bombs carried by heavy bombers would not count in the 6,000 ceiling. They steadfastly refused to extend this principle to cruise missiles. Thus, they rejected the USA's proposal that a heavy-bomber carrying cruise missiles would count as carrying only six or ten warheads regardless of the number of actual missiles it might carry.

There was the same philosophical impasse regarding sea-launched cruise missiles (SLCMs). The two sides agreed that a ceiling should be set on these weapons, one that would be in addition to the 6,000 limit on other warheads; but they were far apart when it came to numbers. The Soviets proposed that each side have no more than 400 long-range nuclear-armed SLCMs and another 600 conventionally-armed ones. The USA apparently offered no figures at all, but argued that any SLCM limit was unrealistic since it could not be verified. The US Navy was building almost 4,000 SLCMs, of which more than 700 would be armed with nuclear weapons. The American negotiators could be expected to want to protect most of these as contributing to nuclear stability.

When Reagan and Gorbachev ceremoniously exchanged the ratification documents for the INF Treaty on June 1 in the Kremlin, they figuratively started the clock on a sequence of events bound to stretch into the next century. Some obligations were to commence immediately, many more within weeks or months. Teams of Soviet and American inspectors were to carry out the unprecedented on-site inspection provisions of this accord.

The treaty to ban all Soviet and American land-based nuclear missiles with ranges between 500 and 5,500 kilometers went into effect just short of 6 months after it was signed by Reagan and Gorbachev on December 8, 1987, during their last summit in Washington.

As soon as the two leaders exchanged the ratification documents, their governments were bound to halt immediately all production, flight-testing, or training launches of the several types of missiles covered by the treaty. The best-known of these were the Soviet SS-20 missiles, each with 3 nuclear warheads, and the American Pershing II and Ground-Launched Cruise Missiles (GLCMs). The superpowers were now committed to a process that would see all of these medium-range missiles destroyed over the next three years, while the shorter-range missiles, such as the Soviet SS-23s, were to be gone by no later than December 1, 1989. Starting June 1, the USA and the USSR also had to give each other advance notice before missile bases and support facilities were taken out of service or before missiles or their launchers destroyed. They also had to report to each other within two days of moving any missile or launcher from one location to another.

*Getting On With Inspections.* These notification requirements were tied to the relatively rigorous on-site inspection provisions of the treaty. As early as June 2, the two sides exchanged lists of verification inspectors. There were three lists from each side. One covered the inspectors who performed the brief inspections—lasting in most cases only hours or two days at most—to check the numbers of missiles and launchers at their bases or storage depots. These inspectors were also to watch as the missiles and launchers were destroyed, as well as making spot checks to confirm that former missile bases had not been secretly returned to operation. Missiles and launchers were only to be destroyed on the superpowers' home territories, but the other types of inspection were also to take place in the other European states where there were missile bases covered by the treaty. These were East Germany and Czechoslovakia for the Warsaw Pact and West Germany, the United Kingdom, the Netherlands, Belgium, and Italy on the NATO side.

The inspectors on the second list were appointed to man the gates at the two missile production plants where the treaty allowed continuous monitoring. American inspectors were stationed outside the Votkinsk Machine Building Plant, in the Udmurt Autonomous SSR of the Russian SFSR, while a similar Soviet team was to monitor the entrance of the Hercules Plant Number 1, at Magna, Utah. The factory at Votkinsk built the rocket motor for the SS-25 Intercontinental Ballistic Missile and once produced the very similar SS-20 motor. The Hercules Plant once made Pershing II rocket motors.

Finally, the two sides exchanged lists of members of the aircrews that were to man the planes bringing the inspection teams. Each of these three lists could contain as many as 200 names. Unless someone listed had been convicted of a crime on, or had previously been expelled from, the other side's territory, the inspectors and aircrews on lists one and three had to be accepted by the other party and provided with the necessary visas and travel documents within 30 days. Each side could, however, turn down, without explanation, anyone on the permanent monitoring list, so long as they did so within 20 days. The Americans rejected 8 prospective Soviet inspectors.

The inspection program shifted into high gear on July 1. By then, the two sides had updated the extensive exchange of information that took place in Washington the previous December.

*Changes in Numbers and Locations.* The new data showed that some changes had indeed occurred in the intervening seven months. For one thing, the Soviets had pulled all their SS-12s out of East Germany and Czechoslovakia, as well as least some of the shorter-range SS-23s that were stationed in East Germany. They had blown up some of these missiles to test their destruction procedures. The Americans had test-fired 19 Pershing II missiles during crew training exercises, so their total missile inventory was somewhat lower as well—although, in the American case, the reduction was at least partially offset by eight old, unserviceable Pershing 1A missiles that were "found" after the December data exchange.

During the 60 days between July 1, and August 29, 1988, American and Soviet inspectors conducted "baseline" inspections of every missile operating base and support facility reported by the other side, except for missile production plants. The Americans visited some 130 Soviet facilities, of which 123 were in the USSR itself, six in the GDR, and one, a former SS-12 base, in Czechoslovakia. Since the Americans had far fewer missiles bases than the Soviets, there were not so many stops for the Soviet inspectors. They visited around 30 American missile facilities: 18 or so within the USA and 12 in Western Europe. The purposes of these inspections was to confirm the data that was exchanged by the two sides. As many as 100 inspectors could be in the Soviet Union or the United States at one time, as the treaty allowed 10 simultaneous inspections to be conducted by 10-man inspection teams.

At the same time that the baseline inspections were starting, the monitors set up their equipment outside the Votkinsk and Magna plants. While it took longer to build the permanent monitoring facilities allowed by the treaty, the so-called portal inspections started on July 1. According to the treaty, these two plants could only have one entry/exit point for missile rocket motors—or for anything large enough to carry one. The inspectors were to ensure that no banned missile motors came out of the plants, going so far, if need be, as to look inside a suspicious container.

*The Start of Destruction.* In theory, missile destruction could have started as early as July 11; this would have been the case if the Soviets had decided quickly to take advantage of the treaty option to destroy some missiles by launching them. Each side was allowed to destroy as many as 100 longer-range missiles in this manner during the first 6 months that the treaty was in effect, that is, until December 1, 1988. Ten days advance notification had to be given before these destruction firings so that the other side's inspectors could be present. Most of the missiles were to be destroyed either by burning or being blow up with high explosive charges. Each side had to give 30 days advance notice before performing these methods of destruction. In the event, the Soviet Union began destroying shorter-range missiles on August 1, and announced that the first SS-20 medium-range missiles would be scrapped on August 28. The Americans notified the Soviets that they would begin their missile destruction process on September 8.

The treaty set certain deadlines for destruction. The 84 Soviet ground-launched cruise missiles, the SSC-X-4s, which had been produced but not yet deployed, had to be destroyed by December 1, 1988. All the shorter-range missiles, the SS-12 and SS-23s, had to be destroyed by December 1, 1989. The medium-range missiles were to be taken out in two stages. All the missiles and launchers covered by the treaty had to be eliminated by May 17, 1991.

*Short-Notice Inspections for 13 Years.* From August 29, 1988, until the end of the destruction period and for an additional 10 years thereafter (that is, until June 1, 2001), American and Soviet teams received the right to make "short-notice" inspections at the former missile bases and facilities as well as at other, active missile bases and most support facilities so long as some missiles were still deployed. The number of such inspections allowed each year was to be reduced in three stages. For the first 3 years each side would be able to call for 20 snap inspections per year; for the next 5 years their quota would be reduced to 15 per year; and only 10 such inspections by each side would be allowed during the last 5 years.

All on-site inspection rights were to end in 2001, 10 years after the last legal INF missile was to have been destroyed. Since each side would be watching the other's missile test ranges by spy satellites throughout this period, the rationale for ending the on-site inspections was that any illegal missiles that might have been hidden away would not have been tested for a decade and could not be considered to be reliable or militarily useful.

It was this passage of time, more than the unprecedented on-site inspection provisions of the treaty, that would ultimately protect NATO from the possibility of Soviet cheating. For, as dramatic as all these inspections might be, on their own they were not enough to ensure that the Soviets were sticking to the rules. Covert SS-20 missile production, for instance, at some location not mentioned in the INF data exchange would not be found by any of these inspections. There was little incentive, however, for the Soviets to go to all the trouble of evading the treaty, since they had ample means of filling in for the now banned weapons with perfectly legal nuclear systems.

# 6
# THE PROBLEM OF CONVENTIONAL IMBALANCE
Douglas Clarke

*"Reasonable Sufficiency"* and *"Asymmetries."* When talking about conventional forces, the Soviets defined "sufficiency" as being the "amount and quality of armed forces and armaments which would be enough to reliably ensure collective defence of the socialist community."[1] The level was based upon the perceived threat, and the military leaders saw no diminution of that threat. The Soviet Commander-in-Chief of the Warsaw Pact forces Marshal Kulikov, for example, referred to "reactionary imperialist forces" that had not given up their attempts to gain military superiority over the Soviet Union and its allies.[2]

While admitting that there were "asymmetries" between the conventional forces of the two military alliances, the Soviet military nevertheless claimed that there was an overall conventional balance. In other words, the Warsaw Pact's advantage in tanks, for instance, was canceled out by what they saw as a NATO advantage in jet fighter-bombers. NATO analysts agreed that the Warsaw Pact was considerably stronger in tanks and guns, but few Western analysts agreed that these advantages were substantially offset by other NATO strengths. This is why the NATO heads of state said at their summit in Brussels that future stability in Europe would require "highly asymmetrical reductions by the East" entailing, for example, "the elimination from Europe of tens of thousands of Warsaw Pact weapons relevant to surprise attack, among them tanks and artillery pieces."[3]

The initial Soviet response to this NATO statement was predictably negative. The Soviet military could not be expected to welcome dramatic changes in their force structure, particularly not unilateral ones. Recalling the armed forces' manpower reduction under Khrushchev, General Ivan Tretiak, the head of Soviet Air Defense Forces, said that this "rash" step "dealt a terrible blow at our defence capacity" and that the effects were still being felt. Any "changes in our army should be considered a thousand times over before they are decided upon," the general cautioned.[4]

*Civilian Defense Intellectuals.* The military's pre-eminence in security philosophy was challenged by a group of civilian defense intellectuals centered in two sections of the USSR Academy of Sciences—the United States and Canada Institute and the Institute for World Economy and International Relations

(IMEMO). Andrei Kokoshin, a deputy director of the US and Canada Institute, published an article analyzing the reasons why a new system of military balance in conventional arms was necessary in Europe and what this balance should look like.[5] He concluded:

> The Warsaw Pact's defensive capabilities must substantially exceed NATO's offensive capabilities, while NATO's defensive capabilities must substantially exceed the Warsaw Pact's offensive capabilities, at reduced levels of military confrontation between the two alliances.

Kokoshin believed that the Warsaw Pact's military doctrine and its various proposals for reducing conventional arms would bring this about; but he stressed that there had to be a "total correspondence" between the political and "military-technical components" of this doctrine, that is, Soviet force structure and equipment would have to reflect the doctrine.

This same theme was emphasized by three other scholars from the US and Canada Institute—Vitalii Zhurkin, Sergei Karaganov, and Andrei Kortunov—who stressed that "reasonable sufficiency" required that "the armed forces structure,... the military build-up as a whole, and operational strategy (clearly even tactics, especially in Europe)" had to be in full conformity with the declared defensive character of the military doctrine.[6] They went, however, significantly beyond this, arguing for a degree of unilateral Soviet reductions and suggesting that it was not necessary for the Soviet Union to achieve a balance of forces in every region or even to aim at having forces large enough to match "the total forces of all potential adversaries."

*Trading NATO Planes for Warsaw Pact Tanks.* In a wide-ranging interview[7] with two American reporters on November 11, PUWP First Secretary Wojciech Jaruzelski said that the Warsaw Pact would be prepared to reduce the number of tanks in Central Europe if NATO were willing to cut its bomber force in return. Referring to what he called a Western "belief" that Warsaw Pact forces were superior in tanks, the Polish leader said: "We believe that the NATO countries have a predominance in certain kinds of aircraft, especially bombers."

Jaruzelski suggested that the two military alliances should cut back on the types of offensive weapons systems (those better suited for an attack than for defense) that each side found the most threatening. He thought the first steps could be taken with Warsaw Pact tanks and NATO bombers.

This proposal was an amplification of one aspect of a four-point arms control program for Central Europe that Jaruzelski first put forward in May 1987. He called then for the reduction of conventional weapons with "the greatest strength and strike precision, which could be used for a sudden attack." The other points dealt with a reduction of all types of nuclear weapons, a change in military doctrines so that they would be recognized as being strictly "defensive," and as yet unspecified "confidence-building" measures.

The Polish leader's May proposals would apply at first only to a limited number of countries: the GDR, Poland, Czechoslovakia, and Hungary on the Warsaw Pact side; the FRG, the Netherlands, Belgium, Luxembourg, and Denmark on the NATO side. He thought that in the longer term they could be extended from the Atlantic Ocean to the Ural Mountains.

In a speech in Prague on April 10, 1987, Gorbachev first raised the idea that there might be "asymmetries" in the armed forces of the two opposing military alliances. These should be corrected by having the side with greater numbers reduce, rather than the weaker side build up. NATO leaders welcomed Gorbachev's words not because they agreed with them, but rather because they interpreted them as the first, albeit indirect, Soviet admission of Warsaw Pact superiority in conventional forces. The official Eastern position was and continued to be that the two sides' forces were essentially equal. A release issued by *Novosti* on November 12 claimed that the two sides were "roughly equal" in conventional arms. Although numbers of divisions and weapons might differ, there was equality in what the Soviet press agency termed "combat potentialities."

Thus, the two sides were looking at the problem of conventional armed forces from two widely different perspectives. The Warsaw Pact saw essential equality and looked to improve the security atmosphere by adjustments in numbers of individual types of weapons that particularly bothered one side or the other. By inference, to maintain what it saw as the existing overall equality, reductions by one side would have to be balanced by some sort of cut by the other: hence Jaruzelski's tanks-for-bombers idea.

Most Western analysts agreed with Jaruzelski that the Warsaw Pact—and especially the Soviets—found NATO's fighter-bombers particularly threatening. They believed, however, that it was because these aircraft could carry nuclear weapons rather than because of their conventional role, for most of the medium-range bombers and so-called fighter-bombers were what military specialists termed "dual-capable." This meant that they could carry nuclear as well as conventional bombs. One US State Department official described the Soviet effort to mix tactical nuclear systems into talks on reductions in conventional weapons as a way "to pursue their objective of denuclearizing Europe through the back door. . . ."[8]

*Gorbachev's Mediterranean Proposals.*  Addressing the Yugoslav National Assembly on March 16, 1988, Gorbachev proposed limiting the size and "naval potential" of the American and Soviet fleets in the Mediterranean, requiring advance notices of warship movements and exercises, and introducing unspecified "principles and methods" to protect shipping lanes, particularly those in international straits.

This was not the first time that the Soviets had focused their "peace offensive" on the Mediterranean. Foreign Minister Eduard Shevardnadze had announced in June 1987 (also in Belgrade) that the USSR would be willing to stop transporting nuclear weapons by ship through the Mediterranean if the US would do the same.

Nor was it the first time that naval forces had been singled out. The military aspects of Gorbachev's proposals in October 1987 for an Arctic "zone of peace" dealt almost exclusively with similar restrictions on naval activity. The Soviets tried, unsuccessfully, to convince the Stockholm conference on European security to apply the same sort of confidence-building measures to naval and air activities that were being agreed for land forces. Soviet spokesmen pointed to NATO's superiority in capital ships (that is, battleships, cruisers, aircraft carriers, and the like) as one of the reasons why the conventional forces of the two sides were roughly equal despite the Warsaw Pact superiority in tanks and guns.

There were both significant similarities and differences between the Soviet Mediterranean Squadron and the US Sixth Fleet, the American naval force in the Mediterranean.

If the numbers were roughly the same—about 45 to 50 ships—the American force had a considerable advantage in tonnage and firepower: this is what Gorbachev might have been  thinking of when he spoke of "naval potential." The Sixth Fleet always had at least one and often two aircraft carrier Battle Groups. These potent fighting units consisted of one of the US Navy's giant aircraft carriers, whose 86 aircraft provided an integrated mix of attack, fighter, reconnaissance, early warning and antisubmarine capabilities, and cruisers, destroyers, and frigates that accompanied and protected the carrier. The A-6, A-7 or F-18 jet fighter-bombers aboard the Sixth fleet carriers posed a nuclear threat to the Soviet Union.

A lack of similar airpower was one of the Mediterranean Squadron's main disadvantages. One of the biggest problems facing the commander of the Soviet Mediterranean Squadron was how to supply his force with the oil, ammunition, and supplies it needed. While the Sixth Fleet could use the many NATO facilities in the area, the Soviets had largely to fend for themselves. As a result, nearly half of the ships in the Mediterranean Squadron were not warships but had a logistical or supporting role.

One of Gorbachev's suggestions was that the US and Soviet naval forces in the Mediterranean give advance notification of their movements. The Americans were likely to interpret this as an attempt to saddle them with a restriction that the Soviets could not avoid, for according to the terms of the 1936 Montreux Convention, which governed the peacetime passage of naval vessels through the Bosporus and the Dardanelles, the Soviets had to notify Turkey eight days before sending a warship through these Turkish straits. They were also limited in the numbers and types of ships they could bring out of the Black Sea.

*The Warsaw Pact Appeal from Sofia.* A Warsaw Pact foreign ministers' meeting in Sofia on March 29 and 30, 1988, issued a lengthy appeal on arms control, which was mainly devoted to repeating older positions. It did suggest, however, that talks on reducing conventional arms in Europe might be speeded up through an exchange of data and it offered a solution to the troublesome problem of "dual-capable" weapons. Nevertheless, the appeal seemed aimed less at Western governments than at influencing the Western public.

The foreign ministers proposed separate talks on reducing, and ultimately eliminating, tactical nuclear weapons in Europe. They specifically included in this category the "nuclear components of dual-purpose systems." Tactical nuclear weapons were those with ranges of less than 500 kilometers, weapons that were sometimes called "battlefield" nuclear weapons. Most of these were "dual-capable" or "dual-purpose," which meant that they could fire or carry either a nuclear or a conventional high explosive warhead.

For over a year in Vienna, representatives of NATO and the Warsaw Pact had been trying to agree on a framework for new talks on reducing conventional arms and forces in Europe. These new negotiations were to be known as conventional stability talks, and they would eventually replace the moribund negotiations on cutting forces in Central Europe that were known in the West as Mutual Balanced Force Reduction (or MBFR) talks. The main sticking point in these preliminary negotiations had been how to handle these dual-capable weapons. The NATO representatives, determined to resist Soviet efforts to denuclearize Europe, rejected all East European efforts to focus on the nuclear missions of these dual-capable systems in the future negotiations on conventional arms. The Warsaw Pact, on the other hand, insisted that these nuclear forces be included in the future talks.

The Sofia formula offered a way around this impasse. In their appeal, the foreign ministers indicated that they accepted the principle of dealing with the nuclear components of these dual-capable weapons in negotiations that were separate from those on conventional weapons.

The only other possible new kernel among the chaff of old proposals was the suggestion that the Warsaw Pact and NATO should exchange data "as soon as possible" on their armed forces and conventional arms in Europe.[9] This proposal was rendered a little suspect, however, during the press conference after the meeting, when it was disclosed that the reason for wanting the exchange was to dispel the "myth" of Warsaw Pact supremacy.[10] Nevertheless, the ministers stated that their countries were prepared to "uncover and eliminate on a reciprocal basis" such asymmetries and imbalances "both on an all-European scale and for individual regions." This might clear the way for more realistic appraisals of the military balance in central Europe.

*Gorbachev's Offer.* At the Moscow summit, Gorbachev proposed to Reagan on May 30 that NATO and the Warsaw Pact each remove 500,000 soldiers from Europe. As explained by Soviet Foreign Ministry spokesman Gennadii Gerasimov, the reduction would be part of a three-stage process. First, there would be some sort of inspection to verify the size of each side's conventional forces in Europe. This would apparently be coupled with negotiations to decide exactly which kinds of units should be eliminated. Then the two opposing military alliances would each pull out 500,000 soldiers. Finally, the remaining forces would be turned into what Gerasimov called "defensive character forces."

Such substantial—but equal—troop reductions had been advocated by the Warsaw Pact for several years. The idea, in roughly its present form, stemmed from a speech Gorbachev made in East Berlin on April 18, 1986. His ideas were elaborated two months later at a meeting of Warsaw Pact heads of government in Budapest, where they became part of what was later called the "Budapest Appeal."

This appeal called for an initial mutual withdrawal of between 100,000 and 150,000 soldiers over 1 to 2 years. Once this was completed, the two sides would make further reductions so that eventually their opposing forces would be roughly 25 percent smaller. The Warsaw Pact leaders estimated that the reductions would "comprise over half a million people from each side," in other words, they would be of approximately the same size as suggested in Moscow. However, now the cut would be in one step, rather than the two-tiered Budapest approach.

While there was considerable debate over the quality and quantity of the opposing forces, virtually all Western analysts agreed that any equal cuts would be to NATO's disadvantage. Some studies indicated that the Warsaw Pact would need to remove five divisions for every one given up by NATO in order for the situation of the Western alliance to improve.

By making a new proposal on the control of conventional arms at the Moscow summit, Gorbachev was seen by many as playing more to Western public opinion than helping to move conventional arms control forward. NATO leaders considered that a more appropriate place for such ideas was Vienna, where negotiators from NATO and the Warsaw Pact were trying to work out the ground rules for new talks on conventional arms stability in Europe.

During his visit to Poland, Gorbachev proposed a pan-European disarmament summit, suggested setting up a permanent European "war risk reduction center," and offered to cut the strength of Soviet jet fighter-bombers in Eastern Europe if NATO would give up its plans to move 72 American F-16 jets from Spain to Italy.

The American jets Gorbachev was talking about were the 72 F-16 fighter-bombers belonging to the American 401st Tactical Fighter Wing stationed at Torrejón Air Base, just outside the Spanish capital, Madrid. Under the terms of the defense agreement between the United States and Spain, these aircraft would have to be withdrawn from Spain by 1991. The Italian government had agreed to provide a new home for the 401st Tactical Fighter Wing at an airbase in the south of Italy.

In his speech to the Polish Sejm, Gorbachev said that the USSR would be prepared "to withdraw our matching aircraft from forward-deployment sites in Eastern Europe if NATO agrees not to base its 72 F-16 fighter-bombers, rejected by Spain, in Italy." Presumably, by "matching aircraft" Gorbachev meant some of the Su-17, -24, and -25 and MiG-27 jets based alongside Soviet troops in some of the Eastern European countries. Like the American F-16s, the primary mission of these aircraft in wartime would be to attack ground targets with bombs or missiles. According to the London-based Institute for Strategic Studies, 450 of these combat jets were stationed outside the Soviet Union on the Warsaw Pact's western flank: 315 in East Germany, 45 in Czechoslovakia, and 90 in Hungary.[11]

Geography suggested the unacceptability to NATO of Gorbachev's offer. The American F-16s would have to return to the United States in 1991 if NATO were to forego the Italian basing option. In the USA they would be at least some 10,000 kilometers away from their wartime operating areas. The Soviet aircraft, on the other hand, could still reach their targets in minutes.

The Soviet leader's offer also seemed to contradict a long-standing Soviet position on whether or not there was a balance of conventional arms in Europe. Gorbachev himself maintained that there was such a balance between the Warsaw Pact and NATO, although, for historical reasons, one side might have more of one type of weapon while the other had more of another.

Western authorities disputed both the Warsaw Pact claim that NATO had a lead in attack aircraft and the idea that such fighter-bombers could be weighed against tanks in determining a balance of conventional forces. At least in the early stages of any reduction of conventional arms in Europe, NATO was certain to oppose trading combat aircraft for tanks or for planes. The principal impediment to conventional stability in Europe was in what Western leaders perceived as the Warsaw Pact's potential for a quick armored thrust across Central Europe. This potential was measured in tanks, artillery and missiles. Until Gorbachev was willing to tackle this problem head-on, there would be little progress in conventional arms control.

# 7
# ROMANIA BLOCKS PROGRESS AT CSCE
Vladimir Socor

Romania became more isolated from both the East and the West at the Conference on Security and Cooperation in Europe (CSCE) as a result of Romanian resistance to movement toward a final document at the review meeting in Vienna. Nicolae Ceauşescu's envoys rejected the chapters on human rights in the draft final document forming the basis of the negotiations. The draft was submitted by the neutral and nonaligned states in the middle of May as the conference entered its final stage. The provisions on human rights held center stage in these negotiations, since economic issues were less contentious and detailed issues of military security were to be dealt with mainly in other forums of the CSCE.

*Commitments on Human Rights Unacceptable to Romania.* While the Soviet and several East European delegations found some of the draft's provisions acceptable in principle and engaged in detailed negotiations over the others, the Romanian delegation alone declared those provisions unacceptable across the board; it accused the neutral and nonaligned delegations of making concessions to the West on human rights. Professing to resist interference in its internal affairs, Romania formally notified the negotiators that it would withhold its consent to the draft's key sections: those on religious rights, human contacts and humanitarian matters, freedom of movement, the rights of ethnic minorities, and procedures for reviewing the implementation of the provisions of the final document. Romania also notified the conference that it would not agree to language that went beyond that of the final document of the Madrid meeting of the CSCE in 1983 (a document widely regarded as general and noncommittal). Withholding consent from a draft amounted to killing it under the rule of unanimous consent that governed the CSCE process.

Western criticism of Romania's stance and the reported attempts of its Warsaw Pact allies to persuade it to change its course had no effect. If anything, the Romanian delegation  toughened its position after its leaders' return from a week of consultations in Bucharest in early June 1988, with fresh instructions from Ceauşescu. Acting on those instructions, the envoys announced Romania's rejection of several provisions on which there was already a measure of agreement between East and West, including a mechanism for the permanent review of human rights problems. Both East and West took this situation seriously in view of Romania's obstructionist record at previous CSCE review meetings on human rights. Both sides wanted a successful outcome to the Vienna conference with a balanced final document that would keep the CSCE process on track and both shared an interest in preventing Romania from derailing it.[1]

*Trying to Dilute the Mandate of CSCE Review Meetings.* The Romanian authorities attempted to rewrite the agenda of this and future CSCE meetings and to discontinue the process of reviewing compliance with Basket Three of the Helsinki Final Act. In his public address on June 2 Ceauşescu claimed that "the Vienna conference has no authority to adopt normative measures" that would "in some way or other open the way to interference in the internal affairs of other states." Moreover, it had "become apparent that a better organization of work at the conference is essential" in order to refocus its proceedings on "the fundamental problems" of disarmament, economic cooperation, and social rights. In Ceauşescu's view, future CSCE meetings should be limited to "a few days or a week, and under no circumstances should they last longer than 10 days."[2] The Vienna meeting had been under way since November 1986.

Romania made proposals to that effect at the Vienna conference. It also insisted that the right to work and to guaranteed employment (especially for the young), equal employment rights for men and women, and a guaranteed right to housing be recognized as "fundamental aspects of human rights" in any final document of the conference. According to Western representatives at the Vienna meeting, these Romanian proposals revived older ones of a clearly impractical and propagandistic nature that the other Warsaw Pact states had given up in earlier stages of the conference. The idea of limiting follow-up meetings to just one week seems, however, to have been an original Romanian contribution. These proposals showed Bucharest casting about for any device, hopeless though it might have been, to prevent serious discussion at CSCE meetings of compliance with Basket Three and progress on more specific commitments.[3]

*An Unfolding Pattern.* Romania's role as a consensus-breaker and obstructor of movement on human rights at CSCE meetings can be traced back to  the Budapest Cultural Forum in 1985. Romania caused that meeting to end without a final document by vetoing an Austrian-Hungarian draft that referred all the proposals presented there to the next CSCE follow-up meeting.  At the 1986 CSCE review meeting in Berne on human contacts, Western delegates reported that "Romania was taking the leading role in obstructing agreement" and that Romania's stance was "harder and more vicious than that of the Soviets."[4] Indeed, Romania failed to join the USSR and the other Warsaw Pact countries when at the last moment they presented a draft that offered a modicum of concessions to Western wishes.

Western diplomats concluded that Romania's consistent objective at these conferences had been to obstruct the issuance of any final document or mandate to which Romania could be held accountable. Romania's conduct at the Vienna meeting was basically continuing in that vein, but this time Romania was mounting the challenge on a broader front of issues and was seeking to pre-empt a potential consensus.

*Soviet Pressure on Romania Broached.* Western officials at the Vienna conference were quoted as discounting the possibility that the Romanian stance was prearranged as part of a Soviet-bloc strategy. Some, however, suggested that Romania's obstructionism might well enjoy quiet support from some East European régimes as a convenient cover for their own reservations about any substantive agreements with the West on human rights. Western delegates expressed their concern that Romania might, indeed, have been prepared to act alone in blocking progress on any significant document by resort to the rule on unanimous consent.

According to Western sources at the conference, the Warsaw Pact delegations were openly blaming Romania for causing difficulties through its intransigence and for refusing to support negotiations for a compromise between the East and the West. Soviet and East European diplomats claimed that Romania was out of step with the other Warsaw Pact members and that they had urged it in vain not to pursue its course.

In light of all this, Western delegates to Vienna spoke openly about the desirability of Moscow putting pressure on Romania to desist from blocking movement toward an agreement. The Soviets gave evasive replies when approached by their Western counterparts about this; in several instances they intimated that the USSR lacked the leverage to pressure Romania.[5] Yet no one at the conference was certain that the protestations of the Warsaw Pact states were entirely candid.

# III. FOREIGN POLICIES OF ACCOMMODATION

8

## MOSCOW TAKES DISTANCE FROM THIRD WORLD CLIENTS
### Vlad Sobell

If selfless cooperation proved difficult to attain in the relatively prosperous and evenly developed core of the European CMEA, it was even more difficult to apply to the CMEA's less developed, non-European members—Mongolia, Cuba, and Vietnam. Indeed, the entry of these countries into the CMEA (in 1962, 1972, and 1978, respectively), motivated also by Soviet desire to spread the burden of aid throughout the entire CMEA, was reportedly resisted by the rest of the community.[1] The entry of Vietnam (and implicitly of its two neighbors, Laos and Cambodia) apparently stretched the CMEA's leveling principles to the limit so that no new members could be expected in the foreseeable future. Mozambique attempted to join in 1980 but was turned down by the Soviets, as was Nicaragua in 1985. These had to be content with an observer status.[2]

*Shifts in the Kremlin's Thinking.* In the past, the Soviet Union, in its search for political allies, had proved willing to underwrite developing countries' economies. However, once the process began, the demand for aid tended to grow inordinately. CMEA aid usually started as temporary compensation to the recipient for losses caused by a Western economic boycott. In turn, the Western boycott tended to become more severe and the inflow of Western aid to diminish. The USSR and the CMEA then felt compelled to respond by increasing aid still further, although even then the aid remained significantly below what the recipient would have received had it stayed outside the CMEA orbit, as ultimately the CMEA could not compete economically with the Western countries. Also, Marxist economic policies usually followed by the countries receiving CMEA aid tended to impoverish rather than enrich them, thus providing the CMEA with the prospect of subsidizing its Third World allies indefinitely.

Such a situation ran counter to the spirit of Gorbachev's "restructuring," which sought to expose and tackle vital problems rather than conceal them. The new Kremlin leadership was aware that the USSR and the CMEA had overextended their capacity for sustaining Soviet imperial commitments and that certain corrective measures could not be postponed if the empire were not to disintegrate. The Kremlin also came to realize that global competition with the West was hopeless unless sustained by sounder economics. Accordingly, the USSR made it clear that the recipients of aid must be more thrifty. It also began to promote Soviet-style "restructuring" among them, which should, at least in theory, have improved their prospects for eventual "self-financing." Finally, it displayed greater caution in supporting new clients— a corollary of a profound shift in Soviet foreign policy away from confrontation and toward integration and cooperation with the rest of the world under the slogan of "interdependence." Soviet and East European policies toward Vietnam, Cuba, and Nicaragua reflected this shift.

*Vietnam.* As one of the world's poorest countries (estimated per capita income less than $200 a year) and, after the USSR, the CMEA's most populous country, Vietnam was potentially its heaviest drain. In December 1986 the Soviet Union disclosed that its economic aid came to about $2,500 million a year, in addition to about $1,000 million a year in military aid to sustain Vietnam's occupation of Cambodia.[3] This investment enabled the Soviet navy to use the deep-water port at Camranh Bay and the military base at Da Nang.

Although the USSR and Vietnam signed a new agreement for the 1986-1990 period which, according to Vietnamese sources, envisaged a doubling of Soviet aid, the Kremlin demanded that Vietnam straighten out its economy. In October 1986 Truong Chinh, then leader of Vietnam, said that "the great assistance of the Soviet Union and other socialist countries has been seriously squandered and is in danger of gradually becoming exhausted."[4]

In late 1987, there still was no evidence that the Kremlin had weakened its support for Vietnam's occupation of Cambodia, the main obstacle to China's normalizing relations with the USSR and Vietnam; indeed, Soviet military aid to Vietnamese occupation forces reportedly increased.[5] At the same time, however, the Soviet Union under Gorbachev displayed a readiness to normalize relations with China and sanctioned an East European-Chinese normalization.[6] By mid 1988, there was some reversal in policy on Cambodia.

*Cuba.* The USSR's aid to Cuba was estimated at between $1,000 million and $4,000 million a year.[7] It consisted of purchases of Cuban sugar at artificially high prices, soft credits for CMEA investment projects in Cuba, and until 1986[8] subsidized Soviet oil. In April 1986 a new agreement was signed between the USSR and Cuba, which allegedly was to double Soviet aid and extend $3,000 million in new Soviet credits. At the same time, however, there was to be a slight reduction in indirect subsidies to the Cuban economy. The price paid by the USSR for sugar in the 1986-1990 period was reduced from 915 to 850 rubles a ton, and the nominal (artificially fixed) price of Soviet oil paid by Cuba rose above world market prices.[9] Fidel Castro reportedly assured Gorbachev at the 27th CPSU Congress in early 1986 that measures had been taken to make the Cuban economy less wasteful. In view of the sustained US activity in Central America and the Caribbean,[10] the Soviets had little choice but to step up support for Cuba.

Castro's confidence in his strong leverage in bargaining with the Soviets could be seen in Cuba's indifference to "restructuring." In the spring of 1986 Castro abruptly ended free-market experiments that had begun several years before and ordered a return to the puritanical "socialist values" of the earlier stages of his revolution.

A *New Times* article on Cuba's economic difficulties by Vladislav Chirkov noted Cuba's economic shortcomings, such as shortages of housing, electricity, food, and mismanagement of CMEA aid;  problems caused by "historical backwardness," and  the US economic boycott.  At the same time, Chirkov admitted that many of Cuba's problems were also present in the European CMEA countries and that the CMEA as a whole shared responsibility for Cuba's economic failure.

Chirkov's unprecedented admission of Cuban-Soviet tension drew an irritated attack from the highest quarters of the "unrestructured" Cuban establishment. A subsequent issue of *New Times* contained an article by Carlos Rafael Rodriguez, criticizing the prominence Chirkov had  given to the "negative aspects" of the Cuban economy.  The author accused Chirkov of succumbing to the "temptation to repeat the generalities made by American 'Cubanologists' about Cuba's inability to achieve economic success."

The most interesting aspect of Rodriguez's reply was his strong endorsement of Cuba's defense budget. Chirkov had questioned the wisdom of Cuba's spending so much on defense, given the size of its population.

*Nicaragua.* The shift of the Soviet position on Nicaragua was a clear manifestation of the "new thinking." Nicaragua was receiving sizable economic and military aid from the CMEA (more than $425,000,000 by 1987), and the USSR supplied some 80 percent of Nicaragua's oil on very favorable terms. In early 1987, however, the USSR announced that it would provide only 40 percent of Nicaragua's oil needs and that the shortfall would be made up by supplies from other CMEA members—altogether some 200,000 tons less than needed. Although the Kremlin eventually agreed to ease the Nicaraguan fuel crisis by promising another 100,000 tons, its reluctance was a clear sign that it would not support Nicaragua at the cost of undermining its new policy toward the USA and Latin America.[11]

*Defusing Tension Is a Cheaper Option.* Gorbachev's political success hinged on economic improvement in the Soviet Union and not on the export of a Marxist revolution.  He therefore balked at a "new international economic order" that would allow the Soviet Union's scarce resources to flow into inefficient economies and doubtful projects on its underdeveloped periphery.  The Soviets were also loath to sink funds into exacerbating US-Cuban tension, which would benefit the "unrestructured" Cuban leadership more than it would advance the current foreign policy line of the Kremlin.

The "new thinking" entailed an effort to preserve Soviet strategic gains but with less international tension and hence at a lower cost. Aleksandr Iakovlev, a CPSU Politburo member and spokesman on ideological matters, argued that the traditional Marxist analysis of the capitalist crisis would have to be revised, because capitalism was not about to collapse, but on the contrary remained dynamic. The main driving force of US imperialism was its militarism. Remove the pretext for military confrontation, and US imperialism was weakened. Therefore, without abandoning the notion of ideological opposition, socialism should seek relations based on peace, cooperation, and interdependence rather than be drawn into a further escalation of the arms race and overt global rivalry which was the alleged objective of the USA.[12] Hence, Moscow sought to de-emphasize overt confrontation, improve the Soviet image, and promote relations with influential moderate developing countries such as Mexico, Brazil, Argentina, Egypt, Kuwait, Saudi Arabia, Indonesia, and Thailand.[13]

9
## AFGHANISTAN: ENDING AN UNPOPULAR WAR
Sallie Wise

A majority of the Soviet citizens undoubtedly applauded the withdrawal of their troops from Afghanistan that began on May 15, 1988. The USSR had finally committed itself to disengage from an unpopular and unwinnable war which had become a serious drain on its economic resources and international prestige. The Soviet decision to withdraw troops from Afghanistan after more than eight years of war signaled a reevaluation of Soviet foreign policy. The potential damage to the USSR's stature from withdrawing in less than victorious circumstances was evidently reckoned to be less than that of pursuing a bankrupt policy in hopes of eventually saving face.

The Kremlin's decision to disengage militarily from Afghanistan can hardly have been made overnight. Most likely, it took shape gradually. It is probable that a major factor in the decision was the impact the war was having on Soviet domestic opinion.

*Public Opinion Research.* RFE/RL's Soviet Area Audience and Opinion Research unit (SAAOR) had been tracking the attitudes of Soviet citizens toward the USSR's involvement in Afghanistan for several years. A survey[1] was conducted during most of 1987, a time when the conclusion that withdrawal was inevitable must have crystallized among Soviet leaders. 1987 brought changes on the military front in Afghanistan that in turn reverberated on the domestic front back in the Soviet Union. The possibility of achieving a military victory over the Afghan resistance had apparently faded, and the Kremlin focused its energies on trying to achieve a face-saving settlement on its own terms by diplomatic means. At the same time, Soviet troops in Afghanistan faced the prospect of military defeat by a force of Mujahiddin better armed and organized than previously.

At home, Soviet citizens were exposed to a sobering view of the war through a much more realistic media coverage than in previous years. The climate created by glasnost encouraged Soviet citizens to express their opinions and generated greater official interest in public opinion.[2] Evidence of negative public opinion on Afghanistan surfaced more and more frequently in letters to the editors of official publications. Although glasnost was much more limited on foreign policy issues than on domestic ones, it permitted a little more light to be shed on the state of affairs in Afghanistan. As a Ukrainian technician in his thirties observed, "lots of articles have appeared about Afghanistan in the Soviet press. It's no longer a secret that there's a war going on in which many people are dying."

Nearly half the Soviet urban adult population (45 percent) in 1987 disapproved of official policy, while less than a quarter (24 per cent) still approved and close on a third (31 percent) remained ambivalent on the issue. This represented a considerable shift in opinion since 1986: disapproval of the USSR's role in Afghanistan had increased by 12 percentage points, while approval dropped by 8 points. Whereas in previous years attitudes toward Soviet involvement in Afghanistan had become increasingly polarized, there appeared in 1987 to be a surge of disapproval of official policy across all demographic categories. Given the fact that by 1987 official Soviet policy advocated the withdrawal of Soviet troops if certain conditions were met, the increase in disapproval was all the more striking. While the Kremlin was advocating conditional withdrawal, a large number of Soviet citizens favored unconditional withdrawal from Afghanistan. In the words of an Armenian builder in his thirties, "There is no justification for the Soviet involvement in Afghanistan. This is a war that never should have happened."

*The Role of the Media.* During the course of the war the Soviet media repeatedly changed their tack in reporting on events in Afghanistan. They never were able, however, to "manage" the Afghanistan issue by hitting upon a convincing rationale for the USSR's involvement in the conflict. Rather, media coverage was reactive, acknowledging, at least in part, what many people already knew from eyewitness accounts or from foreign radio broadcasts to be the true situation. According to a Russian scientist, a party member in her forties: "In the first years of the war the mass media carried only positive accounts of the war. After eight years, the tone has changed and one can tell that Soviet aid has not had the desired result."

Over the years there was a noticeable link between opinion about the war and sources tapped for information about it. In 1987, as in previous years, the attitudes of Soviet citizens who relied on foreign radio broadcasts or word of mouth for information on Afghanistan differed significantly from those whose information came from the official Soviet media and agitprop. Those who cited foreign radio as a source of information on Afghanistan continued to display the greatest disapproval of the Soviet role there (71 percent), followed by those who relied on information passed by word of mouth (64 percent). Although a wide attitudinal gap remained between Soviet citizens citing the official Soviet media and those relying more on "unofficial" sources on Afghanistan, disapproval increased noticeably among the former. Approval dropped among users of all official media, reflecting the increasingly sober official coverage of events in Afghanistan.

The Soviet press was consistently the source of information on Afghanistan most widely used. Just as the print medium had been in the forefront of glasnost overall, reporting on Afghanistan in the press was most revealing of any medium. However, television continued to grow in importance as a source of information on the war. This was clearly a result of the increased television coverage of events on Afghanistan.

Heeding calls for greater glasnost about Afghanistan may have been due, to some extent, to the fact that the war was no longer solely a matter of foreign policy. The Afghan conflict had a far-reaching domestic impact on the Soviet public, not only in terms of casualties, but also in terms of long-term social problems. Phenomena such as vigilantism or, conversely, cynicism among youths who had served in Afghanistan, drug addiction, the problems of invalid veterans, and so on, were discussed in the press with increasing frequency and candor. The fact that letters to the editor expressing disapproval of the role of Soviet troops in Afghanistan were printed in a number of publications[3] signaled official awareness of the domestic dimension of the Afghan dilemma. Indeed, in the wake of the decision to withdraw from Afghanistan it seems that a certain amount of soul-searching was taking place to see if the costs of the war had been worth it.[4]

*Non-Russian Republics.* Residents of all geographic areas in the USSR grew more disillusioned with the Soviet role in Afghanistan between 1986 and 1987. As in previous years, disapproval of the Soviet presence in Afghanistan was highest overall among inhabitants of non-Russian areas.

The greatest shifts in attitudes to Afghanistan during 1987 took place among inhabitants of Central Asia. In the past, Central Asian residents were the most polarized in their opinions about the conflict. The rate of approval of official policy in Afghanistan among inhabitants of Central Asian SSRs in 1987 plummeted by 23 percentage points to 18 percent. At the same time, disapproval among Central Asian residents rose 9 points to nearly half (49 percent); they also became more ambivalent on the issue, with one-third expressing no clear attitude (an increase of 14 points). This suggests that the surge in approval of official policy among Central Asian residents noted in SAAOR's data for 1986 was ephemeral. In addition, it appears that some inhabitants of Central Asia who previously had supported the party line on Afghanistan later became less convinced of the wisdom of official policy. An Uzbek service worker in her forties commented: "Our boys are dying for an alien cause."

Residents of the Baltic States continued to have the highest rate of disapproval of Soviet policy in Afghanistan: 67 percent, an increase of 16 points since 1986. A mere 12 percent of Baltic residents expressed approval of the Soviet role in Afghanistan. This group was also the least ambivalent about the war in Afghanistan (21 percent), and was by far the most likely to think the USSR would not achieve its objectives (51 percent).

There was a large increase in disapproval—from 37 percent to 58 percent—among residents of the Caucasian SSRs, a group which previously had been relatively ambivalent on the Afghan issue. Caucasian residents came to resemble Baltic residents in their attitudes to Afghanistan, and now had the second-highest rate of disapproval and second-lowest approval rate.

Inhabitants of the Ukrainian SSR had the same attitudinal patterns on Afghanistan in 1987 as did Central Asian residents. Belorussian residents, however, grew more ambivalent than before. With increased disapproval of the Soviet presence in Afghanistan generalized across all geographic groups, however, differences in attitudes between the RSFSR and non-Russian areas of the USSR became less pronounced.

*The RSFSR.* Residents of all areas of the RSFSR expressed considerably greater disapproval of official policy in Afghanistan during 1987 than previously. Although the RSFSR was still the only region of the Soviet Union where approval of the Soviet role in Afghanistan remained above 20 percent, disapproval nonetheless became, for the first time, the dominant attitude in all areas except Siberia. This rise in disapproval in areas where Russians were the dominant ethnic group suggested that the core of support for official policy in the traditional Russian heartland was eroding.

As in 1986, Moscow and Leningrad residents continued to change their attitudes about the Soviet role in Afghanistan, with respective increases in disapproval of 14 and 18 percentage points. Leningrad residents and, to a lesser extent, Muscovites, had become less ambivalent on the Afghan issue. These findings strengthened the hypothesis that the Soviet elite, based largely in the two metropolitan areas of Moscow and Leningrad, became disenchanted with the stalemate in Afghanistan. Residents of the provincial European and Siberian regions of the RSFSR also showed rises in disapproval of official policy toward Afghanistan. However, while inhabitants of the European RSFSR drew closer to the attitudinal patterns of their cosmopolitan compatriots, Siberia remained the last bastion in the Soviet Union where approval was the predominant attitude to the war.

*Party Members Disillusioned.* The gap between party members and non-members in their attitudes to official policy on Afghanistan narrowed steadily over the years. While party members still had a higher rate of approval and a lower rate of disapproval than non-members in 1987, the differences were much less pronounced than before. This would indicate that party members, whose rates of approval and disapproval were nearly equal (39 percent and 37 percent respectively), came to reassess the Soviet role in Afghanistan. A Russian inspector and Communist party member in his forties said he felt that "the USSR went too far in its military aid to Afghanistan." Indeed, the finding that less than 40 percent of the party members actively approved of the Soviet Union's military role strongly suggests that the erosion of support within party ranks strengthened the case for Soviet withdrawal.

Also, members of the Communist party became more pessimistic about the prospects for Soviet success in Afghanistan in 1987. There was little difference between party members and non-members in their prediction of the outcome of the Afghan conflict. With only 33 percent of the party members believing that the USSR would achieve its aims in Afghanistan, it seems clear that the vanguard of the Soviet population had lost confidence in official policy there. A Belorussian blue-collar worker and party member in his thirties expressed this view: "I don't like this war and neither does anyone else.... Going into Afghanistan was an error, but ending it is a matter of prestige."

*Conclusion.* The rapidity with which the Soviet Union backed away from its conditions for withdrawal early in 1988 suggests that a fallback position on the issue had already been staked out. 1987 was, then, a pivotal year in the evolution of Soviet policy toward the Afghan conflict. It was, moreover, a year when public disapproval of the USSR's role reached a critical point, spreading to virtually all segments of the population, even the Russian heartland. In particular, there was an erosion of approval among the Soviet elite—party members and metropolitan dwellers—for the USSR's continued involvement in Afghanistan. This factor, in conjunction with the somewhat greater attention paid to public opinion in the USSR in general, must have played some part in the decision to withdraw Soviet troops. Indeed, it seems clear that Soviet public opinion on the USSR's involvement in Afghanistan finally came to carry some weight in the Kremlin. Domestic discontent exacerbated the costs of participation of Soviet troops in combat in Afghanistan. The price in terms of human casualties, economic burden, and loss of face at home and abroad, was evidently too high.

10
# SOVIET-VIETNAMESE RELATIONS
Patrick Moore

On August 28, 1988, week-long Sino-Soviet talks on the Cambodian question began between the two countries' deputy foreign ministers in Beijing. Exactly a month earlier, the Jakarta Informal Meeting ended, having brought together, at least for initial talks, the three Cambodian groups in the anti-Vietnamese resistance, Hanoi's client régime in Phnom Penh, and, to a lesser extent, other interested parties in Southeast Asia, including the Vietnamese.

*A Solution in Cambodia?* These and other, less striking developments led some observers to suggest that there was real movement toward a solution of the Cambodian problem, which had begun with the Vietnamese invasion of that country in December 1978 and the overthrow of the Pol Pot dictatorship, which had terrorized its own people since coming to power in 1975, partly with Vietnamese help.

Some writers had argued that Hanoi would sooner or later find itself forced to wind down the conflict, since the war was costly and the Vietnamese economy was tottering on the verge of collapse. They noted that a study by the United Nations, cited by the Vietnamese themselves, ranked Vietnam number 161 out of 164 countries in terms of wealth,[1] and that in any event, Hanoi had pledged to withdraw its remaining troops, generally estimated by Western observers to total between 130,000 and 140,000 men, from Cambodia by 1990. Finally, they pointed out that Vietnam needed to quit Cambodia if it were to overcome its diplomatic and economic semi-isolation that had limited its contacts to the Soviet bloc, India, Sweden, and a few other countries, and establish normal links with the United States, Japan, and its non-communist neighbors.

*Not Eastern Europe.* A final argument used by those who felt that "peace is breaking out" and who foresaw an end to regional conflicts around the globe, including Cambodia, claimed that the Soviet Union wanted to place its relations with its clients in the Third World on a more cost-effective basis. This had been frequently pointed out by Gorbachev and others. The argument went on, however, to make a crucial assumption: that Moscow had considerable leverage over Vietnam by virtue of the roughly $1,000 million it gave Hanoi each year, and would use this clout to convince the Vietnamese to end their costly war and devote their resources and energies to developing their own economy. This assumption was, however, debatable and touched on the fundamental nature of the Moscow-Hanoi alliance, which was not the same kind of relationship that the Soviets enjoyed with their East European comrades. The key difference was military. First, while Vietnam was a member of Comecon and an ally of the Soviet Union, it did not belong to the Warsaw Pact; hence the Soviet Army did not have the same kind of institutional links with the People's Army of

Vietnam that it did with Warsaw Pact armies, with the partial exception of Romania.

Second, the Soviets were hardly in a position to use military power to impose policies on Hanoi, even if they should ever have considered doing so. The most crucial factor was geography: Not only did the USSR and Vietnam not share a common frontier, but between them them lay the great land mass of a China that regarded the Soviet-Vietnamese relationship with deep suspicion if not outright hostility. Furthermore, while the Soviet bases at the former American installations at Danang and Cam Ranh were strategically important for enabling the Soviet Union to project its power directly into Southeast Asia, they were largely the preserve of naval and air forces, not of ground forces. In short, any Soviet influence with the Vietnamese had to come through political and economic means alone, means that did not prove sufficient to prevent the Sino-Soviet rift.

*Different Perceptions.* Moscow and Hanoi, moreover, had profoundly different understandings of their relationship. The leading American expert on Vietnam, Professor Douglas Pike, made this point clear in his book, *Vietnam and the Soviet Union: Anatomy of an Alliance*.[2] The Soviets, Pike noted, viewed their assistance to the Vietnamese revolution over the years as vital, bountiful, timely, and disinterested; the Vietnamese regarded it as incidental, niggardly, tardy, and aimed primarily at offsetting Chinese influence in Vietnam after the Sino-Soviet split emerged in the early to mid nineteen-sixties. The Vietnamese Communists, he wrote, were particularly upset that both Moscow and Beijing agreed at the 1954 Indochina peace conference in Geneva to partition their country into a communist north and noncommunist south, forcing them to engage in another war and wait 21 years before they could assume power throughout the country.[3]

The negative feelings were not limited to official matters: Russians were highly unpopular and even hated, being compared unfavorably in the popular mind with the French and Americans as racist, unfriendly, aloof, and stingy. A number of Western visitors to Vietnam were nearly killed by locals who had mistaken them for Soviets; they saved themselves only by producing their passports or other evidence of origin. One Belgian was not so quick or lucky, and the killer told the police that he had thought his victim was a Soviet. Technicians at a Swedish aid project seemed aware of such attitudes: when they went on the streets of Hanoi, they wore T-shirts with bold letters reading *Khong Lien Xo* (Not a Soviet).[4]

But perhaps Pike's most original contribution to the literature on the Soviet-Vietnamese relationship was his theory that Vietnamese culture contained some particular ethnocentric and xenophobic attitudes that would make any Vietnamese polity a difficult partner, especially for countries with a traditional European understanding of the rules of international relations.[5] In a nutshell, Pike argued that Vietnamese viewed relationships with outsiders as a necessity in a dangerous world, but saw nothing wrong in tricking, taking advantage of, or laughing at the foreign partner. At the same time, they regarded the ally as absolutely obliged to help them, and were baffled and shocked if this assistance was less than expected. The professor suggested that this problem in cultural perceptions lay at the bottom of French and American difficulties with their Vietnamese allies, went a long way to explain Hanoi's "ingratitude" toward and repudiation of its long-time ally in Beijing, and, above all, did not bode well for the future of the Soviet-Vietnamese relationship.

*Current Problems.* Thus it seems that not only did the alliance rest on weaker institutional foundations than those which Moscow had with the Warsaw Pact countries, and that the Soviets did not have the ultimate military option in influencing Hanoi, but that the two sides viewed the relationship in different terms. A number of issues, moreover, surfaced to put yet further strains on the alliance.

The first and most important was China. In short, Hanoi viewed the Soviet Union as a useful or even necessary counterweight to an unfriendly China, Vietnam's traditional cultural model but also traditional chief enemy. As long as Moscow and Beijing were at loggerheads, Hanoi could feel comfortable. At least since 1982, however, the Vietnamese had been hinting that they felt the Soviets might "sell them out" in order to normalize ties with China. This become all the more relevant later when Beijing made it clear to Gorbachev that the one main "obstacle" in the way of good relations and a summit meeting was Cambodia. To remove this obstacle, the Chinese seemed to be saying not that the Soviets would have to actually force the Vietnamese to withdraw from Cambodia, but simply that they would have to make efforts to do so. This formulation enabled Moscow and Beijing to normalize relations without Hanoi being able to block them by staying in Cambodia.

The second issue was Vietnamese squandering of Soviet aid, which was a source of concern to Moscow even under Brezhnev. In 1980, the Soviets found equipment sent to Haiphong in 1968 still lying about, and there was an apparent case of arson to cover up pilfering at the port of Haiphong, which resulted in the destruction of $28,000,000 worth of goods.[6] Under Gorbachev, criticism of the squandering and stress on the need to use Soviet aid more effectively, became standard in both the Soviet and the Vietnamese speeches when representatives of the two countries met.[7] The Vietnamese apparently recognized the problem, but they did not seem particularly successful in any aspect of their economic reforms, including this one. Soviets made it clear that Vietnam and other Third World clients should concentrate on their traditional economic pursuits and small industries rather than on building up a modern industry.[8] Products mentioned included rubber, coffee, tropical fruits, and raw materials—precisely the approach taken by the French colonialists; the parallel was unlikely to be lost on any Vietnamese, however economically sound the advice. If the Soviets, however were to become impatient and slash the amount of assistance they provided to

Hanoi, they would find themselves with even less chance of influencing the behavior of their client; reports suggested a growing impatience with and frustration over the economic relationship on both sides.[9]

*Whither?* The Soviet-Vietnamese alliance thus seemed to be a marriage of convenience—if the relationship was ever that close to begin with. Strains were visible, and it was unlikely to prove durable, particularly if China and the Soviet Union drew closer together and if Hanoi somehow disengaged itself from the Cambodian conflict and thereby acquired new diplomatic and economic options. But, whichever way it decided to leave Cambodia, it was likely to do so of its own accord and in line with its own national interests, and not because of Soviet pressure.

## 11
## NEW THINKING IN THE BALKANS
Stephen Ashley and Louis Zanga*

The conference of the six Balkan Foreign Ministers, the first meeting at such a high level in the troubled history of the peninsula, was held in Belgrade from February 24 to 26, 1988. It was, the participants and foreign observers agreed, a major success. As had been anticipated, the delegations preserved harmony and dignity in the sessions by avoiding direct criticism of other participants and referring to their bilateral disputes in only abstract or allusive terms. The conference focused its three days of speeches and discussions on the development of regional cooperation in trade, industry, energy generation, transport, communications, tourism, environmental protection, education, sports, and culture.[1]

This same pragmatic approach guided the drafting of a well-balanced final communiqué that Turkish Foreign Minister Mesut Yilmaz described as "a major effort of compromise."[2] It synthesized various proposals for promoting multilateral cooperation and contained an agreement "in principle" that meetings of Foreign Ministers should be held at unspecified intervals. By not determining the regularity of future conferences, the communiqué deferred to the wishes of the

---

* Author of the section on Albania

Albanian delegation, which had also objected to Romania's call for a summit meeting of Balkan Heads of State.[3]

*Bulgaria's Attitude Toward the Conference.* Bulgaria was formally invited to attend the Belgrade Foreign Ministers' meeting by former Yugoslav Foreign Minister Raif Dizdarević in a circular letter sent to his five Balkan counterparts on April 6, 1987. In spite of the fact that Bulgaria had repeatedly stated its willingness to contribute to multilateral Balkan cooperation in areas that were not sensitive, its response was cautious. By the end of the summer, however, Sofia's misgivings appeared to have been dispelled, possibly because preliminary diplomatic exchanges had begun to move toward an informal agreement that the conference would avoid controversial issues and respect the principle of noninterference in other countries' domestic affairs.

Subsequently, the Bulgarian government, Foreign Ministry officials, and the media spoke in increasingly positive terms about the foreign ministers' meeting. At the BCP national conference in January 1988, Deputy Foreign Minister Lyuben Gotsev said that Bulgaria regarded the Belgrade meeting as the fruit of Soviet foreign policy initiatives that had improved the international climate, reducing tension between NATO and the Warsaw Pact. He said that Bulgaria would go to Belgrade in order to prove that the principles of "new thinking" could be applied in relations among "lesser" states and that neighboring countries should cooperate and not seek "to complicate the atmosphere" in the Balkans.[4] Other official commentaries repeated another theme of Gorbachev's foreign policy, calling for efforts to improve security and relations on "the Balkan floor of the common European house." At the same time, Bulgarian spokesmen attempted to claim some of the credit for the successful convening of the Belgrade conference by stressing that Bulgaria's good relations with Greece had served as a model for other Balkan states.

As no sensitive issues affecting regional defense or the bloc loyalties of the participants were discussed at Belgrade, it would be wrong to see Bulgaria's support for the conference as a major reversal of its traditional Balkan policy. A certain shift of emphasis did, however, become discernible; the Bulgarian government had been showing more concern for multilateral initiatives in the previous two years, almost certainly as a consequence of its acceptance of "new thinking." On August 11, 1986, the BCP daily *Rabotnichesko Delo* argued that "the growing interdependence and connections between the Balkan states" required a higher level of regional cooperation. It said that the Balkan countries could not hope to compete in the world economy without a greater pooling of resources and talent, and that the peninsula's growing environmental problems could only be solved through multilateral agreements. *Rabotnichesko Delo* also adapted a characteristic element of "new thinking" when it said that "no Balkan state can guarantee its security at the expense of another Balkan state."

*Toward Reconciliation with Turkey.* This statement was aimed primarily at Turkey. Since January 1985, when relations between the two countries began to deteriorate, the Bulgarian media claimed on several occasions that Turkish politicians had made indirect threats of war against Bulgaria. To the surprise of most observers, on February 23, the two foreign ministers, Petar Mladenov and Mesut Yilmaz, signed a protocol committing their governments to work toward signing a Declaration on Good-Neighborliness, Friendship, and Cooperation. Bulgaria had been demanding that relations be normalized (despite refusing to reconsider its policy toward its Turkish minority, which it continued to describe as "reborn Bulgarians"). Turkey's change of policy might be explained partly by its desire to ensure the success of the Belgrade conference and strengthen its rapprochement with Greece; another major factor, however, was undoubtedly Prime Minister Turgut Özal's awareness that confronting and seeking to isolate Bulgaria had failed to improve the lot of the Turkish minority and that negotiations might yield greater benefits.

The Turkish government had always hoped that its policy of confrontation and protest would lead to negotiations. During a state visit to Morocco in April 1987, President Kenan Evren said that his aim was to pressure Sofia into seeking a peaceful resolution of their conflicts.

Until the meeting in Belgrade between Mladenov and Yilmaz, Bulgaria's response to these overtures had been ambiguous. After maintaining silence over the fate of the Bulgarian Turkish minority throughout 1985, the USSR seemed to play a significant part in persuading Bulgaria to be more flexible. It repeatedly urged the two countries to improve their relations; on November 25, 1987, Albert Chernyshev, the Soviet Ambassador in Ankara, said that he supported negotiations to establish good relations between Bulgaria and Turkey.[5]

Bulgaria subsequently made a number of gestures to ease tension and prepare for the signing of the protocol. From January 1987, it allowed 64 children of ethnic Turkish descent to join their parents in Turkey (10 were permitted to leave on February 23, the day the protocol was signed). In October 1987 it allowed Mustafa Suleymanov, a Bulgarian Turk who had taken refuge in the Turkish embassy in Moscow, to emigrate to Turkey and in return secured the repatriation to Bulgaria of Metodi Davidov (Mehmed Demirel), who was being detained in Turkey on charges of espionage.

While expressing approval of the new protocol, Yilmaz's predecessor as Turkish Foreign Minister Vahit Halefoglu revealed that it had been prepared during secret discussions that had been going on between the two Foreign Ministries for over a year, presumably since his meeting with Mladenov in Vienna in November 1986.[6] It seems likely that the reunification of families and the exchange of accused agents were agreed upon during these secret talks. Bulgaria probably also used them as a forum to protest over the Turkish television series "To Be Reborn," which was canceled after the second episode, in December 1987, when Bulgaria released the ethnic Turkish girl Aysel Özgür, whose case had been featured in the series.

The protocol called for the creation of two mixed commissions to work toward a full normalization of relations. The first would review all existing bilateral disputes, including those over "humanitarian issues," and prepare the draft of the declaration, presumably to be modeled on the declaration signed between Bulgaria and Greece in September 1986, which would include a nonaggression clause and an agreement that the two governments would confer during any crisis in the Balkan region. The second commission was to boost bilateral cooperation in trade, transport, communications, and tourism, tapping the massive unfulfilled potential for exchanges between the two states. It was also agreed to institute regular meetings between the Bulgarian and Turkish foreign ministers.

*Albania's New-Look Diplomacy.* The foreign ministers conference had a special significance for Albania: it was the first time Albania participated in a multilateral Balkan gathering, the clearest evidence to date of the country's pragmatic approach to foreign policy and its genuine interest in becoming an active member of the Balkan community of nations. Albania's new-look diplomacy was demonstrated masterfully by its foreign minister, Reiz Malile.

In sharp contrast to his ideologically-inspired and assertive speeches at past annual United Nations General Assembly meetings, Malile's approach in Belgrade was conciliatory, pragmatic, and more realistic. He was firm on key issues and conciliatory in his language. "A star," "astonishing," "an elegant, French-speaking diplomat," were some of the more euphoric appraisals of Malile by foreign journalists; the TASS reporter also had positive things to say of him.

Malile succeeded in giving the clear impression that Tirana wanted to pursue a nonisolationist policy through more active participation in Balkan affairs. He was firm when necessary, for example, in reiterating Albania's continued opposition to multilateral meetings at the highest level. He said that the time was not ripe for a Balkan summit meeting (which had been proposed by Romania) and that it was wrong to hold high-level "parades" that would give the false impression that all disputes had been settled. Nevertheless, he did not minimize the value and benefit of multilateral cooperation but rather emphasized the necessity of bilateral relations, as complementing each other.[7]

There was little new in Malile's proposals about cooperation in the Balkans; they reflected Albania's general line that cooperation with foreign countries, particularly neighbors, could contribute to the country's domestic development. He urged the development of small-scale trade across the borders, which would not only be of economic benefit but would also serve humanitarian aims, he said. This statement followed trade agreements with Greece and Yugoslavia. Barely a week after Malile's speech in Belgrade, a chamber of commerce was opened in the southern city of Gjirokaster, the specific aim of which was to promote trade between the Greek and Albanian border areas.[8]

The only really novel proposal in Malile's speech was his suggestion that the "Committees of Balkan Understanding" be revived. This was a scheme launched by the Greeks in 1961. Malile said that these committees should include parliamentarians, writers, journalists, and members of mass organizations as representatives of public opinion.

It was the first time that Albania had been represented at a conference of Balkan states. The Yugoslav hosts in particular seemed very pleased at the Albanians' attendance. The Albanian-language daily *Rilindja*, published in Priština, interviewed journalists from Tirana,[9] and the correspondent of the Tirana daily *Bashkimi* was quoted as saying that "we are neighbors and must be friends."

The Yugoslav press commented that Malile's speech had been "delicate" and "pragmatic" and that he had avoided stirring up any controversy by skillfully skirting the Kosovo issue through declaring that the national minorities should help build bridges between states.[10]   Malile used the conference to meet separately with some of his Balkan counterparts. He  granted an interview to *Rilindja*, in which he said that Albania was in favor of a "high standard of integrity" in relations with Yugoslavia. He reiterated his claim that the minorities acted as bridges and, with specific reference to Kosovo, said that "we have not demanded and do not demand anything." This was an apparent response to the Yugoslavs' allegations that Albania had territorial claims on Yugoslavia.[11]

Three conclusions could be drawn from Albania's participation in the Balkan Foreign Ministers' conference. First, Albania could no longer be referred to as "an isolated Balkan island." Second, by its attendance for the first time at a multilateral conference, Tirana had reentered the European political scene. Third, an important step forward had been taken toward the long overdue reconciliation between Yugoslavia and Albania.

## 12
## SOVIET CULTURAL FIGURES
## INTERVIEWED ON RADIO LIBERTY
### Wayne Brown

Three prominent Soviet theatrical figures visited Radio Liberty's studios in Munich on January 29, 1988, and took part in a discussion on new trends in the Soviet theater and cinema for the program "Over the Barriers." Mark Zakharov, chief director of Moscow's Lenin Komsomol Theater and secretary of the USSR Union of Theater Workers, and two of the Theater's leading actors, Oleg Iankovskii and Aleksandr Abdulov, had come to Munich to take part in a Moscow theater festival. This was the first broadcast of its kind in the Radio's history.

The three participants interviewed by Radio Liberty's Vladimir Matusevich stressed the value of seeing with their own eyes the enthusiastic reception accorded the plays in Munich. Zakharov pointed out that since Soviet correspondents had always reported only the positive aspects of a play's reception abroad, it had been impossible "to understand the real success or failure of this or that theater on the basis of what our press printed."

The most significant development in the Soviet theatrical world, according to Zakharov, was the relaxation of state censorship in some—though not all—theaters throughout 1987. Censorship had stifled interesting initiatives by many artists, writers, directors, and actors. Now, he said, "No one interferes in our affairs," and the only criterion for a play at his theater was whether it was any good.

Zakharov went on to say, however, that the relaxation of censorship had brought with it new responsibilities: "We have come to know the burden of freedom," he said, or at least of "relative freedom." His theater now had to engage the public's interest not only by presenting problems in an incisive manner but by dealing with more profound themes, such as the exploration of man's nature and spirit.

Matusevich asked Zakharov what he thought of Polish film director Krzysztof Zanussi's remark that censorship was helpful, in a certain sense, because it forced a serious artist to circumvent it and dig to get at the heart of a subject. Mentioning the title of the Radio Liberty program on which he was speaking—"Over the Barriers"—Zakharov replied: "A barrier, a certain ban, a certain counteraction, a certain feeling of struggle can greatly develop certain qualities in a person and move him to some serious undertaking." He added that "a theater works interestingly and well only in the earth's volcanic zones, where the air is saturated ... with some kind of electrical charges of social torments, searching, sufferings, deliberations."

Acknowledging the Soviet leadership's contribution to the changes taking place in Soviet cultural life, Zakharov said that "great energy has come from such people as Gorbachev, [and] Iakovlev—our leaders in the Politburo." He added that he thought they would do a lot more to help. In conclusion, he expressed optimism for the future but cautioned that "the process will be very slow."

Andrei Voznesenskii, one of the Soviet Union's leading poets, talked about the past, present, and future of Soviet literature in another interview with Radio Liberty. He and three other Soviet literary figures were in Munich at the invitation of the Bavarian Academy of Fine Arts. The others were Bella Akhmadulina, Anatolii Pristavkin, and Andrei Bitov. Voznesenskii, who gave the interview to an RL editor on February 14, 1988, spoke about his impressions of the Moscow theater festival in Munich. He said Munich audiences had seen "a new Russia full of dispute," and the reception had been overwhelming.[1]

He talked about the rehabilitation of the late writer Boris Pasternak and the late bard Vladimir Vysotskii, and their persecution. Referring to the serialization of Pasternak's novel *Doctor Zhivago* in the literary monthly *Novyi mir*, Voznesenskii called the book "a masterpiece of literature" and said it contained no "crude politics." He noted that Pasternak had been forced to refuse the Nobel Prize for Literature. He said the prize should be reinstated because it rightly belonged to Pasternak. Voznesenskii said Vysotskii—an enormously popular singer and actor—might still have been be alive if during his lifetime he had received just "one-thousandth" of the recognition he was now being given; there were still some people who "shriek with hatred when they hear his [Vysotskii's] words." He called these people "the brakes of perestroika."

Voznesenskii also spoke of "the revolution by culture," a concept he coined. He said fresh ideas and new views were needed to change the economy and democratize Soviet society. He said the artist, the writer, and the poet were providing those ideas and views so that "the revolution penetrates to the people." He talked about previously forbidden works that were now being published in the Soviet Union and about efforts by cultural figures to promote the process under way. He said it was very important for a new generation to come onto the scene.

## 13
## LITERARY BATTLES IN THE USSR
### Julia Wishnevsky

Iurii Kariakin, a well-known philosopher and literary scholar, wrote: "The last two or three years are unprecedented in the entire history of our literature. Never has so much literature, and of such [quality], appeared in such a brief space—all at once!"[1] He referred in particular to the belles-lettres, both poetry and prose; literary criticism, his own genre, was least in his mind.

According to a tradition dating back to the first half of the nineteenth century, Russian literary criticism influenced not only literary taste but social issues too. All the so-called revolutionary democrats of the 1840-60 period were literary critics. Their work had a decisive influence on the rise of opposition to the tsarist régime. The first hot blast of Khrushchev's "thaw" was Vladimir Pomerantsev's essay "About Sincerity in Literature."[2] Conversely, the stagnation under Brezhnev began after the rout of the editorial board of *Novyi mir*, the primary causes of which were the publications of literary critics.[3]

*Restructuring and the Tradition of Novyi mir.* According to a former contributor and critic, Iurii Burtin, in the second half of the nineteen-sixties, *Novyi mir* was "the chief organ of democratic opposition" to the general line of the then leadership of the CPSU. Burtin said the question of *Novyi mir's* oppositional stance was very topical because of Gorbachev's policy of perestroika. He spoke of the need to revive "criticism that translates the images and characters of the writer into the language of social thought." Burtin came to the conclusion that "a system [which is based on] the ownership of the means of production by the state" was pernicious to the morality of the people, and that it was necessary to exchange it for "some kind of substantially different economic mechanism."[4]

The rout of *Novyi mir* at the beginning of 1970 was but one episode in the persecution of writers in the Soviet Union. This history began with the formation of "Associations of Proletarian Writers" in 1920, progressed through Stalin's Terror, the years of Ezhov and Zhdanov, periodic campaigns against Formalism and the decadent influence of Western ideology in the nineteen-fifties and nineteen-sixties, until it wallowed in the quiet murk of the bureaucratic cabals of the Brezhnev, Andropov, and Chernenko eras. The terrible truth about how all this came about was now being revealed in literary journals.

The excursions into history were not merely academic; they served to help understand how the system of managing literature came about and flourished, and how political smears and denunciation became the chief weapon against independent writers and editors occupying key positions in the Writers' Union. Benedikt Sarnov depicted this system in his eloquent article "The Fight for the Right to Write Badly" He wrote that people who like to give orders and defend their right to write badly from [their] commanding positions have not disappeared.

"*The Right to Write Badly.*" Sarnov's article appeared after a memorable session of the Secretariat of the Writers' Union of the RSFSR in March 1987, during which the writers Petr Proskurin, Iurii Bondarev, Mikhail Alekseev, and others demanded "a new Battle of Stalingrad" with critics who had dared to assert that they wrote only moderately well.[5]   A collective appeal to the Central Committee of the CPSU was directed against *Ogonek*, the journal in which Sarnov's article was published, and against its editor, Vitalii Korotich. Seventeen writers reportedly accused Korotich of abusing glasnost, engaging in "incitement, lies, and dangerous social demagogy."

Viacheslav Gorbachev, deputy editor of the journal *Molodaia gvardiia*, subsequently demanded the sacking of the chief editors of *Ogonek, Literaturnaia gazeta, Nedelia, Moskovskie novosti, Sovetskaia kultura*, and *Oktiabr*. He divided Soviet writers into two categories: those printed in his own journal, *Moskva* and *Nash sovremennik*—all "epoch-making and great"—and the rest, tending toward a *nabokovshchina*.[6]

The fight for the right to work in bad faith also affected criticism and literary scholarship. The textbook *The History of Russian Soviet Literature*, edited by Professor Petr Vykhodtsev, which was used by all university students of twentieth century Russian literature still repeated the characterizations of the works of Boris Pasternak, Mikhail Bulgakov, Osip Mandelshtam, and Mikhail Zoshchenko,   made during the Zhdanov era. Marina Tsvetaeva was not mentioned at all. Even the orthodox classics such as Samuil Marshak, Valentin Kataev, and Ilia Erenburg were mentioned only in passing, yet Sergei Vikulov and Stanislav Kuniaev, and the Stalinists Anatolii Sofronov and Vladimir Firsov, merited separate chapters. Only in 1987 did Vadim Sokolov criticize Vykhodtsev's textbook in *Iunost*.[7] In this he was supported by the most important literary weekly, *Literaturnaia gazeta*,[8] as well as the most authoritative professional journal, *Voprosy literatury*.[9]

*Literature about Stalin and His Times*. The relaxation of censorship after the 1986 Congress of Soviet Writers unleashed a veritable flood of poetry and prose on the theme of Stalin and Stalinism, followed by a steady stream of literary criticism on the subject.

The most topical theme in the present context was the collectivization of agriculture between 1928 and 1932. The fate of the children of families whose fathers were dispossessed and exiled as kulaks was the subject of the poem "*Po pravu pamiati*" (By Right of Memory)[10] by the late Aleksandr Tvardovskii, chief editor of *Novyi mir*.

In his novel *Deti Arbata* (The Children of Arbat), veteran novelist Anatolii Rybakov depicted the assassination on Stalin's orders of Sergei Kirov, the head of the Leningrad party organization, in December 1934. Set in the early nineteen-thirties, Rybakov's novel portrayed the very first steps in the process of the annihilation of the generation of Old Bolsheviks who made the revolution in 1917.[11] The specific period of the *"ezhovshchina,"* the Great Terror of 1937-38 that traditionally bears the name of the NKVD chief of the time, was depicted in Anna Akhmatova's poem *"Requiem,"*[12] in Azeri writer Iusuf Samedoglu's novel *Den kazni* (Day of Execution),[13] and in the late  Iurii Trifonov's unfinished novel *Ischeznovenie* (Disappearance).[14]

The overnight deportation of entire nations accused of collaborating with the Nazi invaders during World War II provided the backdrop for Anatolii Pristavkin's *Nochevala tuchka zolotaia* (A Golden Cloud Passed the Night).[15] Another forbidden topic until Gorbachev's accession to power was the persecution of geneticists following the discussion of biology that started in the Soviet Union in the nineteen-thirties and ultimately led to the complete suppression of genetics in 1948.[16] Vladimir Dudintsev's second novel, *Belye odezhdy* (White Coats),[17] which portrayed the arrests of the geneticists, became a symbol of the era of glasnost in exactly the same way as his first book, *Not by Bread Alone,*[18] became one of the first literary sensations of Khrushchev's thaw.

Another of Trifonov's works, *Nedolgoe prebyvanie v kamere pytok* (A Brief Stay in the Torture Chamber), recalled one of those numerous hate meetings during the "struggle against cosmopolitanism" in the late nineteen-forties and early nineteen-fifties.[19]  The father of the popular song-writer and novelist, Bulat Okudzhava, was a prominent Communist who perished during the purges of the late nineteen-thirties. In two autobiographical stories set in the nineteen-forties, *Devushka moei mechty* (Girl of My Dream) and *Iskusstvo kroiki i shitia* (The Art of Cutting and Tailoring), Okudzhava told of a young man whose father was shot and whose mother was arrested as the wife of "an enemy of the people."[20] Another russified Caucasian, Fazil Iskander, depicted the effect of Stalinism on the lives of the people in the mountains of his native land in the late nineteen-thirties.[21]

The depiction of the ordinary young men in the stories by Okudzhava and Iskander contrasts with the portrayal of Stalin himself in *Deti Arbata* and that of one of Stalin's ministers in the late Aleksandr Bek's novel *Novoe naznachenie* (New Appointment).[22] In her *Requiem*, Akhmatova, the widow and mother of victims of the terror, conveyed the desperation of the mothers waiting in lines outside the prisons of Leningrad in 1937.

Three different literary works depicting the horrors of  collectivization appeared in 1987. The first, Nikolai Kliuev's poem *Pogorelshchina* (The Burnt Land)[23] was written under the immediate impact of events, in 1928.  A poet with a peasant background, Kliuev showed the influence of Russian gnostic sects.  He saw the ruin of a northern Russian village in mystic terms; the disaster of collectivization signified for him the victory of the Devil, the serpent, over the peasant saints and angels.

Boris Mozhaev's novel *Muzhiki i baby* (Peasants and Peasant Women),[24] written in 1978-80, was more a journalistic piece than a novel; quotations from contemporary leaders of the Communist party occupied quite an important place in his narrative. He demonstrated the mass peasant resistance to collectivization and depicted the destruction and profanation of churches, the spoliation and "dekulakization" of neighbors, and the forcible deportation to Siberia of innocent children and the elderly.

Both Mozhaev and Vasilii Belov in his novel *Kanuny* (Eves),[25] expressed their preference for the voluntary forms of peasant cooperatives created before the October Revolution but destroyed during collectivization forced on the peasantry by Stalin. This point of view confirmed the official position of the Gorbachev leadership as conveyed in *Pravda*.[26] Other ideas of Mozhaev and Belov appeared, however, to be different. Some of Mozhaev's heroes interpreted collectivization, for example, as God's punishment of the peasants who had looted residences of landowners after the revolution in 1917.

*The Voices of Reaction. Molodaia gvardiia*, a Stalinist and extreme Russian-nationalist Soviet journal, became the principal opposition journal questioning the line of the Gorbachev leadership.

In an article printed in *Molodaia gvardiia* in July, 1987, the journal's deputy chief editor Viacheslav Gorbachev implied that Stalin's purges had not been so terrible. He claimed that the process of collectivization had been "different in different parts of the country," suggesting that in some parts of the USSR the dispossession and exile of the families of "rich" peasants in the early nineteen-thirties had been justified.[27] In any case, he said, Stalin was not personally responsible for the crimes of his era. He had been a victim of his own bureaucracy[28] and a tool in the hands of his secret police chiefs, Nikolai Ezhov and Lavrentii Beriia.[29]

An article by another of *Molodaia gvardiia*'s favorite contributors, Aleksandr Ovcharenko, lionized Stalin's close associate, Viacheslav Molotov.[30] Ovcharenko disclosed that the plot of Ivan Stadniuk's novel *Voina* (The War) was based on Molotov's unpublished memoirs. According to another contributor, Viktor Krechetov, truly great literature existed in the USSR in Stalin's time.[31]

*Molodaia gvardiia* opposed the publication of Pasternak's novel *Doctor Zhivago*[32] and strongly disapproved of exhibitions of the works of previously banned artists such as Vasilii Kandinsky[33] and Marc Chagall.[34] According to Nikolai Doroshenko, one of the journal's experts on the subject, a true Russian patriot should be ashamed of such decadent Western artists as Kandinsky, Chagall, and Pablo Picasso.[35]

Rock music was a particular bête noire of *Molodaia gvardiia*. In its September 1988 issue, critic Anatolii Doronin stated without a trace of humor that "rock music is not simply music but the religion of Evil."[36] In a diatribe against rock music, Arkadii Lisenkov and Iurii Sergeev claimed that the term "rock'n'roll" has "Negro roots" and that these words, "borrowed from Negro slang," contain "improper sexual implications." In the view of these two writers, rock music is based on "the denial of any human sense, honor, and beauty."[37]

In another article in *Molodaia gvardiia,* Aleksandr Nagorniuk, a legal expert, expressed his sympathy for two members of the Komsomol who had encountered punks in a cinema, decided to teach them a lesson in Soviet patriotism, and ended up by beating two of them to death.[38]

In March 1987, the journal printed an article in which its deputy chief editor alleged the existence of a conspiracy between Zionists and freemasons, whom he described as the living incarnation of Satan. This conspiracy, Gorbachev said, was responsible for the destruction of the Russian family and for the corruption of the Russian nation by sex, alcohol, and drugs.[39] In a review of Burliaev's film *Lermontov,* Anatolii Doronin hinted that Judeo-masonic conspirators had murdered the two greatest nineteenth-century Russian poets—Aleksandr Pushkin and Mikhail Lermontov.[40] Reviewing a novel about the eighteenth-century Russian court, Sergei Perevezentsev claimed that freemasons had always sought to dominate the world.[41]

*Molodaia gvardiia* appealed to that sizeable group of readers who shared Stalinist, anti-Western, and ultra-nationalist convictions.[42] There were at least two other monthly journals—*Nash sovremennik* and *Moskva*—whose editors propagated similar views, but *Molodaia gvardiia* was the most outspoken. Its print run was 640,000, and the combined print run of *Nash sovremennik* and *Moskva* was 650,000. However, the print run of *Molodaia gvardiia's* relatively liberal counterpart, the reform-minded Komsomol monthly *Iunost,* was over 3,000,000.

*Reactionaries Tighten Hold on the Writer's Union.* "Some of our comrades [among Soviet writers] have even gone so far as to propose the liquidation of the USSR Writers' Union as being an unnecessary organization," exclaimed Vladimir Karpov, the first secretary of the writers' organization, in his opening speech at a plenum of the union's board held on March 1 and 2, 1988, in Moscow.[43] Not surprisingly, Karpov did not approve of what he termed such an "extremist" proposal. In his speech, he reiterated the validity of Lenin's article "On the Party Organization and Party Literature" of 1905, which had constantly been invoked to suppress creative freedom in the USSR since the times of Stalin. Iurii Verchenko, the union's secretary for organization, said that the provision that Socialist Realism was the leading "creative method" for all Soviet writers would be retained in the draft of the union's new statute.

Since the Eighth Congress of Soviet Writers in June 1986, control over the Union of Writers had steadily been passing to the most conservative—for the most part, extreme Russian nationalist—elements in this very powerful organization.

At the 1986 Congress, such reform-minded writers as Andrei Voznesenskii, Ales Adamovich, Daniil Granin, and Academician Dmitrii Likhachev held the upper hand.[44] Immediately after the congress, censorship of literary works was virtually abolished; the conservative editors of many journals were replaced by moderates. Vitalii Korotich took over *Ogonek*, Sergei Zalygin *Novyi mir*, and Georgii Baklanov *Znamia*; and the journals proceeded to publish a flood of literary works that had been banned by the censors over the previous sixty years.[45]

At the April plenum, however, at least six of the speakers—Iurii Bondarev, Stanislav Kuniaev, Iurii Prokushev, Vladimir Krupin, Nikolai Shundik, and Viacheslav Shugaev—were known militant Russian nationalists with close ties to *Nash sovremennik*, the monthly of the RSFSR Union of Writers, which could be described as a mouthpiece of the extreme Russian nationalist "Pamiat" society.[46]

Kuniaev and Krupin defended "Pamiat" in their speeches. Indeed, Kuniaev devoted his entire speech to attacks on those who criticized "Pamiat" and anti-Semitism, among them the poet Evgenii Evtushenko, writer Fazil Iskander, journalists Elena Losoto of *Komsomolskaia pravda* and Pavel Gutionov of the government daily *Izvestiia*,[47] and economist Gavriil Popov. Kuniaev accused Evtushenko of lack of respect for his own people, while another speaker, Maia Ganina, castigated what she alleged was the Russophobia of other peoples—in particular, Georgians and Jews.

Prokushev chose a Russian as the target for his attacks—none other than Nikolai Bukharin, who had been rehabilitated only a few weeks before the plenum. According to Prokushev, Bukharin's article *Zlye zametki* (Malicious Notes) of 1927, in which the author criticized the poetry of Sergei Esenin, "had buried Esenin's poetry for three decades," thereby "robbing the Russian national culture."

Prokushev also suggested that instead of criticizing Stalin, Khrushchev should have repented his own part in Stalin's repressions. Prokushev went on to claim that Stalin's great enterprises, built by prisoners in Siberia in the late nineteen-thirties, ultimately had saved all the Soviet peoples from Hitler's camps.

Stalinist nostalgia was evident also in a number of other speeches. Bondarev attacked those who "mourned over" Russian history and claimed that everything was bad both before and after the revolution of 1917. According to Bondarev, these "mourners" were responsible for the loss of orientation of Soviet arts and also for the sexual misbehavior of the young. He read aloud a letter from a student advocating group sex and then proceeded to attack Professor Iurii Afanasev, the director of the Moscow Institute of Historical Archives and a leading critic of the Stalinist falsification of Soviet history. Bondarev called him "an apostle of sensations and slander, who almost comes to blows in every lecture hall."

The most outspoken Soviet writers were not present at the plenum. Whereas there had been sharp polemics between conservative and reform-minded writers in April 1987, this time there were none. When Russian nationalists viciously attacked writers of the "thaw" generation of the nineteen-sixties such as Evtushenko, Voznesenskii, Okudzhava, and Andrei Bitov, nobody answered them back.

The USSR Union of Writers had a membership of 11,000. Many of them were not writers but pensioned-off representatives of the *nomenklatura* who did not write books but nevertheless enjoyed considerable influence in determining the atmosphere in the body. The leaders of the union enjoyed special privileges, including the opportunity to have their books printed and reprinted and to receive payment regardless of sales.[48] Such people were determined to keep these privileges intact. As *Ogonek* put it:

> Political accusations have been replaced by concern about the "threat to the nation" from "Zionists and masons," by false nostalgia for a "persecuted Russian culture," and by maniacal hatred of people who, in the most difficult years, preserved their integrity.[49]

## 14
## RESTRUCTURING IN SOVIET HISTORY
### Vera Tolz

From 1986 on, official policy on the treatment of Soviet history changed dramatically, and some major "blank spots" were filled. However, some historical episodes continued to be ignored in the Soviet press, or discussed  very superficially.  Equally, a political figure or historical event might be covered in the press, but in a overtly biased way—the role of Leon Trotskii in the revolution and the creation of the Red Army, being a case in point.

*Identifying "Blank Spots."*   Many historical issues required analysis of relevant archive material.  For example, *Komsomolskaia pravda, Literaturnaia gazeta*, and *Nedelia* provided some details of the arrest of Stalin's Secret Police chief, Lavrentii Beriia at a Politburo meeting in the summer of 1953 and of his subsequent execution.[1] This coverage was a great step forward.[2] The archival materials, however, remained unavailable, as did the most important documents about Stalin's purges.

*The Lenin Period.*  Press revelations of Stalin's crimes had long been balanced with praise for the government under Lenin. Stalin's policies were depicted as departing from Lenin on almost every significant issue. Thus violations of legality and terror instituted during the first years of the Bolshevik power were almost entirely ignored.

There was hardly any mention of the fact that the one-party dictatorship, which made Stalinism possible, was established by Lenin. In his play, *Dalshe..Dalshe..Dalshe...*, Shatrov had Lenin's opponents accuse the Soviet leader of putting an end to party pluralism in Russia. The author, however, made it immediately clear that he personally did not regard these accusations as justified. He had the leader of the left Socialist-Revolutionaries, Mariia Spiridonova, state that Lenin had initially intended to allow other democratic and socialist parties freedom to operate in Russia, but that these parties "constantly used all the freedom accorded them ... to overthrow the existing régime." In short, according to Shatrov, it was not the Bolsheviks who made party pluralism impossible in the USSR, but the other parties that were active in Russia at the time of the revolution. Any kind of discussion of the opposite point of view—i.e., that from the very beginning Lenin did not want to share power with other parties—remained taboo.[3]

Numerous articles that appeared in the press in later years about Lenin's New Economic Policy, in part a precursor of Gorbachev's economic reforms, ignored the fact that the economic liberalization introduced by Lenin was accompanied by political repression. Thus, writings on the NEP avoided reference to the June 1922 Moscow trial of Socialist Revolutionaries—the first open trial conducted by the GPU. Maksim Gorkii described the trial as a measure intended to "annihilate the intelligentsia in our illiterate country."[4]

Among other measures adopted during the NEP was the expulsion of a large group of prominent Russians in August, 1922. Daniil Granin, in a historical novel entitled *Zubr* (The Aurochs), published in 1987 in *Novyi mir*, praised Lenin for his kindness in offering the intellectuals who did not accept the revolution the chance to leave Russia while still retaining their Soviet passports.[5] Granin described the expulsion as a humanitarian act. In reality, a number of intellectuals were arrested, and most of them were forced subsequently to emigrate.[6] Some of them had to sign an acknowledgement that, should they be found on Russian territory, they would be executed.

In calling for a return to "Lenin's principles of legality,"[7] Soviet authors customarily ignored Lenin's notion that legislation should serve the immediate interests of the leadership. Lenin stated that "the court should not be a substitute for terror...; it should substantiate and legalize it."[8]

Similarly, repressions against the clergy under Lenin were no less harsh then in subsequent periods of Soviet history. For instance, the famine of 1921 was extensively used by the authorities as an excuse for a crackdown on the Church. The authorities made the decision to confiscate Church treasures on the pretext of raising funds to aid victims of the famine. The Church showed willingness to cooperate, but Lenin personally gave instructions to the party leadership to use the opportunity of the famine to deal with the clergy as harshly as possible.

*The Stalin Period.* Under Khrushchev, Stalin was officially considered a loyal Leninist up to 1934. In contrast, under Gorbachev, Stalin's career came to be regarded as flawed from the end of the nineteen-twenties onwards. Yet several notorious cases that Stalin's secret police fabricated at the end of the nineteen-twenties and the beginning of the nineteen-thirties were still to be reviewed.

Stalin's role in the the 1934 assassination of the Leningrad party chief Sergei Kirov merits the description of "a blank spot." In his play *Dalshe...Dalshe...Dalshe...*, Mikhail Shatrov mentioned that Stalin was believed to have organized the assassination of Kirov.[9] Academician Aleksandr Samsonov said in an interview with *Knizhnoe obozrenie* in February 1988 that an analysis of documents should be undertaken to clarify the issue of Stalin's complicity in the assassination plot.

Although in August 1988 the Estonian party newspaper *Rahval Haal* published, for the first time in the USSR, the secret agreement between Stalin and Nazi Germany that led to the Soviet takeover of the independent Baltic States, some historians and propagandists still continued to question the secret protocol's authenticity.

On May 28, 1988, Radio Moscow in English hinted that the Soviet Union might have been responsible for the killing of thousands of captured Polish officers at Katyn forest, near Smolensk, during World War II. The hint came in a report on a ceremony, which took place on May 27, at a monument to the dead Polish officers, with Soviet officials in attendance. The radio said that the monument, at the site of the mass graves where the bodies were found, bore an inscription ascribing the massacre to Nazi forces. The radio said:

> This was the accepted view held by the Soviet Union and its wartime allies for many years after the war ... But now the affair has to be put down as a 'blank spot' in history.

The Katyn issue was on the agenda of the work of the joint Soviet-Polish commission of historians that was set up in 1987 to clarify "blank spots" in the history of relations between the two countries.

In October 1987, a leading advocate of the revision of Soviet history, Professor Iurii Afanasev, urged that the truth be told about the Katyn massacre; his comments appeared in an interview with the Polish weekly *Polityka* (No. 40).[10]

In March 1988, a letter by fifty-nine Polish intellectuals called on Soviet cultural figures, scientists, and scholars to make a public stand on Katyn.[11] The letter was criticized in the Soviet press (*Literaturnaia gazeta*, March 30), but its text was not published in the Soviet Union.

Academician Aleksandr Samsonov, the author of numerous works on the history of World War II, pointed out that Stalin's orders in the fall of 1941 had misled the Soviet armies defending Kiev and resulted in their capture by the Germans. Samsonov said that while this fact was mentioned in memoirs by senior Soviet officers, historians had yet to analyze the event properly. Moreover, the general issue of the capture of Soviet soldiers by the Germans and the official attitude towards these prisoners of war was regarded by Samsonov as an area that had not been adequately dealt with by Soviet historians. In an earlier interview with the propaganda organ *Argumenty i fakty*, Samsonov singled out the fate of General Andrei Vlasov as "a blank spot." Vlasov, a notable commander, was captured by the Nazis in 1942 and subsequently headed the so-called Russian Army of Liberation.[12] At the beginning of March 1988, *Komsomolskaia pravda* published a lengthy article on Vlasov. The article, however, was not an objective analysis of Vlasov's actions, but an emotive account criticizing Vlasov's personality written by Konstantin Tokarev, a war correspondent who was acquainted with Vlasov.[13]

*After Stalin's Death.* Soviet history after Stalin's death attracted less attention than the period before. Neither the uprising of East German workers in June 1953, which was suppressed by Soviet tanks, nor the events of the 1956 Hungarian revolution and its suppression by the Soviet Union were revised during the campaign for glasnost.[14]  The Soviet press proved more positive in its attitude towards the Prague Spring of 1968; from time to time, however, Soviet newspapers criticized the West for drawing parallels between events in Czechoslovakia and Gorbachev's perestroika.

The Khrushchev era attracted considerable attention from 1987 on. Soviet authors complained, however, that Khrushchev's "complicated personality" had not found a researcher equal to the demanding task.[15]  While Khrushchev was credited with the rehabilitation of many of Stalin's victims, the political repressions and harsh antireligious campaign conducted by Khrushchev were mostly ignored by Soviet sources. Khrushchev's secret speech at the Twentieth Party Congress remained unpublished in the USSR despite the numerous appeals of Soviet intellectuals.[16]  Details of Khrushchev's fall in 1964 were yet to be revealed.

The Brezhnev era attracted much more attention in the Soviet press than the period under Khrushchev, but the contributions were mainly by journalists, not historians.  Some important phenomena, such as the dissident movement and Jewish emigration, were referred to in the press in vague terms, but not analyzed. The Soviet invasion of Afghanistan remained "a blank spot," despite incipient revelations about its origins.

*A Verdict on Lenin and Russian History.*  An article by economic journalist Vasilii Seliunin, published in *Novyi mir*, presented Russian history, including the Soviet period, as a chain of missed opportunities which had resulted in the failure to develop democracy and create an effective economy. One instance of an opportunity missed, according to Seliunin, was the institution of "War Communism" by Lenin in 1918, which aborted the nascent progressive trends in the development of Russia at the end of the nineteenth century. Seliunin clearly stated that a system of forced labor and concentration camps was set up by Lenin under the régime of "War Communism" which Stalin "only revived."[17]

Before the article by Seliunin appeared, Soviet intellectuals had only rarely hinted in the press at the connection between the Stalinist terror on the one hand and Lenin's struggle against counter-revolutionaries and the policies of "War Communism" on the other. Among these instances was an article in *Literaturnaia Rossiia* (October 9, 1987), in which Aleksandr Misharin discussed "the roots of the personality cult" by reference to the summary execution of landowners after the Revolution.

In 1988, more material about the terror under Lenin was published. In April, *Sovetskaia kultura* published an article by Doctor Nikolai Popov of the Institute of the United States and Canada, in which he stated that the concentration of excessive power in the hands of the Bolshevik party started under Lenin and that this made possible the creation of "a perfect totalitarian state" by Stalin.[18]

At the same time, the conservative and nationalistic journal *Nash sovremennik* published an article by literary critic Vadim Kozhinov entitled *Pravda i istina*, which paid much attention to Lenin's terror.[19] However, he attempted to prove (by falsifying statistics) that more people were killed under Lenin than under Stalin, and thereby to rehabilitate Stalin. Kozhinov made no secret of his intention to imply a connection between the number of deaths under Lenin and the high number of Jews who belonged to Lenin's first Soviet government. In short, Kozhinov—who sympathized with the ideas of the Russian nationalist group "Pamiat"—attempted to present terror in Russia after the revolution as a plot by Jews against Russians. Kozhinov's ideas, and the dubious means by which he tried to advance them, were extensively criticized by liberal Soviet intellectuals.[20]

In contrast, Seliunin attempted to analyze Lenin's post-Revolutionary policy and its connection with Stalinism from a scholarly position. Compared with other Soviet authors who touched on the topic, he was much bolder and condemned Lenin's policy of "War Communism," introduced in June, 1918, as extremist.

Seliunin disputed that "War Communism" was adopted by the Bolsheviks in response to the chaos and devastation caused by the First World War and the Civil War. He argued that "War Communism" reflected ideas Lenin had even before the October Revolution. Quoting extensively from Lenin, Seliunin showed that in Lenin's mind a successful Socialist revolution entailed the destruction of free trade and the market, and the introduction of state control over the means of production. But by destroying the market economy, Seliunin said, Lenin had killed any financial interest people had in their work. Systems of forced labor was the inevitable result.

Quoting Lenin and the first chief of the Cheka, Feliks Dzerzhinskii, Seliunin showed how terror against counter-revolutionaries gradually developed into terror against whole classes of people (including peasants and workers), and finally came to be regarded as a solution to economic problems. The concentration camps, first instituted by Lenin and Dzerzhinskii, became an important element in the Soviet economy. Citing Lenin's and Dzerzhinskii's statements on the need to use concentration camps to extract labor from those who refused to cooperate fully with the state's plans to reorganize the economy, Seliunin said:

> So we see that limits on the use of repression expanded boundlessly. First it was used to suppress opponents of the revolution, then it shifted to potential opponents, and finally it became a means of solving purely economic problems.

Seliunin paid special attention to the peasant question after the Revolution, but argued that even before the Revolution, Lenin had regarded collective peasant labor as a model for economic activity. He also maintained that the destruction of trade relations in the countryside was another of Lenin's goals. However, when Lenin had tried to make these ideas reality after the Revolution, he met with strong resistance from the peasantry; the Bolsheviks managed to suppress peasant uprisings during the Civil War only by recourse to the Red Army. Apart from his adoption of "military measures" to solve the peasant problem, Seliunin also criticized Lenin for ordering the confiscation of land from rich peasants in 1918. Lenin's order of 1919 which initiated a policy whereby peasants would no longer engage in individual labor but participate collectively in sovkhozes and communes was also subjected to strong criticism: Seliunin reminded readers that, despite all the benefits which accrued to the peasants on joining agricultural collectives, communal agricultural labor remained extremely unpopular among the peasants. He described as naïve Lenin's assertion that providing communes with tractors would encourage peasants to join them.

In sum, Seliunin was certain that neither collectivized agriculture, nor total state control of industry and state ownership of the means of production, could be successful. The economic system introduced by Lenin immediately after the Revolution, according to Seliunin, was a step backward from the Capitalist system that preceded it and a return to the use of "slavery." Moreover, "total state control over the means of production" inevitably led to violations of the civil rights and freedoms of the individual. Further, Seliunin said that Lenin himself recognized that "War Communism" was mistaken. The introduction of the New Economic Policy (NEP) in 1921, which entailed elements of free market economics, was the victory of realism over ideology, he said. Seliunin emphasized several times that, in suppressing NEP in 1927, Stalin was in fact returning to the ideas of Lenin's "War Communism" period.

Seliunin's article gave a detailed analysis of Russian history before the Revolution. The author identified the roots of authoritarianism in Russian history in the system of pervasive state control over individuals under the tsars which included the use of serf labor in agriculture and manufacturing. He also paid attention to the progressive elements of a capitalist system in Russia which became noticeable after Alexander II's political and economic reforms in the eighteen-sixties. Seliunin made it clear that he believed the October Revolution had arrested progressive developments at the time and exacerbated the trend toward authoritarianism in Russia.

In his analysis of Russian authoritarianism, Seliunin concentrated on two main periods—the reigns of Ivan the Terrible and Peter the Great—and rejected the traditional assessment by orthodox Soviet historians. Stalin had regarded Ivan the Terrible as a model. However, since Stalin's death, historians tended to be more harsh in their judgement. Also, the results of Peter the Great's reforms had been uniformly and positively regarded by historians until Iurii Afanasev and Nikolai Popov began to identify Peter the Great as a precursor of Stalin.[21]

Seliunin argued that Ivan the Terrible, who had first turned free peasants into serfs, and Peter the Great, who had introduced the use of serf labor to manufacturing, not only strengthened the conservative political set-up in Russia but also made it structurally impossible for the Russian economy to function effectively. Ivan the Terrible devastated the countryside, while economic achievements under Peter the Great were very temporary, Seliunin argued.

According to Seliunin, political conservatism as reflected in the concentration of all the power in the hands of the state and ultimately the tsar, usually had the negative economic consequence of killing any initiative from below. Seliunin quoted US historian Richard Pipes' conclusion in his book *Russia under the Old Régime* (which was sharply attacked in the Soviet press) that as a result of the concentration of power in the hands of the state, the Russian people became "lumpen from the economic point of view" and "slaves of the state" politically. While agreeing with him in general, Seliunin said, however, that Pipes ignored those periods in Russian history in which attempts were made to break with tradition. He cited the reforms introduced by Tsar Alexander II which freed peasants from serfdom as positive evidence for his case. He attached greatest significance to the reforms in agriculture introduced at the beginning of the twentieth century by Petr Stolypin, chairman of the Council of Ministers in 1906-1911.

Seliunin praised Stolypin highly for advocating private peasant ownership of the land and for his attack on the communal system which then existed. Seliunin also said that Stolypin was the first Russian official who clearly understood that individual rights and forms of ownership were connected. Stolypin stated that without giving a peasant the right to own land privately, it would be impossible to free him politically. Seliunin was in full agreement with Stolypin on this point, arguing that Stolypin's reform of agriculture brought quick success, a debatable proposition.

According to Seliunin, when Lenin instituted "War Communism" and reintroduced communal ownership of the land, he took a step backward from the success of Stolypin's reform. Lenin, according to Seliunin, added nothing to the positive results of Stolypin's reforms but reinstated the old Russian form of land ownership—in Seliunin's mind, a regressive step. He added that, apart from an undynamic system of agriculture, the Soviet state inherited other serious shortcomings from pre-Revolutionary Russia—namely, a powerful bureaucratic apparatus and control over industry concentrated in the hands of the state. The result, Seliunin said, was that Soviet citizens were now "social parasites" who only demanded—whether a free flat or cheap food—from the state, but were not willing to take any initiative themselves.

Seliunin's article was the harshest verdict on Russian history yet to have appeared on the pages of a Soviet periodical. He depicted Russian and Soviet life as a series of episodes in which conservative forces prevailed and killed burgeoning democracy, individual freedom, and popular initiative in the economy. Lenin was among the historical figures accused by Seliunin of helping conservative, antidemocratic tendencies to flourish.

# V. THE ECONOMY ON THE ROAD
# FROM SOCIALISM

## 15
## THE SOVIET ECONOMY AFTER SEVENTY YEARS
### Philip Hanson

Most economic systems evolved so gradually that nobody would think of them as having birthdays. The Soviet economy is an exception: it was born in 1917, when the Bolsheviks seized power in Petrograd. The leading Bolsheviks did not have any very precise ideas about how the economy should be organized. They were clear, however, that it was to be based on social ownership of resources. At the outset Lenin, at least, had a vision of the whole of the nation's production being managed like a single, giant factory. In May 1918, he wrote that socialism required

> large-scale capitalist engineering and planned state organization which keeps tens of millions of people to the strictest observance of a unified standard in production and distribution.[1]

For all but seven of its seventy years the Soviet economy was indeed organized on the principles that Lenin advocated in 1917-18: state ownership and detailed central administration. The only departure from this régime was one initiated by Lenin himself, the New Economic Policy of 1921-28. That interlude, during which small-scale private enterprise and a heavily "guided" market mechanism played an important part, was being held up in 1988 by many Soviet writers as a model to which the country should return.[2] Yet it was only a tiny part of Soviet history.

The centralized system took shape in the first few years of Stalin's industrialization drive. By 1932 the main institutions and operating procedures of the modern Soviet economy had been created: state and cooperative ownership of almost all productive assets, with the cooperatives just as subject to central control as state enterprises; central control over prices and wages; material-balance planning; centralized allocation of materials; obligatory annual plan targets for all production units; branch ministries as intermediaries between the central planners and the enterprises.

The advantages claimed for this system had mainly to do with growth. The debate in the Soviet press that preceded the collectivization of agriculture was primarily about rapid industrialization.[3] State ownership would do away with "exploitative" incomes from property, but equality was an aim only for the distant future, when full communism would be achieved. For the time being, as Stalin's speeches made clear, the overriding aim was to make the Soviet Union a modern industrial power as quickly as possible, so that the only Socialist state in the world could stand up against those who were presumed to be its enemies. There was also an implicit aim: the system had to be one that was compatible with the party leadership's monopoly of power.

Only gradually did the enormous human costs of collectivization and forced industrialization come to be discussed publicly in the Soviet Union. In 1987, one Soviet economist wrote that the economy would have grown more steadily if the market mechanism had never been abandoned.[4] Another wrote that the price paid for industrialization "could be to some extent explained, though not justified, only by extraordinary, inhuman circumstances that have ceased to exist since at least the mid-nineteen-fifties."[5]

In the nineteen-fifties and nineteen-sixties three main claims were made for the Soviet economic system. The first was that it allowed a more equitable distribution of economic well-being than that obtained under capitalism. The second was that it provided full employment and economic security for its citizens. The third, and most important, was that it exhibited a capacity for faster economic growth in the long term than the main capitalist economies.

The first of these claims was, and remained, contentious. Neither the meaning of "equity" nor the measurement of distribution of economic welfare was an unambiguous matter. The gulf in material welfare between a member of the Politburo and an inmate of a severe-régime labor camp might have been greater than anything observable in the West; the gap between the top and bottom 5.0 percent of households, on the other hand, was possibly less in the USSR than in many capitalist countries. Even the latter kind of comparison, however, could not easily be made. Soviet data on the distribution of incomes were poor. Moreover, privileged access to supplies was crucial in a shortage economy, so that money income data were in any case an inadequate guide to consumption levels. Several Western studies showed that there were large inequalities in Soviet society.[6]

The contention that the Soviet system guaranteed full employment and a high measure of economic security for the great majority of Soviet citizens was borne out by historical experience. Both were linked, however, to the system's in-built excess demand for labor, which was another feature of a shortage economy. Both were also accompanied by a relatively low average level of material welfare. Consumption levels grew quite strongly in the nineteen-fifties and nineteen-sixties, but remained well behind those of Western Europe or the United States. At that time, though, this weakness seemed likely to be cancelled out in the long run by superior Soviet economic growth.

When the Soviet economy was entering middle age, therefore, the crucial issue in East-West economic competition seemed to be growth rates, and here the Soviet system appeared to have the edge. Nobody seriously disputed that the centrally administered economy used resources wastefully, produced goods of relatively poor quality, and was riddled with shortages. Neither was there much disagreement over whether Soviet growth relied to an unusual extent on sheer capital accumulation and the mobilization of ever-increasing quantities of labor; the record of Soviet productivity growth was unimpressive. Several Western economists argued, though, that if the Soviet economy continued to grow faster than Western economies, these defects would eventually be dwarfed by the sheer volume of Soviet output—including consumer-goods output.[7]

In the first edition of their book of readings on the Soviet economy, published in 1962, Morris Bornstein and Daniel Fusfeld included a table showing dates at which Soviet GNP would overtake US GNP, with various plausible extrapolations of growth in the two economies. They put the level of Soviet GNP in 1960 at about half that of the United States; with US output growing at 2.5, 3.0, or 4.0 percent a year from that date and Soviet output at 6.0, 7.0, or 8.0 percent, the dates for "overtaking" ranged from 1973 to 1996.[8] Even in the early nineteen-seventies it could reasonably be pointed out in the standard American textbook on the Soviet economy, that the long-term growth of Soviet GNP (5.1 percent a year from 1928 to 1972) was faster than that shown by any capitalist economy, including Japan, between the beginning of industrialization and the nineteen-sixties.[9] None of these Western assessments were based on the official Soviet growth statistics, which had been shown in the nineteen-fifties to be grossly exaggerated. The assessments were based on Western estimates of Soviet growth.

At the age of seventy, the Soviet economy's prospects were less bright than they had been at its half-century mark. Growth had been slowing since the late nineteen-fifties, but the slowdown had become more pronounced during the nineteen-seventies. Instead of being on course to overtake the United States in total output, Soviet production had ceased to catch up since the early nineteen-seventies. The Soviet annual statistical handbook for 1974 showed the USSR's national income (on Soviet definitions) to be 66.5 percent of that of the United States.[10] The equivalent officially published Soviet assessment for 1985 was 66 percent.[11] Unpublished Soviet assessments put the comparative level of output closer to that estimated by the CIA in terms of Western-style GNP: around 50 percent.[12]

Numerous explanations were offered, by both Soviet and Western economists, for the slowdown. Part of the story, certainly, was that the labor force was no longer growing rapidly. Another influence was the depletion of the more easily exploitable natural resources in the Western part of the country. But the effects of demography and geography would have mattered much less if Soviet growth had not been so dependent on the continuous mobilization of additional resources. In other words, if growth of productivity (for labor, capital, and natural resources combined) had been higher, the slowdown would have been less marked. Productivity growth had not accelerated to offset the effects of a slower growth of factor inputs. Indeed, according to most analysts, the rate of increase of productivity had slowed. Thus, when the Western economies were severely disrupted by the oil-price shocks of the nineteen-seventies, the Soviet economy's growth also slowed.

In the long run, the main source of productivity growth in any economy is technological change: the introduction and diffusion of new production processes and new know-how generally. There is now a wealth of evidence for the proposition that centrally administered socialist economies perform more poorly in technological innovation than capitalist market economies.[13] In the early stages of industrialization, this may not matter too much, as growth can be driven by mobilizing resources to change the structure of the economy, copying foreign technology on a large scale and incorporating it in new plants. When input growth slows, however, the systemic weakness in innovation becomes more serious.

The Gorbachev leadership put technology at the top of its agenda and also moved in the direction of decentralizing reform. By 1988, however, decentralization in socialist economies had not been allowed to create the sort of competition in which the penalties for failing to keep up with new technology were severe. Probably for that reason, no Socialist economy, reformed or unreformed, had yet become a dynamic technological innovator across more than a very narrow sector of industry.

Historically, the Soviet growth performance was quite impressive but not exceptional. A rough-and-ready linking of various Western estimates for different periods puts real Soviet GNP growth in 1928-86 at about 4.6 percent a year, or about 3.6 percent a year for the whole period since 1913.[14] The latter figure, which makes no allowance for periods of wartime and civil war destruction, is about the same as the long-run growth of the US economy between 1834-43 and 1963-67.[15] Since the nineteen-twenties, the Soviet Union had reduced its economic lag behind the United States, but not by much. In 1928 Soviet GNP per head of population was on the order of a fifth of that of the US, while in 1985 it was on the order of two-fifths.[16] The narrowing of the gap in per capita consumption was significantly less than this.

It was in the consumer sector that the Gorbachev reforms promised to yield the most if they could be implemented. In agriculture, distribution, services and small-scale consumer-goods production, the greatest hope for improvement seemed to lie in the reintroduction of various forms of private initiative (including small, unplanned cooperatives). In Hungary and China, it was changes of this sort that had yielded the greatest gains for household consumption. The Soviet economy appeared to be on the brink of a historic departure from the framework of near-total state ownership and detailed central administration within which it had so far operated. Such a change, however, was bound to be difficult.

16
## INCENTIVES FOR THE PEASANTS
Andreas Tenson


The Politburo of the Central Committee of the CPSU adopted two resolutions of great significance for the development of the private sector of Soviet agriculture. During the session on July 9, 1987, the Politburo decided to permit city dwellers to buy empty rural houses and to use the private plots attached.[1] Previously, according to the Land Code, city dwellers could buy the house but not the land on which it stood together with the adjacent plot; only those registered as living in the countryside had the right to use private plots.

City dwellers, primarily emigrants from the countryside, had fought for years for such a dispensation. The significance of this resolution was enormous and "touches a spot dear to the nation's heart, because it affects the interests of millions of people," wrote Kapitolina Kozhevnikova in *Literaturnaia gazeta*.[2]

The origins of these abandoned houses dated back to the nineteen-sixties and nineteen-seventies, when the philosophy of "agro-cities" prevailed, i.e., the urbanization of the countryside. Lightly populated villages were left to rot on the grounds of "unviability", and the remaining population transferred to centralized farms built up with multistory urban apartment blocks with no chance to cultivate private plots. Unviable villages lacked all infrastructure, even electricity, but the inhabitants passed up the promise of urban apartment blocks on centralized farms, preferring to board up their homes and head for the towns. As a result, by 1988 more than half of the city dwellers were former country folk, "bound by family, economic, and other ties with the places they were born."[3] Meanwhile the number of rural settlements in the country had fallen by a factor of two.[4]

In certain raions of the USSR there are more than 725,000 empty homes. Of that number, almost 500,000 are in the RSFSR ... About 200,000 hectares of land that goes with the houses has fallen into disuse.... In Moscow alone there are a million unsatisfied requests for garden plots [*sadovye uchastki*]; fewer than 10 percent of urban households in the capital and provinces achieve this dream. City dwellers rush into the countryside for the growing season. They are ready to take on homes. To win over the land that surrounds them. To feed their families. To give up their surplus produce for sale. But it's not done to give them an answer, [it is] forbidden; we will not allow them to take the land.[5]

There were also the owners of empty houses, predominantly urban pensioners who returned semi-legally to abandoned villages for the summer. Those in charge of the economy labeled them *dachniki* and fought against the phenomenon, supposedly because the newcomers demoralized the laborers in the villages.

The Politburo's new decree ended a struggle for the rights of the *dachniki* that had been fought bitterly by the authorities to the point where some officials set fire to "illegal" huts at night.[6] In future, in accordance with the decree, a citizen normally resident in a town would have the right to make use of the plot of land attached to the house he owned or rented, for the purpose of agricultural production, up to an area of 600 square meters, including the ground occupied by the buildings. If the plot was larger, it was granted to the owner or the tenant on the condition that the surplus produce be sold to a sovkhoz, kolkhoz, or consumer cooperative.[7] The second resolution taken by the Politburo on July 23, 1987, was perhaps of greater significance. It stated that "for the purpose of increasing the contribution by citizens in the resolution of food supply problems, a review is recommended of the norms of livestock holding (including horses),[8] and of the maximum size of private plots."[9]

The chairman of the USSR State Committee for the Agro-industrial Complex (Gosagroprom), V. S. Murakhovskii, explained in an interview that local soviets would attend to all these questions: "Measures are envisaged that will be directed at exerting pressure on sovkhozes and kolkhozes to provide every possible assistance to laborers [cultivating private plots], in the apportionment of young livestock and poultry, of fodder, and the assignment of pastures, and help in the construction and repair of premises, and the provision of transport."[10]

This decision by the Politburo was connected with the decline in productivity in the socialized sector. Compared with the previous period, in the eleventh five-year-plan, gross average annual grain harvest fell by almost 14 percent.[11] Plan targets were not being met; reorganization of the agrarian sector and the creation of Gosagroprom had not improved affairs. The food supply program had not been fulfilled; the supply of foodstuffs reaching the population was far from satisfactory.

The leadership failed to utilize the reserves of collectivized agriculture. The lifting of the existing limits on the private sector, however, which contributed 25-30 percent of overall agricultural production,was promising in the long term, even though the private sector was in decline. Clearly the decline was connected with the signs, in the summer of 1986, that a new campaign was coming, aimed at private greenhouses, orchards, vegetable gardens, and livestock fattening. "Is it possible that the antistate character of this group of people, so inimical to the country, could not be seen at once?" wrote N. Shmelev in *Novyi mir*.[12] This campaign took place after the Politburo showed a protective attitude towards private plots; it was therefore in opposition to the line of party and government.

A general squeeze and limit on private plot activity led to a fall in the national herd. Iurii Nikolaev wrote in *Sovetskaia Rossiia* that in the country as a whole cattle fell by 400,000 head, pigs by 337,000, and poultry by two million in 1986. "Today a third of all households in the country keep no livestock at all, half the peasant farmyards have no cattle, 70 percent no pigs."

A stereotype explanation was widely offered as to why farmers with private plots no longer wanted to keep animals: supposedly "old peasants no longer have the strength to tend stock, and young households generally have no need of them …" This would be merely a dispiriting myth about the feckless peasant, if it had not been for the mass investigation into the actual state of private plot agriculture in one hundred oblasts, krais, autonomous republics, and in tens of thousands of kolhozes and sovkhozes. The investigation was conducted into more than six million farmyards. The notions that the rural inhabitant did not want to keep livestock were proved to be completely groundless: 85 households out of 100 that did not have poultry would have liked to raise them, but conditions did not permit this.[13]

In the opinion of such specialists, the backwardness of the agricultural sector of the economy was caused by the absence of owners to take personal charge of the land. At some time, social holdings lost the relative freedom they had enjoyed and they were now directed by the organs of central government; these were inculcated with the principles of management and organization applied to industry. Consequently, peasants turned into day-laborers and lost all interest in their work. *Kolkhozniks* drifted to the city out of apathy and indifference. The problem had been discussed for decades. Many experiments attempted by the authorities without taking the human factor into account were shortlived—Khrushchev's corn campaign, the specialization and concentration scheme, the Moldavia experiment, the Ipatovo method, and finally the creation of raion agroindustrial productions associations (RAPOs). Now the collective or family *podriad* (contracted production assignment and remuneration—contracting hereafter) was in jeopardy. Although essentially an extension of the promising experiment with "normless links" (*beznariadnye zvena*), contracting did not change the general situation.

Specialists agreed that families needed not contracting, but the right to long leases on land and the chance of unfettered ownership without supervision from above. But a law on land use was necessary for this measure to be carried out, and not the existing declarations which did not protect tenants who leased their land.

The published draft of the new Model Kolkhoz Statute[14] contained articles which came to the same conclusion as the juridical commission of the Supreme Soviet of the USSR. In Section III, "The Land and its Use," Article 10 spoke of "granting plots of land for lease and other forms of secondary use to members of the kolkhoz, other citizens, and also to kolkhozes, enterprises and organizations." In Section IX, "The Personal Subsidiary Economy of the Kolkhoznik's Family," there were no articles that limited the size of the plot and the number of livestock permitted.

A number of authors emphasized the problem in articles on the topic of land use. Shmelev wrote that

> in a number of cases it might even be possible to disband kolkhozes and sovkhozes, and leave it to local authorities to conclude agreements with collectives made up of family members. Or, say, to RAPOs, consumer cooperatives, or timber enterprises.[15]

Supporters of leasehold based on the family foresaw two difficulties: would there be a sufficient number of people who would want to take up private enterprise, and what was to be done with the kolkhoz bureaucracy? Ananev thought that people who fled the countryside and kolkhoz for the city would return as soon as there was a legal guarantee and confidence that "... somebody is not going to come to you tomorrow and say: you've become kulaks, come on—hand it over!... " Bashmatchikov wrote that

> many urban families today agree with the idea of the leasing alternative in agriculture. They are pushed towards it by difficulties with food supply in towns,... the sense of creativity in farm work, the prospects of work without the daily tutelage of a multitude of superiors, and the possibility of receiving relatively high incomes.[16]

On the question of what to do with kolkhoz staff, Ananev wrote that

> family units can form an association in a variety of ways ... in this association, on the basis of a contractual agreement, specialists will work ... soil scientists, agronomists, specialists in animal husbandry, and clearly all this requires a coordinator too—the chairman—who will represent the association.[17]

The question of what to do with the staff of disbanded kolkhozes was not so important. More significant was the problem of the appreciable assistance in agricultural work provided by city dwellers in significant numbers. In 1984, for instance, they performed 313 million man-days of labor.[18] The situation was now changing with the shift by kolkhozes and sovkhozes, and industrial enterprises too, to *khozraschet* and self-financing. Who would pay the millions who came from the towns to help? This state of affairs was squeezing public sector agriculture, while at the same time stimulating the move to the leasing of land by peasant families, who would have help from friends and relatives for harvest and other busy times.

The extent of the forthcoming changes remained uncertain. However, as Shmelev wrote, "This juncture is indeed crucial for our agriculture. If today does not live up to people's hopes for a reassertion of common sense, apathy may become irreversible."[19]

## 17
## EDGING TOWARD OPEN UNEMPLOYMENT
### Vlad Sobell

*Modifying the Communist Social Contract.* It is generally accepted that despite their lag in technology and their inordinately wasteful production, the communist systems achieved at least one critical advantage over their capitalist rivals: guaranteed full employment. This advantage was perhaps the most telling single argument put forward by East European officials in defense of communism's record in human rights.[1] Some Western theories on the nature of the communist system claimed that the communist parties had struck a tacit social contract with the population, trading resignation to communist rule and a Soviet-type economic system for a high degree of egalitarianism, a lack of inflation, and full employment.[2]

The move away from orthodox communism focused attention on the necessity of modifying if not abrogating this social contract. Its modification had been under way for many years in the countries of Eastern Europe, and there were signs that in 1988 a similar revision was under way in the USSR.[3] Egalitarianism in remuneration came to be considered harmful and was being replaced by the principle of pay according to individual performance. The right to work remained firmly entrenched, but the idea that individuals should expect life-long job security was now rejected; instead, it was anticipated that individuals might find it necessary to learn a new profession or move should their place of work be closed. The commitment to full employment was no longer sacrosanct; instead, concepts such as "rationally justified" employment (the idea that the authorities support full employment only up to a "rationally justified" point; when full employment is excessively costly it ceases to be "rationally justified") had been gaining currency. The commitment to stable prices was also being abandoned, at least implicitly, in view of the need to phase out consumer price subsidies. The most dramatic departure from this commitment occurred in Poland.

*Unmasking Hidden Unemployment.* Prompted by the imperatives of "restructuring" and encouraged by the climate of glasnost, Soviet and East

European officials and the media displayed unprecedented frankness in discussing the drawbacks of the central article of the social contract: the maintenance of full employment. The most significant outcome of the debate was that overmanning, slack labor discipline, and subsidization of inefficient factories were being increasingly recognized for what they were: a form of hidden unemployment. Accordingly, official and unofficial estimates were advanced of what open unemployment might amount to should the régimes demand high productivity and give up their commitment to job security.

For example, Prime Minister Nikolai Ryzhkov said in a speech to the Supreme Soviet on June 29, 1987, that about 13 percent of all state-run enterprises were unprofitable and might have to be closed down; the claim was later repeated by Minister of Finance Boris Gostev. The influential reformist economist Abel Aganbegian said in an interview with *Izvestiia* that "several hundred enterprises would do best to close in the near future" (Aganbegian included in his list 30 old coal mines in the Donbass region of the Ukraine).[4] In 1986 the economist Vladimir Kostakov caused a major furor by claiming that between 13,000,000 and 19,000,000 jobs would have to be eliminated in the manufacturing sector by the year 2000 should the authorities insist on meeting their productivity targets.[5]

Similar statements were made in other CMEA countries. Marian Woźniak, the Polish CC secretary responsible for the economy, said in December 1987 that more than 350 Polish enterprises faced bankruptcy if they failed to improve their performance;[6] and government spokesman Jerzy Urban announced in April that subsidies to inefficient enterprises would be reduced by 15 percent in the course of 1987.[7] In March the prominent Polish economist Jósef Kaleta (Rector of the Oscar Lange Academy of Economics in Wrocław) took issue with official claims that there was no unemployment in Poland and estimated Poland's "latent unemployment" as being at least 5-10 percent (about 12,000,000 people were employed in the state sector of the Polish economy).[8]

The architects of the Czechoslovak and Bulgarian versions of "restructuring" sounded confident about the prospects for ending subsidization of inefficient plants; indeed, potential bankruptcies were implicit in their blueprints for reform. They tended to be reticent, however, when it came to the delicate task of specifying just how many closures there might be. It is reasonable, nevertheless, to assume that hidden unemployment in these countries was about the same as in Poland and the USSR.[9]

The Hungarian authorities, on the other hand, were facing the problem with unparalleled openness. The continued operation of obsolete plants was recognized as a major cause of the worsening economic crisis; Hungarian studies on hidden unemployment concluded that its rate was as high as 20-25 percent and that in some branches less than 50 percent of capacity was being utilized. The program of industrial reorganization planned by the authorities envisaged that well over 200,000 employees in Hungarian industry (13 percent of the industrial work force) would be affected by 1990; industrial employment was to decline by 90,000 and about 70,000 workers were to be moved to other industries. Hungary was also leading the way with plant closures and introduced unemployment benefits to make the process less painful. Nevertheless, officials expected more and more social problems, especially among young people, because of the increasing number of people seeking jobs and the reduced number of vacancies.[10]

*The Official Reaction.* When confronted with the prospect of open unemployment, Soviet and East European officials tended to dismiss it as not being a serious issue. In an interview with the French paper *L'Humanité*, Gorbachev denied that perestroika would lead to unemployment: "In a planned economy the two things are not connected," he said.[11] Bulgarian Communist party CC Secretary Emil Hristov responded to the same question in a similar way:

Unemployment is unnecessary for the rational development of the economy. We are confident that we can achieve the desired effect solely by applying the economic mechanism that is to be phased in over the next few years.[12]

Hungarian officials, who could no longer deny the existence of open unemployment, were more frank; but, again, they tended to emphasize the allegedly transitional nature of unemployment as well as the allegedly humane nature of the communist approach to the problem. Károly Németh, President of the Presidential Council, said in August that

We wish to retain full employment; but this is not exclusively an issue of political resolve or good intent. In certain areas and professions we must expect transitional employment problems. They must be treated and solved everywhere in a socialist, humane manner.[13]

*Is Western-Style Unemployment Possible Under Communism?* Without detracting from the genuine hardship and inconvenience that awaited the individuals affected, the official position on the significance of unemployment was to a large extent justifiable. There is reason to believe that as long as the entire economic system was dominated by the central authorities rather than by the market, the aggregate demand for labor was bound to remain significantly in excess of supply, so that the occurrence of large-scale, structural unemployment was most unlikely.

Measures to modernize the East European economies would not be applied indiscriminately to all enterprises across the board (as normally happened under the market system); instead, they would be applied selectively by central planners by means of the termination of subsidies. The planners did not and could not intend to subject all enterprises to this treatment but only those (or those industrial branches) whose inefficiency constituted the heaviest drag on the economy as a whole. Thus, only those branches were likely to be phased out where inefficiency was well above the average; and only those plants would have to reduce their personnel whose overmanning was far in excess of the average. The remainder (the bulk of existing enterprises) would continue to operate as before, under the protection of central planning, without the need to compete for survival with domestic and foreign rivals, and productivity would remain well below that of the market economies; overmanning and an inordinate demand for labor would also remain the norm throughout the economy as a whole. Under these conditions, the workers squeezed out of the least efficient plants and industrial branches would be likely to find alternative employment with ease compared with their Western counterparts.[14]

Given these circumstances, the social problems likely to appear as a result of economic reforms were essentially an outcome of organizational rather than systemic problems, as was the case in the West. These problems included the chronic shortage of housing, insufficiently developed transport and communication systems, a lack of retraining facilities, and inadequate facilities for matching those looking for work with suitable vacancies, all of which collectively hindered labor mobility, as well as the reluctance of the unemployed to look for work in other parts of the country; East European populations were psychologically ill-prepared for such an eventuality. (It was a systemic problem only insofar as the lack of housing and the other factors inhibiting labor mobility were by themselves considered inevitable, systemic properties of central planning.)

*The Utility of Open Unemployment.* This is not to say that the gradual emergence of Western-style unemployment in the countries of Eastern Europe could be entirely ruled out. Should the East European leaderships eventually conclude that their reforms could be effective only if they resulted in a transition to a full market system, then Eastern-style unemployment (an organizational problem) might gradually become a Western-style, systemic problem. It is too early to judge the eventual outcome of the modest steps undertaken in this direction.

The possibility of unemployment should not be seen only from the negative point of view, however. Painful as it is for the individuals affected, open unemployment can be a useful factor in stimulating labor discipline and productivity. The postwar record has shown that Western societies willing to live with open unemployment have generally been more prosperous and technologically dynamic than the communist ones that opted for hidden unemployment. The populations in Eastern Europe seemed mature enough to understand this lesson. A speaker who suggested at a public meeting in Hungary that an unemployment rate of up to 2 percent would be beneficial was reportedly applauded by his audience.[15]

18
# REVIVAL OF SOVIET COOPERATIVES
## John Tedstrom

Cooperatives were one of Lenin's concessions to market economics during the early years of Bolshevik rule. They remained a significant element in the Soviet economy up to 1960, although their contribution to total output decreased over time.[1] Because the lost production of the cooperatives was by and large not replaced by production from state enterprises, activity in the black market increased during the Brezhnev years. As part of his overall program to revitalize Soviet society, Gorbachev began to champion the virtues of cooperatives, claiming that they could improve the supply of consumer goods and services and help "squeeze out the shadow economy."[2] Beginning with a Politburo statement in support of the cooperative movement in February 1987, Gorbachev took a number of concrete steps to reestablish the cooperative as a legitimate part of the Soviet economic system.[3]

A decree on the development of new forms of cooperative enterprise was adopted by the USSR Council of Ministers early in 1987, and set some basic guidelines for the formation and operation of cooperatives.[4] It was not, however, effective in preventing local authorities from impeding the development of the cooperative movement. The press was filled with letters and stories about the difficulties entrepreneurs faced in trying to establish cooperatives. Often, local officials would not allocate them space; or, if space was allocated, it was in many instances not suitable for the proposed activity of the cooperative. In those cases where local authorities were inclined to support the establishment of a cooperative, moreover, they were frequently at a loss as to how to go about it. Moscow apparently had not passed on the necessary concrete rules and regulations. This created a good deal of confusion and frustration for all involved.[5]

The resulting pace of development in the cooperative sector was not impressive. By January 1, 1988, only some 23,000 cooperatives were registered in the entire country. That figure is somewhat misleading, though. As of late April 1988, only about 14,000 cooperatives, employing some 156,000 people, had actually begun to operate. The rest were waiting for space or were refitting the space they had been allocated. The total expenditure for cooperative-produced goods and services in the USSR during 1987 was estimated at 350 million rubles.[6] Furthermore, Prime Minister Nikolai Ryzhkov noted in his address to the USSR Supreme Soviet on May 24 that in 1987 the output of cooperatives had accounted for only 0.03 percent of total production of consumer goods in the Soviet Union; in the catering sector, 0.3 percent; and in the volume of marketed consumer services, only 0.5 percent. He went on to say:

> On average, across the country consumer services worth
> 25 kopecks per person were rendered by cooperatives.
> [This works out to about 70 million rubles for consumer
> services, which leaves about 280 million rubles spent by
> consumers on cooperative-produced goods.] In Azerbaijan,
> Kirgizia, and Turkmenistan the figure was up to 10
> kopecks. Only in Estonia did these services come to more
> than 3 rubles.

Ryzhkov argued that if the cooperatives were to make a significant contribution, these figures must be ten or, in some fields, a hundred times as great.[7]

To accelerate the development of the cooperative movement, a draft law on cooperatives was published in March 1988.[8]   While the draft law did go a long way toward improving the economic environment for cooperatives, a number of problems were not resolved either in theory or in practice. These difficulties were fully revealed in an open debate over the cooperative movement that took place both in the specialized economic literature and in the news media. Three broad, interrelated problems for the cooperatives could be identified from the debate: lack of concrete legislation guaranteeing the rights of cooperatives, problems in cooperative-state relations, and a mixed and skeptical public attitude toward cooperatives.

*Lack of Concrete Legislation.* Because the draft law was only a draft, it carried no legal weight. Local authorities who continued to impede cooperative developments were therefore not subject to legal prosecution. A good deal of bureaucratic foot-dragging and outright resistance (especially at local levels) to the cooperative movement tended to go unchecked as a result. The would-be entrepreneurs simply had no legal recourse. This question could only be resolved with the formal adoption of the law on cooperatives by the Supreme Soviet. In the other areas of difficulty—that is, cooperative-state relations and public opinion—the problems could not be so easily handled.

*Cooperative-State Relations.* There were three points of contention that concerned cooperative-state relations. First, the intended relationship between the cooperatives and official organizations such as local soviets was open to interpretation. For example, while the draft law claimed that cooperatives had only to register with these local bodies, it was clear that in reality many cooperatives were having to gain either explicit or implicit *permission* to become established. Another example of confusion over this issue concerned the question of how closely bound kolkhoz cooperatives would be to the central agricultural bureaucracy and to *goszakazy*. Second, there was great concern over the issue of prices. It was not clear to what extent cooperatives would be able to freely determine their own prices or to what extent the state would prevent them from charging "excessive prices" as mentioned in the draft law. Third, many cooperative managers complained strongly that since most of the Soviet supply network was still controlled by Gossnab (State Supply Committee), it was hard for cooperatives, which operated outside the plan unless they were under contract to or attached to *(pri)* a ministry or state enterprise, to get supplies.

*Public Attitudes Toward Cooperatives.* Following the reemergence of cooperatives in the Soviet economy, the public attitude toward them was quite mixed. On the one hand, press reports indicated that many cooperatives were doing a brisk business and that cooperative markets were full and busy. On the other hand, there were many letters and editorials in the press that opposed cooperatives on both economic and ideological grounds. The most frequent complaints were that the prices charged by cooperatives were excessive and that the high incomes sometimes earned by cooperative members were anathema to the Socialist concept of equality.

Because public support for cooperatives was important for their successful development, the authorities moved quickly, if not decisively, to address some of the public's concerns and to bolster support for the cooperative movement. On April 1, 1988, a new, progressive income tax scheme for cooperatives became effective. The marginal income tax rate was as high as 90 percent on income over 1,500 rubles per month.[9] (See the discussion on taxes below.) Instead of increasing support for cooperatives, however, the new tax scheme only served to fuel the debate. Many officials as well as economists felt that the taxes were too steep and would lower entrepreneurial incentives. As for the economists, in an interview with *Trud* on April 24,1988, Gelii Shmelev openly advocated revising the tax rates downward. This opinion was subsequently supported by Abel Aganbegian and Nikolai Shmelev, both well-known, reform-minded economists.[10]

In sum, a good deal of controversy had surrounded the draft law on cooperatives, and the bargaining and debating over a number of its points continued up to the last minute. While some of the problems were resolved, others were not. The version of the draft law that Ryzhkov presented to the Supreme Soviet reportedly took into account many of the opinions and proposals advanced since the draft was first published in March. Still, it was clear that on a number of controversial issues, a consensus had not yet been reached.[11]

*Cooperative Independence.* One of the most hotly debated issues was the guarantee of independence from the state for the cooperative. This was underlined by the sharp debate over kolkhoz cooperative independence. This particular debate continued until the last minute and was apparently resolved the night before Ryzhkov's speech to the Supreme Soviet on May 24. The debate occurred in a joint session of the Commission for the Agro-industrial Complex and the Commission for Legislative Proposals of the USSR Supreme Soviet.[12] In the original version of the draft law, Article 31 made a reference to state orders for kolkhozes and other agricultural cooperatives. Members of these cooperatives feared that the language was so vague that local authorities could use Article 31 to strip the cooperatives of their independence from the state. A number of variants of the article included the words "state order" but that also stressed the voluntary nature of cooperative-state relations were proposed. Many delegates feared, however, that even a voluntary state order would ultimately become a mandatory state command, and those proposals were defeated. The final version of the article contained no mention of state orders and was thus not an obstacle once the draft was presented to the Supreme Soviet. Much of the credit for this victory of the *kolkhozniki* must go to Aleksei Ponomarev, chairman of the Soviet of the Union's Commission for the Agro-industrial Complex, who led the successful campaign and who was subsequently selected to make the final presentation of the full draft law to the Supreme Soviet for ratification.

*Prices.* In addition to the change in Article 31, there were also changes in the part of the original text on prices. Ryzhkov strongly asserted in his speech that when the law of supply and demand was violated, it would aggravate "speculative and other negative phenomena in the market." He went on to assert that through the formation of cooperatives on a broad scale, conditions of competition would be created in the socialist market that would in turn retard inflation.

On the whole, cooperative prices were to be essentially free-market prices. There were exceptions, however. First, centrally determined prices were to hold when a cooperative was selling output in fulfillment of a state order. Second, centrally determined prices would also hold in cases where a cooperative used state-supplied natural resources to produce its output. Finally, centrally determined prices were to form the basis of retail prices when cooperatives traded products they had acquired through the central allocation system.

Through a varied application of the provisions for centrally determining prices, the state could create incentives or disincentives for cooperative production. For example, by holding state sector prices for natural resources low, the state could force cooperatives to sell at lower-than-market prices, thus making production unprofitable. Thus, through manipulation of prices, the state would still be able to influence the mix of goods and services offered by the cooperative sector.

*Supplies.* The revised draft law also tried to take into account the severe problems that cooperatives (as well as state enterprises) encountered with the Soviet supply system. Stating that this was the most important problem for cooperatives at that time, Ryzhkov claimed that 84 percent of the cooperatives in Moscow Oblast were still having "considerable difficulties" in obtaining supplies. Ryzhkov's long-term solution was for the cooperatives to become involved in all phases of production from the mining of raw materials to final production. In the short term, he asserted that Gossnab would have to become a more effective supplier for the cooperatives.

Both of these proposals were unrealistic. First, it was highly unlikely that the authorities would allow significant cooperative involvement in the extractive industries, which they considered national security interests. Moreover, cooperatives were intended to be small and medium-sized undertakings and were therefore unlikely to be able to finance such capital intensive ventures as oil or coal mining or processing. Even if they could, they would not be able to benefit from economies of scale necessary for profitable production in those and similar industries. Second, as far as his short-term solution was concerned, when Gossnab could not satisfy centrally planned needs within the state sector, why should it be expected to supply cooperatives effectively? Supply problems were likely to remain one of the chief complaints of cooperative managers for quite some time.

*Taxes.* The debate over taxes had been without doubt the most heated. Ryzhkov's speech to the Supreme Soviet implied that the question of taxes was still not yet fully resolved, though the goals for the tax policy had been clearly developed in the idea that "flexible tax policy is a reliable tool for regulation in the hands of the state making it possible to stimulate production of goods for which there is increased demand and to restrict production of other goods that are less necessary."[13] Ryzhkov also asserted that progressive taxes helped to keep prices low. Finally, with respect to the scale of taxes, he indicated that "decisions will be made according to the interests of the cooperative movement and the principles of social justice in society."[14]

The tax scheme that caused such a stir was a fairly straightforward, progressive one, with increasing marginal taxes assigned to incomes over 500 rubles per month. The marginal tax on income between 501 rubles per month and 700 rubles per month was 30 percent, for example. (See Table.)

Besides this, there was a tax levied on the profits of cooperatives. This tax was much lower than the income tax on cooperative members' incomes in order to encourage profits to be reinvested into the cooperative instead of passed out as wages. Still, the tax on cooperative profits could be stiff. As the law stood, in its first two years a cooperative would pay between 2 percent and 5 percent of its profits in a flat tax. At the end of two years, that tax would be raised to 10 percent. Moreover, 12 percent of the profits would go to social insurance and on average 10 percent would go towards the formation of a fund for "the industrial and social development of the cooperative."[15]

After Ryzhkov's speech on May 24, disagreements arose in both chambers of the Supreme Soviet over the issue of taxes, and it was announced on May 25 that the vote on the draft law would be postponed. Some twenty-three deputies were reported to have spoken out against the draft law at a meeting of a commission of the Supreme Soviet, primarily because of their objections to the tax policy.[16] The meeting went on late into the night of May 25. Politburo members Viktor Nikonov and Georgii Razumovskii were in attendance, as was Finance Minister Boris Gostev, the author of the tax decree.[17] Finally, on May 26, it was announced that a number of changes had been made in the draft law, including important revisions in the tax scheme. For the short term, local authorities were given the power to grant tax breaks and other incentives to cooperatives, their members, and employees (subcontractors) on a case-by-case basis. For the longer term, it was announced that a new law on taxes was in the drafting stage.

## Income Tax on Cooperative Members' Incomes

| Monthly Income | Total Tax |
|---|---|
| Up to 500 rubles | The same rate as that established for the income of blue- and white-collar workers. |
| 501-700 | 60 rubles, 20 kopecks, + 30% of the amount over 500 rubles. |
| 701-1000 | 120 rubles, 20 kopecks, + 50% of the amount over 700 rubles. |
| 1001-1500 | 270 rubles, 20 kopecks, + 70% of the amount over 1000 rubles. |
| 1501 and over | 620 rubles, 20 kopecks, + 90% of the amount over 1500 rubles. |

Source: *Argumenty i fakty*, No. 18, 1988, p. 8.

It was not clear just how the local authorities were to determine who got what tax breaks. Moreover, it is doubtful whether local authorities who had thus far resisted the development of cooperatives would suddenly grant them incentives to spur their development. This applied especially in those areas where cooperative taxes constituted a relatively small revenue base for the local soviets. Many questions were left unresolved, and in all probability the deputies simply agreed to pass the law on cooperatives and deal with the tax question later.

Despite the temporary delay caused by the debate over taxes, the law was unanimously passed on May 26. Significantly, virtually all of the revisions to the new law were in the direction of further liberalization and should thus have benefited the development of cooperatives. While there were still a number of issues to be resolved and a number of obstacles to be overcome, this law stood as one of the most significant elements in Gorbachev's economic reform. The text of the new Law published in *Pravda* on June 8, contained a number of articles and provisions that are worth examining.[18]

*Role and Types of Cooperatives.* Cooperatives were established as one of the fundamental elements of the Soviet Socialist economy (Article 1, Point 4). Two types of cooperatives were allowed by the Law: producer cooperatives and consumer cooperatives. "Producer cooperatives produce goods, products, and jobs, and also provide paid services to enterprises, associations, institutions, and citizens." Consumer cooperatives engaged in "trade and consumer services, and the requirements of cooperative members for housing, dachas, garden plots ... and sociocultural and other services." Although the general distinction between producer and consumer cooperatives was that producer cooperatives engaged more in "industrial" activities and consumer cooperatives operated more in the services sphere, all cooperatives were essentially granted the right to engage in any activity. The Law also recognized what it referred to as "mixed cooperatives," or cooperatives that operated in both the industrial and the service sectors of the economy (Article 3, Point 2).

*Legal Protection of Cooperatives' Property.* One of the sharpest departures from traditional Socialist practice was the guarantee that private property could now be owned by the cooperatives. The Law stated that "Cooperative ownership ... enjoys legal ownership on par with state ownership" (Article 8, Point 1). Essentially, the cooperatives were free to do with their property (both material and financial) what they wished. They could sell it, lease it, or transfer or merge it with the property of any other enterprise, organization, or institution or with any citizen's property as they saw fit.

*Cooperative Independence.* This was one of the most controversial issues in the debate over cooperatives. The Law unequivocally stated, however, that "Interference in the economic or other activity of a cooperative by state or cooperative organs is not permitted, save where envisaged by this law." As envisaged by the Law, the state's involvement in cooperative affairs did not extend to oversight of management or operational issues. Rather, the state coordinated plans, collected taxes, and ensured that the cooperative was not breaking any laws.

*Creation of a Cooperative.* The Law stated flatly that "The creation of a cooperative is not contingent on any special permission from soviet, economic, or other organs" (Article 11, Point 1). Now, if local authorities persisted in slowing the establishment of cooperatives, they would be in violation of the law and subject to legal prosecution.

*Termination of Cooperatives.* This point underscored the liberalism of the Law. A cooperative might terminate its activities through merger, amalgamation, subdivision, separation, transformation, bankruptcy, or simple liquidation of its assets. This gave the cooperative virtually all of the alternative forms of action available to businesses in the West when they faced new developments in their markets or in their financial position (Article 15, Points 1, 2 and 3).

*Planning.* The Law stated that cooperatives would have to draw up their own five-year operating and financial/budgetary plans. These plans were then to be broken down into annual plans. This was to be done "independently," and the plans were to be ratified by a general meeting of cooperative members. The cooperatives' plans were then to be coordinated with relevant local organs. This in theory was supposed to be a meeting of two equal parties (Article 18, Points 1, 2, 3 and 4).

*Prices.* When goods and services were produced entirely with the means of the cooperative itself, prices would be set by the cooperative on the basis of supply and demand. The Law also stated that "Competition in the goods (jobs and services) market should help reduce the cost of goods (jobs and services) and cut prices (tariffs) (Article 19, Points 1 and 2).

*Taxes.* Although the details of the tax policy were not a concern of this Law, it did outline a few points on taxes. Tax rates on cooperatives were to be differentiated on the basis of the type of cooperative and the aims of their activities. Cooperative tax rates were fixed for a period of five years "to boost its interest in increasing output." Income taxes for cooperative members and employees (subcontractors) were to be on a progressive scale. When cooperatives sold their goods and services at state-established prices, their members and employees (subcontractors) were to be taxed at the same rate as state enterprise employees. All cooperative tax revenues were to go to local soviets and other local organs that could grant tax breaks to stimulate the development and the production of cooperatives (Article 21, Points 1 and 2). A report carried by *Izvestiia* quoted the Minister of Finance, Boris Gostev, as saying that the marginal tax rates on members' incomes would be lowered but that the tax on cooperative profits might be raised.[19]

*Kolkhozes.* Essentially kolkhozes were treated just as any other cooperative with respect to planning, pricing, and property. So it would appear that theoretically, kolkhozes had been freed from mandatory state orders. The price for these sales was to be determined by market forces, unless the kolkhoz was selling to a state enterprise in fulfillment of a state order. Then the price would be centrally determined. If the kolkhozes were in reality granted the independence the Law indicated, and if state procurement orders were kept to a small share of kolkhoz output, this would be a historic turn of events in that it would effectively mean the end of procurement (Articles 33, 34, 35 and 36).

*Conclusion.* The new Law provided one of the few occasions since the nineteen-twenties in which a national debate in the Soviet Union clearly had an impact on the formation of a law. While public opinion may have been taken into account on previous occasions, this time representatives of the peoples' interests (namely, those representing the kolkhozniks and the Supreme Soviet deputies concerned over the tax question) delayed voting on a draft law presented to the Supreme Soviet and made significant changes and amendments to it—virtually all in the direction of economic liberalization. Besides this, the Law formally legitimized cooperatives as an integral element in the economy and created many of the necessary legal and economic conditions for their efficient development. Though the contribution of the cooperative sector was as yet small, the development of cooperatives could eventually have a significant effect on the Soviet economy, especially in the spheres of consumer goods and services.

## 19
## ALARM OVER PERESTROIKA
John Tedstrom

In an article published in *Novyi mir*, Soviet economist Nikolai Shmelev painted a picture of a reform process that had serious and noble intentions but lacked direction and cohesiveness.[1] In addition, he attacked those citizens who opposed restructuring (perestroika)—either overtly or covertly—and those who had too quickly become disillusioned, cynical, or complacent. Shmelev recognized that, if the reforms were to succeed, they would have to enjoy the mass support of the Soviet people. He offered Soviet policymakers a number of recommendations, including the proposal to set up an extra-ordinary commission ("cheka") to oversee perestroika, and hints at the economic gains to be made from reducing the military budget.

Shmelev was asked to write the article by the editors of *Novyi mir* after they had received several hundred letters in connection with his famous earlier article "Advances and Debts." That article, published in *Novyi mir* in the summer of 1987,[2] remained one of the most biting critiques of the Soviet economic system to date. In it, Shmelev called for reforms considerably more radical than those proposed by Gorbachev and subsequently embodied in the "Basic Provisions" approved at the Central Committee plenum of June 1987, which defined, at least for the time being, the goals and limits of Soviet economic reform. The editors of *Novyi mir* noted that about 90 percent of the readers' letters supported Shmelev's arguments.[3]

In his new article, Shmelev criticized the Soviet reform experience from two perspectives. He identified a number of socioeconomic phenomena such as foot-dragging and bureaucratization engendered by the difficult and complex reform process, but also directly criticized the economic basis of Gorbachev's program for restructuring, as embodied in the Twelfth Five-Year Plan.

There was growing anxiety, Shmelev complained, at all levels of the population. This anxiety was caused, he said, by a number of negative phenomena that were seriously impeding the progress of perestroika. First on Shmelev's list was the reaction of the bureaucracy, now waking up from its initial confusion and mounting a counterattack against the reforms. Although this was by no means a new revelation, Shmelev implied that bureaucratization had been intensifying as the reforms progressed further and threatened interests in the party and government apparatus.

Second, Shmelev noted that the situation in the consumer sector had failed to improve and had possibly even deteriorated since the beginning of perestroika:

> Lines in stores and empty shelves exist as before: the production of food from state sources has increased only marginally, the quality of domestic consumer goods has not changed, and imports (including essential items such as tea and coffee) have declined markedly.[4]

Shmelev blamed this situation largely on the failure of individual labor activity and cooperatives to overcome the myriad barriers placed in their way.

> The individual and cooperative sector ... intimidated by the local authorities and grave organizational difficulties (paperwork, red tape, extortion, the hostility of the police, and the impossibility of securing regular supplies) has not yet raised its head.[5]

The result of all this was increasing cynicism and disillusionment among Soviet consumers, who were resentful of the continued drive for stricter labor discipline.

Third, Shmelev asserted that people were frightened by rumors about price increases for consumer basics such as food and housing. This anxiety was understandable, to say the least, although a reform in this field was necessary to relieve the state budget of the burden of colossal subsidies in the consumer sector (some 57 billion rubles for meat and dairy products alone in 1986) and to bring the goods-money market towards equilibrium.

Shmelev argued that any acceleration that had taken place in the Soviet economy since 1985 had been due largely to an increase in the production of goods that were not needed. This theme was expressed by a number of reform-minded economists such as Yevgenii Iasin and Seliunin.

Shmelev saw the only way out in an improvement in the consumer goods sector, as a way of increasing incentives for labor and relieving the goods-money imbalance. For the longer term, he prescribed basically free-market solutions, including decentralizing the agricultural sector and substantially increasing imports of consumer goods, especially from capitalist countries. These imports could be funded, he asserted, by selling off some of the Soviet Union's gold reserves and increasing international borrowing. Significantly, he also hinted that the USSR could cut military expenditures—which, the Soviet press implied, constituted some 19 percent of Soviet GNP.[6] He also suggested that the consumers should be allowed to invest in industry by buying stocks and bonds.

Finally, Shmelev strongly encouraged those wishing to establish joint ventures, particularly with Western firms. He called for Soviet policymakers to abandon their dogmatic views on majority Soviet ownership, high rates of taxation, and the prohibition on joint ventures selling directly in the Soviet market.

Many of the criticisms he leveled were not new. They were, however, expressed in a harsh, open, and authoritative language that was still relatively rare among publishing academics in the Soviet Union. His criticism of the contradictory and irreconcilable goals of the Twelfth Five-Year Plan—universally associated with Gorbachev—was particularly bold.

# 20
# OWNERSHIP AND REFORM
## Philip Hanson

"Socialist ownership," Alexander Zinoviev has said, "is a contradiction in terms."[1] The émigré novelist and philosopher was drawing attention to the roots of the Russian word *sobstvennost* (ownership). Like the words "property" and "ownership" in English, it has connotations of exclusiveness. What is my own, or has been appropriated by me, is not yours. A milder observation to the same effect seemed to enter the canon of officially approved Soviet phrases—that is to say, it had been uttered by Gorbachev himself: state property was treated as nobody's property.[2]

In the first half of 1987, the published debate on reform in the USSR expanded to include a questioning of state ownership.[3] In the light of what had already happened in practice in Hungary and China, not to mention what had been publicly discussed in those countries and in Poland for several years, the Soviet debate was not breaking any new ground in the Socialist world. A look at Soviet public debate and policy, however, in comparison with, say, Hungarian developments over some twenty years of reform, reveals the rate of change to have been quite rapid. Not only had the public discussion of ownership continued, but the new draft law on cooperatives was extremely liberal in intent.[4] There were no ceilings on the size of cooperatives or on earnings in them; no major sector of production was declared off-limits for cooperatives, and they were encouraged to raise funds by issuing shares.

This new and rather liberal Soviet approach to questions of resource ownership was surprising to observers focusing on past Soviet history. It was less surprising when the experience of other Socialist countries was considered. The reform process in the Socialist world had run into severe problems so long as the aim had been to decentralize or "marketize" the state sector. This forced reformers (or in some cases, perhaps, provided them with the opportunity) to put changes in traditional Socialist ownership on the agenda. That experience apparently influenced at least some top Soviet policy-makers. The main channel through which that influence was communicated seemed to be the USSR Academy of Sciences' Institute of the Economics of the World Socialist System (IEMSS), headed by Academician Oleg Bogomolov.[5] The reasons why the ownership issue had arisen, and the role of Bogomolov's institute in the Soviet debate, are considered below.

*State Ownership as an Obstacle in Economic Reforms.* In March 1988, more than 170 economists from East and West met in Győr, Hungary, to discuss "Alternative Models of Socialist Economic Systems." Most speakers accepted the idea that past attempts at economic reform had failed. Many went on to argue that real reform required changes in resource ownership.

In both Poland and Hungary, this proposition had been acceptable for several years. In Győr, one of the best-known Hungarian reform economists, Tamás Bauer, observed that successes in the Hungarian reform process had come mainly from the expansion of the legitimate private and cooperative sectors, while attempts to make the state sector efficient and competitive had largely failed. Bauer went on to argue, however, that there was little scope for further gains of this nature; that privatization and the market reform of the state sector were not perfect substitutes for one another; "comprehensive reform" of the state sector was needed if further progress were to be made.[6]

Włodzimierz Brus, one of the early proponents of reform in Poland but resident in the United Kingdom since the nineteen-sixties, attributed the shortcomings of the Hungarian New Economic Mechanism to the extent of continued regulation from above. He accepted the Hungarian economist János Kornai's account of enterprise behavior in the reformed state sector: Hungarian state enterprises no longer received output targets or supply allocations. Nonetheless they still paid more attention to the central authorities than to customers and suppliers. They expected to be bailed out of any trouble by "the authorities." Therefore they operated with soft rather than hard budget constraints. The powerful stimulus of a threat to their survival if they failed to control costs and produce competitive products was missing. Only the end of dependence on higher authorities would force them to behave "competitively," in the full sense in which that word can be used in a capitalist economy. (This was not the "perfect" competition of the textbooks, but actual or potential oligopolistic or otherwise "imperfect" competition.)

Brus went on to argue that even a less regulated market would not be enough to generate substantially more efficient and dynamic behavior on the part of producers, so long as only the market for products had been liberalized. East European experience suggested that some sort of capital market needed to be created.

Brus argued as follows. In the absence of a capital market the central authorities would continue to allocate investment funds. This would maintain their leverage over the behavior of enterprises. Moreover, freedom of market entry was thereby reduced and, consequently so was the strength of competitive pressures in the long run. This whole line of argument entailed a view of central planners' control of investment allocation as generally damaging compared with market allocation—a proposition that Brus and many other East European reformers did not accept in the nineteen-fifties and nineteen-sixties. By the nineteen-eighties, however, it was almost a commonplace among Hungarian and Polish economists. What is more, Brus, one of the founding fathers of market socialist reform ideas in Eastern Europe, acknowledged that his earlier views about the necessary extent of reform did not go far enough.

In the East, as in the West, belief in the power of the central government "to get things right" in the economy had declined. There was an increasing tendency to see the center's role as best confined to setting a general framework of institutions and otherwise concentrating on social infrastructure. Brus raised the question of whether further deregulation of product markets and the development of a capital market were compatible with "the existing structure of ownership" and with the political system; he implied that they were probably not. "Outside the state sector," he said, "[including in genuine cooperatives], the market finds a ready-made motivation syndrome linking personal (or personal through group) interest with business performance."

In other words, the problem of how to motivate producers to behave competitively under state resource ownership had not been solved: how to induce them to economize on resources, seek new markets, and develop new products and processes as vigorously as they would do under capitalism. Private and cooperative businesses, however, for which the state had no responsibility and which would have to survive and prosper by their own efforts, did provide that motivation. That was the lesson of Hungarian agriculture and services and, most dramatically, of Chinese agriculture. In China "the agricultural structure and the property-use rights have been transformed to re-establish peasant farming without abolishing collective land ownership." The most dramatic extension of the Chinese approach was made in Poland, where private businesses leased from the state were to be allowed to employ up to 2,000 people.[7]

The crucial problem had to do with motivation: above all, motivation to minimize costs and motivation to seek new profit opportunities and innovate or at least keep up with the level of quality and technical innovation of one's competitors. The experience of Hungary suggests that so long as higher state bodies, whether ministries or some other kind of agency, represented the owners of a business and had in effect a responsibility for its survival, it was difficult—perhaps impossible—to prevent them from interfering in its work.

Hungarian economists discussed various ways to get around this: separating the state as owner from the state as economic regulator by creating state holding companies on the lines of Italy's ENI; requiring the managers of state enterprises to be elected by their work force and thus weakening their dependence on "the authorities" for their careers, and so on. Superior performance by the various sorts of nonstate enterprises had, though, become an increasingly salient feature of the Hungarian economy.

At the same time, the provision that enterprises, whether state or cooperative, could retain substantial funds to invest in the expansion of their activity, did not assist the flow of investment funds between different activities. For a state enterprise in particular, it was difficult either to enter a new line of production by spinning off a new company, or simply to invest in other firms whose business might offer a higher rate of return than the plowing back of profits into the original enterprise. These considerations prompted Hungarian policy-makers to reform the banking system, separating commercial banking from the central bank and setting up potentially competitive commercial banks through which funds could be channeled between users. These considerations also combined in such a way with concerns about motivation as to prompt both Hungarian and Chinese policy-makers to allow the issue of bonds and equity shares—the latter generally restricted to workers in those firms issuing the shares.

Even this development, however, fell short of a full-scale capital market. These bonds and shares could not be widely traded. Resistance to the idea of capitalist incomes had thus far prevented the creation of a large secondary market in equities. In other words, there was resistance to the idea of someone deriving income from an activity in which the recipient of the income was not himself "productively" engaged. Mario Nuti has pointed out that this limitation had three damaging consequences for a capital market. Share investments were not easily turned into cash, and this was a disincentive to save; no market valuation of the assets of firms would emerge, which hindered pricing and investment allocation; and there was no mechanism for resource reallocation by takeovers and mergers.[8] Nuti proposed an ingenious scheme by which these restrictions might be removed, without entailing a total departure from "socialist" ownership. The question that most speakers at the conference in Győr were too cautious or too polite to raise was whether this whole line of development was "socialist."

*Soviet Debates and Policies.* The conservative economic journal *Voprosy ekonomiki* published a round-table discussion on reform reportedly held in June 1987.[9] The speakers dwelt on lessons from history for Soviet economic reforms. The general tone was, by Hungarian standards, antediluvian. The emphasis was on past Soviet—and indeed Russian—history. Only one person, K. Mikulskii, said anything at all about ownership. He came from the Institute of the Economics of the World Socialist System (IEMSS), headed by Oleg Bogomolov. Mikulskii said that the process of creating an effective economic system included an increase in individual and cooperative forms of enterprise.

In May 1987, Bogomolov, in an interview with *Izvestiia*, spoke of the desirability of introducing a variety of personal and cooperative ownership forms in the Soviet economy.[10] He stressed the differences between different property rights: formal ownership as distinct from the power to decide how an asset should be used. That distinction was crucial to several Hungarian-style arrangements and to Chinese agriculture, where an asset such as land or buildings remained in a formal sense state property but was leased to a family or partnership to operate for their own profit and at their own risk.

Bogomolov later published a key article on reform in the Socialist world in the party's theoretical journal, *Kommunist*.[11] He laid far more emphasis on matters of personal motivation, and hence of the ownership and control of assets, than the traditional "optimal planning" school of reformers associated with TsEMI (the Central Economics-Mathematical Institute of the USSR Academy of Sciences) usually did. New forms of capital ownership needed, he said, to be developed alongside state ownership. He listed them as individual, family, and small-group ownership. There should also be mixed forms: state-cooperative, state-individual (e.g., cafés operated by families on a lease from the state), and state-capitalist (i.e., joint ventures with Western firms on Soviet soil). The reason for introducing such innovations, he maintained, was that they strengthened the links between the power to control the use of assets and the incomes of those who did the controlling, i.e. motivation.

Not only was Bogomolov believed to be an informal advisor to the leadership, but IEMSS received the responsibility for drafting policy proposals on the introduction of cooperatives and individual enterprise in agriculture. Much of the ideological minesweeping required to clear the way for radical proposals on property rights was contained in an obscure publication of IEMSS dated 1987 and entitled *Problems of Ownership in the Countries of Real Socialism* of which only 495 copies were printed. Even in this book, the chapter on individual enterprise, by N. L. Lvova, concluded that private ownership, i.e. private ownership of productive assets associated with the employment of nonfamily labor, was not appropriate in socialism and was due to die out in those socialist countries where it had so far survived.

It was a long way from this kind of ritual exorcism to the pragmatic reasoning characteristic of Hungarian and Polish economists and, indeed, of many senior Polish and Hungarian party officials. Opposition to these revisionist ideas—not to mention resistance to their implementation—was clearly very great, but Soviet economists and ideologists made a start on this journey to a still uncertain destination. What is more, the law on cooperatives was evidence that radical ideas about ownership had already been absorbed by policymakers.

The Albanians claimed that the destination of the Soviet reforms was capitalism, and they were not necessarily wrong in this assessment. Still, the Soviet legislation adhered to certain taboos. Individuals and cooperatives could not own land, though they might be able to lease it for long periods. Unless they were grouped into cooperatives, individuals could not employ other individuals. People could not own equity in enterprises in which they did not work, though they could possibly hold fixed-interest bonds of enterprises other than their own.

Two specters seemed to haunt the drafters of this legislation. One was the specter of the pure rentier, the coupon-clipper whose income was composed entirely of Marxian surplus value. The other was the specter of the big-time entrepreneur, who could either build up a business and sell it for a fortune if he so chose, or achieve the same result by playing the markets.

The first of these specters would scarcely be recognized in the capitalist world in 1988. Pure rentiers were a dwindling species, and the Western world economy could adjust readily enough to their extinction. The second specter, though, represented something fundamental: the large secondary market for shares, where productive assets were valued, providing information for the whole system of market prices; and where capital flowed between different production activities and high incentives for risk-taking were in part created.

Perhaps market reform in the socialist countries could stop short of evoking the second specter and still improve efficiency. The resulting system could then still be claimed for socialism, though it would be socialist in a rather attenuated sense. The limitations on the capital market would probably be accompanied by high marginal tax rates, as they would be to start with in the Soviet Union. There could well continue to be a requirement that all working-age people have jobs and a further requirement that most of those jobs be in the state sector.

The result would be a system that was viable in the sense that it provided more prosperity and technological dynamism than the traditional system; it might still be unable to match the West in these respects, but it would be held up as more "just" because it avoided extremes of wealth. It is possible that the more imaginative reformers had some such ultimate end in mind: a scheme for beating the West without—quite—joining it. If so, it was still only a gleam in their eyes.

# VI. THE CASUALTIES OF REFORM

## 21
## THE IMAGE OF THE KGB
### Viktor Yasmann

In 1988, the KGB began to publish regular information bulletins in *Argumenty i fakty*, the weekly newspaper for propaganda workers. It was announced that the bulletins, which appeared under the rubric "The KGB Informs and Comments," were to become a permanent feature. This was the first time since the nineteen-twenties that state security organs had addressed the public in print. The column seemed to be mainly a defensive exercise in public relations. The prestige of the KGB among the Soviet public had reached a nadir with the publication in the media of ever more horrifying facts about Stalin's terror. Furthermore, since the beginning of 1987, articles criticizing the KGB's performance of its functions (though none challenging its legitimacy as an institution) had been appearing in the press.

—In November 1986, an article in *Sovetskaia Rossiia* told of a group of drunken young men who had opened fire with hunting rifles on a memorial to soldiers killed in World War II. One of the organizers of the attack on the monument was Pavel Guliaev, who had served in the border troops of the KGB.[1] The newspaper received many shocked and angry letters from readers after its account of the incident appeared.

—In January 1987, wide publicity was given to the case of journalist Viktor Berkhin, who was illegally arrested while investigating corruption among party officials in Voroshilovgrad Oblast in the Ukraine, and was subjected to harrowing interrogation sessions while in custody. Berkhin had been arrested on the orders of A. Dichenko, the head of the Voroshilovgrad Oblast KGB. The affair led to a public apology in *Pravda* by USSR KGB Chairman Viktor Chebrikov. Berkhin was released, and Dichenko, who probably held the rank of major general, was dismissed from the KGB.[2] Long after these events took place, the press continued to discuss the Berkhin case; it was revealed, for example, that two friends of the reporter had been framed by the KGB for refusing to testify against him,[3] and Berkhin's death several months after his release was also reported.[4]

—In October 1987, *Literaturnaia gazeta* made public the unfortunate experiences of Police Captain Aleksandr Malyshev, who was chief of the Odessa

Department for Combating Embezzlement and Speculation until his superiors, finding him too energetic and tenacious, dismissed him from his position and put him under arrest on fabricated charges. In doing so, they resorted to the services of Iu. Bobovskii, senior commissioner of the KGB in Odessa Oblast, who became Malyshev's main interrogator.[5] In January 1988, the Party Control Committee of the CPSU Central Committee published its own verdict on the Malyshev affair in *Pravda*: Bobovskii was expelled from the KGB;[6] his immediate superior in the Odessa Oblast KGB, A. Dovzhenko, was demoted and received a strict party reprimand, as did a number of senior law enforcement officers in Odessa; Malyshev was restored to his position.[7]

—In November 1987, *Izvestiia* criticized the border troops of the KGB for damaging, in the course of inspection at border checkpoints, Soviet-manufactured cars destined for sale abroad.[8]

—In February 1988, *Literaturnaia gazeta* sharply criticized the KGB's practice of confiscating videocassettes at the border.[9]

—In March 1988, the luxurious life style of Aleksei Boiko, chairman of the KGB in the Turkmen SSR, came under scrutiny in *Izvestiia*.[10]

—In April 1988, *Krokodil* published a letter from a reader, P. Anodin, in which he suggested that the magazine was waging a KGB-inspired vendetta against the émigré writer Vasilii Aksenov.[11] Early that year, *Krokodil* had printed a pro-American passage from Aksenov's novel *In Search of Melancholy Baby* and invited readers' comments.[12] The readers responded with a flood of bitterly angry letters condemning the writer as a deserter and a traitor to his country.[13] Anodin, however, questioned the magazine's motives: "Could it be that *Krokodil* has a special assignment from the KGB organs?"

The press materials criticizing the KGB expressed a wide variety of complaints whose publication, two or three years earlier, would have been unimaginable; yet in no instance was the legitimacy of the KGB as an institution called into question. The message from the Kremlin was clear: the security organs were not immune from criticism for activities that ran counter to the interests of perestroika, but equally, they were in no danger of being done away with altogether.

The KGB's public relations campaign was directed towards several goals, one of which was to portray the organization as a fearless fighter against corruption. An article in *Moscow News*, for example, on the investigation into the rampant corruption in Uzbekistan under Sharaf Rashidov mentioned that when Rashidov learned who had called in the investigators from Moscow, he had the leadership of the republican KGB removed.[14]

In order to challenge the popular perception of the NKVD's repressive machinery, the story was circulated that a large number of Chekists in Dzerzhinskii's mold had preferred to sacrifice themselves rather than take part in the monstrous crimes of Stalin's terror. Sociologist Igor Bestuzhev-Lada, writing in *Nedelia*, estimated that 20,000 NKVD members "became victims of a bacchanalia of illegality." Only a few of them, he went on to say—among them high-ranking officers of the NKVD who were henchmen of Stalin—were removed by the dictator because they were witnesses of his crimes; the rest suffered simply because they refused to make a career of murder.[15]

The KGB's efforts to create a new public image were closely connected with a basic question—the legitimacy of its existence. There was no Soviet law spelling out the role and functions of the KGB.

The KGB, like the Communist party itself, became   a less than homogeneous organization. The ideological polarization within the party regarding the pace and character of Gorbachev's reforms was also evident among the ranks of the security organs. The strategy of exposing some members of the KGB to a measure of public criticism was being pursued with the aim of purging that institution, like the party itself, of corrupt members or those unwilling to adapt to a changing society. Just as in the case of the party, Gorbachev wanted to make the KGB a more efficient organization—not to undermine it, but to strengthen it.

## 22
## THE LOSERS AND THE YES-MEN
Bohdan Nahaylo* and Elizabeth Teague**

During the Chautauqua conference on US-Soviet relations during the last week of August 1987, Academician Tatiana Zaslavskaia answered the question: "Where is resistance to reform concentrated, and how strong is it?" She said:

"You need to understand who gains most of all from these reforms and who loses. An important result, a social result of the reforms will be the creation of conditions where every worker will be able to work to the full extent of his ability and knowledge. And second, every man will receive for his work what he puts into it—pay according to work done.

"Who loses from this system? First of all those people who essentially cannot increase their output: the elderly, the badly educated, the passive in spirit; but the young, the educated, and energetic people gain—the active part of society.

---

*The interviewer of Zaslavskaia

**On the Bovin Interview

"Moreover a substantial number of people who at the moment receive an income without reason will lose. A large part of the administrative apparatus really does more harm than good with its work. A large part of these people will be freed from the sector of administration and moved to the production sector. They do not want this and are resisting. The second group, which consists of a fair amount of workers, are privileged workers who receive [remuneration] by tradition, irrespective of how they work—that is, they may have a high income, without having to exert themselves much for it.

"I still have not spoken about the black economy which in general consists of non-labor incomes. Resistance comes from all those groups who may lose out. These groups are fairly numerous, and resistance is very perceptible, especially on the side of the administrative apparatus, of the state, soviets and party…. Yes, it is possible to overcome this resistance with the joint actions of the political leadership and the basic mass of workers who want reform."

On November 6, 1987, the semiofficial Hungarian newspaper *Magyar Hírlap* published an interview with Aleksandr Bovin, a political commentator of the Soviet government newspaper *Izvestiia*. Bovin's theme was the need for Soviet society to come to terms with "the terrible remnants of the cult of personality" which, he said, continued to exert its influence even at the present day.

The most terrible thing Stalin succeeded in achieving was to frighten people, and to implant the fear of the bosses in every person, in every Communist, in every official. The fear of opposing the leadership…. People were terrorized, and this feeling is still alive. That is why I say that, until we learn to say "No," there will be no restructuring.

While calling on the Soviet population to cast aside its fear of the "bosses," Bovin identified three groups of Soviet citizens who were apparently not too frightened to resist perestroika. Bovin divided them into three groups: (1) those blinded by ideological blinkers; (2) those who stood to lose personal power and privileges; and (3) those too stupid to "restructure" themselves. He did not acknowledge or resolve the apparent contradiction between his advocacy of the right to say "No" and his disapproval of those groups in Soviet society who were, albeit covertly, saying "No" to perestroika.

The first group, Bovin said, was a small one whose members opposed Gorbachev's reforms on ideological grounds. "They feel we are abandoning our principles; that self-accounting and private work … are deviations from the Socialist path, because socialism is not a goods-producing society and even less a society based on private production." Bovin said this group included members of the ideological and economic apparatuses, "including—how should I put it?—elderly people commanding great respect."

Bovin called the second group "the pragmatic opponents of restructuring." These, he said, constituted a much wider stratum of society and represented "the greatest obstacle" to reform. They included "people who occupy high positions in society and who over the course of many years have become used to their position and to a rather high material standard of living." Such people, Bovin went on, "do not want to take responsibility, because greater personal responsibility is accompanied by a lot of inconvenience. These people do not want glasnost because they are not used to being criticized."

Then, Bovin said, there was a third group of people whose "ingrained habits" made them incapable of working in a new way even if they wanted to. This group was, the journalist said, only a small one.

Bovin lamented the imprint left on the whole of Soviet society by the Stalin terror. Resistance to perestroika, he said, "is inherent in all of us, in each and every person, and in each and every Communist":

Man cannot leap out of his skin, out of history, out of his own biography. The braking mechanism is present in all of us, in our conscience, in our backbone.... We are all a little afraid of being carried away by taking too radical steps.... This fear that is inherent in all of us leads to the danger of half-solutions, and half-solutions are the most destructive. Half-solutions are what destroyed the reforms of 1965 and the guidelines of the Twentieth Party Congress.... Things were only carried out halfway. We began something and then gave it up, then began again and gave up again. Now we see the result. That is why I say that the most dangerous enemy of perestroika is within us.

23
GORBACHEV AND THE SOVIET SOCIAL CONTRACT
Aaron Trehub

The idea that a social contract existed between the Soviet leadership and the Soviet people has, over the years, gained wide acceptance in the West. Although its composition has remained problematical, the contract could be said to rest on "egalitarianism, stability, and security."[1] These principles, however, came under threat from Gorbachev's program of perestroika. Egalitarianism began to yield to the principle of pay according to performance; stability, to the prospect of an end to state subsidies for housing and food; and security—above all, job security—to the possibility of being "freed" (laid off) and having to look for work in a different sector of the economy, perhaps even a different part of the country. The post-Stalin social contract was being annulled, and it is probably safe to say that the fate of perestroika depended on whether the contract that replaced it would prove acceptable to the Soviet population.

*Egalitarianism.* Egalitarianism, perhaps the most important element in the Soviet social contract, was possibly also the most pernicious from the point of view of economic progress. By pandering to the popular notion that everybody should be equal, the state achieved political stability, but at the price of alienating the most enterprising members of society. Under Gorbachev, the emphasis shifted to "activating the human factor," and the egalitarian ethos was coming under attack.

One of the most-criticized manifestations of egalitarianism was the practice of wage-leveling, or *uravnilovka*, which, by divorcing pay from performance, weakened the material incentive for high-quality work. Wage-leveling was first attacked by Stalin in 1931; it later became a favorite target of proreform economists and sociologists.[2]

Since Gorbachev's rise to power, a number of measures aimed at linking pay to performance were taken. At the beginning of 1986, the salaries of scientific workers (*nauchnye rabotniki*) were made dependent on the quantity and quality of output, not seniority or academic degree; moreover, raises and bonuses were to be financed out of the existing wage fund, without additional allocations from the center.[3] In September 1986, a decree on reforming the wage system in the production sector[4] stipulated that workers' pay must be linked to job performance and that raises and bonuses must be paid for out of enterprise profits.[5] By 1990, more than 75 million Soviet workers were to be working under the new system.[6]

Although there were some administrative hitches in the transition to the new wage system, the main problems were psychological. Many work collectives had difficulty understanding that pay raises and bonuses, instead of being more or less automatic, now had to be earned through better work and higher productivity. Nor had leveling been eliminated; in some cases, raises and bonuses were handed out to an entire collective, regardless of the differences in performance among the workers. Eradicating the practice of wage-leveling would require nothing less than "a shift in people's psychology," meaning, presumably, the jettisoning of the idea that large differences in income were a violation of "social justice," at least as most Soviet people seemed to understand that concept.[7] This shift had yet to occur; as Gorbachev said in his speech at the plenum of Central Committee in June 1987, "The tendency toward wage-leveling has stubbornly continued to gain ground."[8]

*Stability.* The fundamental stability of Soviet life was symbolized by the artificially low prices for housing and foodstuffs. Rents for state apartments had not changed since 1928 and, together with utility payments, accounted for less than 3 percent of the average Soviet family's budget.[9] Prices for bread, sugar, and eggs had remained unchanged since 1954; those for meat and milk, since 1962.[10] Of course, this at first glance enviable state of affairs was achieved through enormous state subsidies: in 1985, the state subsidized housing to the tune of 8 billion rubles, while the subsidies on meat and milk alone amounted to almost 50 billion rubles.[11] According to Gorbachev, "the total amount of subsidies from the state budget today exceeds 73 billion rubles a year."[12]

This seemed likely to change. Price reform became a hot topic in the Soviet Union, and the question of subsidies was perhaps the most sensitive point. Some prominent economists—e.g., Abel Aganbegian and Tatiana Zaslavskaia—argued that food and housing subsidies undermined economic efficiency and "social justice" (since not everyone had access to, say, subsidized meat or apartments) and should therefore be eliminated as quickly as possible.[13] Others were more cautious. Valentin Sergeevich Pavlov, the chairman of the USSR State Committee for Prices, admitted that the existing price system yielded a distorted picture of the economy and would have to be changed; he refused, however, to comment on whether food subsidies were going to be eliminated in the near future, saying that "the question is too complicated, too sensitive."[14]

Assurances that rises in the price of food and housing would be compensated by wage hikes and transfer payments were received with skepticism. In a letter published in *Literaturnaia gazeta*, two postgraduate students argued against raising food prices, saying that around 40 percent of Soviet families had monthly incomes of less than 100 rubles a person and that their standard of living would inevitably drop if food subsidies were removed, regardless of transfer payments. [15] Another reader said she was afraid that a rise in prices would make people turn away from perestroika. "It should not be forgotten," she continued, "that the people in this country have been raised for decades on the ideals of social equality."[16]

*Job Security*. Enshrined in Article 40 of the Constitution of the USSR (1977), "the right to work" was constantly touted as the greatest achievement of Soviet socialism. As perestroika progressed, however, it became clear that the right to work, or rather, the popular understanding of the right to work, was impeding the drive for economic efficiency. Soviet economists took to criticizing the identification in the popular mind of the right to work with full employment; indeed, one influential economist, Stanislav Shatalin, even called full employment "a superseded stage of extensive development."[17] Shatalin and his colleagues proposed replacing full employment with "rational full employ- ment"—i.e., a level of employment consistent with economic efficiency, not political expediency. Their main target was the endemic practice of overmanning.

Overmanning, or underemployment, had a long history in the Soviet Union. Feliks Dzerzhinskii, who in the mid-nineteen-twenties served simultaneously as head of the Soviet secret police and chairman of the Supreme Council of the National Economy (VSNKh), said:

> The presence in workshops and factories under the current labor régime of superfluous workers who are unnecessary for production is a crime before the working class, for every superfluous worker ... hinders the others.[18]

The same point was made by the economist Nikolai Shmelev in his celebrated article in the issue of *Novyi mir* for June 1987.[19] When asked about this article, Gorbachev admitted that it presented an accurate picture of the Soviet economy, but rejected Shmelev's suggestion that the Soviet Union used unemployment as a means of strengthening labor discipline.[20]

Gorbachev's goal was to eliminate overmanning while avoiding unemployment. However, the economist Vladimir Kostakov, a specialist in the planning of labor resources at USSR wrote in *Kommunist*, that the Soviet Union was "not ready, on either the economic or psychological plane, for drastic changes in the use of labor resources."[21]

Even if the shift to "rational full employment" proceeded smoothly, many thousands of workers would be faced with the prospect of having to move to other sectors of the economy—especially the low-paying service sector—or even other parts of the country. What Zaslavskaia called "a qualitative change in the conditions of employment"[22] was bound to be a difficult experience for many workers and their families.

*Little Change in Daily Life.* In a lecture published in March 1987 in *Nauka i zhizn*, Aganbegian, the man widely reputed to be Gorbachev's most influential economic adviser, raised important questions about the effectiveness of his social policy.

Aganbegian began with what he called the most urgent social problem in the Soviet Union—housing. By the beginning of the nineteen-eighties, housing construction in the USSR was stuck at around 2 million apartments a year, not nearly enough to meet the party's goal of providing every family with an apartment or house of its own before the end of the century. There had been some progress in this sphere since Gorbachev came to power. Housing construction in the USSR rose from 1.9 million apartments in 1985 to 2.3 million in 1987—a 20 percent increase. The goal, said Aganbegian, was to build 3 million apartments a year by the beginning of the nineteen-nineties. Even if this goal were reached, however, it would only just cover the creation of new families through marriage (there were 2.7 million marriages in the Soviet Union in 1986). In the meantime, some 13 million Soviet families and single people continued to live in communal apartments, trailers, dormitories, or rented rooms.

The food situation was even more discouraging. Aganbegian pointed out that the Soviet Union lagged behind other developed countries in the consumption not only of meat but also of dairy products, fruits, and vegetables. Indeed, per capita consumption of the latter in the USSR amounted to only one third of the medically recommended norm, a circumstance that had a dire effect on the health of Soviet children. Furthermore, Aganbegian said that a quarter of all Soviet meat was raised on imported feed grain, which the Soviet Union paid for with oil. The fall in the price of oil on the world market in 1986 forced the USSR to cut imports of grain and meat, to the detriment of the Soviet consumer. In 1988, food rationing was in effect in many parts of the country. Quality was also a problem. According to an article in *Literaturnaia gazeta*, Soviet sausage was so bad that cats refused to eat it,[23] and even bread, which used to be a cheap food-stuff of dependably high quality, had apparently become worse—and more expensive.

Gorbachev and his advisers often spoke of the need "to activate the human factor," which basically meant getting people to work harder. Leaving aside the question of whether the human factor was all that eager to be activated, the main problem was how to go about the whole business. The best way seemed to be to produce (or import) things that people would want to buy with their hard-earned rubles. In other words, consumer goods. And this is where perestroika had fallen down on the job. Aganbegian acknowledged that the performance of light industry, the branch responsible for the production of consumer durables, had been "unsatisfactory." This was hardly news to Soviet consumers, who filled the press with complaints about the lack of everything from videocassette recorders to panty hose. To some extent, the poor performance of light industry reflected the low priority it enjoyed in the eyes of Soviet planners. Aganbegian pointed out that the sector received only 8 percent of all capital investments and that 40 percent of its equipment was outdated and in need of replacement. Whatever the cause of the sector's problems, the result was what Aganbegian called "a dangerous gap" between supply and demand, with empty store shelves and bloated savings accounts.

Aganbegian referred the state of the health service, the reform of the pension system, working conditions in factories, and the practice of laying off workers in the interest of greater economic efficiency, which was delicately described as part of the shift to "rational full employment." Although modest progress was made in these areas, the bottom line was not very encouraging. For example, infant mortality in the USSR was still between two and three times higher than it was in other developed countries, and life expectancy was substantially lower. The reform of the pension system, a measure that would affect the lives of some 60 million citizens, was still at the draft stage. Working conditions at many factories were still disgraceful and dangerous. And the shift to "rational full employment" had given rise to a number of unforeseen difficulties. On the plus side, Aganbegian said that "the spiritual life" of the country had improved and that the media had become more interesting. He warned, however, that this was not enough to ensure the success of perestroika. "Many Soviet families are not experiencing any particular changes in their daily life," he concluded.

The same point was made with somewhat more urgency by the economist Nikolai Shmelev, who stated flatly that there had been "no really tangible changes in daily life" for many Soviet citizens. [24] Even more disturbing, "there is a widespread opinion ... that the situation in food and consumer goods stores has not only not improved in recent days but has gotten worse." What was needed, Shmelev went on to say, was a tangible improvement in the daily lives of the people and "not sometime [in the distant future] but in the very near future."

How was this to be achieved? Shmelev made two suggestions. First, "all administrative restrictions" on private agriculture should be removed, a measure that recalled the tsarist minister Stolypin's "wager on the strong." Second, while farmers were recovering from the aftereffects of a half century of collectivized agriculture, the Soviet Union should import foodstuffs and consumer goods, even if this meant going into debt with capitalist countries. The main thing was to saturate the market with goods that consumers wanted to buy. Shmelev said that this would help to alleviate the problem of alcoholism, since "full shelves in food and consumer-goods stores ... would give the people something besides liquor to spend their money on." But the success or failure of Gorbachev's antidrinking campaign was not all that was at stake here. Shmelev warned that "if we do not manage to achieve something substantial in the next year or two, something that everybody can feel, then the fate of perestroika may be in danger."

## 24
## POVERTY AND HOMELESSNESS IN THE SOVIET UNION
### Aaron Trehub

In June 1988, *Sotsialisticheskaia industriia* published an interview with Marina Mozhina of the Central Mathematical-Economics Institute of the USSR Academy of Sciences in Moscow. The subject of the interview was "Who Lives below the Poverty Line?"[1]

Discussing the results of a survey of 62,000 Soviet families conducted each year by the USSR State Committee for Statistics (Goskomstat), Mozhina said that 10 percent of the Soviet population could not get by from one payday to the next without borrowing money and that 25 percent had no savings at all, since they spent everything they earned on basic necessities. Her most striking revelation, however, was that 20 percent of the Soviet population—that is, approximately 57 million people—had a monthly income of around 70 rubles. This meant that they lived on the brink of what Mozhina, employing the official Soviet euphemism, termed "underprovisioning" (*maloobespechennost*)—in other words, poverty.

According to Mozhina and other Soviet writers on the subject, the Soviet poor fell into four main groups: families in which the fathers had low-paying jobs, young couples with children, single mothers, and pensioners. In 1979, there were almost 8 million single-parent households in the USSR, most of them headed by women, and the number had almost certainly grown since then.[2] But it was the last group—pensioners—that accounted for the bulk of the Soviet poor.

There were some 58 million pensioners in the Soviet Union in 1988, out of a total population of 285 million. The pension system was based on legislation passed in 1956. This legislation was clearly obsolete and in need of revision. The main problem was that it did not guarantee the constitutional right to material security in old age for the simple reason that in many cases the pensions were too low to ensure a decent standard of living, even by Soviet standards.

According to the Soviet statistical yearbook, the average pension in 1986 was 75 rubles a month.[3] It seems likely, therefore, that many pensioners—probably millions—lived under, at, or near Mozhina's poverty threshold of 70 rubles a month.

This assumption was indirectly confirmed by a decree adopted soon after Gorbachev came to power. In May 1985, the CPSU Central Committee, the USSR Council of Ministers, and the All-Union Central Council of Trade Unions issued a decree stipulating that pensions of less than 60 rubles a month that had been assigned more than ten years previously were eventually to be raised to the approximate level of pensions paid to later workers in similar fields and with similar qualifications.[4]

An idea of how the Soviet poor lived can best be gained by reading articles in the Soviet press. One such article appeared in the weekly newspaper *Semia* (Family).[5] It described the daily life of the Titarenkos, a family of twelve in Alma-Ata, the capital of the Kazakh SSR. Mr. Titarenko earned 120 rubles a month as a chauffeur in a motorized police detachment; Mrs. Titarenko got 45 rubles a month as a "hero-mother" with ten children; and the family drew an additional 72 rubles a month in child-support payments. This added up to a total monthly income of 237 rubles, or just under 20 rubles a head.

The biggest problem was food. Mr. Titarenko scoured the city for soup bones to supplement the family's basic diet of milk and potatoes. Meat was a rarity on the Titarenko table, as were fresh fruits and vegetables.

With regard to housing, the Titarenkos were relatively lucky. For many years, the family had lived in two small rooms in a communal apartment. In 1986, they finally received a five-room apartment of their own. The rent was 40 rubles a month, or 17 percent of the family's monthly income (according to official statistics, the average Soviet family spent only 3 percent of its monthly income on rent and utilities). With 65 square meters for twelve people, the apartment was cramped, and the family had to sleep two and three to a room. Nevertheless, the Titarenkos' housing situation was better than that of many other Soviet citizens.

The Titarenkos were poor but not destitute. The same could not be said of many Soviet pensioners, especially the 10 million or so living alone.[6] In 1987 *Sobesednik*, the weekly supplement to the youth league newspaper *Komsomolskaia pravda*, printed an article describing the living conditions of single pensioners in Moscow.[7] One blind woman, a former singer, supplemented her pension by doing piecework in her room (she packaged combs for sale). This way, she earned enough to keep herself in packaged soup, which she prepared with cold tap-water, and candy. She was dependent on her neighbors, and when they refused to run errands for her, went hungry. Another pensioner had not left her communal apartment for three years; she too was dependent on her neighbor, an alcoholic, who ran errands for money.

There were also homeless people in the Soviet Union. They were called *"bichi"* (this word is generally considered to be an abbreviation of *"byvshii intelligentnyi chelovek,"* or former member of the intelligentsia), *"bomzhi"* (from the police abbreviation for "of no fixed residence"), or, simply, *"brodiagi"* (tramps). They could be found in abandoned houses, cellars, coal bins, and garbage dumps, around railway stations, or in special detention centers run by the police of the Ministry of Internal Affairs (MVD). Here they were held for a month while their identities were checked and attempts were made to fix them up with a job, a residence permit, and a place to live. These attempts were seldom successful, however, and when the month was up the *"bomzhi"* were put back on the street.

The Soviet homeless came from various backgrounds. Among the inmates of the detention center in Tashkent, a journalist encountered a proud husband who had walked out on his wife after he discovered she was cheating on him; a disillusioned engineer; a senile old woman who had gone out one day and forgotten her way home; and an insane young girl who imagined herself to be a deposed queen. It seems that a large number of homeless people were ex-convicts who took to the road after being denied residence permits in their native cities. Many of the homeless were alcoholics and had trouble holding down a job. For this reason, they fell into the category of "parasite," the term reserved for people who were not, in Soviet legal parlance, engaged in socially useful labor and therefore liable to prosecution under Article 209 of the RSFSR Criminal Code or the equivalent articles of the criminal codes of the other Union republics. Although homeless people could be found in every part of the Soviet Union, including the northern port cities and the settlements of the Soviet Far East, they were especially common in the southern republics, where the climate was mild, the authorities relatively lax, and odd jobs easy to come by.

Although the official fiction that there were no homeless people in the USSR was implicitly contradicted by articles in the Soviet press[8] during "the era of stagnation" (the Brezhnev years), it took glasnost to put paid to it for good. In May 1986, *Literaturnaia gazeta* published an article about homeless people and vagrants in the Semireche region of Kazakhstan.[9]

In February 1987, the popular weekly magazine *Ogonek* printed a vivid article on homeless people in the USSR.[10] The author, provincial journalist Aleksei Lebedev, had long wanted to experience life among the homeless at first hand. In February 1986, he hid his internal passport and other documents, donned an old overcoat and, with three rubles in his pocket, descended for six months into the lower depths of Soviet society. He described in detail the special detention centers for vagrants that could be found in every large Soviet city and railway station, the places where homeless people sheltered, the temporary jobs they took to survive, and the fine distinctions between different classes of vagrants, from hopeless alcoholics and rubbish-heap dwellers to quasi-professional drifters. He also said that vagrants were a public health menace, claiming that they accounted for a large proportion of patients in venereological hospitals of the compulsory type. "God forbid," he wrote, "that the AIDS virus should take hold in this stratum."

The first explicit admission that there were homeless people in the Soviet Union appeared on February 10. The government newspaper *Izvestiia* inaugurated a column featuring letters that would have gone unprinted a few years previously.[11] The first letter was from one Leonid Kirienko in Sverdlovsk. "Judging from articles in the press," he wrote, "editors believe that homeless people exist only abroad. Well, there are enough of them in our country." Kirienko should have known: he had been homeless since 1980. Although he admitted that he was to blame for his plight, he objected to the label of "parasite." "A parasite," he wrote, "is somebody who sits at home and has a residence permit but doesn't want to work. A person without work and without shelter is not a parasite but a lost and dying man who should be helped back onto his feet again." The Sverdlovsk police directed the homeless man to a couple of local factories, but neither offered him a job. After the second unsuccessful interview, Kirienko vanished without a trace.

*Izvestiia* returned to the subject a few days later, in an article entitled simply "*Bomzh*."[12] It told the story of Petr Maslov, a skilled worker and decorated war veteran from Saratov Oblast who took to drink and became a tramp, eventually winding up in a small city in Uzbekistan. Here he was literally picked out of the gutter by an Uzbek worker, who took him home and gave him a corner to sleep in (illegally, since Maslov had no identity papers). "*Bomzh*" had a happy ending; The author, Plutnik was able to locate Maslov's thirty-two-year-old son, who travelled to Uzbekistan from the RSFSR to take care of his long-lost father.[13] "Kirienko was right," concluded Plutnik, "There are homeless people in our country too."

Lebedev said that there were "hundreds of thousands" of homeless people in the Soviet Union.[14] This estimate may even have been on the conservative side, given that fact that there were 4.5 million officially registered alcoholics in the USSR,[15] over 5 million mentally ill people,[16] and, according to a secret MVD report obtained by Agence France-Presse, at least 500,000 known "parasites."[17]

Ironically, the problem of homelessness in the Soviet Union was finally being acknowledged at a time when the prospects for alleviating it were bleaker than ever. The reason for this was the shift of Soviet enterprises and factories to economic accountability (*khozraschet*). In theory, Soviet enterprises had long been obliged to hire vagrants sent to them by the police and the job placement offices. In practice, as Kirienko found out, this obligation was usually ignored, for understandable reasons. In the past, the danger had been that vagrants and "parasites" would disrupt labor discipline and prevent the collective from fulfilling its plan and getting its bonus. In conditions of *khozraschet*, when enterprises had to pay their own way or face bankruptcy, the disincentives to hire the down-and-out were even stronger. Gorbachev's attempt to make Soviet enterprises more efficient seemingly complicated the task of rehabilitating the homeless.

While experts pondered the problem of poverty, some Soviet citizens were taking matters into their own hands. Branches of the voluntary society "*Miloserdie*" (Mercy) were established in Moscow, Leningrad, and other Soviet cities.[18] Although these organizations were formed primarily to help elderly people and single pensioners, it was possible their activities would eventually be extended to other poor people as well.

In the age of perestroika, the outlook for the poor was not bright. The state was slow to recognize the problem and slow in doing something about it. Moreover, Gorbachev's economic reforms—in particular, the prospect of price increases on staple foodstuffs and housing—spelled trouble for the "underprovisioned" members of Soviet society. Nevertheless, the admission that there was widespread poverty in "the first country of socialism" was a sign that the Soviet leadership was adopting a more mature approach to social problems.

## 25
# STALLED REFORMS PROVOKE LABOR UNREST IN POLAND
## Louisa Vinton

*Government's Austerity Program Under Attack.* On January 13, 1988, Poland's official trade union federation, the National Alliance of Trade Unions, issued a harsh statement[1] rejecting the government's prices and incomes program for 1988 on the grounds that it would entail a decline in living standards. The federation demanded a more accurate calculation of the impact of price hikes and commensurate wage and pension increases to insure full compensation. On January 20 the government announced that it would raise wages and pensions by 6,000 zloty—more than 3 times what it had originally planned—when the new prices took effect. Although this was roughly what had been demanded, the government insisted that Union pressure had not influenced its decision.

The government's initial plan to increase prices by an average of 40 percent had been scaled down to a rise of 27 percent after the defeat, on November 29, of the referendum on economic and political reform  In the referendum, voters had been asked to approve or reject two vaguely-worded proposals for a "radical curing of the economy," which would be accompanied by a "two-to-three-year period of rapid changes," and the introduction of a "Polish model of deep democratization."  Of Poland's at least 26,000,000 or more eligible voters, only 44.3 percent  voted "yes" on the first question and 46.3 percent  on the second. Overall turnout was only 67.2 percent , the lowest for any elections since 1945. Although 66 percent  of those voting actually approved the first question and 69 percent  the second, Poland's referendum law required that 51 percent  of all eligible voters cast positive votes for a measure to be agreed to.

Official unions charged that the government's previous efforts to effect economic change through price manipulation had neither corrected the causes of the crisis nor led to any improvement in the material situation of working people. In the previous year, the unions argued, real wages in the socialized sector had fallen while inflation had risen. The rate of compensation proposed by the government to cover price hikes in 1988, the statement said, had evoked "social indignation," while the government's pledge to increase prices by only 27 percent  was viewed with "distrust and disbelief."

A chorus of protest from the trade unions had become the traditional accompaniment to unpopular government measures in Poland. The charter of the National Alliance of Trade Unions granted it the right of "consultation" over government decisions affecting the quality of life of the working people, and it expressed its displeasure with all price hikes in 1987-1988. In March 1987, for example, pressure from the unions was credited with the reduction of the price hikes from 13 percent to 9.6 percent. Additionally, the federation compiled an alternative reform program, which, it said, gave greater priority to improving supply than to limiting demand through higher prices.

Much of the unions' opposition was probably for the sake of appearances, intended to create the illusion that the government had been persuaded to scale down its proposals to humane proportions. The official unions had always proclaimed their adherence to the government's economic goals and stressed that they were not adversaries of the government but "partners with a different viewpoint." They staunchly opposed the idea of union pluralism and accepted "joint responsibility" for the national economy. Solidarity representatives treated the unions' undertakings with great skepticism; Zbigniew Bujak, for example, suggested that the controversy had been orchestrated to allow a "big show of compromise" as part of the "sophisticated formula" that the régime had developed to forestall social protest against price hikes.[2]

Yet in questioning the government's revised postreferendum reform program, the unions' tone was unusually aggressive. Some of the harshest criticism of the government's reform measures appeared in the federation's weekly *Związkowiec*, in which one writer described price hikes as an "economically ineffective illusion of activity" that, without some remedy for the "general wage and income mess," would change nothing even if prices were raised by 200 percent a year.[3] Union economists argued that the government's program rested almost exclusively on price manipulation and wage limitation while its pledges to create conditions conducive to efficient production and to link wages to productivity amounted to mere exhortation.

*Price Hikes and Economic Reform.* The government argued that steep price hikes were necessary in order to create market equilibrium, limit inflation, and end subsidies, which now consumed more than a third of the national budget. Critics argued that the same rationale had been cited since the beginning of the economic reform program in 1981, yet while prices had risen, supplies of most goods still failed to meet demand. Prices of food and fuel alone rose by up to 400 percent in 1982, 25 percent in 1983, and 19 percent in 1986; these were again the chief targets for the price hikes of February 1: coal was to rise by 200 percent, gasoline by 60 percent, hot water and central heating by 100 percent, and basic food items by 40 percent. Yet subsidies had not been cut and were expected to rise again in 1988; they had even been extended to products from which subsidies had been removed, such as sugar.[4]

According to the government, raising prices to reflect the "real" value of goods and services was a way of introducing market mechanisms into the Polish economy. As Ernest Skalski, one of the most severe critics of economic policy noted, however, this was working backwards: "the market creates prices, but prices do not create the market." Raising prices without permitting autonomous economic entities to interact and create a market could only yield "actually-existing prices," that is, the sum total of arbitrarily established costs. Without changes in the system, "the actual aim of this sort of measure is not to make prices reflect real values but to limit and reduce consumption." Such sacrifices served, in Skalski's view, to keep Poland's notoriously inefficient heavy industries running, in a cycle in which nothing of public use was produced, but a continued "exchange of state coal and state steel between state mine and state mill" was ensured.5

*Tygodnik Mazowsze* agreed, commenting that "not 'radical' price hikes but radical changes in the system offer a chance for the second stage of the reform to mean something more than 50 percent inflation."6

*Labor Unrest.* In April 1988, three major labor protests in the space of a few days indicated the precarious state of social peace in Poland. Strikes or strike alerts called in large industrial plants in Nowa Huta and Stalowa Wola and among transport workers in Bydgoszcz, demonstrated workers' deep discontent at wage levels, which most people evidently felt were insufficient to maintain living standards after the year's dramatic price increases. Government officials, fearful of organized protest along the lines of Solidarity in 1980 and 1981, tended to yield quickly to workers' demands, although they took a hard line at Nowa Huta. Indeed, initial official pliancy may have encouraged further demands by other workers and seemingly compromised the single aspect of the government's reform program on which the authorities had taken action: the limitation of consumption by controlling wages and increasing prices.

Several hundred transport workers in Bydgoszcz staged a successful strike on April 25, halting public transportation for more than twelve hours. Bus drivers in the neighboring town of Inowrocław reportedly went on strike in support of the Bydgoszcz drivers. Workers demanded hourly wages commensurate to those paid to transport workers in Warsaw (meaning a 100 percent increase) and changes in the management. The strikers set up a 10-person "protest committee" that negotiated on behalf of the transport workers. It was led by Krzysztof Wojt, a Communist party member and chairman of the local official trade union organization; but the official union of transport workers was not involved either in the organization of the strike or in the negotiations with the management. Local officials granted workers a 63 percent pay raise, considerably less than the workers had initially demanded, and a salary bonus for the month of May. No action was taken on the striking workers' other demands.7 The government said afterward that the strike had been called in violation of the law.

On April 26, at least 4,000 workers at the Nowa Huta steel mills also went on strike, apparently inspired by the success of the Bydgoszcz bus and tram drivers. Talks between strikers and management broke off late in the night, and Poland's official press agency attacked the strikers for acting illegally and allegedly attempting to increase tension before May Day, traditionally a focus for labor protest in Poland. By the following day at least 10,000 workers were reportedly participating in the strike and a strike committee had been formed. The Nowa Huta workers demanded a 50 percent increase in monthly salaries, an amnesty for strikers, and news coverage of the strike. The addition of an extra

6,000 zloty to the 6,000 wage hikes awarded to all workers in February as compensation for price increases was also demanded not only for employees of the Nowa Huta plant itself but for all those employed in the socialized sector of the Polish economy, about 12,000,000 people in all.

It was unclear what sort of organization lay behind the Nowa Huta strike, although there were indications suggesting the involvement of the independent Workers' Commission of Metalworkers, which was associated with a large, Cracow-based opposition network. Members of the strike committee said that the strike had begun spontaneously. The striking workers demanded the reinstatement of some of the Solidarity activists dismissed earlier from the plant. As in Bydgoszcz, some rank-and-file members of the official trade unions participated in the strike. Official representatives of these unions had meanwhile begun separate negotiations with the Nowa Huta plant management, which ended talks with the strikers; although the leader of the plant's official union organization had expressed support for a limited wage increase for Nowa Huta workers, the efforts of the official union were disavowed by the strike committee. Such efforts could, indeed, be interpreted as an attempt to usurp the authority of the strike committee, steer discontent into official channels, and distract attention from workers' demands that were not strictly limited to pay levels.[8]

In addition, a strike was called for April 29 by workers in the southeastern city of Stalowa Wola on April 26. A few days earlier, on April 21, a Solidarity-organized rally at the steel plant there was attended by approximately 5,000 of the plant's 18,000 employees, who threatened to strike if wage increases of 20,000 zloty a month were not awarded. After this rally two members of the plant's Solidarity organization, Wiesław Wojtas and Wiesław Turasz, were apparently dismissed; their reinstatement was added to the demands of those threatening to strike.[9]

The actions in Bydgoszcz, Nowa Huta, and Stalowa Wola were only the most spectacular examples of a steady wave of labor protest from a variety of workers from all regions of Poland that had been evident since the government's announcement of major price increases on February 1, the most dramatic of which, for coal and electricity, took effect on April 1. On February 29, for example, a strike was organized at the ZNTK rolling-stock works in Wrocław by the factory's covert Solidarity organization; after three hours the management had granted most of the strikers' demands. This strike was reported in the official media;[10] but dozens of other strikes, with similar results, were noted by foreign correspondents and the independent press.

These strikes extended to groups that did not enjoy the negotiating advantage of a large and highly concentrated labor force. Poland's health-care workers, for example, the lowest paid group of employees in the socialized sector of the economy, had been conducting a protest campaign since the beginning of February, when the pay hikes granted by the Ministry of Health proved too low to bring their wages even up to the national average.[11] The government responded only with gestures, but efforts by health care workers to pressure the government proceeded undaunted. On April 7 about 300 health care workers organized a demonstration outside the Ministry of Health, and more than 20,000 workers signed a petition demanding higher wages.

The authorities attempted to use the purported hard logic of economic calculation to persuade the Polish public that strikes would only cause a further deterioration in already declining living standards. After the conclusion of the Bydgoszcz strike, officials stressed that the revenue to cover the higher wages granted to bus and tram drivers would be obtained by increasing fares on public transportation, a statement possibly intended to stir resentment on the part of the general population toward striking workers. Increasing pay levels were not, however, the source of Polish inflation, as was pointed out in the official press; wages had been steadily declining as a proportion of production costs, which had increased dramatically. The government's failure to introduce structural changes that would make production more efficient, and its consequent preference for a price policy that limited consumption rather than increasing production had left workers who wished to defend their standard of living with a single option: to press for higher wages.

The establishment's chief objective in dealing with labor discontent was political rather than economic: to quiet individual work forces and to remove organized dissent from the public eye as quickly as possible, even if this meant compromising the government's stated resolve to maintain discipline in wage awards. Indeed, in spite of much tough talk on the subject of wage levels, including a proposal to grant the government "temporary extraordinary powers" to enact economic reform measures that was mooted by party leader General Wojciech Jaruzelski in March, official statistics indicated that wage levels had increased by 45 percent in the first three months of 1988, more rapidly than prices, which rose 42 percent. Such economic results suggested that the year's price hikes, which were imposed to initiate what the government had heralded as a radical economic reform program, had no perceptible reformative impact. This led many critics to argue that the government did not really have an economic reform program at all.

Solidarity leader Lech Wałęsa said on April 26 that "the situation is getting hotter and hotter, and something could happen anywhere at any time."[12] The pessimism of the Polish public was very deep, reflecting not only the perceptible decline in the standard of living, which had been widely documented in the official press, but also feelings of frustration that the government was botching its attempts at economic reform while refusing to allow anyone else to participate in reform efforts. The involvement of local leaders of the official trade unions in strikes was one revealing indication of the extent of social discontent.

*The Strike at Nowa Huta Continues.* On April 27, talks between the 16-man strike committee at Nowa Huta headed by Andrzej Szewczuwaniec and management representatives were broken off. The plant's director, Eugeniusz

Pustówka, announced that he would not negotiate further with the independent committee representing the striking workers. The Cracow regional prosecutor declared the strike illegal, and management reportedly posted notices informing strikers that legal measures, including imprisonment, could be taken against them.

Quiet intimidation and a publicity campaign against strikes were undertaken to forestall other strikes elsewhere in Poland. While police were not evident in any concentration near the Nowa Huta plant, they seemingly tried to detain or intimidate strike organizers, both at Nowa Huta and at Stalowa Wola. Police attempted to serve summonses on members of the Nowa Huta strike committee. At Stalowa Wola the Solidarity activist Ewa Kuberna, who was apparently active in organizing the large rally at the plant on April 21 at which a strike alert was called, was detained by police on April 28. That same day, three Solidarity activists, Zbigniew Bujak, Janusz Onyszkiewicz, and Bronisław Geremek were detained near Lublin by police.

The mass media, at first hesitant to mention the strikes, had been stressing since April 28 that the Nowa Huta strike was illegal. *Trybuna Ludu* condemned its organizers, charging that "for them, the most important issue is not the achievement of better material conditions for workers but the heightening of tension before May Day."[13]   The official press stressed that "unjustified" wage hikes merely fueled inflation and jeopardized the government's economic reform program.

*The Government Attempts to Wear Down Striking Workers.* The Nowa Huta strike continued over the May Day weekend, apparently unaffected by the rapid conclusion of a similar strike at Stalowa Wola. Alarmed by the doggedness of the Nowa Huta strikers, whose numbers reportedly grew to 16,000, the authorities adopted a variety of measures to end the strike there and prevent others from arising.  Government officials seemed intent on controlling labor unrest by combining financial incentives with various forms of intimidation. On May 2 new protests over wages and trade union pluralism began at the Lenin Shipyards in Gdańsk and at the Dolmel electronics plant in Wrocław; these suggested that the government had failed to gain control over the situation.

As the seventh day of the Nowa Huta strike began, striking workers seemed tired but determined to press on with their demands. Management had refused to negotiate with the strike committee since the morning of April 28 when the local prosecutor ruled the strike to be illegal. On April 29 management claimed that financial penalties would be applied to strikers who failed to end their action by late that evening. Over the May Day weekend, the official unions, which were attempting to steer workers' discontent into the officially-sanctioned channels for labor disputes, held a series of negotiations with the plant's management. No agreement was reached, as management refused to grant one of the union's demands. The union, which the official media insistently referred to as an "independent self-governing trade union," a title adopted by many branches in an attempt to gain the allegiance of former Solidarity members, sent the case to court for arbitration. It urged strikers to return to work and said that the strike was illegal and the strikers' demands excessive.

The government's concern that strikes might spread quickly was eased somewhat by the conclusion of a day-old strike at the Stalowa Wola heavy machinery plant on April 30. Strike participants said that the plant management had given in to their demands for a raise of 20,000 zloty a month (about 50 percent of their wages) and agreed to reinstate several hundred workers dismissed on the first day of the strike. The management had rejected the strikers' demands for trade union pluralism and the rehiring of two activists dismissed after a Solidarity-organized demonstration on April 21, strike organizers said. Meanwhile, PAP reported that there had been no negotiations with the strikers; and a plant spokesman interviewed by Radio Warsaw claimed that the pay concession was the result of pressure from the official trade union at the plant, not the strike.[14]

The government had insisted since the onset of this wave of labor unrest that the nation's economic well-being was of the utmost importance and that economic laws could not be contested. Wage decisions were the prerogative of individual enterprises, which under the economic reform, according to government spokesman Jerzy Urban, were "independent and self-financing." Workers' pay demands could not be met, the government argued, because the productivity of most enterprises did not justify increasing wages. While these tenets were fundamental to the economic reform plan, their implementation had fallen behind the government's rhetorical enthusiasm for them. The central issue seemed to be political and was a matter of control; the authorities had freely agreed to steep pay increases whenever they were enough to defuse labor discontent without appearing to be a concession to Solidarity or other independent organizations.

In the interest of labor calm, moreover, the government demonstrated that it considered its economic laws to be flexible. At a news conference held with Jerzy Urban, Minister of Labor Ireneusz Sekuła suggested that wages could be boosted by manipulating taxes even in enterprises with low productivity.

The official media tried to draw a distinction between supposedly misguided workers and the opposition activists, who were said to be manipulating the others for their own purposes. Radio discussions with officials at the Nowa Huta plant suggested that the striking workers' pay demands had in fact already been met and that their "impatience" was unfounded; one Solidarity activist at the plant was accused of attempting to "coerce" workers into joining the strike. The official media resorted to a familiar vocabulary to discredit strike organizers, suggesting that they were in the employ of hostile foreign powers and that their aim was "to undermine the economy, thwart the realization of the reform, increase inflation, worsen living conditions, and arouse social dissatisfaction."[15]

Wałęsa was attacked repeatedly, and the official press reverted to the argument that Solidarity bore responsibility for Poland's economic plight.

*The Strikes Spread.* On May 2, as 12,000 workers on strike at Nowa Huta reiterated their demands, workers at the Dolmel electronics factory in Wrocław successfully pressured the management into making wage concessions; several thousand shipyard workers began an occupation strike in Gdańsk. Although the government publicly acknowledged that there had been labor unrest in both Gdańsk and Wrocław, it denied that strikes were underway and suggested that the inspiration for work stoppages had come not from the workers concerned but from outside forces anxious to destabilize the economy. A reported nine members of Solidarity's National Executive Commission, including Bujak and Bogdan Lis, were taken into custody on May 2, for what government spokesman Jerzy Urban referred to as "warning talks."

According to local opposition activists, approximately half the 3,500 workers at Dolmel halted plant operations for 4 hours on May 2. They ended the stoppage when management granted their demands for a 20,000-zloty pay increase, a doubling of the 6,000-zloty monthly compensation payments awarded to all workers in the state sector in February, and a pledge that workers involved in the strike would not be penalized.[16]

In Gdańsk, workers demanded not only a substantial wage increase, but also the restoration of Solidarity, the release of all political prisoners, and the reinstatement of all workers dismissed for their Solidarity activities since the declaration of martial law. Wałęsa, an employee of the shipyards, lent his moral support to the strike, although he said that he was not involved in its organization. A strike committee was formed, headed by Alojzy Szablewski, who headed the Lenin Shipyard Solidarity organization in 1980 and 1981. Agency reports said that support for the strike had expanded and that members of later work shifts arriving on May 3 had joined the strikers. As in Nowa Huta, the shipyard management refused to negotiate with the strike committee on the grounds that the local official trade union was the legitimate representative of the work force. The strike was declared illegal.

On May 1, the Nowa Huta strikers responded to charges by government officials that their demands were unfeasible and their strike was economically destructive. (The media reported that the first four days of the Nowa Huta stoppage had cost the nation three billion zloty and that the strike was hindering the manufacture of cars, televisions, and refrigerators.) Expressing the conviction that the Nowa Huta management did not have the authority to respond to the full range of their demands, the striking workers invited Deputy Prime Minister Zdzisław Sadowski, the official responsible for the implementation of the government's economic reform program, to take part in the negotiations. Not only did they criticize the management for failing to introduce economic reform measures but they also stressed the need for better environmental protection at the plant, thus widening the range of issues that the Nowa Huta strike was raising.

Every strike in Poland had manifest political significance, even if the workers' demands were strictly wage-related, for strikes inevitably contested the control of the Communist party establishment over all economic and political decisions. In April and May, however, it was nevertheless clear that the authorities would prefer to deal with strikes, however illegal, that could be solved through the simple granting of a substantial pay increase, as the quick settlement at Wrocław's Dolmel plant on May 2 indicated. Judging from the demands of the striking Gdańsk shipyard workers and the new demands formulated by the Nowa Huta strike committee, the aims of the strikes seemed to be widening. This reflected the realization that real political and institutional changes, and not the mere addition of several thousand zloty, the purchasing power of which was constantly declining, were what was needed to begin to remedy Poland's economic malaise.

This at least was the view expressed by Solidarity in a statement issued on May 2.

A strike wave is covering the country. These are more than just local conflicts. They have spread across Poland because of the economic crisis and the lack of convincing reform policies that would offer prospects for the future.

*The Gdańsk Strike.* Special antiterrorist units raided the Nowa Huta steel works early on May 5, expelling striking workers and detaining many of the strike leaders. At the same time, the Gdańsk shipyard was surrounded by a police blockade. The conduct of the police in Gdańsk was ominous: food supplies were cut off and riot police periodically staged mock charges at the shipyard gates. These conditions suggested that the methods used at Nowa Huta might be repeated, though the extensive foreign media coverage in Gdańsk and the presence of Solidarity leader Lech Wałęsa in the shipyard clearly made this less appealing an option for the authorities. In this context, the opening of negotiations with the strike committee at the shipyard on May 7 was a departure in official tactics, especially as the official media had called the strike illegal and denounced its organizers as outsiders who were manipulating workers' grievances for political gain.

Since the number of striking workers at the shipyard was dwindling steadily, it is unclear why management agreed to talks. Pressure from the Church, particularly from Bishop Tadeusz Gocłowski of Gdańsk, apparently played a role. On Saturday, after several hours of negotiations between management representatives and the strike committee and their advisers, an agreement seemed possible. According to the strike committee, management offered a pay increase of 15,000 zloty a month and an amnesty for striking workers. While stressing their limited jurisdiction, management representatives also agreed to transmit to higher political authorities the workers' demands for the restoration of Solidarity and the release of political prisoners. The start of negotiations relieved tension somewhat at the shipyard, which the strike committee had earlier in the day compared to a "fortress under siege."

Anxiety returned on May 8 when talks were broken off, with management representatives apparently retracting their offer of wage hikes, instead opting for the promise that workers would be paid what the enterprise could afford (not an optimistic prospect given official reports of the shipyard's insolvency). Neither were other offers agreed to on May 7 repeated the next day, and an ultimatum for workers to leave the shipyard suggested that legal prosecution or an attack by riot police could ensue if the workers remained.

With only a hard core of several hundred workers remaining in the shipyard, negotiations were reopened late on May 8 after the intercession of Minister of Internal Affairs and Politburo member Czesław Kiszczak, whose intervention was reportedly conveyed to the shipyard strikers by Władysław Siła-Nowicki, a prominent attorney who, though affiliated in the past with Solidarity, had since agreed to serve on General Wojciech Jaruzelski's Consultative Council. Siła-Nowicki enjoyed a number of informal privileges and had been permitted to cross the police cordon in Gdańsk unimpeded. When negotiations reconvened, the strike committee supplemented wage and amnesty demands with a proposal for the formation of a commission to oversee the fulfillment of any agreements reached; striking workers insisted that they be represented on this commission. The formation of the commission was apparently intended as the price for dissolving the strike without obtaining a guarantee for the legal reinstatement of Solidarity; but the remaining strikers rejected this plan, refusing to abandon their demand for Solidarity's restoration.

After these fitful and unsatisfying negotiations, the workers finally opted to reject all partial offers and to "suspend" the strike unconditionally. They apparently decided that to settle for anything less than the complete recognition of Solidarity would represent a distortion of their aims. A solemn procession of several hundred strikers left the shipyard on May 10.

The attempts by the authorities to negotiate an end to the Gdańsk strike, however, informal and uncertain, may have been in part the result of protests raised at the methods used at Nowa Huta. Concern not to antagonize the influential Roman Catholic Church may also have played a role. On May 6, the Polish Episcopate criticized the government for using force at Nowa Huta, which violated an unstated agreement that no moves would be made to crush the strike by force while negotiations involving five Church-affiliated mediators were under way. The intellectuals dispatched to Nowa Huta expressed their shock and regret at a press conference on May 6; one remarked that she felt she had been deliberately manipulated to lull the striking workers at Nowa Huta into a lack of alertness.

*Strikes and Reform in Poland.* "As of today the reform has failed."[17] This was Wałęsa's comment on the authorities' use of force in Nowa Huta, as he waited for them to take similar action at the Gdańsk shipyards. Many Western observers used similar phrases, seeing the wave of strikes as an indication of the perils inherent in attempts to implement economic reform in the Polish economic and political conditions. It is likely, though, that Wałęsa had something else entirely in mind: that by resorting to force the government had abruptly shattered all illusions about its commitment to any reform that would entail substantive changes in existing political or economic practice.

This is not to say that government had not developed a program of economic reform. Indeed, since late 1986, General Wojciech Jaruzelski's government had devoted great energy to a new effort to create an elaborate vision of Poland as an economically efficient and institutionally pluralistic country. Implicitly acknowledging that similar plans for bold renewal initiated in the early years of Jaruzelski's tenure had resulted in very little, the government in 1987 introduced a "second stage" of economic reform, which, as the official media loudly proclaimed, included the introduction of market rules and better possibilities for private initiative. The government's reforms were said to be aimed at creating a "socialist market economy."

Poland's jails were carefully kept free of political prisoners. The government's plans for economic change were bolstered by pledges to decentralize political power; more public associations were to be permitted; and local government bodies were to be granted extensive control over local financial affairs. Elections were to be made more democratic as well; the official press said that once reforms were implemented, participants in elections would "select" candidates rather than merely "vote" for them. All these measures were publicized in what was meant to appear as a spirit of great radicalism. At the same time, censorship over the official and Catholic press was relaxed to such an extent that almost anything could be published, from *Ład*'s description of the idea of central planning as "a lunatic's raving" to the publication of articles by Adam Michnik in *Tygodnik Powszechny*.[18] Judging from the press, Poland had become a significantly freer place.

This world of reform and liberalization, however, existed mainly on paper, and was evoked through the frequent reiteration of assertions and pledges, rather than through measures with any tangible impact on Poland's political or economic life.

The government's move to impose a set of dramatic price increases, implemented after a lengthy campaign to prepare the public for them, was received with hostility by workers, who continued to eke out a living in a situation untouched by economic reform. The price hikes were seen as yet another attempt to place the burden of the economic failure of the Polish system on the backs of the general population; economic reform plans were seen as a form of deceptive packaging.

As Ernest Skalski argued in *Tygodnik Powszechny*, the authorities' tendency to indulge in reform rhetoric while actually engaging in economic half-measures had resulted in a dramatic and potentially dangerous gap between the authorities' "artificial world of reformist utopia" and the perceptions of people living in the "real, complicated world."[19] The government spokesman's assertion, for example, that because the economic reform would tie wages to individual productivity, income would drop only for "sniveling whiners" and "lazy fools" could only antagonize workers for whom no such new rules had taken force. A similar assertion by the government spokesman that the housing situation was not as bad as Western journalists suggested ignored the grim reality experienced by most Poles: in Warsaw, the waiting period for a cooperative apartment was about 56 years; the cost of an apartment was the equivalent of 48 years' average salary; at 1988 growth rates, housing construction would not reach the level attained in 1978 for another 65 years.[20]

This fundamental divergence of views should have been clear to the government long before the eruption of labor discontent in late April. The failure of the government's November referendum was an important signal, not that the public did not want reform, but that it did not accept the proposed methods. Opinion polls conducted late in 1987, showed that 70 percent of all Poles considered the economic situation bad or very bad (compared with 40 percent in 1984), 80 percent believed that serious social conflicts were likely, and only 7 percent believed that the government's economic reform would succeed.[21] A sociologist writing in *Polityka* in April concluded that the Polish mentality in the late nineteen-eighties was characterized by three main elements: the conviction that "civilizational degradation" (and not just hard times) was imminent; the feeling that all effort was senseless; the obsessive concern with making ends meet; and the consequent permeation of money into all areas of thought.[22]

Feelings of despair and frustration, combined with a deep-seated fear that before long even the utmost effort would not be enough to secure sufficient income to support a family, were exacerbated by the price chaos set off by the increases in centrally controlled prices introduced in February and April. The average monthly wage was running at about 36,000 zloty (including overtime); by comparison, in April a head of cabbage cost 1,000 zloty, the price of a toilet seat jumped to 16,000 zloty, and domestic color television sets were on sale for 400,000 zloty (Japanese imports cost 1,750,000 zloty).[23] The striking workers themselves stressed that they were not demanding luxuries, merely an income that would meet their needs and those of their families without requiring countless hours of overtime (some of the Bydgoszcz bus drivers who went on strike on April 25 had been working 65-hour weeks).

Against this background, the strikes were not only an expression of desperation but a determined effort to stamp everyday realities onto the government's papier-mâché world of economic and political reform.

Economically, they represented a demand that the government do something rather than simply attempt to persuade the public that something had been done; politically, they were a vote of no confidence. A genuine attempt to negotiate with the strikers would have served as an acknowledgment of the hard reality experienced by workers and an indication that there was some substance to the government's elaborate reform claims. But government spokesman Jerzy Urban had declared flatly that the strikes were "unjustified both politically and economically," thereby negating not only the strikers' methods but also their perceptions of the reality in which they lived. The government's adamant refusal to engage in any form of negotiation suggests that its chief priority was control and not reform.

As the various facades of economic and political reform were exposed, the official rhetoric of reform began to show the strain. In responding to the strikes, the authorities at first insisted that wage decisions were the prerogative of individual enterprises, in keeping with the principles of the economic reform; wage hikes would cause bankruptcy for the firms involved, it was argued, and therefore could not be granted. This did not stop the authorities from approving extensive wage hikes wherever they would placate irate work forces. Even in seeking to justify the use of force to suppress the Nowa Huta strike, the government attempted to cling to the arguments used to create its "artificial world of economic utopia." The decision to attack the strikers was explained as a means of restoring production; economic losses were mounting dramatically, the government said, and the striking workers—only a handful in official accounts—were jeopardizing the economic viability of the enterprise.

At the same time, much of the official propaganda employed to fight the strikes reverted to the well-practiced methods of other eras: the evocation of external enemies determined to create economic chaos, the depiction of discontent as the work of provocateurs playing on the naïveté of the working class, and the accusation that political opponents were in the employ of foreign powers. Behind this reversion to old-style rhetoric was a return to what were essentially the police methods of the martial law period. This could not be concealed by government spokesman Jerzy Urban's assurance that the Nowa Huta operation "did not mean that Polish problems and conflicts were solved with the use of force."[24] The methods used at Nowa Huta indicated that the many years spent enacting the government's economic reform had really changed only the official style of expression.

*Invitations to Open a Dialogue.* In an appeal written shortly after the strike at Nowa Huta began, the editors of *Tygodnik Powszechny* said that "social protest is in itself an offer of dialogue; this is most important and must not be wasted."[25] During the strikes, the authorities were unwilling to engage in any such dialogue; but after the immediate danger passed, several officials suggested that the government wished "to broaden the political basis for dialogue," as Jerzy Urban put it, and to consult with some members of independent public groups on Poland's pressing problems. While on an official visit to Spain in late May Foreign Minister Marian Orzechowski stressed that Poland was embarking on "an expansion of the democratic process" and that the authorities were committed to a "dialogue with Polish social forces," including the Church, the opposition, and those who belonged to Solidarity.[26]

Such intentions were widely aired after the strikes. Politburo member Jan Głowczyk, speaking at a joint plenum of the PUWP and the United Peasant Party, referred to the need for a form of "social contract"[27] that would provide the impetus to restore the economy to health. During the debate over "special powers" in the Sejm, the PUWP deputy Ryszard Wojna expressed the hope that these powers would provide "the impulse for the cementing of an anticrisis pact."[28] Asked what this would mean in practice, Wojna said that Deputy Prime Minister Zdzisław Sadowski, the government official responsible for economic reforms, would meet with "several dozen people whose names carry the necessary weight in opposition circles." Sadowski, he said, would explain the philosophy behind the government's reform plans and would then open the floor for discussion.

The idea of an "anticrisis pact" was first raised by the former Solidarity adviser Bronisław Geremek in an interview published by the new PRON paper, *Konfrontacje,* in February 1988. Geremek suggested that Poland's condition was so desperate that the opposition would be willing to limit its ambitions and respect the party's leading role should the authorities in turn respect society's right to self-organization. This, Geremek stressed, would not entail any threat to the party's monopoly on power. (It is ironic that the seeming hopelessness of Poland's economic plight led many members of the moderate opposition to offer the authorities advice about how to cope with the general crisis while retaining their power.) At the time, government officials roundly rejected both Geremek's concept and similar ideas proposed by other prominent intellectuals.[29]

The strikes seemed to prompt the fashion for "anticrisis pact" terminology, but they did not seem to have altered the official position on such proposals. In an interview published on May 16 in *Trybuna Ludu,* Politburo member Józef Czyrek gave the authoritative explanation of what this "broadening of the proreform coalition" or "anticrisis pact" might mean.[30] Czyrek claimed that only those who represented the principle "the worse [the country's situation becomes], the better [our chances]" would be excluded from a dialogue with the government. But, he suggested, the authorities would retain the right to decide just who this included (those involved in the "illegal" strikes, he said, could not take part, because the strikes "objectively worked against the reform.") In reference to freedom of association, Czyrek insisted that "pluralism already exists" in Poland; it could be extended, he said, but within limits, for conflict and confrontation were alien to socialism. Czyrek granted that there could be "oppositionism" in socialism, but only with respect to actual decisions or specific government policies.

The authorities' distinction between a "constructively-oriented opposition" (with whom one could talk) and an "antisystem opposition" (with whom one could not) suggested that the authorities understood the shaping of a "proreformist coalition" not as a compromise between differing standpoints but as a tactic to draw formerly alienated public groups into participating in government programs. While the Polish authorities acknowledged, at least in their dogma, that economic reform could not succeed without political democratization, they seemed to view this democratization as a process that would mobilize support without requiring concessions. This was clear, for example, in Jerzy Urban's description of the "anticrisis pact" as reflecting the opposition's recognition of "the correct view that Poland does not have any other better way out than supporting the economic reforms announced by the government."[31]

Given the caginess of the authorities, the success of any reform in Poland seemed to depend not only on the successful negotiation of meetings at which government officials exchanged views with representatives of independent groups but also on a fundamental change in the authorities' understanding of the goal of such encounters. A philosophical as well as political leap was required of the authorities, one that would allow the treatment of opposition figures as representatives of important social groups rather than as trophies to be won and displayed on the government's side. This would take some doing; as the British writer Timothy Garton Ash noted shortly after the strikes, "Poland today shows how extreme embitterment and insecurity can make an elite almost pathologically incapable of opening a genuine dialogue with the authentic representatives of a large part of its own society."[32] While some members of moderate independent groups appeared to be willing to attempt some form of dialogue with the government, they were very cautious about the danger of manipulation; and their conciliatory mood could quickly turn sour.

*The August Strikes.* In spite of voluminous discussion of "anticrisis pacts" and "proreform coalitions," the practical measures needed to achieve a genuine social compromise were not taken. Economic conditions continued to deteriorate as well, and inflation climbed above 50 percent. The public's frustration with the government's failure to resolve Poland's longterm crisis was painfully evident in August, as a second wave of strikes hit Silesia and the Baltic coast.[33] The depth of dissatisfaction was evident in the fact that coal miners, the highest-paid occupational group in Poland, were the most important force behind the August 1988 strikes.

At their height, these strikes extended to at least 14 coal mines in Silesia, the Szczecin and Gdańsk ports, the Szczecin public transportation system, the Lenin Shipyard and three other shipyards in Gdańsk, and the Stalowa Wola steelworks. In contrast to the strikes of April and May, the primary demand of striking workers in August was the restoration of Solidarity. In some cases, this was the only demand. In an apparent repeat of the tactics used earlier in the year, the authorities declared all strikes illegal and rejected all discussion on the issue of trade union pluralism. Such official intransigence, combined with an abrasive media campaign and police intimidation or intervention managed to limit the scope of the strikes, but a hard core of strikers still stood firm more than two weeks after the strikes began on August 15.

This deadlock was broken on August 30, when Solidarity activists announced that the Minister of Internal Affairs and Politburo member Czesław Kiszczak would meet with Solidarity leader Lech Wałęsa, who was among the strikers at the Lenin Shipyard, on the following day.[34] This meeting, which coincided with the eighth anniversary of the signing of the Gdańsk Accords, had great symbolic significance: it brought together Wałęsa, who had led the movement for relegalizing Solidarity and the other independent organizations banned since the declaration of martial law, and the party and government officials whose chief responsibility it was to combat this movement.

Government officials portrayed the meeting with Wałęsa as only one of a large number of consultations undertaken by the Minister of Internal Affairs to prepare for the "round-table" discussions with "representatives of various social and workers' groups" that Kiszczak had proposed in a television appearance on August 26. In reversing the entrenched practice of martial law, which scoffed at Wałęsa as the "former leader of a former movement," however, the authorities made a weighty, if only tacit, gesture of recognition of both Wałęsa and Solidarity. Having secured from Kiszczak a pledge that the authorities would consider the relegalization of Solidarity at the proposed round-table talks, Wałęsa called for, and after some persuasion secured, an end to the remaining strikes.

In the decision to negotiate with Wałęsa, it remained unclear, as Adam Michnik pointed out, whether the government wanted "to end the strikes at any price, or whether it whether it want[ed] a real dialogue with Solidarity."[35] Uncertainty as to the intentions of the authorities remained after the strikes ended, and as preparations for the round-table discussions began. In the official media, there was great enthusiasm for the idea of dialogue and radical—if vague—new solutions. Many officials acknowledged the need to draw the opposition—or at least what they called the "constructive" opposition—into participation in decision-making on the nation's problems. At the same time, the government spokesman and other officials, including the head of the official trade union federation, echoed the position taken by the party at the Central Committee's eighth plenum: there would be no change in the authorities' stance on trade union pluralism or the status of Solidarity.

This ambiguity on the government side was countered by a clarification and unification of positions on the Solidarity side. On September 10, Solidarity's national Executive Commission met in Gdańsk with strike leaders from various regions and opposition activists. The group expressed full support for Lech Wałęsa and his decision to enter into talks with the government. The group's statement said that "only legalization of Solidarity will allow trade unions to be effective in joining in the reform of the country." A second advisory meeting in Gdańsk, this one attended by over 80 prominent independent intellectuals and opposition activists, came to identical conclusions the following day. Solidarity's reinstatement, the group declared, was "the most important condition for the beginning of a true dialogue." The intellectuals added that trade union pluralism alone would not solve the county's crisis: "what is needed is the freedom to create self-governing bodies and associations of all types."[36]

A political compromise on the part of the authorities that would concede some of these points appeared essential to gain the public's trust and engage popular energies in coping with Poland's dismal economic plight. As many Solidarity activists pointed out, a failure to respond to the desire for independent representation articulated during the August strikes would simply make a more radical eruption of discontent more likely in the near future. Still, similar opportunities had been ignored after the year's first round of strikes, and it was far from certain that the authorities would accept the limitation of their powers that a true social compromise would require, even when dictated by their own longterm self-interest.

# VII. THE CHALLENGES OF NATIONALISM

## 26
## RESURGENCE OF RUSSIAN CHAUVINISM
### Julia Wishnevsky

The Russian nationalist movement came into being and received official sanction in 1965, soon after the removal of Nikita Khrushchev.[1] Initially, views expressed by members of the group encountered sharp opposition in Soviet journals,[2] but by the beginning of the nineteen-eighties the Russian nationalists had managed to silence their critics. Thanks to the relaxation of censorship after 1985, the more liberal opponents of the movement started to speak their minds again. Furthermore, some traditional enemies of the Russian nationalists received important promotions under the new régime, and one of their critics, Aleksandr Iakovlev, reached the very top of the Soviet hierarchy.[3]

One of the main forces behind this right-wing movement was the anti-Semitic and anti-Western "Pamiat" society, a group of self-proclaimed Russian patriots whose chief preoccupation was the exposure of an alleged conspiracy of Zionists and Freemasons against all things Russian.[4] Yet the movement also counted among its ranks many members of the Soviet establishment whose language, ideas, and—what is more important—imagined enemies were indistinguishable from those of "Pamiat." Outspoken supporters of the movement assumed control of such important official bodies as the Secretariat of the Board of the RSFSR Union of Writers,[5] and in Moscow alone they dominated three official literary journals with a joint circulation of over a million.[6] They also had extensive influence over *Literaturnaia Rossiia*, the weekly newspaper of the RSFSR Union of Writers.

*The Sverdlovsk Theater Case.* From early in 1987, the Sverdlovsk opera house and, in particular, its Jewish producer Aleksandr Borukhovich Titel, had been the target of vicious attacks by members of the "Otechestvo" society, the Sverdlovsk equivalent of "Pamiat". The conflict between the theater and "Otechestvo" was covered by the Soviet media, and the materials available provided an insight both into the emergence and activities of such societies and into the role played by Russian nationalists in Soviet cultural developments in general.

The newspaper *Sovetskaia kultura* described the "trial" of Brazhnik and Titel by members of the Sverdlovsk "Otechestvo." The target of their wrath was a production based on Aleksandr Pushkin's *Tale of Tsar Saltan*. The witnesses for the prosecution—members of the chorus and local journalists—had contrived to detect hidden Zionist, masonic, and even Nazi symbols in the sets and costumes of this fairy tale for children. Somebody, for example, had purloined a Russian folklore headdress decorated with snowflakes from the theater wardrobe, and the assembly was busy counting how many points there were on each snowflake. The number seemed to vary, but one was found with six points, and this resulted in the accusation that Brazhnik and Titel were using "foreign"—i.e., Zionist—symbols on the stage of a Soviet theater. Another member of "Otechestvo" imagined he could see a swastika on Tsar Saltan's throne and demanded the dismissal of the two men from the theater and their arrest and trial.

The demands for the trial of Titel and Brazhnik "for crimes against the Motherland and the nation" were repeated in letters by members of "Otechestvo" to the editor of the local evening newspaper *Vechernii Sverdlovsk* and supported by an M. Pinaeva, who used her position as a radio broadcaster to warn her listeners about an alleged conspiracy of freemasons.[7] Her husband, the Sverdlovsk journalist B. Pinaev, followed his wife's example in a letter to the editor of the Russian nationalist monthly *Nash sovremennik*.[8]

In his letter, Pinaev repeated the charges by "Otechestvo" against *Tale of Tsar Saltan* and accused its producers of slandering ancient Russian principalities. He claimed that Titel and Brazhnik had contrasted the Russian principality of Tsar Saltan, who bore a swastika on his throne, with the non-Russian principality of the heroine Swan Queen, who displayed on her head the Star of David in the guise of a snow-flake. Pinaev also claimed that, in their production of Pushkin's *Boris Godunov*, Titel and Brazhnik had portrayed sixteenth-century Russia as a dark cave, contrasting it with the sweet-smelling garden of Poland.

Pinaev's charges brought a rebuff from the leadership of the RSFSR Union of Theater Workers in the form of a letter signed by actor Mikhail Ulianov, the chairman of the Union's board, and ten other leading Soviet theater workers.

Even more important, in a joint resolution signed by Mikhail Gorbachev and Prime Minister Nikolai Ryzhkov, the Central Committee of the CPSU and the USSR Council of Ministers announced the award of one of the 1987 State Prizes for literature, art, and architecture to the Sverdlovsk Academic Theater of Opera and Ballet.

*Nationalist Gathering In Leningrad.* "Nothing can be changed in our country without a renunciation of Marxism as a profoundly Zionist doctrine." These were the words of one of the participants in a Russian nationalist gathering organized by the three most prestigious academic bodies in the former capital of the Russian Empire—Leningrad University, the Institute of Russian Literature of the USSR Academy of Sciences (better known as Pushkin House), and the Alexander Herzen Pedagogical Institute, held late in 1987. "What is the role of Jews in the conspiracy against the Russian people?" another participant inquired. "They don't leave any signatures," replied Fedor Uglov, a member of the USSR Academy of Sciences. A fourth participant said: "I think some ministries and government departments are under the control of our enemies across the ocean."

The above statements were cited in a report on the conference by Leningrad writer Gennadii Petrov that was published in the CPSU Central Committee's cultural newspaper, *Sovetskaia kultura*.[9] Petrov's report, which was sharply critical of the opinions expressed by the speakers, was one of many indications of growing public concern over the fierce right-wing opposition to perestroika.

The conference in Leningrad was of particular interest because of the variety of personalities reportedly involved. Ostensibly devoted to the role of Siberia in Russian literature, the conference was chaired by Nikolai Skatov, the director of Pushkin House, and Professor Leonid Ershov, the head of a department at Leningrad University. The latter opened the proceedings with a ritual attack on the poet Andrei Vosnesenskii, a frequent target of Russian nationalist critics. The backgrounds of the other speakers were significant.

In his report in *Sovetskaia kultura*, Petrov cited Leningrad critic Nikolai Utekhin as openly declaring an "ideological struggle" against all writers who did not share the views of the right-wing opposition movement. In January 1968, an anti-Semitic denunciation written by Utekhin and his fellow members of the literary club "Rossiia" stopped the publication of the works of three young Leningrad poets—one of whom was Josef Brodsky, the 1987 winner of the Nobel Prize for Literature.

"There is not, nor has there ever been, a more gifted people in the world than our Russian people," Petrov quoted the next speaker, Mikhail Antonov, as saying. Antonov came to prominence owing to his polemics with advocates of the introduction of a market economy in the Soviet Union, such as Anatolii Strelianyi and Nikolai Shmelev.[10] Antonov argued that the only way to cure the country's economy was to strengthen the workers' moral fibre—i.e., to teach them Russian patriotism.[11]

From 1968 until 1971, Antonov was confined in a prison-like special psychiatric ward for belonging to a chauvinistic group headed by A. Fetisov. According to the samizdat publication *Chronicle of Current Events*, Fetisov's group

> presents the historical development of mankind as having taken the form of a struggle between order and chaos, chaos having been embodied in the Jewish people, who created disorder in Europe for two thousand years, until the German and Slav principles—the totalitarian régimes of Hitler and Stalin—put a stop to this chaos. Fetisov and his supporters consider these régimes to have been historically inevitable and positive phenomena. The economical program of the group includes, in particular, the deindustrialization of the European section of the U.S.S.R., the transfer of industry and a mass deportation of workers to Siberia, and the reestablishment of a system of patriarchally run communes on the territory of European Russia.[12]

According to Petrov's report in *Sovetskaia kultura*, Antonov's declaration was followed by a statement from Professor Petr Vykhodtsev. "Somebody needs the cultural conscience of our people to be deformed." "Somebody needs our culture and art to acquire alien national roots."

Economist Mikhail Lemeshev was quoted in Petrov's report as suggesting at the meeting that the systematic destruction of sacred objects of Russian culture had been a deliberate policy whose aim had been to make the Russians forget their national history. Petrov, in his turn, accused Lemeshev of having deliberately created an atmosphere of hysteria at the conference.

At a meeting of "Pamiat" in Moscow in February 1987, a speaker by the name of Lemeshev had called Gorbachev a puppet of his foreign policy adviser Georgii Arbatov, who was a Jew. On that occasion, Lemeshev went on to denounce Christianity because of its Jewish origins and to call for the restoration of Russian Orthodox churches as places of worship for the old Russian pagan religion.[13] It cannot, however, be established for certain that Lemeshev was the same man who spoke at the conference in Leningrad.

In his speech, Mark Liubomudrov, a theater critic of *Nash sovremennik*, accused certain Soviet cultural figures of responsibility for the deaths of prominent Russian writers and artists. Petrov commented that "one had to be there to appreciate the special emphasis speakers placed on non-Russian names." Liubomudrov said: "We understand how the mechanism for the destruction of Russian talents works" and compared the struggle against this mechanism to a third world war.

F. Morokhov, a lecturer at the Academy of Civil Aviation, called in his speech at the conference for the creation of a society to protect Russian geniuses, and the first he named as in being need of such protection was Liubomudrov. He went on to express his concern for thirteen Soviet astronomers who were allegedly fired for their criticism of the theories of Albert Einstein, a Jew.

Academician Fedor Uglov, a Lenin Prize winner, is reported to have named certain Soviet officials who, he claimed, were deliberately seeking to rot the Russian nation by abetting alcoholism. Uglov had previously published articles demanding total prohibition.[14] He maintained that the most dangerous alcoholic drink was kefir, a dairy product with an alcoholic content of 2 percent. Members of "Pamiat" railed against "the Judeo-Masonic conspirators" who recommended kefir as a baby food.[15]

"Pamiat" was represented at the conference by the journalist and photographer Dmitrii Vasilev. He arrived at the meeting in disguise, mounted the podium, ripped off his false beard and wig, and posed for the cameras that had suddenly appeared. "That is our way to the truth in this time of democracy and restructuring!" Vasilev proclaimed in explanation of his masquerade.

In his speech, Vasilev claimed that the Russians lived on reservations like Red Indians. He declared that the acute shortages of goods and foodstuffs in shops were a carefully planned man-made phenomenon, and complained about the exploitation of the natural wealth of the Russian soil for the benefit of "somebody across the ocean."

*Sovetskaia kultura*'s reporter was dismayed about the enthusiastic bursts of applause from the audience. The meeting took place in the largest hall at Leningrad University, and the audience was composed of students and faculty. One of the listeners said the discussion elevated the human spirit; another suggested that it constituted a turning point for the entire Russian patriotic movement.

## 27
## UPHEAVAL IN THE BALTIC REPUBLICS
### Saulius Girnius

In 1988, the pace of change began to accelerate. Topics that had been handled with great delicacy and trepidation at the beginning of the year came to be discussed quite bluntly. Not only dissidents but an ever greater number of intellectuals and members of the cultural unions, making use of official channels, began to state their views on important questions and expand the range of their criticism to include not only the security agencies and the bureaucracy but the Communist parties themselves. Demonstrations to honor Stalin's victims or to mark national holidays became almost commonplace; and the authorities even sanctioned some of them, trying to prove their commitment to perestroika and making sure that they retained some control of the proceedings. While the condemnation of Stalin and of Brezhnev's years of stagnation grew more strident and the calls for radical change more insistent, the issues that dominated the discussions remained the same: greater cultural and economic autonomy, the dangers posed to the national existence by Russification, the falsification of history, and ecology. At the start of the year the Estonians were the most outspoken critics and the boldest innovators, but in May and June Lithuanians and Latvians began to catch up.

*New Forums for Expressing Views.* Although the press and other public media remained the central means for the expression of views, three other forums were added for communicating thoughts and grievances to the authorities: public commemorations, the cultural unions, and informal groups that supported reform.

In 1987, Baltic dissidents began to organize public commemorations of important historical events, such as the traditional days of national independence and anniversaries of national tragedies: for example, the mass deportations to Siberia and the signing of the Molotov-Ribbentrop Pact. The first such demonstration took place in Latvia on June 14, 1987. Similar protests were organized in Lithuania and Estonia. There were at least three such commemorations in each republic.[1]

The authorities still seemed unsure about how best to handle such meetings. They passively observed the demonstrations on August 23, 1987, in Tallinn, Riga, and Vilnius commemorating the signing of the Molotov-Ribbentrop Pact in 1939; but they then launched a propaganda campaign against the organizers of the meetings. On November 18, 1987, Latvian Independence Day, the Latvian authorities organized an official demonstration to protest against US interference in local Latvian affairs and brought in large numbers of militiamen to intimidate an unofficial demonstration that still attracted more participants than the official demonstration. A number of the organizers of the demonstration in Latvia on June 14, 1988, were expelled to the West and others were put under house arrest; the authorities appeared to consider this approach more effective. The Lithuanian authorities mobilized hundreds of militiamen on February 16, 1988, Lithuania's National Day of Independence, hoping that a massive show of force would preclude any commemoration; and they placed some of the organizers of the commemoration under house arrest. Nevertheless, commemorations still took place.

Later the authorities changed their tactics again. They began sponsoring official meetings, at times even letting known dissidents address them; but they always tried to play down criticism of the party and to steer the meetings in a particular direction. Thus, in response to a call for a meeting in Vilnius on May 22 to honor the victims of the 1948 mass deportations, the authorities held an official commemoration on May 21 that emphasized the sufferings of party members at Stalin's hands. The Latvian authorities officially sponsored the commemoration in Riga of the deportations of June 14, 1941, but the Mayor of Riga, Alfreds Rubiks, took great pains to emphasize that many nationalists and Nazi fifth columnists had been arrested at that time.

*The Role of the Cultural Unions.* At a plenum held on April 1 and 2, the Estonian cultural unions called for a radical change in relations between the central and republican governments; it also recommended that the CPSU condemn the Stalinist repression and rehabilitate all its innocent victims. In addition, it demanded that all nationalities in the Soviet Union be given genuine cultural independence.

The cultural unions also submitted a resolution to the leaderships of the ECP and the ESSR. Arguing that the Estonian nation was threatened with extinction, the resolution proposed a number of reforms and strongly condemned the leadership in Estonia. It specifically blamed ECP First Secretary Karl Vaino and Chairman of the ESSR Council of Ministers Bruno Saul for failing to solve the country's problems. The resolution also dealt with a number of strictly

Estonian matters, such as recommendations to decentralize cultural life in the ESSR, give more financial support for scholarship on subjects relating to the national heritage, and increase academic and cultural contacts with ethnic Estonians living outside the republic.

In Lithuania, the Union of Writers was in the forefront of the movement for greater openness. Writers, and not historians instituted the debate on the falsification of history that functioned as the cutting edge of the campaign for change. The range of issues that writers raised  increased substantially. For example, on February 10, 1988, they sponsored a meeting that discussed in very critical terms the republic's ecological situation, and on April 4 they held another meeting on nationality problems. The latter meeting was particularly significant, for several writers openly stated that the Russians were a privileged nationality and expressed their concern at the plight of Lithuanians living in neighboring Soviet republics. Expressions of such concern would previously have been considered unjustified interference in the internal affairs of a fraternal republic.

The Latvian cultural unions passed a resolution to be submitted at the CPSU conference, which was printed in *Literatura un Maksla* on June 10. The resolution asked that Latvian be made the official state language of the Latvian SSR, that Latvia become a member of the United Nations and UNESCO and have its own team in the Olympics, and that soldiers from Latvia serving in the Soviet Army be stationed in Latvia. History was not forgotten, as the resolution suggested that the secret protocols of the Molotov-Ribbentrop Pact be published and that those responsible for the mass deportations of 1941 and 1949 be stripped of any honors they had received. The resolution also noted that the ecological situation in the republic had deteriorated as a result of great industrial expansion.

*Informal Groups.* In April 1988, The People's Front in Support of Perestroika was set up by a number of reformist and nationally-minded Communist intellectuals. The organizational structure of the group was similar to that of the Communist party, but membership was not limited by party, religious affiliation, or nationality. In many respects it was an embryonic opposition party, still loyal to the CPSU but outside the jurisdiction of the ECP. It nominated a list of reformist candidates to the CPSU conference in June but only succeeded in getting a small number of them elected. It is possible that the opposition of the People's Front in Support of Perestroika to the ECP leadership was a factor in the decision to call the June 16 plenum of the ECP CC that deposed Karl Vaino and elected Vaino Valjas as First Secretary of the ECP. The extent of the popular support for the People's Front was made clear on June 17 when it organized a meeting in Tallinn to discuss the Estonian party's draft program for the forthcoming CPSU conference in which an estimated 150,000 people participated.

On June 3, about 500 Lithuanian intellectuals met at the Lithuanian

Academy of Sciences and set up the Lithuanian Restructuring Movement. They elected 36 people to head the organization. The specific aims of the movement were unclear, but it seemed determined to retain some independence from the party. It did not allow Steponas Imbrasas, the Head of the Lithuanian Central Committee's Academic and Educational Institutions Department, to attend its first meeting on June 12. Imbrasas and Justas Vincas Paleckis, the Head of the Central Committee's Cultural Department, attended a second public meeting the next day, but they were criticized for being too evasive in their responses to questions. The meeting decided that it was still too early for it to support, as a group, the planned unofficial commemorations of the June 14 deportations; and it was suggested that each member should decide for himself whether to take part in them. The authorities complied with the movement's request to be given a hall in which it could hold its own commemoration of the deportations.

*The Central Issues.* At the beginning of 1987 Estonian and Latvian intellectuals made the unequal status of the Russian and native languages in the schools and public life one of their major criticisms of government policy. In Lithuania, where language was not as burning an issue (Lithuanian was the language of instruction in about 84 percent of all schools), the original focus of dissatisfaction was the falsification of history and the national cultural heritage. In all three republics concern was frequently expressed about the deterioration of the environment and the prospect of an even grimmer future. In Estonia the chief danger was seen in the authorities' plans for phosphorite mining; in Lithuania it was the continued construction of the Ignalina atomic power plant; in Latvia, the construction of a hydroelectric power station on the Daugava. Under pressure, the central Soviet authorities made concessions. Plans for the hydroelectric power station and the phosphorite mining were shelved and the size of the planned atomic power plant was reduced. Criticism by Gorbachev and in the Soviet press of the dominant role of central planning and suggestions for the devolution of responsibility for the economy to smaller units met with an enthusiastic response from many Balts convinced that they were disproportionately penalized by the system.

While criticism of historical writing and of language, economic, and ecological policies was harsh and in many respects unprecedented, it was only the tip of a much larger iceberg, namely, the conviction that under the present system of government the very existence of the small Baltic nations was threatened. Because of substantial immigration from other republics and an extremely low birth rate, there was a real danger of national extinction. Latvians probably constituted no more than 50 percent of the population of Latvia and Estonians about 60 percent of the population of Estonia, while the decline in the Lithuanian birth rate led to concern. With the easing of censorship and in light of developments in Armenia and Azerbaijan, Balts—and particularly the Estonians—began to state publicly what some had long thought in private: that the various problems facing their nations could only be solved by demanding and getting the maximum amount of political and economic autonomy. In view of the low birth rate, immigration would have to be controlled if the proportion of the titular nationality were not to fall even lower. Such restraints would be hard to defend if the central authorities retained the right to embark on the construction of massive plants whose demand for workers could not be satisfied by the local labor pool. Equally, ecological problems were unlikely to be solved if planners in Moscow remained free to dictate where and what kinds of factories were to be built.

Estonia took a clear lead in demanding more autonomy. The Estonian cultural unions' resolution noted that the all-Union ministries generally ignored local economic, ecological, social and cultural interests and needs, which resulted in an unprofitable economy, uncontrolled migration, and a greater risk of ecological catastrophe. The resolution blamed these centrally created conditions for the increase in tension between the nationalities in the USSR, which local bureaucrats attempted to put down as expressions of chauvinism. The unions also recommended a radical change in the electoral system that would involve multicandidate elections and the holding of referendums on important social questions. The resolution called for the decentralization of the economy and specifically supported the proposal made in September 1987 by four social scientists to turn Estonia into a closed economic zone.

The meetings in Lithuania sponsored by the Union of Writers became forums for the criticism of certain aspects of government policy that might otherwise not have been publicly enunciated. It seems that the other cultural unions in Lithuania supported the views expressed at the Writers' Union meeting on nationality questions. On May 28 the Lithuanian literary weekly *Literatura ir Menas* published a statement addressed to the Soviet party conference in June. The statement, signed by the chairmen of all the cultural unions and the Cultural Foundation, made a number of recommendations that were similar to those made by their Estonian counterparts. It recommended that the deputies to the Lithuanian Supreme Soviet and local soviets should be elected in multicandidate elections and have greater responsibilities toward their constituents. The statement called for the passage of a law that would clearly define relations between the central and republican governments. Each republic should create an independent economic program for restructuring that would allow for the coordination with the central authorities of all construction or expansion of industry that might be ecologically dangerous or result in the mass immigration of workers. The statement urged that all restrictions on scientific, technological, and economic relations with foreign countries be abolished. It called for making Lithuanian the official language of the republic and for establishing schools that would teach in the native language of all national minorities and for the writing of an objective history of the republics and of the USSR.

*Conclusion.* The support of the titular nationalities for greater autonomy was understandable. What was surprising was the passivity of the other inhabitants of the republics in light of such demands. Those who had not yet learned the native language could not relish the idea of Estonian or Latvian becoming the official language of the republic. Suggestions in Lithuania that an extra grade be added to schools in which Russian was the language of instruction, so that the pupils could improve their Lithuanian would hardly be greeted with much enthusiasm by those affected. Nor would there be much support from non-Estonians for the noted Estonian writer Lennart Meri's proposal that Estonian—and only Estonian—families with three children be given a supplement of up to 300 rubles a month to be raised from taxes on all inhabitants of Estonia. The ecological protests against the construction of a subway in Riga might not seem important to non-native workers wanting better urban transportation. By mid-1988 there had as yet been no backlash from the Russian immigrants to these demands from the native Balts; possibly, however, there had not been time for their implications to sink in. The prospects of such radical changes must also have worried many Balts in influential party, administrative, and economic positions, particularly since criticism of past policies was becoming more explicit and the names of those responsible were finally being named. All in all, it made for a heady, if not volatile, atmosphere.

28

NO AUTONOMY FOR CRIMEAN TATARS

Ann Sheehy

In June 1988, the state commission which had been set up under the chairmanship of Soviet head of state Andrei Gromyko in July 1987 to look into the grievances of the Crimean Tatars, rejected their demands for national autonomy. The Crimean autonomous republic, established in 1921, had been abolished when the Crimean Tatars were deported en masse from the Crimea in May 1944 for alleged wholesale collaboration with the German occupation forces. A communiqué on the work of the commission stated that "the commission has reached the conclusion that there are no grounds for establishing a Crimean autonomy."[1]

The decision of the commission was criticized by Crimean Tatar spokeswoman Elvira Ablaeva on the grounds that without autonomy none of the national rights of the Crimean Tatars could be guaranteed.[2]

The re-creation of their autonomous republic in the Crimea was one of the two main demands of the Crimean Tatars, the other being permission for mass resettlement in their traditional homeland. The communiqué confirmed that Crimean Tatars were no longer barred from taking up residence in the Crimea on the grounds of their nationality, as they had been in practice previously, but it implicitly rejected their demands for mass resettlement.

The Crimean Tatars had been campaigning without success for the restoration of their autonomy and permission to resettle in the Crimea for more than thirty years. In 1967, the authorities acknowledged that the accusation of wholesale collaboration with the Germans had been unjust and even issued an order permitting the Crimean Tatars to reside anywhere in the Soviet Union. In practice, however, the Crimean Tatars soon discovered that any of their number who tried to settle in the Crimea were likely to be expelled, often with crude force. Some were eventually allowed to return to the Crimea under an organized resettlement scheme, but by 1987 only some 20,000 out of an estimated 300,000 or more had been able to return to the Crimea from their exile in Central Asia. A few thousand more had settled in the adjacent Krasnodar Krai and Kherson Oblast.[3]

The state commission under Gromyko was set up after several hundred Crimean Tatars converged on the Soviet capital in the summer of 1987 and staged protest demonstrations on Red Square and elsewhere in central Moscow. A meeting of leading Crimean Tatar activists with Gromyko shortly afterwards failed to reassure them in any way that their demands would be met.[4] The Crimean Tatars continued to stage protests in Uzbekistan, Moscow, and the Crimea, and at the beginning of May 1988 they announced that a large delegation would arrive in Moscow on June 20 and repeat the mass demonstrations of the previous summer if their demands were not met.[5] The state commission had thus to conduct its work against a background of continuing protests.

The communiqué was the third report on its activity. The first report, issued in October 1987, called for cultural concessions to the Tatars; criticized discrimination against them in matters of housing, employment, and study; and at the same time said that the regulations on residence in the Crimea and other health resort areas of the country needed to be more precisely defined.[6] The second report, issued in February 1988, reviewed the implementation of measures in all three areas, including discrimination as regards place of residence.[7] Some of the cultural concessions were being implemented even before the October report was issued. It was also announced that a limited number of Crimean Tatars would be able to return to the Crimea under a new organized recruitment scheme.[8]

The only entirely new aspect of the June 1988 communiqué on the work of the commission was its rejection of the demand for the re-creation of the Crimean ASSR. The communiqué started by saying that all the restrictions that infringed the rights of Crimean Tatars in the choice of place of residence, employment, and study had been lifted. Since the middle of 1987, it continued, some 2,500 Crimean Tatars had been granted residence permits and provided with employment in the Crimea, and sovkhozes and other organizations were being set up to provide further job opportunities. The communiqué then went on to say that measures had been taken to satisfy more fully the social and cultural needs of Crimean Tatars. These included teaching the native language in schools in Uzbekistan, Krasnodar Krai, the Crimea, and other areas, as well as an increase in the size and circulation of newspapers and more radio and television broadcasts in Crimean Tatar.[9]

These were definite gains for the Crimean Tatars, but the elimination of discrimination against them as regards residence in the Crimea did not mean that they were now free to flock to the peninsula. Since 1977 it had been difficult for Soviet citizens of all  nationalities to obtain residence permits for the Crimea, and the new regulations governing residence in the Crimea and other resort areas of the country adopted by the USSR Council of Ministers did not make things any easier. The Crimean Tatars complained that the new regulations virtually barred them from settling in fourteen towns and raions of the Crimea and eleven in Krasnodar Krai.[10] The media stressed that the Crimea did not need labor and that it was as a gesture of goodwill that the new organized recruitment scheme had been set up. It would bring a mere 300 families to the barren northern steppes in 1988, 200 from Uzbekistan, and 100 "who moved to the Crimea earlier but for one reason or another were not provided with housing and jobs."[11]

The commission justified its rejection of Crimean autonomy on the grounds that: (1) the present administrative-territorial division of the country made it possible to accomplish successfully the tasks of economic and social development of all the ethnic groups in the country; and (2) the population of the Crimea had trebled in the postwar period and now consisted overwhelmingly of Russians and Ukrainians. The second argument had some force in that the majority of the population of the Crimea in 1988 would probably have objected strongly to the formation of a Tatar republic there, but the Crimean Tatars were bound to vehemently contest the validity of the first, as Ablaeva had already done.

Gorbachev, like his predecessors, was faced with an almost insoluble problem. What would be a satisfactory solution for one  nationality would be totally unacceptable to the other or others.  Moreover, restoring autonomy to the Crimean Tatars at this late stage would open a Pandora's box.  The authorities were presumably hoping that the Crimean Tatars would eventually weary of the struggle. The Crimean Tatars had, though, shown a remarkable persistence in the past and continued to stage protest demonstrations after their demand for the recreation of the Crimean ASSR was formally rejected by the Gromyko commission.

## 29
## THE ARMENIAN IMBROGLIO
### Elizabeth Fuller and Kevin Devlin*

*Nagorno-Karabakh.* The Nagorno-Karabakh Autonomous Oblast, a moun-
tainous enclave of approximately 4,400 square kilometers situated in the
Azerbaijan SSR, had at the time of the Soviet census of 1979 a population of
162,181, of which 123,076, or 75.9 percent, were Armenians and 37,261, or
22.9 percent, Azerbaijanis.[1] The area was formally assigned to Armenia under
the terms of an agreement signed in December 1920—i.e. at the time of the
crushing of Armenia's independence. This agreement was, however, never put
into effect, and in 1923 Nagorno-Karabakh was granted the status of an
autonomous subdivision within the Azerbaijan SSR.[2] In late 1986, according to
dissident Sergei Grigoriants, an open letter to Gorbachev demanding the
incorporation of Nagorno-Karabakh into Armenia was delivered to Secretary for
Propaganda of the Central Committee of the CPSU, Aleksandr Iakovlev. In the
course of a year, 75,000 Karabakh Armenians appended their signatures to the
appeal.

*The Armenian Memorandum.* The text of the document was later obtained
by Giulietto Chiesa, the Moscow correspondent of *L'Unità*, the daily newspaper
of the Italian Communist party, and was printed there in extensive extracts.

When this "Memorandum to the CC of the CPSU" was first sent to the
Kremlin, Chiesa said, the authorities had not appreciated that this issue could
become "an enormous political problem"; the petition therefore "went unheard,
in order to avoid creating precedents." In its historical survey of the past seven
decades, the memorandum dealt with this argument:

> The Nagorno-Karabakh question has been submitted more than once to
> the judgment of the CC CPSU and the Supreme Soviet of the USSR.
> However, on every previous occasion we have heard demagogic
> conclusions to the effect that, if we settled the question of Armenian
> territory in accordance with justice... we would create a precedent which
> must be avoided, since there are other unresolved "territorial" issues
> within our state. The fact is that in our country there are no examples
> that are really analogous; apart from the socialist republic of Armenia
> there are two autonomous portions of Armenian territory, the

---

*Author of the sections on the Armenian Memorandum and the Kaputikian
and Balaian interviews.

autonomous republic of Nakhichevan and Nagorno-Karabakh. They are located administratively in another republic, and this brings about open and hidden conflicts between two neighboring peoples.

The memorandum claimed that the "Azerbaijani working people" recognized that this "violation of historical justice" had in the present generation compromised a centuries-old tradition of friendship between the two peoples.

In their "historical justification" of the Armenian claim to the territory, the compilers of the document went back over 2,000 years, invoking the Greek geographer and historian Strabo, who lived around the time of Christ and who placed Karabakh (with its ancient names of Orkhistina, Arzakh, and Khacen) within "Great Armenia." Testimonies to Armenian occupation of the territory occurred throughout the medieval period, up until "the struggles of liberation against Persian and Turkish despotism" in the 16th and 17th centuries, when "the orientation toward Russia developed and became the patrimony of the whole of Armenia"

From the 10-page text, "replete with historical and biographical quotations and references", the message emerged that (in Chiesa's words) "Karabakh has for centuries been the spiritual center of the Armenian nation." With this went an attempt to demonstrate that "the creation of a [Christian] Armenian state, with Karabakh as its center, was one of the principal objectives of Russia's southern strategy." The text accordingly stressed the role of Armenia—and of Karabakh —in the prolonged struggle between the Russian and Turkish empires.

In June 1921 Nagorno-Karabakh was declared "an integral part of the socialist republic of Armenia." Already by this time, however, a sharp and bitter struggle over the issue was raging on among the Bolsheviks, and the memorandum charged that Azerbaijani Communists and Turks had been acting together against Armenia and that attempts to exacerbate the ethnic conflict had been part of what Chiesa called "a conspiracy against Armenia by two enemies."

As reported by l'Unità, the text described how, when the Azerbaijani party leadership had "refused to apply the party and state decision," Kirov and Ordzhonikidze had sent a telegram from Tbilisi to Baku saying that "no Armenian village" was to be transferred to Azerbaijan and had decided that the "now incandescent problem" was to be settled by the Central Committee in Moscow. On the following day, July 5, 1921, however, Stalin blocked this move and "personally took the decision that openly contradicted ... Leninist nationality policy": Nagorno-Karabakh was to remain within Azerbaijan while being given wide regional autonomy.

"At this point," l'Unità commented, "the document changes its tone and style, taking on the form of a very violent nationalist pamphlet, in which it is now difficult to distinguish the objective data of the situation from the accumulation of sectarian bitterness." For example, the Azerbaijani leaders of the time were accused of having expelled almost the entire Armenian population of the autonomous republic of Nakhichevan, "where there are now only 2 percent of Armenians, compared with an initial 70 percent."[3] The text also claimed that Azerbaijani families had been "systematically transferred" into Nagorno-Karabakh.

Dealing with earlier approaches to Moscow, the document said that in 1966 an appeal on behalf of the Armenian population, signed by 45,000 people, had been sent to Moscow. It had asked for "the re-establishment of historical justice and the reunification of the Armenian region with the Armenian socialist republic." Later it had noted that "a letter signed by tens of thousands of people was sent to the 27th [CPSU] Congress."

The text concluded by invoking the authority of Lenin:

A correct decision on the destiny of the Armenian region is also necessary for the Azerbaijani people. In fact, the very injustice of the situation is inflicting harm on the friendship between the two peoples by stirring up exacerbated nationalism. The great Lenin warned against this.

*Demonstrations Take Mass Form.* After a one-year interval, a reply to the open letter was received in early February 1988, from a lower-level Central Committee functionary indicating that the demand had been refused.[4]

The refusal sparked off demonstrations. On February 11, 1988, Armenians in Stepanakert, the capital of Nagorno-Karabakh, put up posters and distributed open letters calling for the return of the territory to Armenia. On February 13, schoolchildren and students at the Stepanakert Pedagogical Institute boycotted classes. Then on February 20, a group of deputies to the Nagorno-Karabakh Oblast soviet passed a resolution, which was subsequently published in the local press, calling for a reexamination of the issue of incorporating Nagorno-Karabakh into Armenia.[5]

On February 18, demonstrations began in Erevan to protest the construction of a chemical plant at Abovian, near Erevan[6] and to draw attention to the issue of Nagorno-Karabakh. On February 21, a session of the Politburo of the Central Committee of the CPSU passed a resolution ruling that "demands for a revision of the existing national and territorial structures are not in the interests of the workers of Armenia and Azerbaijan and constitute a breach of inter-nationality relations."[7]

CPSU Central Committee Secretary Georgii Razumovskii and Politburo candidate member Piotr Demichev were promptly dispatched to Stepanakert, where Razumovskii told a party meeting on February 22 that there could be no question of changing the existing territorial boundaries.[8] That evening, while between 50,000 and 70,000 persons demonstrated in Erevan to demand that Nagorno-Karabakh be given back to Armenia, Karen Demirchian, the first secretary of the Communist party of Armenia, appeared on television in the

republic to report on the decision adopted by the Politburo two days previously.[9]
A TASS dispatch of the same evening, datelined Baku, cited Azerbaijan SSR
Gosplan Chairman Aiaz Mutalibov as having rejected arguments that
Nagorno-Karabakh was economically backward and, for that reason, should be
made a part of the Armenian SSR.

On February 23, a crowd of between 100,000 and 120,000 again gathered in
Erevan, chanting the slogan "One People, One Republic" and calling for a strike
to reinforce their demands. The demonstrators also demanded that a session of the
republic's Supreme Soviet be convened to discuss the issue of Nagorno-Karabakh. Police followed the demonstrators without intervening.[10]

Demonstrations continued in Erevan and in other Armenian cities from
February 24 to 26; estimates of the numbers of people involved ranged from
several hundred thousand to over a million. Industrial strikes and school boycotts
were also reported.[11]

On February 26, in response to this unprecedented display of civil
disobedience, an appeal for calm by Gorbachev to the populations of both
republics was read on Armenian and Azerbaijani television and radio. Gorbachev
admitted that the Central Committee of the CPSU had been "disturbed" by
events in Nagorno-Karabakh. He stressed that "we do not wish to evade a sincere
discussion of various ideas and proposals" but that this "must be done calmly,
within the framework of the democratic process and legality." He further made
the point that "all the republics, many oblasts, and even some of our towns ...
are multinational," thus implying that the situation of Nagorno-Karabakh could
not be considered unique or exceptional. Gorbachev singled out as the most
pressing issue the need "to concentrate on overcoming the existing situation, to
solving concrete economic, social, and ecological problems that have
accumulated in Azerbaijan and Armenia, in the spirit of the policy of perestroika
and renewal."[12]

*Armenian Representatives Meet with Gorbachev.* On the evening of
February 26, the Armenian writers Zori Balaian and Silva Kaputikian flew to
Moscow for consultations on the Nagorno-Karabakh issue with Gorbachev and
Iakovlev.[13]

The new Moscow correspondent of the Rome daily *La Repubblica*, Ezio
Mauro, obtained interviews with Kaputikian and Balaian. In the interviews[14]
the two paid tribute to the Soviet leader's reformist course and expressed the
hope that the crisis would be settled peacefully without causing him political
harm.

Kaputikian began by referring to Nagorno-Karabakh as "the soul of this
great Armenian body, dismembered and scattered throughout the world." It was
not, she went on, only a matter of territory: "Our problem is not one of territory
but of historical and national identity, of Christian culture." When she had met
Gorbachev on February 26, she said, she had not wanted to reopen the old debate
about Karabakh belonging to Armenia, because that would have been an offense

to the Armenians' dignity—like claiming that her hand belonged to her body. She had gone there aware that for the first time in 67 years "Moscow's eyes were on us," and that it was up to her to make the Armenian drama understood in the Kremlin.

According to Kaputikian, Gorbachev said that he knew of, and understood, their problem and wanted to settle it personally. He continued:

> Today, however, I have a lot of important nationality questions to deal with. I promise you that there will be a new beginning in Karabakh. I am not in a position today to decide on the restitution of this region to Armenia, because the situation is very difficult, but I will keep the problem under my direct personal control.

The general secretary told her that the forthcoming CC plenum would discuss the nationalities question: "That plenum will give you, too, an answer, but right now you have the guarantee that the problem of Karabakh will be at the center of my attention." This was in her mind when she subsequently returned to Erevan to face the enormous crowd:

> Why are we here today? Because someone has finally allowed us to raise our heads, to take to the streets. We must do all we can to avoid harming Gorbachev. Our hopes today are vested in him.

Balaian opened his interview with *La Repubblica* by saying that, during the demonstrations in Erevan, "all of us were aware that our movement, which developed as a result of Gorbachev's new policy, could be exploited as a weapon against perestroika." Remarking that he had heard it suggested that the Armenian demand for the return of Karabakh represented a desire to release centrifugal strains in the Soviet Union, he said:

> I want to state openly that this is an absurdity—or, to be precise, a provocation. It is also in order to defeat provocations of this sort that we are ready today to accept a partial solution to our problem....

> Our people understood everything, from the first day, even as the demonstrations were continuing. Not one stone was thrown; not one anti-Soviet slogan appeared in the parades; no one on the streets had a bottle of vodka, although the shops were open.

Discussing the possible elements of a compromise solution, Balaian referred to various grievances of Armenians in Nagorno-Karabakh, mentioning the suppression of vine-growing, old Christian churches closed, destroyed, or made into mosques, television broadcasts and schooling in Azerbaijani only, and no

Armenians among leading officials. He added: "On all of this, a compromise could be sought that would do justice in Karabakh, at least partially."

On the afternoon of February 27, a meeting with demonstrators was held in Erevan at which Balaian and Kaputikian reported on their talks with Gorbachev. Balaian disclosed that in response to a resolution passed at a plenum of the Central Committee of the Armenian Communist party on the previous day, a special commission was to be set up in Moscow to examine the whole issue of Nagorno-Karabakh. Kaputikian quoted Gorbachev as promising that "a just solution" would be found. On receipt of this information, the "Organizing Committee," headed, according to one report, by the president of the Armenian SSR Academy of Sciences, Viktor Ambartsumian, decided to postpone further demonstrations for a period of one month to give the Moscow commission time to formulate its decisions.[15]

Human-rights activists in Moscow reported on February 29, that the first concessions to the Armenians of Nagorno-Karabakh had been made public. These included relaying Armenian television programs to Nagorno-Karabakh; transferring local schools to the jurisdiction of the Armenian SSR Ministry of Education; and restoring the Armenian monastery at Shusha.[16]

*Backlash In Azerbaijan.* On February 27, USSR Deputy Procurator Aleksandr Katusev disclosed in an interview on Radio Baku that two young Azerbaijanis from Agdam Raion, located on the eastern border of Nagorno-Karabakh, had been killed at some unspecified point during the unrest.

Between February 27-29 groups of Azerbaijanis attacked Armenians on the streets of Sumgait (population 234,000), a city known for its petrochemical industry some fifteen miles northeast of Baku on the Caspian Sea. A total of thirty-one people, of various nationalities, including women and elderly men, were killed.[17]

The full extent of the bloodshed in Sumgait only became apparent after a period of several days. The original TASS announcement about the unrest merely stated that "a group of hooligans" had resorted to "rampage and violence" and that "measures had been taken to normalize the situation."[18] A more explicit account was furnished to Western reporters in Moscow on the same day by Sergei Grigoriants, who revealed that "thugs" had approached people on the streets and inquired whether they were Armenians. Those who admitted to being Armenian were beaten up; some were knifed.[19] A death toll of thirty-one was reported by TASS only on March 4, five days after the event.

Disturbances also took place in the city of Kirovabad (population 270,000), where troops were reported to be patrolling the streets on March 3;[20] in the town of Shamkhor, to the northwest of Kirovabad;[21] and in the capital of Azerbaijan, Baku.[22]

*Attitudes Harden.* On March 21, *Pravda* published a detailed account of the historical background to the Nagorno-Karabakh dispute and of the recent events in Armenia and Azerbaijan. In an allusion to the first secretary of the Armenian

Communist party, Karen Demirchian, the newspaper noted that the question of Nagorno-Karabakh had been raised in the past when the republic's party leadership had found it advantageous to distract the public's attention from unresolved economic and social issues and from its own "unsuitable" work style.[23] *Pravda* further criticized shortcomings in the conduct of "internationalist upbringing" by the party leadership in both Armenia and Azerbaijan during "the years of stagnation." It was as a result of shortcomings in this sphere, *Pravda* continued, that "feelings of national egoism" emerged that ultimately brought thousands of people onto the streets and squares of Armenia. The Azerbaijani leadership was also criticized for neglect of the socio-economic development of Nagorno-Karabakh and for infringement of the national rights of the area's Armenian population.

*Pravda* explained the rationale for the decision in 1923 to create the Nagorno-Karabakh Autonomous Oblast by suggesting that at that time, the economy of Azerbaijan had been more developed than that of Armenia. The newspaper went on to stress the ties that had developed over the years between Azerbaijan and Nagorno-Karabakh. It also implied (as Gorbachev had done in his media address of February 26) that the situation of the Nagorno-Karabakh Armenians was not unique or exceptional and that for Moscow to set a precedent by agreeing to transfer the Nagorno-Karabakh Autonomous Oblast to Armenia would merely encourage other ethnic groups with similar grievances to begin agitating for comparable concessions.

Whereas Gorbachev had remarked approvingly on the orderly conduct of the mass demonstrations in Erevan, *Pravda* implied that many of those who had taken part had been indoctrinated, if not bullied, by the organizers into participating. Particular emphasis was laid on the meticulous organization of the demonstrations: the participants were regularly supplied with food and drink; discipline was enforced; "leaders suddenly turned up at enterprises, establishments, and institutions of higher education who knew in advance where to take people and at what time, and what slogans to chant"; and "substantial funds" were found to be available.

*Pravda* concluded that the whole campaign for the reunification of Nagorno-Karabakh with Armenia had "a distinct anti-Socialist tinge"; it gave rise to "nationalist manifestations"; and its organizers, wittingly or unwittingly, were acting in accordance with the theory of "those trans-Atlantic sovietologists who state that socialism in the USSR can be defeated only by breaking it down into national components."

The attack in *Pravda* was followed by an article in *Izvestiia* on March 22, that accused one of the more moderate members of the Karabakh Committee, the thirty-year-old economist Igor Muradian, of aspiring to the role of "leader of the people" and quoted him as having asserted that "Armenians in Nagorno-Karabakh have faith in neither Moscow, nor the Central Committee, nor supreme justice, nor the Russian people, nor anything else." *Izvestiia* further accused the leadership of the Karabakh Committee of issuing "an ultimatum to party and Soviet authorities containing a threat to look for support beyond the country's borders" and of demanding that the Azerbaijan SSR be charged at the International Court in The Hague with "annexing Armenian territories."

In Azerbaijan, both the Russian and native-language press sought to bolster Azerbaijani claims to territorial and administrative control over Nagorno-Karabakh and to present Azerbaijan as the wronged party in the dispute. An article attributed the events in Nagorno-Karabakh in the first instance to shortcomings in planning, administration, cadre policy, and internationalist upbringing;[24] another article entitled "Who Incites Passions?" condemned the role played by Western radio stations, including the Armenian and Azerbaijani services of Radio Liberty, in exacerbating the dispute over Nagorno-Karabakh.[25]

Meanwhile, the party leadership in Stepanakert delivered a clear message of defiance to the Azerbaijani CP Central Committee in Baku. At a plenum of the Central Committee of the Oblast Party Committee on March 17, a resolution was passed pressing for the transfer of Nagorno-Karabakh to Armenia.[26] On March 16 and 17, thousands of people demonstrated again in Stepanakert, where factories and schools also remained closed.[27]

Reaction to the Nagorno-Karabakh campaign in the Armenian Russian-language press was confined to the publication of letters expressing whole-hearted support for "the brotherhood of peoples." In an extensive article published in *Sovetskaia kultura,*[28] the chairman of the Board of the Union of Armenian Theater Workers, Hrachia Kaplanian, disclosed how he had attempted in vain to protest the appendage of his signature to one of what he termed "the stereotyped, standardized responses in which successive writers give assurances of friendship for the fraternal people." When he telephoned the Armenian press agency to complain, he was asked not to raise a scandal. Similarly, *Pravda*'s Armenian correspondent, Iu. Arakelian, protested that he had never seen the article in *Pravda* of March 21, although his name was appended as one of the coauthors.[29]

Western news agencies in Moscow reported that demonstrations took place in Erevan on March 21 and 22, to protest *Pravda*'s version of events as "ugly and provocative."

*Attempts to Defuse Crisis.* March 26 was the date set by Armenian demonstrators in late February for resuming mass demonstrations to demand the return of Nagorno-Karabakh, failing the promulgation by then of "the just solution" promised by Gorbachev. In the event, however, tentative plans for a mass meeting on that date to discuss future tactics in the campaign for reunification were thwarted by a combination of official intimidation and reprisals, as well as caution on the part of the "Karabakh Committee" and the population of Erevan.

On March 23, the Presidium of the USSR Supreme Soviet rejected as "intolerable" attempts "to resolve complicated national-territorial issues through pressure on state authorities" and further condemned "self-styled formations that declare for the recarving of national-administrative boundaries."[30] On the same day, Radio Erevan warned that the meeting scheduled for March 26 "could have explosive consequences." Troops and police were flown to Erevan, and helicopters circled the city.[31] Kaputikian and Balaian, the two writers who had met with Gorbachev in late February, made an appeal to the population on television, asking them to refrain from further demonstrations.[32] Late that evening, the Karabakh Committee[33] voted to call off the meeting scheduled for March 26. The following day the leadership of the Karabakh Committee issued leaflets calling on the population of Erevan to register continued support for the return of Nagorno-Karabakh to Armenia by remaining in their homes on March 26 and 27, to give the impression that Erevan was "a dead city."[34]

On March 24, the Politburo published a program detailing massive investment in the economic and social sphere in Nagorno-Karabakh for the period 1988-1995.[35] On the same day, the Armenian authorities issued a ruling that all plans for spontaneous street demonstrations must be communicated to and cleared by the authorities seven days in advance.[36] The republican press also carried a statement that the Armenian SSR Supreme Soviet had banned the Karabakh Committee; its counterpart in Nagorno-Karabakh, the Krunk Committee, was similarly banned by a decree of the Azerbaijan SSR Supreme Soviet.[37] On the night of March 24, four leading Armenian dissidents—Paruir Airikian, Movses Gorgisian, Mekhak Gabrielian, and Gevorg Mirzoian—were arrested.[38]

The inhabitants of Stepanakert proved to be less easily intimidated than those of Erevan. Demonstrations occurred in Stepanakert on March 24 and 25.[39] On March 26, when the city was overrun by some 15,000 policemen brought in from Baku, residents remained in their homes. On March 27, *Pravda* disclosed that most of the factories in Stepanakert were not functioning. Strikes began in Nagorno-Karabakh on March 25.[40] Two Soviet newspapers disclosed that party activists were visiting the homes of strikers in an attempt to persuade them to return to work.[41] The strikes petered out only in the second week in April.

The mood in Armenia was well expressed in a samizdat response by Kaputikian to an open letter by four prominent Russian intellectuals that was published in *Izvestiia*.[42] Kaputikian made it clear that the Armenian intelligentsia reacted with shock, anger, despair, and incomprehension to the rejection by the Presidium of the USSR Supreme Soviet of the demands for the annexation of Nagorno-Karabakh to Armenia and to what they interpreted as a consistently anti-Armenian, pro-Azerbaijani stance by the Moscow authorities. She implied that many of her compatriots were inclined to think that this "prejudice" on the part of the central authorities was secured by massive bribes of the sort routinely donated to the elderly Brezhnev by the Azerbaijani leadership.

Kaputikian contrasted *Pravda*'s charges that the campaign for the reunification of Nagorno-Karabakh with Armenia had "a distinct anti-Socialist tinge" and gave rise to "nationalist manifestations" with Gorbachev's assertion during his trip to Yugoslavia that the campaign was neither anti-Socialist nor anti-Soviet in character. She pointed out that the mood of demoralization in Armenia, not only in connection with the failure of the Karabakh campaign but also as a result of the general climate of corruption and the deteriorating ecological situation, had led to a dramatic increase in emigration. As for those who chose to remain, she said "it is impossible to say whether our faith in perestroika will ever be restored."

*New Demonstrations.* After a month-long period of calm, new demonstrations took place in Erevan, Stepanakert, and Baku. Three events served as the catalyst for the renewed protests: a clash between Armenians and Azerbaijanis in Armenia on May 11,[43] the death of a young Armenian at the hands of Azerbaijanis in the Shusha Raion of Nagorno-Karabakh on the same day,[44] and the sentencing on May 16 of the first of the young Azerbaijanis tried for the violence in Sumgait in late February.[45]

Demonstrations took place in Erevan on May 7 and 12, to demand the release of Paruir Airikian, the veteran Armenian human-rights activist.[46] Airikian was arrested in Erevan on the night of March 24. On May 12 and 13, demonstrations and strikes were reported from Stepanakert to protest the death of the young Armenian and the announcement in the local press that an ethnic Azerbaijani had been appointed deputy procurator of Nagorno-Karabakh.[47]

The sentencing on May 16 of a twenty-year-old Azerbaijani locksmith, Talekh Ismailov, to fifteen years of imprisonment for the brutal murder of an elderly Armenian in Sumgait gave rise to demonstrations in both Erevan and Baku. In the Azerbaijani capital 5,000 students and faculty members took to the streets for several hours on May 16 and 17, to demand leniency for the accused—in particular, that the death sentence should not be imposed. On May 18, the crowd had grown to 100,000, according to a spokesman of the Azerbaijani Ministry of Foreign Affairs, and the demonstrators protested that the fifteen-year sentence was too harsh. They also raised doubts concerning Ismailov's guilt, arguing that he had acted as "one of a crowd"[48] although Ismailov himself admitted to having attacked his victim with an iron bar.[49]

In Erevan, on the other hand, the Karabakh Committee summoned a meeting on May 17 to protest the sentence given to Ismailov as being too lenient and to demand that the Sumgait trial proceedings be televised. Reports quoted participants as declaring the proceedings "a show trial" and as maintaining that those ultimately responsible for allowing the situation in Sumgait to get out of hand were not in the dock.[50] A second demonstration, attended by 200,000 people, took place on May 19.

*Party First Secretaries Replaced In Armenia And Azerbaijan.* On May 21, the respective first secretaries, Karen Demirchian and Kiamran Bagirov, were simultaneously "retired on grounds of ill health."[51] With these retirements, Moscow thus finally delivered a clear signal to what the journalist and member of the Central Committee of the CPSU Nikolai Portugalov called "those temperamental Caucasians."[52] The message was that unrest and mass demonstrations would no longer be tolerated.

Demirchian was succeeded by Suren Gurgenovich Arutiunian, former first deputy chairman of the Armenian SSR Council of Ministers. Abdul-Rakhman Khalil ogly Vezirov, former Soviet ambassador to Pakistan, was elected the new party chief in Azerbaijan. The Baku plenum was attended by prominent Politburo member Egor Ligachev and by Politburo candidate member Georgii Razumovskii, who had ben  one of the two Kremlin troubleshooters in Azerbaijan in February. CPSU Central Committee Secretary Aleksandr Iakovlev was present at the plenum in Erevan, together with Vladimir Dolgikh. The latter had likewise traveled to Erevan in February as Moscow's representative.[53]

Both Demirchian and Bagirov had been in disfavor since before the beginning of the Nagorno-Karabakh crisis. Indeed, some observers advanced the theory that the two men tacitly encouraged the unrest in order to obstruct perestroika and bolster their own shaky positions.[54] Demirchian had been one of the last surviving party bosses of the Brezhnev era and had been under attack since 1984. In June 1987, Gorbachev had charged that the process of perestroika in Armenia was "stuck in a rut."

The possibility that Bagirov might be replaced had been rumored as early as 1987, presumably because of the chronic corruption in the republic, which Bagirov's predecessor, Geidar Aliev, had fought in vain to eradicate.

*Radicalization of the Campaign.* July witnessed the deterioration into civil disobedience and violence of the hitherto orderly five-month campaign in Armenia for the transfer of Nagorno-Karabakh. The failure of the Nineteenth All-Union Party Conference to propose a solution to the deadlock over the future of the region was met with anger, disappointment, and incomprehension in Armenia. On July 3, a group of delegates to the conference addressed a mass meeting in front of the opera house in Erevan. Although the delegates appealed for calm, members of the Karabakh Committee chose to mount a final push for the annexation of Nagorno-Karabakh.[55]

The Armenian activists called for a general strike in support of the following five demands: 1) the separation of Nagorno-Karabakh from Azerbaijan; 2) the transfer of the trial of those accused of participation in the anti-Armenian riots in Sumgait in February from the Azerbaijan SSR Supreme Court to the Supreme Court of the RSFSR; 3) an end to the "blockade" of Nagorno-Karabakh; 4) publication of details of an incident at a garment factory in the town of Masis on June 23, in which fifty-one female employees were exposed to an unidentified toxic substance; and 5) publication of all relevant information concerning events connected with Nagorno-Karabakh.[56] On July 8, it was announced that the trials of those involved in the Sumgait pogroms would be transferred to regional courts in the RSFSR.[57] The following day, Soviet television screened a report on the Masis incident.

Participants in the mass meeting on July 3 also decided to occupy Zvartnots

Airport, from which hundreds of demonstrators were violently evicted by Ministry of Internal Affairs troops on the evening of July 5. In the course of the storming of the airport, one passenger died of a heart attack, and thirty-six people, including several members of the security forces, were injured. A young man who was shot at close range with a plastic bullet when demonstrators attacked security forces on the highway leading to the airport died later in a hospital.[58] Armenian human rights activists quoted the chairman of the Armenian SSR Council of Ministers, Fadei Sarkisian, as stating that the order to storm the airport came from Moscow. This statement was subsequently denied by the official Armenian news agency ARMENPRESS.[59] Tens of thousands of people attended the funeral of the two victims on July 7. The city of Erevan was bedecked in black flags on the weekend as a sign of mourning.

The violent intervention by troops at the airport served to compound the general mood of anger and alienation in Armenia. A professor at Erevan State University was quoted as saying that tensions were now running higher than at any point since the campaign had begun.[60] Balaian, for his part, characterized the airport confrontation as "the final straw" and expressed concern lest "mistakes breed more mistakes" given the "very complicated psychology" prevalent then in Erevan.[61] The mood of alienation was, according to some reports, now manifesting itself for the first time in the form of anti-Soviet or anti-Russian slogans.[62] According to Moscow dissident Sergei Grigoriants, many Armenian party members had threatened to hand in their party membership cards if the republican party leadership failed to clarify the circumstances surrounding the storming of the airport.[63]

On July 10, more than 120,000 people attended a mass meeting at a sports stadium in Erevan and decided to prolong the week-old general strike at least through July 11.[64]

However, not all of those involved in the Nagorno-Karabakh campaign were in sympathy with the strikers. Kaputikian, who had served as a moderating influence within the unofficial "Karabakh Committee," was quoted as disclosing that many Armenian intellectuals had severed their connections with the committee because "the anti-Russian tone that the movement has assumed does not represent Armenians' feelings."[65]

*Supreme Soviet Rejects Annexation.* On July 18, the Presidium of the USSR Supreme Soviet ruled that Nagorno-Karabakh should not be ceded to Armenia. The decision followed a heated, and at times acrimonious, eight-hour debate during which speakers from Armenia and Azerbaijan were repeatedly interrupted and accused of irresponsibility and a lack of willingness to compromise by Gorbachev himself.

The Soviet domestic media carried detailed coverage of the proceedings only after an interval of twenty-four hours.

At a press conference on the evening of July 19, the first deputy chairman of the Presidium of the USSR Supreme Soviet, Petr Demichev, Soviet General Prosecutor Aleksandr Sukharev, and USSR Minister of Internal Affairs Aleksandr Vlasov outlined possible measures—including the imposition of a curfew and the use of military and special police units—that might be taken "to ensure stricter labor discipline and rigid observance of the Constitution of the USSR and Soviet laws, resolutely preventing any activities directed at kindling national enmity and attempts to exploit democratic rights for antidemocratic purposes."

In his address to the meeting, Gorbachev traced the roots of the dispute over Nagorno-Karabakh to past errors in the spheres of economic and social development, ecology, personnel policy, and ideological work. The situation had been manipulated by anti-perestroika forces in Armenia and Azerbaijan, he charged, who had abused the "banner of democratization" to exert "shameless pressure" on workers' collectives, the populations of the two republics, and the state organs of power to the point where "passions are now running out of control," and "a threat to the lives and tranquillity of the populations of Armenia and Azerbaijan has emerged." In this situation, Gorbachev argued, it was imperative to find a solution to the dispute that would not be detrimental to the population of either republic. Failure to do so, he implied, would jeopardize the future of perestroika.

Genrikh Pogosian, the first secretary of the Nagorno-Karabakh Oblast party Committee, was the only speaker at the session to press the demand that Nagorno-Karabakh be ceded to Armenia. Armenian Central Committee First Secretary Suren Arutiunian reiterated the proposal that the area be temporarily subordinated to the central authorities. The chairman of the Presidium of the Armenian Supreme Soviet, Grant Voskanian, argued that the vote of that body on June 15 in favor of the unification of Nagorno-Karabakh with Armenia should not be interpreted as constituting any territorial claim on Azerbaijan but was based on the constitutional right of the people of the oblast to self-determination. Predictably, Suleiman Tatliev, Voskanian's Azerbaijani counterpart, rejected this argument, accusing the people of the oblast of "total insubordination" and asserting that there were no economic, political, or legal grounds for the transfer of Nagorno-Karabakh to Armenia. The majority of speakers from other Union republics were no more sympathetic to the Armenian case. Ukrainian First Secretary Vladimir Shcherbitskii must have been expressing misgivings shared by his counterparts in other Union republics when he pointed out that "what happens in Transcaucasia has a tendency to spread across the whole country."

According to TASS, the final resolution ruling that the Nagorno-Karabakh Autonomous Oblast should remain a constituent part of Azerbaijan was adopted unanimously (*edinoglasno*)—a formulation implying that the Armenian representative in the Presidium, Grant Voskanian, did not dissent.

The only concessions to Armenian demands contained in the resolution were recommendations that the implementation of existing plans for the economic, social, and cultural development of the oblast be accelerated; that the process be monitored by representatives from Moscow; and that a special commission be created to study "related issues."

## 30
## RELIGIOUS POLICY UNDER GORBACHEV
### Oxana Antic

The manner in which religious issues were treated in the Soviet press in 1987-88 clearly reflected Gorbachev's style of leadership. On the one hand, there were articles of the "traditional" type that teemed with stereotype statements about the decline of religion—"The number of believers in the population as a whole is decreasing;" "the religious crisis is deepening;"[1] "in our country religion has been squeezed out of a leading position in public life;"[2] and so on. On the other hand, with the approaching anniversary of the Christianization of Kievan Rus, the Russian Orthodox Church came to occupy an important place in the mass media.

Leading newspapers began to report on religious conferences and congresses in the Soviet Union: *Izvestiia* gave extensive coverage to an international conference in Kiev on the Christianization of Rus at which representatives of more than twenty Christian churches took part.[3] The Soviet embassy in Bonn gave a reception for Church representatives in West Germany. Members of the hierarchies of both the Catholic and Lutheran Churches and prominent figures in religious organizations were among the hundred guests invited.[4]

In March 1987, a new monthly, *Religiia v SSSR*, commenced publication in Moscow. The journal was put out by the publishing branch of the Novosti press agency in six languages—Russian, German, English, Portuguese, Spanish, and Arabic.[5] Cooperation between the Soviet authorities and representatives of the Russian Orthodox Church abroad became the general policy. Kliment, Bishop of Serpukhov and administrator of the Patriarchal parishes in Canada and the United States, attended a reception given by the USSR Mission to the United Nations to mark the sixty-eighth anniversary of the October Revolution.[6] At the end of 1986, at the invitation of the Soviet authorities, Bishop Vasilii (Vladimir Rodzyanko) of the Orthodox Church in the United States, led the first official group of foreign pilgrims to visit the USSR.[7]

*New Role of the Press.* Newspapers began to report about the infringement of the rights of believers. *Moscow News* gave extensive and sympathetic coverage to some of those who had suffered; a correspondent of the newspaper, Vladimir Shevelev described the measures used by the authorities in the town of Oktiabrskii against Orthodox believers who, in accordance with the law, wanted to register a new parish.[8] Under the headline "Believers Insulted," *Literaturnaia gazeta* printed a complaint by "a church council and a group of Orthodox Christians" from a village in the Chuvash ASSR describing how, despite permission being granted by the raion authorities to build a new church, the deputy chairman of the raion executive committee "turned up with a detachment of police,... brandished her fists," and forbade further construction work.[9]

In August 1987, in *Moscow News*, Aleksandr Nezhnyi recounted a clash between believers and the authorities in Kirov. The journalist stigmatized "old opinions that have turned into dogma," that "have usurped the law and changed it." The believers in this town had been forced to fight for nearly twenty-five years for the right to set up a second parish. In particular they appealed in writing to Moscow forty-three times; they sent a letter of complaint signed by two thousand believers, to the editor of *Moscow News*. In his report on the incident in Oktiabrskii, Nezhnyi, like his colleague Shevelev, portrayed the believers with sympathy and the authorities with blatant irony.

Also in August 1987, *Literaturnaia gazeta* came out again in defense of the rights of believers. In a long article, "Miracle in Grushevo," K. Sergeev described an event that took place in the village in Lvov oblast when, according to believers, the Virgin Mary was seen on the cupola of the defunct church. The journalist recounted how the local authorities infringed on the rights of the pilgrims: they secretly took photographs of several pilgrims and gave the photos to the chairmen of the relevant kolkhozes so that they could carry out "educational work" on "their *kolkhozniks*." The registration numbers of automobiles driven by believers coming into the village were recorded and several pilgrims were asked to show their documents.[10]

The *Moscow News* correspondent Vladimir Shevelev traveled to the towns and villages in the Western Ukraine and visited the place where it was claimed the Virgin Mary had appeared. In an article entitled "The Inertia of Simplification" the journalist urged that the occurrence be examined from a serious scientific angle.[11]

Alongside articles supporting the rights of believers, however, there were still campaigns in the press persecuting both religiously active individuals and whole religious groups. Several regional newspapers carried articles abusing believers. A Lithuanian Catholic priest,[12] a Pentecostalist presbyter,[13] and members of unofficial Baptist parishes were called "political agitators," "obscurantists," and "provocateurs."[14]

A new Council for Religious Affairs attached to the RSFSR Council of Ministers was set up in November 1986.[15] The body functioned as part of the Council for Religious Affairs. According to Western sources, Professor Leonid Kolesnikov had been nominated as the chairman of the new Council. Kolesnikov declared that the main task of the Council would be "to do research into the needs and wishes of believers and to assist the solution of their current problems."[15]

*Official Statistics on Churches.* In an interview in the journal *Nauka i religiia*, the chairman of the Council for Religious Affairs under the USSR Council of Ministers, Konstantin Kharchev, criticized both  violations of religious legislation by some clergy and violations of the rights of believers by the authorities.  Two tables of collated data on religious communities in the USSR over the preceding twenty-five years and data on religious services over the last twenty years were published as a footnote to the interview (see Tables 1 and 2).

Believers in the USSR were said to constitute "about 10-20 percent of the population, depending on the region," i.e. between 28 and 56 million. The first table contained a list of the eight principal religious faiths in the country and data about the communities of these faiths since 1961.  According to Soviet law a religious community or association had to consist of not less than twenty believers.

The chairman of the Council for Religious Affairs announced that the number of religious communities had decreased by 34 percent over the preceding 25 years.  In 1988 their overall number was just over 15,000.  The total number of christenings declined over the years from 1,017,228 in 1966 to 774,747 in 1986, christenings of children of school age quadrupled and, in 1986, attained a figure of 40,469.  Also worthy of attention was the relatively large number of christenings among adults. The number of marriage services grew in comparison with 1966, but in 1981 it was far bigger than in 1986.  In the intervening five years, the figure declined by 26,000, and, in 1986, 79,840 couples were married. The number of funeral services grew constantly.

Kharchev pointed out that, since the Central Committee Plenum of April 1985, 173 communities of various faiths had been registered.  He added, however, that 107 had been disbanded.

*Effort at Moral Regeneration.*  The spiritual crisis afflicting people in the Soviet Union became a source of profound anxiety to the authorities, and there were signs that the effect of faith in God on moral stabilization was viewed positively by the state.  A church elder was allowed to express his views on the moral fiber of young people in a newspaper. *Pravda* published a statement by Archbishop Mikhail of Vologda and Velikii Ustiug who had taken part in a writers' discussion on the spiritual crisis among young people. The archbishop called on adults to exert greater influence on young people and to pass on the valuable traditions of the past to the new generation.[17]

The introduction of new festivals and rites to take the place of religious festivals evidently had failed to produce the desired result in the eyes of organizations responsible for ideology.  A report by a Radio Moscow correspondent on preparations for Christmas in East Germany referred favorably to such Christmas traditions as Christmas fairs and noted that Christmas was a profoundly family festival, one that strengthened the family—"something we are very much in need of now."[18]

## TABLE 1

### Number of Religious Communities in the USSR

|  | 1961 | 1966 | 1971 | 1976 | 1981 | 1986 |
|---|---|---|---|---|---|---|
| Russian Ortho-dox Church | 11,742 | 7,523 | 7,274 | 7,038 | 7,007 | 6,794 |
| Catholic Church | 1,179 | 1,116 | 1,087 | 1,070 | 1,102 | 1,099 |
| Islam | 2,307 | 1,820 | 1,087 | 1,069 | 954 | 751 |
| Judaism | 259 | 238 | 220 | 181 | 130 | 109 |
| Evangelical Chris-tians-Baptists | 2,917 | 3,054 | 2,964 | 2,981 | 3,078 | 2,976 |
| Pentecostalists | 1,006 | 904 | 965 | 775 | 863 | 843 |
| Seventh Day Adventists | 399 | 372 | 350 | 381 | 434 | 445 |
| Jehovah's Witnesses | 607 | 468 | 480 | 411 | 411 | 378 |
| Total (including other faiths) | 22,698 | 17,507 | 16,323 | 15,687 | 15,713 | 15,036 |

Source: *Nauka i religiia*, No. 11, 1987, p. 23.

TABLE 2

Number of Religious Ceremonies Conducted
(data supplied by religious organizations)

| | 1966 | 1971 | 1976 | 1981 | 1986 |
|---|---|---|---|---|---|
| Christenings: | 1,017,228 | 963,188 | 808,478 | 830,586 | 774,747 |
| Christenings of children of school age | 10,261 | 29,335 | 25,682 | 40,253 | 40,469 |
| Christenings of adults | - | 21,680 | 26,818 | 45,178 | 51,684 |
| Confirmations | - | 23,049 | 24,383 | 27,333 | 25,145 |
| Weddings | 60,516 | 79,356 | 74,988 | 106,259 | 79,840 |
| Funerals | 848,805 | 990,618 | 1,096,190 | 1,125,058 | 1,179,051 |

Source: *Nauka i religiia*, No. 11, 1987, p. 23.

*Concessions to the Church.* Three monasteries were returned to the Russian Orthodox Church—the Danilov Monastery in Moscow,[19] the Optina Pustyn Monastery in Kaluga Oblast[20] and the Monastyr Tolgskoi Bozhei Materi in Iaroslavl.[21] In Moscow on June 13, 1988, the foundation stone was laid for the Cathedral dedicated to the Millennium of Christianity in Russia. The cathedral, situated in a new district of Moscow, was dedicated to the Holy Trinity.[22] The All-Union Council of Evangelical Christians-Baptists was given permission to receive 100,000 Bibles from England[23] and to open the first amateur video recording studio in Moscow, equipped with the most up-to-date equipment.[24] The authorities were also examining a plan to set up an open museum of Old Believer culture near Moscow.[25] Mikhail Kulakov, the chairman of the Council of the Church of Seventh-Day Adventists in the RSFSR, proposed in an article in *Moskovskie novosti* that, with the participation of Adventists living abroad, a joint enterprise be set up to manufacture baby food. Kulakov, a member of the board of the Lenin Children's Fund, believed that such an enterprise could also produce for export and thereby replenish the Children's Fund with hard currency.[26] American Rabbi Arthur Schneier managed, with money from abroad, to arrange for a kosher take-away restaurant to be set up in Moscow.

Practicing Jews now had the opportunity to buy kosher products imported from Hungary.[27]

*Mother Theresa in the USSR?*  The visit by Mother Theresa, the founder of the Missionaries of Charity, to Moscow in August 1987 had, by mid-1988 still had no further consequences.  Inspite of Western press reports,[28] the Soviet authorities did not give Mother Theresa permission to open a sister house of congregation in Moscow; but the fact of her visit alone illustrated the progress of glasnost in the religious arena.

On the day prior to her arrival, three representatives of the "independent Christian community" in Moscow addressed an open letter to her. They drew Mother Theresa's attention to the "all-encompassing ambit of the planned changes to legislation on religion and observance" taking place in the Soviet Union, adding that they hoped that in consequence the church would be given the opportunity to fulfil one of its chief duties to God and mankind—charitable works. "Our Church is denied this opportunity," wrote the authors of the open letter to Mother Theresa.[29]

The Soviet press agencies and newspapers also gave thorough coverage to the visit.[30] TASS reported on the day following the visit that Mother Theresa had received an invitation from the president of the Soviet Peace Committee, Genrikh Borovik, and that in the course of conversation they had considered the problem of "combining activities to foster peace with the struggle against poverty, hunger, and disease, from which hundreds of millions suffer throughout the world."[31] Furthermore, Mother Theresa expressed a desire to go to Kiev to visit the new settlements for those who suffered the Chernobyl disaster: "Representatives of the order of the Missionaries of Charity—and I am the founder of this order—always strive to get to those parts of the globe where tragic events are taking place." Mother Theresa reported during the interview that she was ready to discuss cooperation between the foundation established in the Soviet Union for aid to orphans and her charitable order of missionaries.[32] Concerning Mother Theresa's visit to Kiev, *Literaturnaia gazeta* reported a few days later that she had commented very favorably on the fine new houses given to the Chernobyl evacuees, and the care and concern lavished on them.[33] In the Soviet Union, Mother Theresa stressed that she had not officially asked the authorities for approval to send a mission from her congregation to the Soviet Union, although it was clear from the start that this had been the aim of her visit.  Her noble initiative found support in the Soviet Union not only among believers but among all those concerned about social problems, especially that of the situation of patients in hospitals. The chairman of the council of the Church of Seventh Day Adventists in the RSFSR, Mikhail Kulakov, remarked in an article in *Moskovskie novosti* that believers might help the community by building some kind of clinic for alcoholics, or by taking on the duties of hospital orderlies, for example.[34] A physician writing in *Literaturnaia gazeta* echoed him in an article about the state of the hospitals. He indicated that the visit by "the virtuous Mother Theresa" had reminded him "that [to give] succor to the suffering is work in which the church has engaged willingly from time immemorial."[35]

*Unofficial Religious Groups.* In 1987, there was little change for the better in the situation of unregistered religious groups. Although several religious "prisoners of conscience" were released from camps before completing their sentences, and the members of a whole congregation had been promised exit visas, the process of glasnost and democratization had scarcely touched the lives of the majority of members of unofficial Churches. State harassment continued unabated.

Throughout 1987, members of unregistered congregations of Evangelical Christian Baptists, who were called "Baptist schismatics" or *"initsiativniki"* by the press, were subjected to an increasing degree of persecution. This was accompanied by a smear campaign in the press. Believers had large fines imposed on them for attending prayer meetings; in one village more than twenty Baptists were fined fifty rubles each. In both towns and villages prayer meetings were broken up, particularly at Eastertime.[36]

At the beginning of 1987, there were a number of trials against Baptists. The court presiding over one of the trials of Baptists issued an order to the raion executive committee to carry out the demolition of "a prayer house built without authorization."[37]

Some 30,000 Pentecostals applied to emigrate. Many had been fighting for decades for the right to do so. Appeals for help were received in the West from whole communities, families, individual believers, and even children. In January 1988, a West German newspaper published an appeal to Chancellor Kohl from Ania Walter, the eleven-year-old daughter of the leader of the Pentecostal congregation in Chuguevka, Pastor Viktor Walter. Ania asked for help in obtaining the release of her father, who had been sentenced in 1985 to five years of imprisonment.[38] The congregation in Chuguevka, the majority of whom were of German extraction, consisted of 130 persons, including children. They had been campaigning for many years to be allowed to emigrate to West Germany and had staged numerous hunger strikes and demonstrations.[39] At the end of February 1988, the news was received unexpectedly that all the members of the congregation had been promised permission to emigrate. Furthermore, of ten members of the congregation who were sentenced in 1984 and 1985 to various terms of imprisonment, four had their sentences shortened. Pastor Walter's sentence was shortened by a year.[40]

Activists from various Christian denominations working together with individual believers submitted proposals to the government on how religious legislation could be changed to allow Churches to live in accordance with religious teaching. Particularly active in this campaign were a number of Orthodox Christians, including the priests Gleb Iakunin and Nikolai Gainov and the layman Aleksandr Ogorodnikov.[41]

The efforts of these Christians were not entirely fruitless. In September 1987, Iakunin told Western journalists that the government had replied. He showed the journalists a letter from the USSR Ministry of Justice dated September 9, 1987, stating that a government commission was examining the proposals received "in the framework of an improvement in state religious legislation." Iakunin said: "We want the state to stop interfering in religious affairs, we want an independent Church."[42]

Russian Orthodox activist Aleksandr Ogorodnikov, who had spent more than eight years in prison, announced in Moscow in February 1988, that representatives of the unofficial Christian community were planning to hold a seminar devoted to problems of the Church to which representatives of foreign Churches would be invited as official guests of the Moscow Patriarchate. Ogorodnikov said that his group feared that the Moscow Patriarchate and the Soviet authorities would stage "pompous celebrations" in a bid to push the real problems of the Church to the bottom of the agenda.[43]

Glasnost even made it possible for the Orthodox "catacomb Church," the True Orthodox Christians, to issue a statement. In the first issue of the journal *Za pravoslavie i monarkhiiu*, which began publication in samizdat form, two priests of this Church appealed to the first hierarch of the Russian Orthodox Church abroad, Metropolitan Vitalii, to accept them as parishioners.[44]

*CPSU against Persecution of the Church. Kommunist*, the journal of the CPSU, published a keynote article that tried to dissociate the CPSU from past persecution while at the same time stressing the continuing importance of Lenin's decrees on religion. The article, which was published under the rubric "Pages of History," was unsigned and may therefore be considered an editorial. It took the form of a historical survey of the religious policy of the CPSU, starting with the publication in 1918 of the decree on the separation of church and state. The principal aim of this survey was to demonstrate the nonparticipation of the party in processes that the article referred to as "distortion of the party line," "a deliberately brutal approach," "the application of administrative measures," and "mockery of articles of faith and cults." The article referred to a series of decrees in which the party leadership condemned such actions, and explained away the continuing persecution of the church and believers as antireligious fervor on the part of local party officials. The article then went on to stress the correctness of Lenin's religious legislation, maintaining that its fundamental principles remained valid in the era of perestroika "for the conditions of the democratization of Socialist society."[45]

This emphasis on the validity of the Leninist decree was clearly a response to the intensive campaign to change religious legislation. Groups of believers, representatives of the unofficial Christian community, had put forward concrete suggestions for changes in legislation that would allow churches, in particular the Russian Orthodox Church, not just to exist but to live in accordance with their doctrines.[46] Several Orthodox hierarchs had also spoken in favor of changes in legislation, albeit in far more general terms. Metropolitan Aleksii of Leningrad and Novgorod stressed in an interview that the laws currently in force had been adopted many decades before, in the years during and immediately following the revolution.[47] The chairman of the newly created Commission on Humanitarian Cooperation and Human Rights attached to the Soviet Committee on European Security and Cooperation, Fedor Burlatskii, told a press conference that "representatives of our Church" had raised the question of improving religious legislation at the first meeting of the commission.[48]

*The Church and Charitable Work. Meditsinskaia gazeta* interviewed the rector of the Leningrad Spiritual Academy, Professor and Archpriest Vladimir Sorokin. The Orthodox priest stressed the need for the Russian Orthodox Church to be allowed to engage in charitable work and to take an active part in decisions concerning a number of the country's most pressing problems. He pointed out that the church and its members had been striving to be allowed to do this for many years but that all its efforts had "met with a hostile reception." Father Vladimir stressed the value of specific, individual charity, such as allowing the Church to patronize a particular hospital, children's home, or old people's home. "Would it really be such a bad thing if a hospital run by believers were to exist alongside a state hospital," he asked. Asked by the newspaper's correspondents what he would be able to do for health care, Father Vladimir replied that he could organize a group of his parishioners who would be willing to go to a hospital and care for the sick. "A good deed of this kind would inspire believers," he added.[49]

Concern that Christians should have the opportunity to help members of the community was also expressed by members of other churches. In an interview with *Moskovskie novosti*, the chairman of the All-Union Council of Evangelical Christians-Baptists, Vasilii Logvinenko, drew attention to the fact that "our Church is actively involved in charitable activities all over the world." He listed the countries to which Soviet Baptists sent tons of medical supplies (Angola, Nicaragua, and Ethiopia) and asked the inevitable question: "If we help the needy and sick abroad, why is our help not enlisted for our compatriots?"[50] He suggested lifting the restrictions on charitable activities laid down by Soviet law. In an article entitled "Wisdom and Patience Are What Is Needed," the chairman of the Council of the Church of Seventh-Day Adventists in the RSFSR, Mikhail Kulakov, proposed that the Adventists should be allowed to open special sanatoriums for alcoholics not responding to treatment and added that the members of Adventist congregations would be willing to work as orderlies in local hospitals.[51]

*Church Bells and Perestroika.* In an article in *Moskovskie novosti*, the journalist Natalia Davydova described how, to mark the millennium of the baptism of Rus, the bells in some churches were to be rung for the first time in seventy years. During the celebrations, services would be held in all the Moscow churches, and a number of once famous bells would again begin to sound.[52] Georgii Pliasov, a novice and senior bell ringer at the Danilov Monastery, which was returned to the Russian Orthodox Church at its request in 1983,[53] told the journalist that foreign guests attending the celebrations would be greeted with "the beautiful sound of bells." When construction work began on the half-destroyed monastery in 1983, the forty-five-meter high, tiered bell tower was re-erected together with the belfry. Davydova explained that the old bells were no longer there, because they had been removed "during the period of active theomachy." By some miracle, she says, they had been preserved and ended up in the United States, where they remained in the keeping of Harvard University.

The long article was written in a nostalgic, emotional tone:

Within the boundaries of old Moscow—along the Kamer-Kollezhskii rampart—the bells used to ring in 560 churches. But within the administrative boundaries of today's city, which has grown immeasurably since that time, there are 47 active churches. What is more, the bells have not yet come back to life in all of them.

Not only did the bells cease to ring after the Bolsheviks came to power, they began to be destroyed. Old bellringers died, and there were no new ones to succeed them; the ancient art of bell founding, for which Russia had at one time been famous, came to an end. At the end of her article Davydova wrote: "Having practically imposed a ban on bell-ringing, we broke a tradition. Bells have not been cast for fifty years.[54]

In an essay by Leonid Leonov entitled "Thoughts on an Old Stone," which was published only in 1986 with a note saying that it had been written more than six years previously, the following sad lines appear, describing the neglected churches and silent belltowers:

The majority of them are majestic cathedrals, with silent, sometimes heartrendingly miraculous belfries, cruelly worn away long ago by continental bad weather, the cornices overgrown with little bushes.[55]

In the early nineteen-eighties, the newspaper *Sovetskaia Rossiia* began a campaign to save the art of bell founding and the sound of Russian bells. In 1987 one of *Sovetskaia Rossiia*'s own correspondents described with rapture how the Sunday celebration marking the 1,125th anniversary of the founding of Rostov culminated in the striking of the famous Rostov bells: "They rang out at the top of their voices to the joy of the people." A former teacher, Mariia Tiunina, who devoted many years of her life to a campaign to save the Rostov bells, recounted how she had begun to try to preserve the bell-ringing a quarter of a century before.

It seems doubtful that bell-ringing was ever officially banned. Instead, a series of instructions, and directives were issued that in practice allowed local authorities to destroy the tradition of bell-ringing. A clear example of this was the "Explanatory Instruction No. 80" issued by a department of the All-Russian Central Executive Committee on March 13, 1928, which gave local authorities the right in practice to ban "the so-called sound of bells."[56]

*Gorbachev Meets with Leaders of the Orthodox Church.* On April 29, 1988, Gorbachev met with Patriarch Pimen and members of the Holy Synod in the Kremlin. The meeting occupied a prominent place on the front pages of *Pravda*, *Izvestiia*, and other major Soviet newspapers.[57]

As *Pravda* reported, Patriarch Pimen had written a letter to Gorbachev requesting a meeting "in connection with the millennium of the Christianization of Rus." On April 29, 1988, the general secretary of the CPSU received him and a number of metropolitans of the Church in the Catherine Hall in the Kremlin. The Russian Orthodox Church was represented by Patriarch Pimen and five senior Church hierarchs: Metropolitan of Kiev and Galicia Filaret; Metropolitan of Leningrad and Novgorod Aleksii; Metropolitan of Krutitsy and Kolomna Iuvenalii; Metropolitan of Rostov and Novocherkassk Vladimir; and Metropolitan of Minsk and Belorussia Filaret. These metropolitans were members of the Holy Synod, the advisory organ to the patriarch, which had eight members in all—five permanent and three temporary. Metropolitan of Rostov and Novocherkassk Vladimir was a member of the Commission of the Holy Synod for Questions of Christian Unity. In 1984, he was appointed Patriarchal Exarch for Western Europe.[58]

Gorbachev welcomed the Church leaders with a speech devoted mainly to a survey of the Church's history during the seven decades of Soviet power. He expressed regret about the fate of the Church under Stalin, saying: "Religious organizations were also affected by the tragic events of the period of the personality cult," and added: "This period has been evaluated as a departure from Socialist principles, principles that have now been rehabilitated." Gorbachev did not mention the persecution of the Church under Lenin, but was full of praise for the role played by the Russian Orthodox Church in World War II. Promising that "the interests of religious organizations will also be reflected" in the new law on freedom of conscience, Gorbachev said:

At present we are in the process of fully restoring the Leninist principles regarding religion, the Church, and believers.[59]

Reports in the press stated that during the meeting the Church hierarchs not only expressed their full support for "the measures being taken in our country for restructuring and moral renewal in society" but also "posed a number of questions connected with ensuring that the Russian Orthodox Church can engage in normal activities." Gorbachev promised to pass on these requests and ideas to the government.

*Toward Celebration of the Millennium of the Christianization of Rus.*
From the beginning of 1988, there was a marked increase in the number of
publications about the Church in the Ukraine. A number of senior Russian
Orthodox clerics of the Exarchate of the Ukraine gave interviews and made
statements on various topics ranging from a description of preparations for the
forthcoming jubilee, to political speeches including a critique of a resolution by
the US Congress on "religious glasnost" in the Soviet Union.[60] Vladimir
Shcherbitskii, first secretary of the Central Committee of the Ukrainian
Communist party spoke in Kiev in December 1987, underlining the "deepening
interest" of the public, particularly young people, in Kiev and its unique
monuments. [61]

In March, Western press agencies reported that "for the first time in the
existence of the Soviet Union, autonomous Soviet republics have received
permission to import large numbers of Bibles." In particular, foreign Bible
societies were expected to donate thousands of Bibles in Ukrainian.[62] The news
was confirmed by several senior Soviet churchmen.[63] Furthermore, Makarii,
Archbishop of Ivano-Frankovsk and Kolomiia, told a TASS correspondent in
May that "... on the eve of the jubilee, the Gospels will be printed in Ukrainian
at Lvov." Paladii, Suffragan Bishop of the Kiev Eparchy, administrator of the
Exarchate of the Ukraine, told a correspondent for *Literaturna Ukraina* that "...
75,000 prayer books are being prepared for publication, the New Testament in
Ukrainian is coming out in Kiev. Other publications are planned, including a
Catechism."[64]

The authorities undertook several construction projects for the celebration of
the millennium. In January 1988, *Izvestiia* reported that on Old Kiev Hill a
broad avenue had been laid out and the restoration of the noted Desiatinnaia
(Tithe) Church was planned.[65]

Bishop Palladii enumerated the changes which were supposed to demonstrate
the favorable attitude of the government towards the Church: the restitution of
several monasteries, the opening of the Chapel of the Blessed Kseniia of
Petersburg, and the construction of new churches. He also noted that the
regulations requiring the registration of parents of children to be baptized had
been abolished.[66]

With the forthcoming millennial jubilee, a number of articles were printed
which bitterly attacked the Ukrainian Catholic Church—or Brest Church Union,
as the newspapers called it—which had been liquidated in 1946.[67] Nikodim,
Metropolitan of Lvov and Ternopol, criticized "Uniates now living abroad" in
categorical terms.[68]

This seemed especially out of place in view of the effort of both the Russian
Orthodox Church and the Soviet government to find common ground for
negotiations with the Vatican over the fate of the Ukrainian Catholic Church.
Before the start of the millennial celebrations on June 4, Filaret told reporters
that representatives of the Russian Orthodox Church and Roman Catholic

Church would meet in Finland in July to exchange opinions on the Ukrainian Catholic Church. Metropolitan Filaret warned that the aim of the meeting was not to begin "negotiations" but simply an attempt to clarify the position of their respective churches on the matter. In his statement to journalists at the Danilov Monastery, he emphasized the "deep desire" of the Russian Orthodox Church and the Soviet government to improve relations with the Vatican.[69] Pope John Paul II had gone on record in the past in the cause of the Ukrainian Catholic Church which represented the largest "catacomb" church in the Soviet Union with its adherents numbering several millions.[70]

*Outcome and Prospects.* The celebrations marking the millennium of the Christianization of Rus brought prestige to the Russian Orthodox Church at home and abroad. The theme of "Christianization of Rus" was prominent in both the domestic and the foreign media. The celebrations soon passed beyond the purely religious as the official Soviet establishment took a prominent part in the celebrations. On June 10 senior politicians joined members of the Church hierarchy and foreign guests at an official function in Moscow's Bolshoi Theater marking the millennium. These included Deputy President Petr Demichev, Deputy Prime Minister Nikolai Talizin, and Konstantin Kharchev, chairman of the Council for Religious Affairs. Patriarch Pimen gave Raisa Gorbachev an especially warm welcome, remarking that "she has dedicated herself to the noble cause of popularizing the great cultural heritage of our motherland"; his remarks were greeted with loud applause. At the start of the celebrations, the Soviet government's official message greeting the millennium was read out.[71] The following day, President Gromyko held a reception in the Kremlin for a large group of the official contingent and guests at the millennium, Patriarch Pimen among them.[72]

According to the speeches of both churchmen and politicians on the occasion of the millennium, the Russian Orthodox Church had an important place in the moral and spiritual restructuring of Soviet society, and in the regeneration of social values. The Church had fifty million adherents. Many senior churchmen in the Russian Orthodox Church emphasized the significance of the processes taking place in society and the Church's favorable attitude towards them. Filaret, Metropolitan of Minsk and Belorussia, compared glasnost with confession: "Glasnost is the motivating force behind perestroika. This is like social repentance, and—akin to our notion of confession—inner repentance."[73]

The official festivities marking the millennium took place in Kiev between June 14 and 16, 1988. After the conclusion of the main event in Moscow, some of the official guests arrived in Kiev for a ceremony on June 14 at the Shevchenko Theater. The following day, there was a service at the Vladimir Cathedral. That evening at the Shevchenko Theater, there were two concerts—one secular, the other religious—and a wreath was laid at the Tomb of the Unknown Soldier. On June 16 a service was conducted at the statue to St. Vladimir, and the guests visited the Cathedral of St. Sophia—the city's most sacred shrine—and the Monastery of Kiev-Pecherskii, part of which had only just been handed over to the Church.[74]

The Gorbachev leadership seemed to be appealing for the Church's support for perestroika, and this allowed the Church to put forward several demands and begin the struggle for the amendment of legislation which, in particular, forbade churches to perform charitable works. At a press conference with senior clerics which took place in Moscow on May 11, Filaret, Metropolitan of Minsk and Belorussia, said that the Church leadership had presented Gorbachev a list of "the most pressing problems of the Church," and the General Secretary had promised to attend to the matter.[75]

In full support of perestroika, Church functionaries argued for the continuation of the Church's tradition of charitable works and asked that the Church be allowed to open parish schools, hospitals, and various other charitable institutions. In an interview with *Trud*, Filaret, the Metropolitan of Kiev and Galicia, and one of the most influential figures in the Church, stressed that "We're ready for perestroika. We will increase [the number of novices] admitted to monasteries, open hospitals, and the wherewithal for this will be found."[76] Previously, the Church had received permission to build a home for aged clerics at Tolgskii monastery (the return of which was described by the Soviet press as a "Jubilee present"); nuns of the monastery were to take care of those confined to the institution.[77] The clergy and parishioners of the Cathedral of the Epiphany in Moscow began to work together with City Hospital No. 6, "in the name of charity."[78] This, however, took place outside of the law.

The question of new legislation was of concern both to believers inside the Soviet Union and to observers abroad. At a press conference on June 10, 1988, foreign correspondents put a question to Konstantin Kharchev, chairman of the Council for Religious Affairs, asking about the state of progress of plans for a new law on freedom of conscience. Kharchev replied that work on it had been in hand since 1979, but, "in reality, only got under way three years ago. Now, the specific provisions are being worked out, after which the clergy will be the first to be consulted."[79]

Kharchev's remark demonstrated how far the government was prepared to go, or said it was prepared to go, to accommodate the Church. But some Church representatives openly expressed their dissatisfaction. The principal objection was to existing legislation that constrained Church activity, but violations of rights under existing legislation that affected efforts to establish new parishes also caused disquiet. Some spiritual leaders went further and criticized the inimical attitude toward believers in general. Mefodii, Metropolitan of Voronezh and Lipetsk,[80] described the conflicts of the Church with the Soviet authorities in the years following the Revolution, and drew the conclusion that the key to the current difficulties lay in what had happened in the past.

The Metropolitan bitterly remarked that as for many years all that had been heard were words about the need to engage in a struggle with religion, these stereotypes had become such a part of popular consciousness that many people automatically protested whenever there was any talk of believers participating in social life. Metropolitan Mefodii said that the authorities "would prefer to give serious consideration to ... the possibility of an extension of activities to our country of the Catholic order created by Mother Theresa than to meet believers in their own country even half-way."[81]

For several months before the start of the celebrations, members of unofficial Orthodox groups had expressed their apprehension that the purpose of these "pompous festivities" was to push the problems of the Church and believers into the background. Aleksandr Ogorodnikov expressed the hope that the authorities would allow his group to rent premises in June so that a seminar could be conducted on the problems of the Church and its situation in general.[82] The religious activists did not get premises but organized a three-day seminar anyway; on June 6, about twenty people attended a service "for the persecuted and their persecutors" which took place in a private apartment in Moscow.[83] The following day, another group held a press conference at which Father Gleb Iakunin reported that the group had sent an appeal to Patriarch Pimen and delegates to the Synod to reconsider the congratulations sent on behalf of the Church to Stalin on his seventieth birthday in 1949. Patriarch Aleksii had praised "Stalin's attention to the needs of the Church" in especially extravagant terms. Father Gleb felt that the Church should now join those voices that criticized the period of the "cult of personality." A priest, Georgii Edelshtein, argued at the press conference against the system of selecting delegates to the Synod, which was conducted at the highest level of the Church without the participation of priests, deacons, or the laity.[84]

Such opposition aimed at perestroika inside the Church itself. The critical voices of certain senior churchmen suggested that such a restructuring might be possible. The new legislation and the changes that were made regarding the position of the Church were expected to indicate just what positive changes the Church might win from the government and how the government was progressing in the process of democratization of society.

31
## ISLAM IN THE SOVIET UNION
Bess Brown and Anne Bohr*

*Greater Tolerance for Islam?* In 1988, the Soviet authorities still considered Islam to be a brake on the social and economic development of traditionally Muslim areas of the USSR, in particular the Central Asian republics. This necessitated efforts at an "atheist upbringing." On the other hand, the authorities could hardly afford to be perceived to be allowing greater latitude toward Christianity than to Islam.

Official publications often pointed to a connection between social deviation, such as the massive corruption that infected all aspects of life in Uzbekistan, and the retention of religious prejudices and "feudal" social traditions, which were often described as having a religious component. Religion was implicated at least indirectly in the rash of self-immolations of Central Asian women that was the subject of a series of press stories. Many officials, including Gorbachev himself, were critical of the observance of religious rites by party and government figures with traditionally Muslim backgrounds, because such observance was interpreted as evidence of dual loyalty, of separate "public" and "private" convictions and lack of total commitment to party ideals. Official complaints had been voiced for many years that hostile external forces sought to use Islam for subversive purposes against the USSR.

Although the legalization of unregistered mosques was proposed in *Literaturnaia gazeta*, the proposal was conceived as a means of establishing control over "unofficial Islam" rather than as a liberalization measure, and there was little follow-up to it.[1]

In Tajikistan, the rite of circumcision, which had been accepted by almost the entire Tajik population, was put under the jurisdiction of medical facilities, but this was done to ensure that the operation was performed in sanitary surroundings and to get it away from the clergy. The participants in a round-table on antireligious propaganda sponsored by the journal *Kommunist Tadzhikistana* were unable to commit themselves to a recommendation for a mass printing of the Koran, although various speakers claimed that greater availability of the Koran would make it easier for propagandists to counter.[2] This proposal was apparently too controversial to be accepted. The Islamic religion and cultural tradition did not as yet have an effective spokesman at the all-Union level.

*Unregistered Clergy.* At a meeting of an ideological *aktiv* held in August 1986 to discuss international and atheist upbringing, Kakhar Makhkamov, the

---

* Author of the section "Fertile Ground for Foreign Interference?"

Tajik party chief, noted that the level of religious observance among the republic's population had risen noticeably.[3] He observed that the antisocial activity of the Muslim clergy was increasing, and complained particularly that the more reactionary members of the clergy sought to revivify nationalist survivals and resurrect outmoded, harmful customs and rites under the guise of "national traditions." As a result of the failure of local party and government organizations to oppose the actions of the clergy, Makhkamov said, various sects had sprung up, including Wahhabism.[4]

Materials about the activities of unregistered mullahs appeared fairly frequently in the republican press in 1987, and several articles suggested that ideological workers and rural intellectuals in general hesitated to oppose these individuals publicly, apparently fearing an adverse response from fellow villagers or townspeople. An article in early in 1987 told of a kolkhoz foreman who had declared himself a mullah, considered himself a Wahhabi, and enjoyed great esteem among both kolkhoz members and well-educated teachers.[5] He tried to persuade the latter of the need for religion classes in the schools. He also criticized the Soviet role in Afghanistan.  The teachers to whom the foreman-mullah made his pitch were unwilling to speak up and challenge him, though they apparently disagreed with him.

In the early part of 1987, considerable publicity was given to the case of Abdulla Saidov, a self-proclaimed mullah and Wahhabi whose supporters staged a disturbance outside a police station in Kurgan-Tyube following his arrest in August 1986 on charges of slander and possession of narcotics.[6] The mullah reportedly tried to induce believers to make a formal request at the Twenty-Seventh Congress of the CPSU for the establishment of an Islamic state in Tajikistan. He also, according to *Kommunist Tadzhikistana*, came close to issuing a call to arms to the guests at a celebration in April 1986 in the hope of realizing his dream of an Islamic state. Like most of the unregistered clergymen described in the press, Saidov carried on his activities quite openly, aided by the protection of his relatives.

Among the practices of the unregistered clergy that drew the greatest criticism from the authorities were the reproduction and distribution of literature and tapes with an "ideologically harmful" content and the showing of video films of a "religious-propagandistic" nature that came from abroad.[7]

*Influence on Young People.* Makhkamov complained at the *aktiv* meeting in August 1986 that the illegal instruction of young people in Islamic dogma had become more frequent and that young people often wore amulets or crosses and decorated private cars with religious symbols and verses from the Koran. He also claimed that there were young people in all rural areas who observed the fast.

According to the report of the Kulyab Oblast Party Committee plenum in July, at examination time the majority of pilgrims to a holy site in the oblast were students hoping for good grades. The report summed up the party's fears about the effects of religion on young people, noting that "today's pilgrims seeking good grades will be silent tomorrow while the mullah rants, and the day after tomorrow they will go to the mosque." Makhkamov told the ideological *aktiv* that some graduates with degrees in Oriental languages were joining the clergy.

The propagandists' journal, *Agitator*, reported the results of a questionnaire on religious belief that was administered to rural young people in one raion in Tajikistan. It provided statistical support for claims made by party officials about the continuing influence of religion and the very apparent lack of success of "atheist upbringing," while graphically illustrating the popular perception of a connection between religion and morality that so worried party officials.[8]

A third of the respondents reported that they visited religious institutions, many because they were raised to regard this as socially desirable behavior. Some said they went to the mosque out of curiosity or to meet friends and relatives. People who said they went to the mosque to pray numbered 21.4 percent. Of the 70.4 percent who reported that they celebrated the major Islamic holidays, only 23.6 percent said they did so for religious reasons.

Of the young people who responded to the questionnaire, more than a third said they found religion useful: 14.4 percent of the respondents found it useful because it preserved national culture and traditions; 10 percent because it provided solace at times of troubles. Many of the young *kolkhozniks* illustrated the moral quality of religion by relating the story of a kolkhoz family in their raion whose home burned during the cotton harvest. Farm officials were too busy to help, but the local mullah took up a collection for the fire victims at the Friday prayers, and relatives, neighbors, and fellow-Muslims helped rebuild the house and assisted the family to acquire the necessities. To Vasneva this was a sad commentary on the effort to inculcate Soviet social and moral standards.

*Religious Observance in Tajikistan.* At an oblast party conference in Kurgan-Tyube in November 1985 it was stated that in the previous four years, the income of the Kurgan-Tyube and Pyandzh mosques had risen 150 percent.[9] A request by three villages for permission to open mosques was reported at a plenum of the Kulyab Oblast Party Committee in July 1987; it had been passed on to higher authorities by the raion executive committee because the raion government did not want to take responsibility for dealing with the request.[10] At a scientific-practical conference on atheist upbringing held in Kurgan-Tyube the same month, it was noted that the clergy (the report did not make clear whether it was referring only to unregistered members of the clergy) had been making use of prayer houses that had been built in almost every village with funds contributed by the inhabitants.[11] There were communal prayers in the mornings and in the evenings, and in some villages "self-appointed mullahs" even decreed that people who were unwilling to participate in communal prayers should not come to the village at all.

*Fertile Ground for Foreign Interference?* In an article published in

*Literaturnaia gazeta* in January 1988 entitled "Khomeini—A Political Portrait," Igor Beliaev, chief of the newspaper's Foreign Department, sounded the following warning about the Iranian leader's desire to spread the influence of Islamic fundamentalism:

> What is Khomeini's dream? It is that the Islamic Revolution be victorious throughout the entire Muslim world, from Morocco in the west to Indonesia in the east.[12]

He clearly included in this geographic sweep those Soviet republics with a predominantly Muslim population, two of which—Azerbaijan and Turkmenistan—shared a common border with Iran. In an earlier interview with AFP, Beliaev was also reported to have predicted that Teheran would extend its sphere of influence to the North, that is, to the Soviet Muslim republics, after the conclusion of the war with Iraq.[13]

Belaiev's article contributed to the on-going dialogue among Soviet specialists on Islam concerning the reasons for Islam's persistence, indeed, its revivification in the USSR, and the ways in which they saw this milieu as providing fertile ground for exploitation by revolutionary Islamic groups in concert with Western powers. In May 1987 Belaiev began the all-Union discussion of the USSR's "Islamic question" with the publication in Literaturnaia gazeta of a two-part article entitled "Islam and Politics."[14] The article began with a letter from a student from Gorkii asking whether it was true that "...as Western politicians believe, Soviet Muslims are subject to the influence of their coreligionists in other countries, who are waging a struggle against socialism that shows no sign of dying down to this day?" Belaiev replied that "assertions about the export of Islamic revolution are not just propaganda" and, furthermore, the existence of "a kind of Islamic infrastructure" in Central Asia and the Caucasus provided "a very receptive milieu" for foreign interference.[15]

Belaiev proposed the legalization of clandestine mosques, so that "things will become much clearer, both for the authorities and for the faithful." Thus he tacitly recognized that the policy of closing mosques, which was carried out with particular vigor under Nikita Khruschev, had not only failed to reduce the number of believers, but had encouraged the growing vitality of unofficial Islamic activity that was beyond Moscow's control. In a subsequent article in *Literaturnaia gazeta*, the first deputy chairman of the USSR's Council for Religious Affairs from 1978 to 1988, M. M. Rakhmankulov, also argued for granting legal status to all mosques operating outside the purview of the officially-sanctioned Muslim Spiritual Directorates.[16]

There were a number of reasons why Soviet authorities might favor legalization, and Rakhmankulov pointed to several of them. First, the closure of official mosques under Soviet rule only contributed to the proliferation of clandestine ones. Rakhmankulov confirmed what many Western experts had long maintained when he stated that in the republics of Central Asia and the Caucasus in 1988, "there exist significantly more unregistered mosques and mullahs than those functioning on a legal basis". Second, Rakhmankulov stressed that "it is precisely the unregistered mosques that are the refuge of all manner of fanatics and extremists." Third, official Islam had been an important foreign policy instrument in the post-Khruschev era. Consequently, an increase in the number of officially recognized mosques and clergy might well enhance Moscow's projected image to the outside world—and to the Muslim world in particular—as a "friend of Islam". Fourth, Moscow surely would hope to put across legalization of mosques as a benificent gesture on the behalf of Soviet Muslims, and thereby garner firmer popular support for perestroika.

## 32
## RELIGIOUS STRUGGLE IN CZECHOSLOVAKIA
Peter Martin and Kevin Devlin

*Petition for Religious Freedom.* In February 1988, *Pravda* (Bratislava) and *Rudé právo* expressed strong concern over the support for a 31-point petition calling for more religious freedom. According to unofficial sources, 600,00 signatures were gathered. The dailies criticized Cardinal František Tomášek for supporting the petition and accused him of making assertions that were "in true contradiction to reality."[1] The attack by the two papers was intended to discredit the organizers of and signatories to the document and to portray the petition as an attempt to "disturb the course" of talks between Czechoslovakia and the Vatican.

On February 20, *Rudé právo* and *Pravda* continued their attacks on Tomášek, saying that "the state supports the demands for religious freedom and the appointment of more bishops" (two points in the petition) but that it was not prepared to support other demands in the petition, which were propagated by Church radicals concerned not with religious freedom but with "political objectives" and the disruption of Czechoslovakia's Communist society. The dailies denied Tomášek's claim that none of the petition's 31 points were unconstitutional or illegal.

*The Pilgrimage to Prague.* Despite the tension in Church-state relations, Tomášek called for a nationwide pilgrimage to Prague on March 6. In his pastoral letter, which was read from the pulpits on February 21, he said that the pilgrimage would take place in conjunction with the "consecration of the year

1988 to the Blessed Agnes of Bohemia." In conclusion, the pastoral letter called on Catholics to attend the pilgrimage to Prague Cathedral, at least in spirit, in order to show "their determination to follow Christ more faithfully and systematically, following the example of Blessed Agnes."[2]

On March 2, at his weekly general audience in the Vatican, Pope John Paul II noted that the feast day of the Blessed Agnes was being celebrated in Czechoslovakia,[3] and said that this celebration was of "special significance" to Czechoslovak Catholics. The Pope made no mention of her possible canonization, but Vatican sources said that the process leading to full sanctification was very much advanced.

Agnes, the daughter of the Czech King Přemysl Otakar I, was born in 1206 or 1208.[4] She became friendly with Saint Clare of Assisi (a close associate of Saint Francis), who founded the Franciscan order of "the minor brethren" during this period. Agnes and Clare corresponded on how Christian charity could help the urban poor and on "Franciscan ideals" in general. Agnes devoted herself to caring for the sick and the poor. A woman of penetrating intellect, she was skilled in languages and diplomacy.

Fearing that the expected crowd at Saint Vitus's Cathedral might get out of control and that the occasion might turn into a political demonstration, the Czech authorities took measures in advance of the event. The heavy police presence on the streets of Prague and on many highways leading to the city was explained by the authorities as an effort to carry out random technical checks on cars to cut down the large number of automobile accidents.[5] The subway station nearest to the cathedral was closed for "technical reasons," and a tram line to the cathedral was blocked by roadmen who were working—unusually—on Sunday.

For the first time since August 1985, the police in Prague used 48-hour detention orders to hold dissidents without charging them. About 19 Charter 77 signatories and Catholic activists were detained on March 4. Among them were the prominent playwright Václav Havel, the Charter 77 spokesman Stanislav Devátý, the Catholic activists Václav Benda and Václav Malý, and Augustin Navrátil, one of the authors of the petition.

Most of the dissidents were picked up two days before the Mass at a party given by Assistant Under-Secretary of State at the British Foreign and Commonwealth Office David Radford, who was paying an official visit to Czechoslovakia.[6] Reports said that the police scuffled with dissidents as they tried to enter a British diplomat's home. On March 5, the British government protested to Czechoslovakia "in the strongest terms" about the incident. The junior minister at the Foreign and Commonwealth Office, David Mellor, immediately summoned Czechoslovak Chargé d'Affaires Roman Hronek for what was described as a "stormy but brief" talk.[7]

At least 8,000 people took part in the Mass celebrated by Cardinal Tomášek in Saint Vitus's Cathedral on March 6, as part of a 10-year period of celebrations that were planned to culminate in 1997 with the 1,000th anniversary of the martyrdom of Saint Adalbert (Vojtěch), Bishop of Prague. [8] Each of the 10 years was to be dedicated to "a specific sector of spiritual life" based on the Gospel and the Ten Commandments; each of the celebrations was to be under the patronage of one of the nation's saints. In his 15-minute sermon, Tomášek stressed the importance of "spiritual renewal" in the coming decade of celebrations. He told the congregation that they should rise above any harassment. A high point of the two-hour service was a message from Pope John Paul II to what he called "the dear nations of Czechs and Slovaks."[9]

After the Mass, Tomášek appeared three times on the balcony of his palace to wave to the crowd of about 1,000, who cheered and clapped, shouting "Long live the Holy Father," "We want religious freedom," "We want bishops," and "We want the Pope."

*Demonstration and Repression in Bratislava.* The tension between the state and the Roman Catholic Church in Czechoslovakia flared up into violence in Bratislava on March 25, when a peaceful religious demonstration was held. Several thousand Slovak Catholics defied the authorities' ban on the demonstration and gathered in front of the city's National Theater in support of religious freedom.

The date chosen for the demonstration appears to have been without special political significance.[10] It was, however, only days before the third round of talks were scheduled to open between the Vatican and the Czechoslovak state on the nomination of bishops.[11] The rally came during the campaign to gather signatures for the petition in support of religious freedom. It also came three weeks after the pilgrimage to Prague to honor the Blessed Agnes. Moreover, a campaign was being waged by the authorities accusing Catholic activists in Slovakia of "clerico-fascist" leanings and connections with anti-Communist forces in the West.

The local authorities were notified of the Slovak Catholics' intention to hold the demonstration in a letter dated March 10. It came from František Mikloško, a lay Slovak Catholic activist.[11] "The silent demonstration," the letter said, was to support the call for Slovakia's vacant dioceses to be filled "in accordance with the Holy Father's decision" and "for full religious freedom and human rights." The demonstrators would express their support for religious freedom, the letter said, by holding a lighted candle. The letter closed by asking the authorities to "take note of this announcement." According to the letter, the demonstration was to be held on the basis of Article 28 of the Czechoslovak Constitution and Article 6 of Law No. 68 of 1951. News of the demonstration spread by word of mouth among Catholics in Bratislava. Unconfirmed reports said that posters calling for participation in the demonstration appeared in the churches of Bratislava.

The authorities reacted by banning the demonstration. Mikloško countered that the ban was in violation of Article 28 of the constitution and that he could not accept the authorities' view that "public order could not be guaranteed at the rally."[12] He announced that the demonstration would go ahead as planned.

Two days before the demonstration, Czechoslovak television broadcast a lengthy program of interviews with representatives of Churches and religious communities in Czechoslovakia who spoke of the religious freedom enjoyed in the country and condemned the Western notion of human rights.[13] The dean of the Bratislava collegiate chapter of canons, Štefan Záreczký, a member of the progovernment organization *Pacem in Terris*, expressed his "surprise and apprehension" at the planned demonstration. He said that such actions had purely political goals and had very little to do with religion, and that "certain self-appointed organizers want to create an atmosphere of distrust and provoke an undesirable confrontation; they are breeding confusion among honest believers instead of preaching Christ's Gospel; they want to achieve personal popularity by whipping up passions."

On the eve of the demonstration the Slovak youth daily *Smena* attacked "groups of laymen, which, though not large, dexterously manipulate religious slogans in order to weaken our building of socialism."[14] *Smena* said that some Western radio stations had reported on various campaigns by Christians in Czechoslovakia to collect signatures and plans for a silent, candlelight demonstration. The paper concluded that the demonstration had been organized by the World Congress of Slovaks in Canada.

Fearing that the demonstration might attract young people, the Slovak authorities took repressive action in advance. Posters announcing the event were torn down. Students were warned against taking part in the unauthorized demonstration and threatened with losing their place at the university or in university dormitories.[15] Some university faculties reportedly directed students to sign a declaration saying that they had been informed that the rally had "an antisocialist character" and that they would not take part in it. Moreover, students were prematurely sent on vacation on the day of the demonstration.

The demonstration went ahead as planned. People lit candles and sang hymns; the police then called on them to disperse, because, they claimed, "the demonstration was illegal.[17] The appeal went unheeded and the police drove into the crowd with cars six abreast; the demonstrators, however, blocked off some of the cars. The police then resorted to street-cleaning trucks that drove through the demonstrators at a speed of about 10 kilometers an hour, showering them with water.

When this failed to move most of the demonstrators, riot police armed with nightsticks, dogs, and three water cannon were called in. Security forces pushed people off the square and herded them into side streets. Tear gas was used and many people were beaten, including BBC's radio correspondent David Blow. Western observers said that many people had been detained, including television crews from West Germany and Austria who had been trying to film the demonstrators. The correspondent for Austrian television, Otto Hörman, said that he had seen at least 100 demonstrators brought to the same police station where he was held; many had to stand facing a wall with their hands up.

The British Foreign Office made an official complaint, saying that it was "appalled" by what happened. Austrian Foreign Minister Alois Mock expressed "deep dismay" at the violence used by the Czechoslovak police. The Austrian Journalists' Union protested against the "revolting way" in which Austrian journalists had been handled. The United States issued a statement to the Vienna CSCE follow-up meeting declaring that it "deplored the police brutality exercised in breaking up the ... demonstration." On April 15, the European Parliament unanimously approved a resolution condemning "in the strongest possible terms the persecution of Christians." It was appalled at the fact that in the "heart of Europe, just 32 miles from Vienna, where the CSCE follow-up conference is now sitting, a government should cynically ride roughshod over the solemn promises it entered into under the Helsinki Final Act." The resolution said that "this will inevitably have damaging consequences for any steps toward further détente in East-West relations." In Hungary, a group of 42 intellectuals and religious activists sent a declaration to Charter 77 expressing solidarity with "all those who fight for freedom of conscience, religion, and free expression of their views."

In a telephone interview with Austrian Radio on March 26, the Slovak dissident Ján Čarnogurský, who had helped organize the rally, said that it had been "a new form of civil protest," because in the 40 years of the ČSSR "a prior-announced demonstration by citizens ... [had] virtually never taken place before."[18]

On March 27, in a telephone interview with Radio Free Europe, Cardinal Tomášek said that "the demonstration in Bratislava for religious freedom was an expression of the religious revival in Czechoslovakia;" that the rally had been "the voice of believers" and not something that had been manipulated from the West. The day before, Tomášek had told Reuters that "loyalty to the Church is becoming more and more active; it is stronger than in the past, especially among young people."[19]

On April 8, at the CPCS CC plenum in Prague, Secretary General Miloš Jakeš sharply, albeit indirectly, condemned the demonstrations and warned that authorities would prosecute those who attempted actions "aimed at causing unrest and tension."[20] Slovak Prime Minister Peter Colotka spoke of "regrettable illegal actions" aimed at creating pressure and "stirred up by evil-minded propaganda from abroad."[21]

*Czechoslovak Dissident Speaks Out in* l'Unità. Five days after the demonstration, the Italian Communist party's newspaper published an article[22] by Erika Kadlecová, a signatory to Charter 77 who was the Czechoslovak official responsible for religious affairs during the Prague Spring.

She opened her analysis by discussing the significance of the campaign for signatures to the 31-point petition, remarking that over 400,000 signatures had been collected at that stage: "an unprecedented figure for a politically inert, socially anesthetized country like ours." Moves of this sort over the previous 20 years had gained the support of some dozens, at best some hundreds of people, she said; and there was nothing surprising about that:

> Anyone who might be disposed to commit himself to any such action knew that, by that very fact, he was becoming an "outlawed" citizen; although he remained at liberty, he could expect the loss of his job, public denigration through the press, his home being searched, his telephone being cut off, and his passport and driver's license being confiscated. He had to recognize that he was putting at risk not only himself but also his wife, his children, and all friends who did not rapidly distance themselves from him.

The fact that the new petition had been signed by so many people represented "not so much an explosion of Catholic religious feeling as a light[23] of civic hope," she continued.

> This does not have its origin here in our country; it is the reflection of détente in the international situation, and above all of the new phenomena developing in the Soviet Union, which, whether they are of greater or lesser significance in themselves, are bound to stimulate a resumption of movement in the other socialist countries.

The consequent pressure for change would be exercised wherever it was possible to concentrate forces and act with the minimum of risk.

In the ČSSR, religion offered a suitable terrain for such movement, Kadlecová said. It continued to be

> the ideological system most widespread among the population; the Churches are tolerated by the constitution and have well-functioning organizational bases, highly qualified personnel, and legal links with centers and individuals abroad providing aid and encouragement.

This, she said, explained why the petition of the Catholics had been signed by people belonging to other denominations, or to none, even though the latter did not always share all the claims made in the document. Kadlecová concluded her article as follows:

> By now, we are used to the idea that in Czechoslovakia everything is possible, in the worse sense of the term. Today, it is possible to arrive at the conviction that here in our country everything is possible, but in the better sense of the term. We now have Jehovah's Witnesses who

fight for the investiture of Catholic bishops; there are "revolutionary Marxists" who struggle for freedom of conscience; and there are Church officials who oppose the movement for the restoration of the rights of the Catholic Church, going against their own cardinal. The pressure has been so strong that all the cards are being reshuffled.

## 33
## EAST GERMAN CHURCH DEBATES POLICY
### Barbara Donovan

Developments in the Soviet Union and the GDR stirred hopes within the Evangelical Church in the GDR after years of resignation among laity and leaders. Gorbachev's domestic reform program and his "new thinking" in foreign policy, as well as the SED's clear support for the latter and its easing of restrictions on travel in the wake of a warming in inter-German relations, raised expectations and fueled debate. This was evident at the Synod of the Federation of Evangelical Churches held from September 18 to 22, 1987, in Görlitz.

As in the past, the synod was the scene of a wide-ranging discussion about social and political conditions in the GDR. Unlike in preceding years, however, the speeches, although still critical, were tinged with optimism: many speakers saw signs of "a new openness" in the GDR as a result of developments in the Soviet Union. The optimism was coupled with new resolve among a number of participants to push the SED toward change by making specific demands and by initiating open, public discussion of social and political problems. The Church leadership remained anxious, however, not to jeopardize state support for Church activities by pressing too hard for change.

*Church Support for "New Thinking."* The Evangelical Church's support for Gorbachev's initiatives in foreign policy and arms control were first articulated in a document entitled "New Thinking in the Atomic Age," which was released in August 1986.[1] Reviewing Soviet and East German statements on peace and foreign policy, the document stated that there was a "clear affinity between these new starting points ... and our own beliefs on peace and politics." According to the document, the Church's resolution rejecting "the spirit, logic, and practice of deterrence," adopted in early 1986, was now viable. The document encouraged parishes to press for the "new starting points" to be put into practice.

In keeping with these views, the synod at Görlitz welcomed a document entitled "Ideological Dispute and Common Security," which was released jointly by the SED and the West German Social Democratic Party. The synod praised the attempt, as embodied in the paper, to handle disputes peacefully "despite the dividing line between the blocs."

There were other reasons for optimism in the Church. It voiced its support for the easing of restrictions on travel. Moreover, according to some observers, the state had moved toward greater "openness" in society; for example, it permitted an unofficial peace demonstration to take place in early September 1987, and allowed members of the Church's peace groups to participate in the officially organized two-week-long Olof Palme Peace March. At a Church Congress in East Berlin in June, representatives of the state were on hand to answer questions from the audience.

*New Impetus to Criticism.* At the same time, Gorbachev's policies and the small signs of change within the GDR had given fresh impetus to those seeing a need to criticize openly social and political conditions in the GDR. At the synod, the Dean of Erfurt, Heino Falcke, demanded that the current "controlled opening up" of foreign policy, as seen in Honecker's visit to the FRG, be matched by an "openness" in society. He argued that the GDR had to learn to discuss its problems frankly and publicly.

Falcke strongly urged the synod to adopt a petition entitled "A Rejection of the Practice and Principle of Delimitation."[2] The document criticized the contradiction between the GDR's policy of détente and its policy of delimitation, which curtailed personal contacts between East and West. Referring to the frustration caused by restrictions on travel, the document stated that 26 years of the Berlin Wall and 6 years of separation from Polish neighbors had "resulted in our society becoming severely diseased." The widespread response to this petition, Falcke said, showed "that we are touching upon a painful subject."

Moreover, the document stated, "delimitation in practice" contradicted the building of trust between peoples, necessary for a credible policy of peace. According to the document, the Soviet Union had come to recognize this link between internal and international peace; the GDR had taken a number of steps in the right direction, but it was "the responsibility" of the Church to encourage the SED to go further. The petition made a number of specific demands on the SED, such as the resumption of free travel between Poland and the GDR; improved opportunities for travel and contacts between East European countries; the right, regardless of age, job, or family ties, to travel to the West; and open discussion of the specific financial problems that apparently prevented a further increase in travel to the West. According to the document, the issue of travel was only the tip of the iceberg, however. Indeed, it said that a fundamental discussion of the impact of delimitation was necessary within the Church and society to develop solutions to the problems.

*Was the Church Leadership Holding Back?* The proposed petition elicited a tremendous amount of controversy at the synod. Support for the general content of the document came from all quarters, but doubts were expressed as to whether it was an appropriate time for adopting such a resolution. The Head of the

Federation of Evangelical Churches, Werner Leich, warned against burdening the state with unreasonable demands at a time when the Church's relationship with the state was improving. The petition, another speaker said, would only obstruct "the process of increased openness." The call for caution was reinforced by yet another speaker, who told of a meeting with state officials at which they had said that the petition was influenced by "provocative and anarchic elements." The SED further expressed its disdain for the discussion within the Church by giving the synod hardly any coverage in the media, in contrast to much more extensive reporting on the congress held in Berlin in June.

The final resolution adopted by the synod did not formally support Falcke's petition, although it did include a number of similar demands. It called for more contact between East Germans and other Europeans, from both the East and West, and expressed support for "dialogue and openness in society," which would contribute toward reducing "the strains and isolation experienced by individual citizens and whole groups." A synodal letter to the authors of the petition, however, said that "a formal rejection of the practice and principle of delimitation is not timely." As in past years, the synod's final report further criticized restrictions on travel, the GDR's restrictive policy on information, problems in the educational system, and called for the establishment of a social service as an alternative to compulsory military service. The synod also spoke of widespread hostility toward foreigners living in the GDR, a feeling that was also prevalent in the Church.

The Church leadership was evidently facing a challenge. Tension between the leadership and more radical forces within the Church had been evident for the past decade. Much of the resignation that was at the root of this tension was apparently being turned around by new policies from the Soviet Union and the hopes they were raising. At the same time, these changes were giving key members of the Church the courage to speak openly on controversial issues. The leadership was clearly optimistic, but cautious and anxious not to pursue a confrontational course with the state. Such an attitude, however, exposed the Church to criticism for forgoing its "duty to stand by those ruled rather than those ruling." Meanwhile, the SED, worried about raised expectations among the populace, was also putting pressure on the Church in an effort to moderate critical voices within it.

*Signs of Increasing State Pressure.* In 1988, there were a growing number of signs that the state was putting pressure on the Church to curtail its critical discussions of social and political problems in the GDR. This pressure was matched by a new resolve within the Church to insist on the need for such open discussions. Coming against the background of rising public expectations for domestic changes, the conflict reflected an increasingly tense political atmosphere. Leading SED officials appeared to be reappraising the party's policy toward the Church, fearing that political events may have undermined the viability of its policy. Meanwhile, the Church had become engaged in a fresh round of debate over its role in a Communist state.

Church publications, for the first time since the early nineteen-eighties, were subjected to state censorship. In May two regional Church weeklies failed to appear because their editorial staff had refused to bow to state censorship. Two others could only be printed and distributed after certain passages had been taken out or changed. The authorities prevented the distribution of four regional Church weeklies and an issue of the Evangelical News Service; they had all reported on the synod of the Berlin-Brandenburg Church from April 8 to 12, at which emigration and other controversial topics were discussed. At the beginning of April, another Church weekly failed to appear, and one was printed with some passages whited out; the affected passages were from a speech by Bishop Christoph Stier, who had demanded an open discussion of the GDR's problems. The authorities also banned Western correspondents from covering the latest regional synods.[3]

In talks with the Church leadership the SED demanded that the Church curtail its political activities. Erich Honecker and Bishop Werner Leich, head of the Federation of Evangelical Churches, met on March 3, 1988, the 10th anniversary of the first meeting between Church and state leaders in March 1978; the meeting was seen as confirming the SED's current policy toward the Church. It became known, however, that an earlier Church-state meeting had taken place.[4] On February 19, 1988, the Politburo member in charge of Church affairs, Werner Jarowinsky, had held talks with Leich and accused the Church leadership of tolerating practices that amounted to interference in state affairs and disrespect for the law. Jarowinsky said that the Church was being used by the "class enemy and counterrevolutionary forces," which wanted to turn it into an opposition force. He demanded that the leadership distance itself from "hotheads and fanatics." In order to preserve the good relations between the state and the Church, he said, it was necessary that the "realistically minded forces" in the Church regain the upper hand.

*Background to the Conflict.* In the preceding years Church leaders had begun to sense that the SED was becoming more tolerant and that East German society was gradually becoming more open. A number of factors now combined to prompt the party leadership to try to arrest, if not reverse, this trend.

The first of these factors was the Church's gradual expansion of its political role since the early nineteen-eighties. The Church used to concentrate its political activities on peace issues and on protesting the excessive militarization of society. Grassroots groups within the Church, however, soon went on to confront environmental problems and human rights violations. The Church became bolder in demanding political change within the GDR.

The Church's discussions of the GDR's emigration problem was another factor that helped to tip the scales in favor of a harsher state policy toward the Church. Emigration was a sensitive issue. The large number of people who wanted to move to the FRG was not only embarrassing, but also a practical problem for the SED. The GDR's labor force was already threatened by a low birth rate. A more liberal emigration policy would place the GDR in danger of losing a substantial proportion of its scientific and technical elite. Moreover, would-be émigrés began demonstrating openly, which pointed to the potentially explosive nature of the emigration issue. The authorities reacted with harsh measures. Almost 400 would-be émigrés were detained from the beginning of December on, and approximately 20 were given prison sentences averaging 30 months.[5]

Emigration became the most frequent and heated topic of discussion within the Church. A large number of would-be émigrés came to the Church for moral support. Moreover, although the Church's policy was to try to persuade people to stay in the GDR in order to work for change from within, it felt increasingly compelled to be more critical of the SED's emigration policy. In talks with the state, the Church insisted that an open discussion be initiated about why so many people wanted to leave and to encourage the state to attempt to improve the social and political conditions in the GDR. In the words of one leading Church figure, the state would have to come to realize that "change is inescapable."[6] In a move that aroused controversy in both East and West Germany, an East German Church leader blamed the allure of the FRG as being partly responsible for the high emigration figures and suggested that the GDR and the FRG had colluded in establishing quotas on the number of people allowed to emigrate annually.[7] The result of the Church's activities was that the emigration issue received the kind of publicity, in both the domestic and Western media, that the régime had sought to avoid.

Perhaps the most significant factor, however, in prompting the state to apply more pressure on the Church was the nervousness of the SED leadership as a result of the popularity in the GDR of Gorbachev's reforms. Dissidents and Church activists, using the Soviet leader's arguments, became bolder in making their demands. By cracking down on Church activities, the SED clearly hoped to regain any political power that it was perceived to have lost as a result of unofficial debates over Gorbachev's reformism and over changes in the GDR.

*The Church's Reaction.* Church leaders rejected claims that the Church exacerbated conflicts through its public discussions of controversial issues. According to the Church, it had been forced into the role of providing a forum in which the problems and deficiencies of the system could be openly discussed, by the state's reluctance to admit to the existence of these problems, let alone tackle them. Indeed, the Church leaders demanded with new forcefulness that the SED initiate an open and fair discussion about the changes that would be necessary if the tension in East German society were to be abated.[8]

The state's pressure on the Church, however, also succeeded in fueling a dispute within the Church over its role in East German society. This debate, which was gradually gaining force, first surfaced during the Berlin-Brandenburg

Church synod when General Superintendent of the Berlin Churches Günter Krusche accused Bishop Gottfried Forck of being too tolerant of nonconformists and would-be émigrés.[9] In a speech assessing the Church's handling of the conflicts, the Bishop defended the decision to defend would-be émigrés, saying that it was always the Church's responsibility to stand up for justice and equality.

Krusche criticized the Berlin-Brandenburg Church's "undifferentiated support of everyone and everything." This type of activity, he said, put the Church in a position to be blackmailed by nonconformist groups; the Church wound up tolerating a great deal just to prevent things from going from bad to worse. Krusche called for a reappraisal of the Church's relations with its peace, environmental, and human rights groups, saying that a partial disassociation from their activities was unavoidable.

Krusche's remarks were a clear indication that the Church had yet to resolve what role it should play in society. Although his remarks were rejected by the majority of the participants at the synod, they were bound to find support among conservative and skeptical members of many parishes throughout the GDR. The SED clearly hoped to exploit these apparent divisions.

At an Evangelical Church Congress that was held in Halle from June 23 to 26, the deputy chairman of the Federation of Evangelical Churches, Manfred Stolpe, said that the GDR's government had in the past decade "pursued a cautious reform policy; but now a qualitative leap forward is in order." In the Church's strongest appeal to date for the SED to follow Gorbachev's example, Stolpe said that "Without perestroika things will not work any more, [and this also applies] to the GDR." The Church congress also approved 20 "Theses on Societal Renewal," demanding that the Communist party renounce its monopoly on truth and its fundamental claim to superiority over other institutions. The theses also called for the introduction of electoral laws that would allow for a choice in the selection of political candidates, an accountable court system, and a revision of the GDR's criminal law.[10] The Church did not cease to put pressure on the state, however.

*Conclusion.* The SED was unlikely to go back to the pre-Honecker era of Church-state relations, that is, resorting to Stalinist measures to control society. However, the SED had begun to ask itself whether the Church was still able to keep its more critical elements under control and had decided, therefore, to exercise a greater measure of control itself. This was unlikely, however, to ease the political tension in the GDR.

# IX. SPREADING DISCONTENT

## 34
## SOCIAL PROTESTS IN ROMANIA
### Vladimir Socor

Despite the blackout maintained by the Romanian authorities, accounts of the Braşov workers' demonstration of November 15, 1987, reached the Western media from Romanian and foreign eyewitnesses and from Western diplomats in Romania. While differing over some details, almost all of the accounts agreed on the essentials of what took place that Sunday in Romania's second largest industrial center.[1]

Protesting fresh wage cuts and chronic food shortages, several thousand workers from the Red Flag truck plant, instead of going to vote in the local elections taking place nationwide that day, marched out at about 9:00 A.M., heading for the party and administrative headquarters downtown. During the one-hour march, they sang a Romanian hymn from the 1848 revolution and chanted, "We want bread" and "Down with dictatorship." They were joined by workers from the Braşov Tractor Plant, where work stoppages had taken place in some sections during the preceding week in response to wage cuts there as well. Along their way to the central square, and once there, the workers were joined by thousands of the townspeople. Estimates of the size of the crowd varied from 5,000 to 20,000, perhaps reflecting its growth as the events unfolded. Some eyewitnesses reported that workers were handing out leaflets.[2]

Some demonstrators forced their way inside the party headquarters, where they tore apart or threw out of the window furniture, telephones, and files. In the square below, this debris was ignited along with party banners, placards, and Nicolae Ceauşescu's portraits which had been torn down from the walls. Some smaller fires were also started inside the party headquarters. There the workers discovered ample food supplies—including items such as flour, cheese, oranges and chocolates, all of which had been very difficult for ordinary citizens to obtain for years—stocked up for the party bureaucrats. This added to the demonstrators' indignation, so that these supplies too, were ransacked and thrown into the square.

According to the reports, Braşov's RCP First Secretary and Mayor (the two posts were merged in Romania) Dumitru Calancea was beaten and rushed to hospital. Two fatalities among the militia were widely reported. There was no indication of plunder or of damage to nonparty property at any point. The forces of order, after some apparent hesitation, moved in before dusk. Both militia and army troops with armored personnel carriers were used to clear the downtown area. No clashes were reported.

A brief video film shown on November 23 in the evening newscasts of Italian television was the first visual document of the event available in the West. According to those who saw it, the film, shot mostly on the run in downtown Braşov by a Western traveler, showed a large public building damaged by fire and emitting smoke; a street bonfire and several small fires of party flags, propaganda posters, and clearly recognizable official portraits; and a large crowd of demonstrators being pursued by armored vehicles. During this phase, one group of workers was seen holding aloft and defiantly waving a national flag, and knots of men were seen stopping from flight to throw stones at their pursuers. Two photographs published in the left-wing Paris daily *Libération* showed cleanup operations at dusk, on a street strewn with broken glass and debris; uniformed personnel and armor were again in evidence.[3]

*An Accumulation of Grievances in an Industrial Show Place.* The wage cuts, reportedly imposed for the second consecutive month for nonfulfillment of the plan, came against a background of increasingly severe food shortages (bread was rationed to 300 grams a day and few staples were available or affordable). Compounding the impact of the wage cuts, a presidential decree that went into effect nationwide on November 10 reduced the population's use of electricity and heating gas by a further 30 percent, from a level already deemed inhumanely low after successive reductions in preceding years, and imposed draconian penalties for exceeding that quota.[4]

The régime had long used Braşov, a city of 400,000 (formerly very mixed ethnically but by 1987, 80 percent Romanian), as an industrial show place, whose production was mainly export-oriented and whose work force was regarded as belonging to the elite of Romania's working class. The Red Flag truck plant, with 22,000 workers, and the Tractor Plant, with some 25,000 workers, ranked among Europe's largest in their branches and exported some three-quarters of their output. The authorities were proud to point out that close to half of the work force belonged to the Communist Youth League.[5] That the protest should have broken out here was indicative of the depth of discontent among the working class. Its outbreak on election day made the authorities' claim of a 98 percent election victory sound more hollow than ever.

This was not the first mass protest at the Red Flag plant: at least one earlier case had been documented. In November 1983 some of the plant's sections went on strike to protest the first wage cuts under the new system penalizing production shortfalls regardless of whether the causes lay beyond the workers' control. The strike was put down.[6]

*Dissidents' Reactions and Student Meeting.* The mathematician and former top economic adviser, Mihai Botez, a leading figure among Romania's dissidents, issued a statement observing that the events in Braşov ought not to have surprised anyone; indeed, they had been almost predictable. They highlighted the divorce between the rulers and the ruled, testified to the "rejection of the leadership's economic and political strategies," and amounted to "a severe warning to the leaders" from the working class. Arguing that repression would be "the costliest option, with disastrous implications for the country," Botez urged the Romanian leadership to heed the "desperate message" implied in the workers' protest.

The former high-ranking party and state official, Silviu Brucan, a Marxist intellectual and promoter of reform, issued a statement to Western correspondents in Bucharest, the main points of which overlapped with Botez's. Brucan said that the workers' "cup of privations is now full" and that "a period of crisis has opened between the Communist party and the working class." He, too, warned against repression, which would antagonize "world public opinion, that formidable force in defense of human rights. Repression may result in total isolation, this time not only from the West but also from the East." Urging the leadership to make "a sincere effort to come to terms with [the public's] legitimate grievances," Brucan said in conclusion that he was voicing the position of an "overwhelming majority" within the party.[7]

In addition to these individual statements, one public gesture of support for the Braşov workers was reported. According to information originating from party sources in Bucharest and separate reports citing Western travelers returning from Braşov, several hundred students at Braşov Polytechnic held a meeting of solidarity with the workers on their campus on November 22.[8]

*Official Silence and Repression.* For 17 days the Romanian media maintained total silence about the Braşov events and subsequent repressive measures. There were arrests on November 15, and police investigations started as early as November 16 at the Red Flag plant and the Tractor Plant, where at least 200 workers were reportedly picked up for questioning. Some Braşov Polytechnic students were investigated following their protest on November 22, according to the reports. Foreign journalists reported from Braşov that the city was being patrolled by soldiers with submachine guns and dogs. Patrols and cordons were reportedly deployed in greater strength around the party headquarters, the approaches to the Red Flag plant, and the campus. In contrast to all other cities in the country, where public lighting was turned off as an energy-saving measure, Braşov was well lit at night, evidently for security reasons.

The authorities' delayed and disingenuous public response to the protest could only add to that concern. On December 2, an "extraordinary meeting of workers' representatives" at the Red Flag plant "unanimously" endorsed measures to dismiss and subject to judicial investigation both the plant management and "certain elements" among the workers. By simultaneously threatening to hold the dismissed technical management accountable for failing to ensure fulfillment of the plan and for "unlawful wage leveling," the party authorities were clearly attempting to shift responsibility onto hapless executives and circumvent the workers' real problems. Indeed, the meeting's communiqué and its lengthy message to Ceauşescu made no mention of the workers' concerns. Instead, the two documents abounded in pledges on behalf of the workers to mobilize for hard work and fulfill the production plans.[9]

*Bizarre Mini-purge in the Party.* Four members of the RCP Central Committee were expelled from the CC and the party for contravening Ceauşescu's injunction and organizing a Sunday outing instead of working overtime for the fulfillment of the annual plan.

On Sunday, November 22, the first secretary of the RCP in Dolj County (southwestern Romania), Gheorghe Matei, who had been appointed to his post only two months earlier, held a hunting party for leading county officials and a visiting instructor from the Central Committee in Bucharest. Two of the participants were full members and two others were candidate members of the RCP Central Committee. The county party secretary in charge of organizational work was accidentally shot and seriously wounded during the hunt. Had it not been for this mishap, Ceauşescu might never have heard of the hunting party, since the CC instructor had failed to "report" it to the higher authorities in Bucharest.

The hunting party took place only two days after a meeting of the Political Executive Committee on November 20, at which Ceauşescu criticized the performance of the economy and of party organizations in general and demanded that party activists work overtime to mobilize people and resources to make up for shortfalls in plan fulfillment.[10] The fact that the Dolj County leaders went hunting instead of remaining at their posts that Sunday was considered a contravention of the PEC's decisions.

Evidently acting on urgent instructions from Ceauşescu, a joint plenum of the party organizations of Dolj County and the county seat of Craiova voted the next day to dismiss the Sunday hunters from their party, administrative, and managerial posts and to expel them from the party for having allowed themselves to be "taken away from their important tasks in party and state work."[11]

The hunt, coming in the wake of the protest demonstration on November 15 in Braşov which showed the degree of discontent in the country, gave Ceauşescu an opportunity to gain some political advantages out of a seemingly minor incident. He seemed to place the onus of improving the situation on the local party *aktiv* by implying that economic performance could improve if only activists and managers showed the necessary responsibility and dedication in their work. If Ceauşescu's statements were a response to the deeper issues raised by the Braşov events, however, then that response was strikingly out of touch with the country's problems. Instead of attempting to deal with these problems,

Ceauşescu offered his usual solutions of greater mobilization and more political education to support existing policies.

Despite the sense of frustration and dismay underlying his remarks, there was no sign that Ceauşescu was losing confidence. In spite of the events in Braşov, the party leader felt secure enough to launch a new and hectic round of Middle East diplomacy and schedule within two weeks no fewer than four meetings with foreign leaders—PLO leader Yasir Arafat, Egyptian President Hosni Mubarak, Syrian President Hafiz Assad, and Zambian President Kenneth Kaunda. The Romanian leader's quest for personal aggrandizement again seemed to provide a diversion from the real problems at home.

*Social Protests Continue.* Largely unorganized social protests spread to various parts of Romania in December 1987 in the wake of the mass protests in Braşov.[12] The authorities responded with a combination of selective repression and ambiguous promises of economic concessions of little value to the public.

Students demonstrated in the night of December 2 to 3 in the city of Timişoara near the Yugoslav border, according to reports cited in the Western and Yugoslav media. An estimated 600 to 800 students marched from the university hostels to the city center, where some townspeople joined them. The demonstrators demanded "bread and meat," sang the 1848 hymn "Awake, Romanian" (as the Braşov demonstrators had done), and chanted "Long Live Braşov" and "Long Live Moldavia" (the latter evidently a reference to the protest demonstration in February 1987 by students in Iaşi). The demonstration proceeded peacefully, and no damage to property was reported. There was no intervention by the authorities.[13]

Student protests and expressions of support for the workers of Braşov also took place at the University of Cluj, the capital of Transylvania. Also in Cluj, but unrelated to the student protests, two leaflets proclaiming solidarity with the workers of Braşov were disseminated.[14] In Bucharest, what appeared to be two acts of arson occurred within days of each other in and near the headquarters of the RCP daily *Scînteia*. Before dawn on December 4 a fire was started around the base of the Lenin monument in front of *Scînteia* House and the monument was also defaced. On December 15, also before dawn, a fire occurred inside the printing plant of *Scînteia*, destroying that day's first edition, which contained Ceauşescu's opening address on the previous day to the RCP's national conference.

Strikes by industrial and transport workers and other forms of protest were widely reported by Western correspondents to have taken place between late November and mid-December in Sibiu (southern Transylvania), Brăila (lower Danube), and Craiova (southwestern Romania). No certain information emerged about these and other reported strikes and protests.

Protest leaflets were circulating in various parts of the country. One of these was circulated in December by the Romanian Democratic Action group, a Bucharest-based group with an anonymous membership that claimed to have followers in the provinces; the group disseminated a number of other leaflets throughout 1987. Another leaflet disseminated in two versions in 1987, mainly in Transylvania, was bilingual, in Romanian and Hungarian, and originated from a small group in Budapest that called itself Free Romania and whose members belonged to the small but growing community of ethnic Romanians who had emigrated for economic reasons to Hungary, where they were tolerated. These leaflets called for gestures of passive resistance to protest the Ceauşescu régime's policies and to show support for the workers of Braşov. No public protests were known to have been sparked off by these two appeals, however.[15] In the last week of December, eyewitnesses reported from Bucharest that hand-written leaflets pasted on the windows of subway cars and strewn about subway platforms called for an end to the "Ceauşescu dictatorship" and to the "Ceauşescu dynasty"; militiamen scurried to collect these leaflets.

The Romanian authorities maintained complete silence about these developments. Moreover, private Romanian sources spoke of other protests elsewhere in the country, but these were not confirmed by Western reports. Such a proliferation of social protests was unprecedented in Communist Romania. It clearly reflected the mounting social tension generated by material deprivation and public frustration with political immobility and official resistance to change. The unrest remained, however, scattered and unorganized; and the authorities were able to deal with it effectively by avoiding confrontations and isolating the protesting groups from one another. Despite the recurrence of protests, there was still no indication that this affected Ceauşescu's firm hold over the party or that it was about to induce the leadership to reconsider its social and economic policies.

*Repressive Measures Against Protesters.* In response to the increase of dissident activity and social protests, the Romanian authorities took legal action against some of the workers arrested after the Braşov demonstration and cracked down on the dissident community.

In an oblique (and thus far the only) official acknowledgment of the mass protests of November 15, 1987, in Braşov, the Romanian media said on December 2 and 3 that some workers who had "provoked disorder" there would be "brought to account in accordance with the law ... depending on the gravity of their deeds." By the time that the announcement was made, investigations by the Securitate were already in full swing at the Red Flag truck and the Tractor plants in Braşov, with at least 200 workers detained and hundreds of others being brought in for questioning at police offices. Some were sent to Bucharest for further investigation.[16]

A "Committee To Support the Detainees" that was reported to be active in the underground in Braşov in December 1987 claimed to have compiled a list of 425 workers, including several women, who were being held for investigation and possible prosecution. A correspondent for the French daily *Le Matin* witnessed two meetings of committee members in workers' apartment blocks near the Red Flag and the Tractor plants. The committee was trying to raise funds to aid the families of detained workers.[17]

According to reports from Braşov that reached Western diplomats and correspondents in Bucharest shortly afterward, a group trial was held in Braşov, at which at least 60 participants in the protests were sentenced to terms ranging from 1 to 4 years imprisonment for "hooliganism."[18] One subsequent report spoke of 25 workers being sentenced to prison terms of up to three years; it was not clear whether or not this referred to another group trial.[19]

The Bucharest media maintained complete silence about the arrests and trials. At the CSCE meeting in Vienna, the USA, the United Kingdom, and Denmark (which was speaking on behalf of the EEC countries) publicly criticized the repressive measures against the protesters in Braşov; but the Romanian delegation left those statements unanswered.[20]

In their announcement of December 2-3, the authorities also intimated that some participants in the Braşov protests would be dismissed from the factories and sent to other locations, which observers surmised could be mines, where the authorities had long complained of a labor shortage. Forcible relocation had been used before as a method of dealing with protesting workers: in 1977 as many as 4,000 of the striking coalminers in the Jiu Valley were relocated, as were the presumed ringleaders of the strikes in 1986 at two factories in Cluj.

In an apparent effort to silence articulate critics during a period of social tension, the authorities arrested most of the prominent dissidents in early December. By detaining or holding them under house arrest at a time of spreading social protests, the authorities managed to isolate them from protesting groups of workers and students, and to silence an important source of information about the situation in the country.

# 35
# CRACKDOWNS IN THE GDR
Barbara Donovan

On November 25, 1987, East German security forces raided the offices of an environmental library in the Zion Church in East Berlin, detaining five people and confiscating documents, samizdat journals, and copying machines. What at first appeared to be an isolated move against the editors of two samizdat journals quickly turned into a wide-ranging crackdown on dissidents. Officials arrested at least another 12 people attending a Church vigil being held to demand the release of the activists; and a number of other East Berlin dissidents not directly associated with the Evangelical Church were detained, had their apartments searched, or were placed under house arrest. A total of 21 people were arrested in East Berlin, although all were later released from custody. Similar actions were reportedly also carried out in other cities (Rostock, Dresden, Jena, Weimar, Wismar, and Halle) and activists were ordered not to travel to East Berlin.[1]

Criminal proceedings against the four activists arrested during the raid were dropped following more than a week of protest actions and of negotiations between the Evangelical Church and the state prosecutor's office. Two men, Wolfgang Rüddenklau and Bert Schlegel, were charged with "organizing themselves to pursue unlawful activities" and producing "antistate literature"; preliminary proceedings were initiated against two other activists as well. According to the lawyer representing the Evangelical Church, the authorities had not been able to produce firm evidence that a non-Church publication had been printed in the library.

The Zion Church had long been a focus of attention for the East Berlin security authorities. The environmental library, which was founded in 1986, became a central meeting place for both Church and independent peace and environmental groups. Not only did it house a wide range of books not otherwise available in the GDR, but one of the two leading samizdat journals in the GDR, *Umweltblätter* [Environmental Pages] was also printed in the library. The authorities also claimed that *Grenzfall* [Border Case], which was not affiliated with the Church, was produced in the library. The first nonofficial peace march in the GDR, held in September, had its origins in the Zion Church. Moreover, from November 27 to 29, the Church was to have been the forum for a three-day, unofficial ecological congress with participants from other East European states. The seminar was held but was moved to the neighboring parish of St. Elizabeth.

The authorities were clearly intent on curtailing the activities of political dissidents acting from within the Evangelical Church. At the same time, the scope of the action was much wider than it initially seemed and affected the entire range of dissident activities in the GDR. It appears that the samizdat journals were used not just as an excuse to clamp down on the activities of groups within the Church but as a pretext to initiate a general crackdown on unofficial activities. Several factors, including Gorbachev's call for glasnost and the joint SED-SPD paper on ideological disputes, prompted a more open discussion within the Church and at the same time encouraged other dissidents. The state's action was clearly designed as a deterrent.

*A Change in Course?* The raid came after a lengthy period of what seemed to be increasing willingness by the régime to tolerate dissident activities. Following the raid, activist groups issued an appeal that recalled their optimism after the state had allowed them to stage their own peace march and had let Church groups participate in the official "Olof Palme" peace demonstration in September.[2] "This seemingly promising development," the appeal said, "is called into question after the latest events."

Manfred Stolpe, deputy chairman of the Federation of the Evangelical Church, offered another opinion. He believed that the action had to be seen in the context of an SED policy of gradually allowing greater independent activity and thought. Unwilling to see too many changes take place simultaneously, the party and state leadership wanted to create "breathing space" for themselves.[3] This, he contended, would explain the apparent contradiction between the crackdown and the relatively critical atmosphere at the Writers' Congress of November 24-26.

*A "Malicious Disturbance."* The arrest on January 17, 1988, and during the following week of a number of East Berlin's most prominent dissidents constituted the biggest crackdown on the GDR's political opposition in at least a decade. Through what appeared to be a concerted, planned effort, the SED moved to reconfirm its political authority by severely weakening the dissident movement.

The event that sparked the arrests and deportations was the attempt by human rights activists to stage a demonstration parallel to the official annual rally on January 17 commemorating the deaths in 1919 of the Communist revolutionaries Rosa Luxemburg and Karl Liebknecht. Security police arrested some 120 young people who had assembled and begun to unfurl banners or, as the party newspaper *Neues Deutschland* claimed, had intended to "maliciously disturb the mourning." A week later the security forces deported to West Germany 54 of those arrested (together with members of their families) who had previously applied for emigration visas. Most of the remaining detainees were subsequently released. An additional six prominent East Berlin dissidents were, however, arrested on January 25. Eleven activists were eventually sentenced to prison terms ranging from six months to one year for unlawful assembly, and seven of East Berlin's most outspoken dissidents, including the dissident balladeer Stefan Krawczyk, were under investigation for having "treasonable ties with the West."

*An Unexpected Turn of Events.* All of the dissidents, however, were later released from prison. On February 2, Krawczyk, his wife Freya Klier, daughter Najda and the ecological activist Bert Schlegel (who had already been sentenced to six months imprisonment) and his fiancée Ines Czygullon arrived in the FRG; the official news agency ADN reported that this was in accordance with their formally expressed desire to emigrate. In addition, five members of the activist group Initiative for Peace and Human Rights—Ralf Hirsh, Wolfgang and Regina Templin, Bärbel Bohley, and Werner Fischer—together with Vera Wollenberger of the Church from Below, left the GDR. With the exception of Hirsch they were all granted East German passports, theoretically enabling them to return to the GDR after periods ranging from six months to two years. Two environmental activists sentenced to prison terms, Till Böttcher and Andreas Kalk, were released on probation and given permission to stay in the GDR.

The attempt to resolve the controversy elicited by the crackdown in such a manner took many people by surprise. Many factors suggested that the crackdown had been carefully organized. Plans for the unofficial demonstration had been made public as early as January 9, and it is likely that the SED seized upon it as a chance to intervene. Many observers considered that the state's response was out of all proportion to the demonstration and that the SED had used it as an opportunity to deplete the ranks of the dissident movement in East Berlin by deporting many of those involved; to warn those remaining to curb their activities; and to sap the movement of morale and of human resources.

In deporting many of those arrested on January 17, the SED resorted to a tactic repeatedly employed by the East German authorities to rid the country of unwanted elements. In addition, the state was thus able to exploit the division within the Evangelical Church and the dissident movement, between those who wanted to leave the GDR and those who wanted to stay and press for improvements in the system from within. Moreover, by deporting these people, the authorities removed many of those responsible for the embryonic unofficial political opposition movement. Finally, one observer speculated that the authorities might have been anxious to prevent those openly articulating their right to leave (a group working specifically toward this purpose was formed in East Berlin in September 1987) from joining forces with mainstream dissidents.

*Reconfirming Authority.* Although the authorities backed down in the aftermath of the raid on the Zion Church in November, releasing those arrested and dropping charges against them, this time they were clearly initially prepared and had been given permission to take additional steps to prevent any protest from spreading. These steps included the arrest on January 25 of six of the most vocal activists in East Berlin and of four people who began a hunger strike to protest the arrests. The experience of the Zion Church affair appears to have played a key role in determining the manner in which the crackdown was implemented and avoiding the mistakes made before. One political activist recalled that people thought then that "a victory over hard-liners" had been won. After the authorities' second move against dissidents, however, Western journalists reported that the remaining activists had clearly been intimidated.

The question that remained was why such a crackdown took place. Western observers, noting contradictions between Erich Honecker's persistent efforts to improve the GDR's image and this shift toward a tougher stance domestically, speculated that there were policy differences between members of the Politburo or that the security police, headed by Politburo member Erich Mielke, were determined to undermine Honecker's policies. Similarly, one might speculate that the seeming inconsistency between the initial crackdown and the apparent retreat was caused by different priorities within the SED Politburo. If this were the case, then the move would suggest that those advocating the importance of a positive international image for the GDR now carried greater weight in the Politburo than the die-hards.

The extent of the initial crackdown, however, would appear to indicate that there was a basic consensus among the top leaders. The move must be viewed against the background of an SED leadership made uncertain and nervous by the repercussions for the GDR of Gorbachev's reform plans. The SED felt that dissidents were using Gorbachev's slogans and arguments as a means of advancing their own political goals. Gorbachev's ideas quickly became popular in the GDR, and political activists became bolder and enjoyed increasing support. Most significantly, they were receiving a great deal of publicity in the West German media, much of which was available to the East German public on West German television. By cracking down on dissident activities with the sort of force displayed there, the SED clearly hoped to reestablish any political authority lost in the course of the unofficial debates about Gorbachev's reformism, thus emphasizing that it intended to maintain its monopoly on defining the terms of any debate about reform and on deciding when and how—if at all—the GDR would introduce reforms.

*Quelling Additional Discontent.* The decision to allow the emigration to the FRG of Krawczyk and the other prominent dissidents from East Berlin fitted clearly into this pattern. Indeed, it is likely that the emigration of Krawczyk, who had attracted a tremendous amount of attention on account of his outspokenness, was one of the SED's goals from the beginning of the crackdown. The members of the Initiative for Peace and Human Rights were among those dissidents most interested in attracting Western publicity as a means of furthering their interests. Upon arriving in the West, Krawczyk, Klier, Wollenberger, and the activists from the Initiative for Peace and Human Rights told reporters that they had not left the GDR voluntarily. All of them had been faced with a choice between emigration and a prison term.Two dissidents, Barbel Bohley and Werner Fischer were allowed to return.  Nevertheless, the deportations can only be seen as a victory for the SED.

The unexpected decision by the authorities to release all the dissidents detained can also partly be explained as an attempt to quell the rising discontent among young people expressed in the protest meetings in Churches that were held virtually every night since January 17. On February 1, for example, some 2,000 people gathered in St. Bartholomew's Church in East Berlin to hold a service in support of the right to emigrate. Similar meetings, although smaller in size, were reported in more than 30 towns in the GDR. At the same time, leading Church officials in East Berlin and a lawyer affiliated with the Evangelical Church, Wolfgang Schnur, played a significant role in persistently pressing for the release of the detainees in talks with the authorities.

The GDR was plainly unsettled by the effect that the crackdown was having on its relations with the FRG. Although the crackdown had yet to affect on-going negotiations adversely, the events attracted extensive critical coverage in the West German media. Clearly, the GDR was very sensitive to this type of criticism, above all because East Germans had access to the West German media.

Moreover, it threatened to undermine the GDR's carefully cultivated image in the FRG. The GDR quickly went onto the offensive: the party daily *Neues Deutschland* began to put out a barrage of articles critical of life in the FRG.

The SED's turnaround was a significant step toward defusing internal tension and repairing the damage done to the GDR's image in the West. This did not, however, appear to be incompatible with its attempts to weaken the dissident movement in the GDR. The SED succeeded in depriving East Berlin's independent activist community of some of its most prominent members and spokesmen, and its actions reportedly had a demoralizing effect and impaired the self-confidence of many remaining activists. The SED remained wedded to a policy of preventing the emergence of any significant alternative political force. Despite the SED's calculation, emigration became a hot political issue.

*Emigration and Dissent.* On February 13 at least 300 people demonstrated in Dresden for the right to emigrate. The demonstrators carried banners and chanted slogans demanding the dismantling of the Berlin Wall and freedom to leave the GDR. The security forces did not intervene immediately, but there were scuffles between police and demonstrators after the crowd had begun to disperse.

This demonstration was one of a number of events that again brought the issue of emigration to public attention. The wave of deportations following the crackdown in January apparently encouraged people who had unsuccessfully applied to emigrate to protest openly for the right to do so. At the same time, the emergence of emigration as a volatile political issue appeared to exacerbated the conflict that existed within independent political groups and the Evangelical Church between those wishing to leave the GDR and those wishing to demonstrate their dissent at home.

While the two groups were united by the detentions of January 17, the deportation of Krawczyk once more split the camp in two. Those bent on remaining in the GDR reportedly felt helpless and resigned upon learning of the emigration of the man who until then had symbolized the determination of those who wanted to stay in the GDR; the would-be emigrants saw his deportation as an encouraging sign.

## 36
## YUGOSLAV WORKERS MARCH ON PARLIAMENT
### Milan Andrejevich

Almost 5,000 workers from a farm equipment manufacturing company went on strike and marched through Belgrade on June 17, 1987, to protest against the latest federal austerity program. The marchers were joined by another 5,000 people outside the Federal Assembly building. The event was the most radical action by Belgrade workers in the postwar period. A Zagreb daily asked whether the demonstration marked "the beginning of a revolution or a counterrevolution."[1]

This was the third time since November 1987 that striking workers, with support from bystanders and others, had turned out to state their grievances to government officials. The march also indicated the militancy among Yugoslav workers, which had gained momentum in the preceding 18 months as the federal government struggled to find solutions to the worsening economy, a problem rooted in the unwieldy, inefficient, and wasteful socialist economic system. Since February 1987, four separate attempts by the government of Prime Minister Branko Mikulić to launch an economic recovery program had failed. The LCY conference of May 29 to 31, 1988, had lent support to Mikulić's latest scheme, which called for radical economic changes through the introduction of a more market-oriented system.

*Strikes and Protests.* There had been a growing number of officially tolerated strikes. In 1987 about 365,000 workers took part in 1,570 strikes, 22 times as many participants and 8.5 times as many strikes as in 1982. Official trade union figures indicated that in the first half of 1988, there were 799 strikes involving 150,997 workers; 5.7 percent times as many strikes and 48.8 percent as many participants as in 1987.

The demonstration in Belgrade was preceded by peaceful demonstrations in other parts of Yugoslavia, which also reflected the workers' sense of having been cheated by a corrupt establishment. In November 1987 almost 9,000 workers in the Macedonian capital of Skopje marched to the National Assembly building to demand higher pay and the resignation of government officials, whom they accused of financial wrongdoing. The workers were granted half of the 100 percent increase in wages that they had demanded, but there was no major purge of party and government officials. In December 1987 some 1,500 workers from a machine factory in Ljubljana marched to the steps of the Slovenian National Assembly building, where they demanded a 50 percent increase in pay and the reimbursement by the Slovenian government of $32,000,000 owed to the factory by Iraq. Government officials refused to meet with the striking workers, who then met at another location where they decided to organize a strike committee for the purpose of proposing that an independent Social Democratic Party be established as an affiliate of the Socialist Alliance, the party's umbrella organization.

Protest marches involving fewer people were also becoming commonplace. In May 1988, 320 coal miners from the Tuzla area, in northeastern Bosnia, marched 175 kilometers to meet with Federal Assembly officials after mine officials had refused to give them buses for the purpose. Zvonimir Hrabar, who was then President of the Yugoslav Trade Union Confederation, met with the miners in the chamber of the Federal Assembly; they protested their pay cuts and demanded the removal of the mine's board of management.

*The Protest in Belgrade.* The strike in Belgrade was both a protest against proposed reductions in pay and a political demonstration. The action began when almost all the 4,800 employees of the Zmaj agricultural machinery enterprise in Zemun voted on June 16 to march on the Federal Assembly building the next day. The workers' action, which was organized by local trade union officials, was in response to the news of across-the-board pay cuts of up to 40 percent, depending on job classification. Since the beginning of the year wages for many workers had already been reduced. Because of austerity measures, the average salary for Zmaj workers had dropped from about $130 a month earlier in the year to about $100 and was to fall to about $88 in July; the average monthly grocery bill for a family of 4 in Belgrade was double the take-home pay of Zmaj workers. According to official data, the average wage for Yugoslav workers was about $150 a month and 60 percent of them earned less than the average. Zmaj had reduced wages because it had been losing money to competitors in Belgrade and Ljubljana that had obtained the most attractive contracts. Zmaj was Yugoslavia's largest producer of farm machinery.

As in the protest in Skopje, the Zmaj workers' march quickly took on broader political overtones. The state-run media reported no incidents of violence or arrests in the course of the seven-hour strike, which began at 10:00 A.M. As the strikers marched the two kilometers from the factory to the Federal Assembly building, they were joined by several hundred workers from other enterprises in Zemun. The workers shouted "We want bread" and branded government officials as "thieves and traitors." Many sang the national anthem and carried framed photographs of Josip Broz Tito, the flags of the Communist party and Yugoslavia, and banners stating "We belong to Tito and Tito belongs to us." Some of the workers called for the government to resign and accused the leadership of betraying Titoism.[2]

The president of Zmaj's trade union, Rade Pupovać, said that the workers had not marched on the Federal Assembly building "because of anger but rather because they are hungry." Some striking workers expressed other frustrations, however, with chants such as "You [the government and party] have sold out Kosovo" and "Kosovo is Serbia," an expression of their displeasure with the authorities' response to the racial tension between Serbs and ethnic Albanians in Kosovo. Workers also called on students to join them in the protest. According to the Zagreb daily *Vjesnik*, several students stood on the steps of the assembly building and spoke of the need for an alliance between students and workers. One Zmaj worker was quoted as saying that "If in 1968 the workers had joined the students, [the situation] would not have come to this,"[3] referring to the student protests of June 1968 against the "inequalities of socialism."

Shortly after the workers arrived, President of the Federal Assembly Dušan Popovski, a Macedonian, told them that only 300 workers would be allowed to enter the building. When the protesters' shouts only grew louder, Deputy Prime Minister Janez Zemljarić met with workers on the front steps of the building and promised them that the government would discuss all their demands and that he would personally visit the factory the following week to talk with the workers. Zemljarić was booed when he said that their wages had been cut because the firm had failed to cover its losses in 1987 and that "All of us who are working honestly have been harmed by the fact that for years we have been spending [and living beyond our means] ... and we must all share the burden..." Workers responded with shouts of "How much do you earn?"—an apparent stab at those leaders whom the Yugoslav press accused of corruption.[4]

*Economic Roots.* The announcement of the pay cut came close on the heels of a federal government economic program which was approved by the Federal Assembly on May 15; it was intended to reduce wages, government spending and investment while freeing prices, imports, and the foreign exchange rate and devaluing the dinar by 23.9 percent. The program was deemed necessary to revitalize the economy, but was bound to increase the cost of living for many people with already limited incomes. Hence, the Zmaj protest probably reflected the frustration prevalent in many enterprises around the country. This frustration was certain to grow with the expected rise in inflation. The inflation rate for May was 149 percent, far below the average of 170 percent in 1987; but the price increases subsequently caused inflation to rise to almost 200 percent, the highest rate since World War II.[5] In any event, even if the program succeeded in limiting inflation to "only" 95 percent, the workers' standard of living, which had fallen by nearly 35 percent in the preceding six years, was bound to drop even further before it improved.

The demonstration against the government's economic measures were only a part of the wider public discontent with the party, the government, and the system. The Titoist "social contract" had been largely based on a continued rise in the standard of living and the growth of a consumer society, the achievement of which appeared increasingly doubtful. Although Tito, as the creator of the system, was ultimately responsible for the these difficulties, he had become a symbol of fair treatment for the workers under the "socialist" system and was apparently seen in their selective memories as a benevolent father figure who led the nation in better times.

The problem was large and complicated, however. Even if the leadership could muster the political will and strength to introduce long-overdue reforms, there would be at least short-term economic dislocation and most probably continued protests by workers who felt cheated and betrayed.

## 37
## HUNGARIANS PROTEST ROMANIAN POLICIES
### Judith Pataki

Tens of thousands of people marched to the Romanian Embassy in Budapest on June 27, 1988, to protest Romanian leader Nicolae Ceaușescu's plan to raze between 7,000 and 8,000 of the country's approximately 13,000 villages,[1] including those inhabited by ethnic Hungarians.[2] It was the biggest unofficial rally in Hungary since the 1956 Revolution. The number of demonstrators was generally estimated at 40,000, but a member of the Hungarian Television crew said that it had been close to 100,000.[3] The Romanian authorities responded by ordering the closure of a Hungarian Consulate and the expulsion of its staff and the closure of the Hungarian Cultural Center in Bucharest.

*Authorities' Tacit Approval.* Although the demonstration was organized by 12 independent groups, including the Hungarian Democratic Forum, the Network of Free Initiatives, and the Foundation for Transylvanian Artists, it apparently had the authorities' tacit approval. A police statement and articles in the press warned people not to respond to any provocations instigated by outside groups, implying that the régime was not planning to use force against the demonstrators.[4]

A two-page report on the demonstration in the Communist Youth League's weekly *Magyar Ifjúság* of June 24, for example, warned that there might be "foreign" elements at the demonstration who would try to provoke violence. It added that "any disorder during Monday's demonstration would not be unwelcome to the Romanian authorities," since a provocation at the Romanian Embassy would put the Hungarian government in a difficult position internationally. *Magyar Ifjúság* and the June 27 issue of the Patriotic People's Front daily *Magyar Nemzet* said that leaflets calling for Romania to return Transylvania to Hungary and containing other irredentist statements had been circulated in Budapest before the demonstration along with legitimate leaflets about the protest. A "non-Hungarian hand," not the demonstration's organizers, had been behind the distribution of the irredentist pamphlets, *Magyar Nemzet* said. *Magyar Nemzet* also asked the population not to confuse the victims of despotism, the Romanian people, with the despots themselves. Most of the articles in the Hungarian press about the razing of villages in Romania said that the project was not directed against only minority groups, although they would suffer the most since they would be dispersed and could therefore lose their cultural identities. The project should be stopped, the articles said, because it would not help Romanians produce more food and would destroy not only homes, churches, and cemeteries but also the entire rural tradition in Romania and an important element of European tradition.

*The Demonstration.* The demonstration was covered by both Hungarian Television and Radio Budapest and was widely reported by Western news agencies, which particularly noted that the demonstrators had remained peaceful. The government daily *Magyar Hirlap* also praised the protesters for behaving responsibly. The police presence was barely noticeable at Heroes' Square, where the demonstrators first gathered at 7:00 P.M., waving Hungarian flags—no red flags, the symbol of communism, were seen—and carrying signs bearing the names of not only ethnic Hungarian villages but also ethnic German and Romanian villages that were to be destroyed. Signs with such slogans as "Hitler, Stalin, Ceauşescu" and "End the Dictatorship" were also carried, some by ethnic Romanian nationals who had fled to Hungary in the preceding one-and-a-half years. According to eyewitnesses, many young people participated in the event, including ethnic Hungarian refugees from Transylvania, of whom well over 10,000 had escaped to Hungary.

At Heroes' Square the actor István Bubik read a statement by the nonconformist playwright István Csurka denouncing the planned demolition of the villages as genocide. The statement also pointed to the significance of the demonstration, saying that "This moment is glorious and hopeful.... This is the first time that we are demonstrating for Hungary's sake."[5]

Carrying candles and torches, the crowd marched a few blocks to the Romanian Embassy, which was surrounded by Hungarian police. The organizers of the demonstration waited some five minutes outside the gates in an attempt to present embassy officials with a statement asking Romania to honor international agreements on the rights of ethnic minorities. The gates were not opened, however. The crowd was quiet and no disturbances were reported. Since the statement was not accepted by the Romanians, the demonstration's organizers sent translations of the text to other embassies in Budapest.[6]

*Romanian Reprisals.* The day after the demonstration, the Romanian government ordered the immediate closure of the Hungarian Consulate in Cluj-Napoca and gave the consular staff 24 hours to leave the country.[7]

In a speech made to the plenary meeting of the Central Committee of the Romanian Communist party, also on June 28, Ceauşescu denounced the demonstration and hinted that the Romanian Embassy in Budapest might be closed as well. As expected, Ceauşescu blamed the Hungarians for the deterioration of bilateral relations, repeating his standard accusation of chauvinism and irredentism.

On June 29, the Romanian government ordered the closure of the Hungarian Cultural Center in Bucharest. The center had been completed for about 10 years, but never allowed to open. The rented building had been used as a storage area for the Hungarian Embassy.[8] Reports also confirmed that Romanian border guards were returning Hungarian tourists to Hungary for the slightest irregularity, and trips organized by the Hungarian travel agency IBUSZ were canceled by the Romanian side.

In response to the Romanian actions and statements, the Hungarian News Agency (MTI) said that "responsibility for violating the consular agreement ...

between the two countries lies with the Romanian government."9 (In 1984 Romania closed its consulate in Debrecen, Hungary.) MTI added that the "severe" Romanian measure would not divert Hungary from "its principle aimed at deepening the friendship between the Hungarian and Romanian peoples [and at] strengthening the connecting role of national minorities living in their countries."

*Was the Demonstration Warranted?* In view of the intensified conflict between Romania and Hungary, the question was raised a number of times as to whether the demonstration should have been held. When asked by a Radio Budapest reporter on June 30 whether the government had erred in allowing the demonstration to occur, party and government chief, Károly Grósz, replied that

> The government had, and has, no right to forbid a march or a demonstration. The government's role according to the constitution is to prevent unconstitutional conduct and to ensure public order. Had the demonstrators attacked the Romanian Embassy, the authorities would have used force to defend it. International agreements oblige us to do so, but the demonstration was disciplined. The marchers asked for the protection of the survival of their Hungarian brothers and sisters, the protection of universal culture, and within that the protection of the [ethnic Hungarian] Sekler tradition. They did not protest against Romania, against the Romanian leadership or [against] socialism.10

Although Grósz apparently expressed the majority opinion on the issue, the newly elected first secretary of the Budapest Party Committee, Mihály Jasso, for example, questioned the value of such demonstrations in furthering constructive bilateral talks.11

All the major Hungarian dailies did not report on the demonstration until June 29, after Romania had ordered the closure of the consulate in Cluj-Napoca. The newspapers denied that the Hungarian government was behind the demonstration but praised the demonstrators for their responsible conduct. The press also indirectly condoned the protest; for example, *Magyar Nemzet* reported that "as a group of Romanian refugees appeared, the crowd opened up in front of them and greeted them with applause."

On July 1 a new radio station with a broadcasting range of 1,000 kilometers—far enough to be received by all the ethnic Hungarians in neighboring countries—was installed in Székesfehérvár, about 40 kilometers southwest of Budapest. The station, which had a strength of 100 kilowatts and cost 235,000,000 forint, broadcast Radio Budapest's program on short wave.

38
# DISSENT IN THE STREETS
Vladimir V. Kusin

In 1988, what had long been special to Poland began to engulf the bloc. Dissent was taking to the streets, from the Caucasus to Prague, from Tallinn to Ruse. More people than in the early stages of Soviet and East European reform were now willing to stand up and be counted when demanding the redress of their grievances or more extensive change. Demonstrations were fast becoming part of the reformist landscape.

The demonstrators largely focused on matters that did not feature in official programs of reform or were only touched upon. Workers and managers had yet to take to the streets to urge speedier changes in the way the economic system worked; bureaucrats had yet to wave banners demanding the reorganization of government agencies; and the party's rank-and-file had yet to march on a secretariat demanding that the local party boss be dismissed because of his unwillingness to adopt reformist thinking.

Instead, historical and national injustice, political and ideological constraints, economic misery, and various sorts of mismanagement, in the field of environmental protection, for example, had led to protests, unrest, and disturbances. While public demonstrations were a product of reformism and glasnost in the sense that they made them possible, they were a response to Communist rule and misrule in general, not just to Mikhail Gorbachev's reformist design.

*Historical and National Injustice.* The number and size of demonstrations provoked by a sense of grievance arising from historical and national injustice were greatest in the USSR. Five underlying causes were discernible: opposition to Soviet rule in general and to Russification in particular, as in the Baltic states; grievance over injustices perpetrated by Stalin, as in the case of the Crimean Tatars and as reflected in demonstrations in Moscow and elsewhere to commemorate the victims of Stalinism and to demand that a monument be erected to them; resistance by the local elite to interference from Moscow, as in Alma-Ata; conflict between two non-Russian nationalities, as in the clashes between the Armenians and the Azerbaijanis; and the surfacing ideology of Russian nationalism, as projected in demonstrations of the "Pamiat" group. Public appeals to the authorities to allow more extensive Jewish emigration also belonged to the category of national and historical grievance.

Few demonstrations on these grounds were noted in Eastern Europe. A rally in Budapest in June 1988, marking the 30th anniversary of the execution of Imre Nagy, was broken up by the police. The tension over the Hungarian minority in Romania could have become a breeding ground for them; 700 people castigated the Ceauşescu régime for its treatment of the Magyar minority at a public gathering in a theater in Budapest on March 6, 1988. Nevertheless, as far as the overriding national grievance in Eastern Europe was concerned, namely, the incorporation of these countries into the Soviet orbit, people had not so far taken advantage of the more open climate under Gorbachev to demand redress publicly.

*Political and Ideological Constraints.* Poland, the GDR, and Czechoslovakia led the field in public demonstrations about political and ideological matters. The spirit of independence associated with the Solidarity labor union still inculcated almost every unofficial gathering in Poland. Church congregations frequently spilled over into brief demonstrations that were decidedly unfriendly to the régime and to the system. Students demonstrated (and clashed with the police) on March 8 in commemoration of the repression of 1968 and to demand the restoration of their independent union. Enterprising people staged satirical happenings in the streets of Wrocław and elsewhere.

There had always been a massive attendance at religious pilgrimages in Poland. The fact that pilgrimages had become so large in Slovakia, however, caused the Czechoslovak authorities considerable concern; and that more than 500,000 people had signed a petition for religious freedom and that a religious demonstration (albeit small) took place in front of the Archbishop of Prague's palace on March 6, added to their anxiety.  A peaceful religious vigil in Bratislava on March 25, 1988, ended when the police used brutal force.[1] Young people held a vigil in Prague every year on December 8 to recall the death of John Lennon; and there was an unlicensed human rights demonstration in the Old Town Square of Prague on December 10, 1987. The police regularly broke up unauthorized pop concerts and the gatherings organized by Charter 77 and unofficial groups in the youth subculture.

A string of demonstrations occurred in the GDR from January to March 1988, beginning with an attempt by a group of dissidents to join an official procession under their own banner. The main themes of public demonstrations of dissent in the GDR were human rights, the environment (both of which were supported by the Evangelical Churches) and emigration to West Germany.

*Economic Hardship and Ecological Mismanagement.* Poland had led the way in protest demonstrations against price increases in the nineteen-seventies, and the Solidarity era continued to inspire the working class.  Even the mere threat of a strike or a demonstration made many enterprise managers back down after a rash protests from February to May 1988, and grant higher wages than the government had said were to be paid out to compensate for price rises. There were smaller demonstrations against the building of a nuclear facility in Poland. Yugoslavia long had a thousand or more wage strikes a year. The Serbs and the Montenegrins from Kosovo took to the streets in the middle of 1988 to demand strict action against what they perceived as Albanian irredenta in the province. Many Slovenes demonstrated in July-August 1988 against the arrest and trial of four activists who publicized plans by the military for coercive suppression of liberal elements in the Republic.  Unrest in Braşov in the autumn of 1987 put Romania on the map as a country where demonstrations were not unthinkable.

On three occasions the people of Ruse in Bulgaria were on the streets to protest against the flow of poisonous fumes from a Romanian chemical plant at Giurgiu across the border. Environmental concern also occasioned open petitions and demonstrations in the USSR.

*The Régimes' Problem.* In tackling street demonstrations, democratic governments always sought to tread the middle ground between downright suppression and dangerous license. Thus far, Communist régimes had worked on the premise that unofficial demonstrations were by definition bad and had to be either taken over and guided by the government or crushed. Gorbachev's pursuit of democratization meant having to learn to live with street demonstrations and, hence, devise rules for the game. Such rules, generally in force in the West, rested on the principle that very few subjects of a demonstration could give the police grounds for intervention so long as the methods of the demonstrators were peaceful and did not contravene the law (for example, on obstructing traffic or on obscenity).

Given the populace's vast reservoir of pent-up feelings and against the background of the accumulated myriad of wrongdoings, not to mention the authorities' ingrained belief that to demonstrate against a Communist government was the devil's doing, it was not easy for the Communist régimes to strike the right balance between excessive lenience and excessive harshness. How was one to go about ensuring that street demonstrations were no more than an innocuous pastime harmless to the régime, and show this régime in a favorable "democratic" light when it sat on a mountain of past and present injustice?

The issue of street demonstrations was, moreover, influenced by extraneous causes. The fact that the police clamped down on students in Poland, on dissidents and religious activists in Czechoslovakia, on dissidents meeting before the March 15 demonstration in Hungary to mark the outbreak of the nation's revolution in 1948, and on would-be émigrés in the GDR may have had something to do with a fear that if one gave domestic demonstrators an inch they would travel the whole Armenian mile. Furthermore, factions in the leaderships may have disagreed over what constituted the right mixture of acceptance and intolerance, so that the treatment of demonstrators differed from case to case, depending on who held sway at any particular moment. Over the years, all East European régimes had built up  powerful and extensive police forces that perestroika had not dismantled; parts of these apparatuses of surveillance, intimidation, and coercion may have been deactivated for the time being; but their influence behind the scenes on political decisions had hardly ceased to exist. Moreover, secret police activities in the bloc had a strong international dimension, and the KGB still no doubt pulled many strings. It was distinctly possible that the approach of the various governments to street demonstrations was being orchestrated from the center. Finally, many diehard East European leaders must still have had doubts about whether Gorbachev's policies would survive in the USSR; should it be necessary to tighten the screws again later, they might speculate, it would be better not to loosen them much now.

In short, even if the Communist régimes were genuinely and honestly trying to relax their approach to street demonstrations within the general framework of a drive for democratization, there would be many formidable impediments to doing so for some time to come. Meanwhile, demonstrating was contagious, as was seen in the West. Demonstrations were also more difficult to keep within the limits agreed by the participants than other forms of dissent. The contest of wills between the rulers and the ruled would therefore seem to have become more volatile.

# X. KEYWORD: PLURALISM

### 39
### SOVIET "INFORMAL GROUPS" ORGANIZE
#### Vera Tolz

*Officially Sanctioned Conference.* The first officially-sanctioned conference of unofficial groups in the Soviet Union was held in Moscow from August 20 to 23, 1987, by representatives of forty-seven unofficial—or as the Soviet press called them—"informal" Soviet groups.[1] *Moscow News* and *Ogonek*, two of the Soviet press organs that reported on the event, provided positive and, at first glance, informative coverage of the conference. Comparison with Western accounts of the proceedings revealed, however, that certain aspects of the debates were omitted in the Soviet press reports, apparently in order to play down the political overtones of some of the discussions and proposals made at the conference.

During the preceding year the Soviet authorities had started to display a more tolerant attitude towards the activities of the "informal groups," and clear attempts were made to engage them in public life, albeit under strict official control. Both the fact that the authorities allowed the conference to be held and the fact that, as *Moscow News* disclosed, it was prepared under the supervision of the Moscow City party Committee were evidence of this policy.

The main subject of discussions at the conference was the role of public initiative in the period of perestroika, and the majority of the proposals put forward echoed discussions on ecological, cultural, economic, and sociological issues that had taken place in the Soviet press.

*Moscow News* reported that the participants put forward proposals to provide help for invalids and elderly people who did not get enough support from the state and also to build a monument to victims of repressions. The newspaper failed to mention that what was actually proposed was to build a monument to the victims of Stalin's purges. *Ogonek* did not mention this proposal at all but did provide details of other proposals made at the conference. These included projects to support self-management at Soviet enterprises, to combat social inequality, to publicize juridical violations, and to democratize the USSR's electoral system. *Ogonek* also reported that the conference had called for an end to the extremist and nationalist inclinations of certain unofficial groups.

After *Ogonek's* account of the conference was published, the Moscow correspondent of the British newspaper *The Guardian* met with the conference's participants and wrote a detailed report on the event, which included many significant details omitted in the Soviet press coverage.[2]

*The Guardian* carried the full text of a manifesto of "The Federation of Social Clubs," which was drawn up at the end of the conference. Some of the federation's proposals were vaguely discussed in *Ogonek*, but neither *Ogonek* nor *Moscow News* carried the full text of the manifesto. Certain proposals, especially from a chapter covering the federation's aims "in the political field," were not mentioned at all. This applied, for instance, to the federation's call for a clear distinction to be made in Soviet law between antistate activity and criticism of deficiencies in the existing Soviet system.

*The Guardian* also reported on the proposals put forward by the seminar "Democracy and Humanism," one of which was to abolish the one-party system and to introduce political pluralism in the Soviet Union. It said that the majority of participants in the conference had rejected this idea.

The Soviet periodicals also failed to provide any background information on the seminar. This could be found, however, in the unofficial journal *Glasnost*, which was published in Moscow by literary critic and former political prisoner Sergei Grigoriants. According to issue No. 1 of *Glasnost*, the seminar wanted the truth to be told about the USSR's past and present and supported the development of democratic traditions in the country.[3] It called for the de-ideologization of Soviet society and for the abolition of the articles on anti-Soviet propaganda and anti-Soviet slander in the Soviet Union's criminal codes. Many of the seminar's members, such as Malva Landa, Valeriia Novodvorskaia, and Iurii Kiselev were activists in the Soviet human rights movement, especially during the nineteen-seventies.

*Independent Journals Proliferate.* In contrast to previous periods, the editors and compilers of many samizdat periodicals supported the domestic policies of the leadership and were eager to bring their periodicals into the open. Some of the journals were successors to samizdat publications of the nineteen-seventies whose authors paid for their activities with prison terms. Other periodicals were totally new and were being published by representatives of "informal" groups, the number of which had been growing rapidly since Gorbachev came to power.

Compared with the "informal" groups, independent periodicals attracted relatively little attention in the official media. As a general rule, those articles in the official press that dealt with samizdat publications continued to adopt a critical tone. The main target of press attacks was the journal *Glasnost*. Grigoriants failed to obtain official permission for his periodical and, despite his support for restructuring, was accused by *Vecherniaia Moskva* of attempting to discredit Soviet policies.[4] From time to time, independent journals published by Soviet rock groups also came under attack in the official press, generally being accused of being too Western-oriented.[5] Only the Leningrad-based independent journal *Merkurii* escaped criticism in the pages of the official media.[6]

The shortage of information in the official press about independent journals and the one-sided treatment they received when they were mentioned led to the establishment of a special periodical entitled *Zhurnal zhurnalov*. This independent journal, the purpose of which was to collect and disseminate information about samizdat publications, was first published in Leningrad in December 1987. The Samizdat Department of Radio Liberty obtained the text of the first issue, which contained a transcript of a meeting held in Leningrad in October 1987 of editors of independent journals.[7] The meeting was sanctioned by the authorities, and journalists working on official newspapers and journals (*Izvestiia, Smena, Selskaia molodezh, Avrora, Literaturnaia gazeta*, and *EKO*) and for the Novosti press agency attended the meeting. Nevertheless, the Soviet press failed to report it.

According to the account in *Zhurnal zhurnalov*, some major problems connected with independent publications were raised at the meeting. A number of speakers discussed why, despite the greater openness of the official press, the number of samizdat publications had markedly increased. They pointed out that it was still too much of a struggle to get items published in the official newspapers, and it was often not worth the effort. In addition, unofficial journals discussed subjects that were still taboo for the official press. In his bulletin *Express-khronika*, for example, former political prisoner Aleksandr Podrabinek dealt with the situation of Soviet political prisoners. The editor of *Vestnik soveta ekologii kultury*, Mikhail Talalai, said that while his publication was devoted primarily to an issue that did receive coverage in the official press (the preservation of historical monuments), it was at times the first to address certain problems. He cited as an example the preservation of cemeteries, a question that the official press began to discuss only after it had first been raised in his journal.

The granting of legal status to unofficial journals was also debated at the meeting. Some participants insisted that legal recognition of unofficial journals should be included in the new Law on the Press, the draft of which was to be published in 1988. The legal status of samizdat journals was a particularly thorny problem because, as was pointed out at the meeting, the "informal" groups and their periodicals could develop into a sort of "opposition" in Soviet society. According to Sergei Grigoriants, who in 1987 obtained a copy of the draft Law on the Press, the new law emphatically reasserted the state's monopoly on the spread of ideas through the printed word.[8] Subsequently, *Pravda* strongly condemned those "informal" groups whose members aspired to create "opposition parties" in the USSR.[9]

Similarly, the authorities appeared to have no intention of making the reproduction of unofficial journals any easier for their publishers. Like the samizdat publications of the nineteen-sixties and nineteen-seventies, more recent independent publications were laboriously typed with carbon copies. As was emphasized at the Leningrad meeting, access to copying-machines was still very difficult. (On October 2, 1987, on the eve of the meeting of independent editors, TASS strongly attacked the publishers of *Glasnost* for using the printing equipment of a Moscow library without official permission.) Hopes that permission might be given for the creation of cooperative publishing houses had not been realized. One of the participants in the meeting revealed the existence of a secret resolution of the CPSU Central Committee instructing the official press to stop discussing the issue of cooperative publishing houses on the grounds that there were no plans to establish them. (At the end of 1987, the head of the Soviet publishing industry, Mikhail Nenashev, stated in an interview with TASS that cooperative publishing houses would not be set up because the USSR did not have an adequate material and technological bases for them.)

*The Democratic Union.* On April 27, Soviet jurist Boris Kurashvili spoke out in an interview with the Latvian Komsomol newspaper *Sovetskaia molodezh* about the need to create an organization, called the Democratic Union, that would unite socially motivated people who were not members of the Communist party. Kurashvili said that the Democratic Union was not to be a second party in the Soviet Union (the CPSU would still have predominant control) but would fulfill some of the functions that alternative parties usually did—namely, to monitor and criticize the government and party apparatus and to make sure that they executed their duties in the most efficient way.

At the end of the interview, Kurashvili stressed that he thought a Democratic Union might come into being in the near future. Ten days later, a Democratic Union was created but not in the form proposed by Kurashvili. More than a hundred representatives of "informal groups" from various cities in the Soviet Union took the initiative into their own hands and created the Democratic Union, styling it "an alternative political party." (The Democratic Union was the second organization described by its organizers as a party in opposition to the CPSU to have been created in 1988: the first came to being in Estonia in January.)

On May 7, 8, and 9, Western news agencies carried numerous reports of a meeting in Moscow of representatives of many "informal groups" from Leningrad, Moscow, the Ukraine, and Siberia who gathered in three apartments in Moscow to set up the Democratic Union with the intention of uniting the "informal groups" behind a common front.[10] From the reports by Western agencies it is clear that the majority of organizers of the Democratic Union had a dissident background and were criticized regularly in the Soviet press. Some participants in the inaugural meeting on the Union were, however, members of "informal groups," which had so far been tolerated by the authorities.[11] A special session to discuss the Democratic Union's political platform was hosted by Evgeniia Debrianskaia, who was an active member of the seminar "Democracy and Humanism," which had been under attack in the Soviet press for "anti-Sovietism," and who was a prominent figure in the "Group for the Establishment of Trust between East and West," the official attitude toward which had softened a little in 1988.[12]

Speaking to Western journalists, Debrianskaia announced the Union's main principles, which certainly were not likely to find any support among the Soviet authorities. The stated aims were: the establishment of a multiparty system in the USSR; the adoption of a new constitution to replace the existing document, which made the CPSU "the leading and guiding force" of Soviet society; the creation of independent trade unions and a free press; and the withdrawal of Soviet troops from Eastern Europe, the Western Ukraine, and the Baltic states, which the meeting's members described as territories "occupied" by the Soviet Union.

On May 7 and 8, the news agencies reported that the police kept a close watch on the meeting: some participants were questioned and even detained. The police, however, stopped short of making wholesale arrests and shutting down the conference. On May 9, the agencies reported that the police had adopted stricter tactics in an attempt to try to prevent the organizers of the Democratic Union from holding discussions. The police also forced participants at the inaugural meeting on the Union who did not have resident permits for Moscow to leave the city.[13]

The announcement of the creation of the Democratic Union came only three weeks before the Reagan-Gorbachev summit, an event that the Kremlin could be expected not to wish to mar with a major incident that might reflect badly on Soviet human-rights policy. Further, the creation of the Union coincided with the increasing trend towards glasnost in political matters that became noticeable from April onwards. Following the rebuff that conservative forces in the USSR received from *Pravda* on April 5, the campaign for glasnost in the Soviet press entered a new stage, with the possibility of political changes becoming the focus of debate.[14]

It was in the course of this intensified debate over political issues that the interview with Boris Kurashvili appeared. The fact that Kurashvili proposed a sociopolitical group called Democratic Union and that representatives of "informal groups" created an organization with the same name would seem not to be mere coincidence, for, although Kurashvili and the "informal groups" may have had different goals, the idea of a powerful umbrella organization was common to both.

Kurashvili first put forward the idea of a democratic union in an article in *Moscow News* that appeared on March 6. A comparison of Kurashvili's views at the beginning of March with what he wrote at the end of April amply demonstrates how far glasnost had progressed in the USSR within this short time. What Kurashvili had to say there was less innovative than what he said a month and a half later in *Sovetskaia molodezh*. Whereas in March Kurashvili emphasized that his notion of a democratic union should not be compared with an alternative party, in *Sovetskaia molodezh* he claimed that no one should be afraid to see such a parallel. In *Sovetskaia molodezh* Kurashvili also called on all "informal groups" who viewed themselves as Socialist, regardless of their differences, to participate in the work of a democratic union.

# 40
# PRESSURE GROUPS IN EASTERN EUROPE
Vladimir V. Kusin

Taking advantage of the moderate political climate and of the official efforts to secure greater public participation in reform programs, groups independent of the political establishments were being set up throughout the Soviet bloc. These groups could be seen as embryonic components of a civil society in which citizens were free to organize themselves in order to exert influence on decisions made by the state's political leadership. These diverse groups were meeting with a variety of responses from Eastern Europe's ruling elites, ranging from uneasy toleration through intimidation to downright suppression.

All independent groups dissented to some extent from official policies; if they did not, their members would have chosen to operate inside an official body. However, proreform activism was becoming increasingly common within the establishment as well. Nevertheless, one could make a distinction between groups that emerged in opposition to Brezhnev-style policies and those that had emerged since Gorbachev took over as leader of the CPSU. The earlier groups, opposed to the Brezhnev line, received added impetus from the new, official course; meanwhile, new groups were augmenting the agendas of their predecessors.

*Old-Style Dissent.* Five main themes characterized dissidence before Gorbachev: defense against the impact of economic mismanagement; the protection of human rights; opposition to religious restrictions; the promotion of intellectual freedom; and the pursuit of countercultures, for example, among young people.

The country that had long had the most independent groups was Poland, where these various dissident themes were closely intertwined. By comparison, the Hungarian opposition during the end of the Brezhnev era was less clearly organized but produced some seminal sociological research, literature, and economic analysis. Thanks to Charter 77, Czechoslovakia was represented on the dissident map during these years with a strong intellectual (samizdat) involvement, particularly on human rights issues; during the nineteen-eighties, religious activism also gained momentum in Czechoslovakia. The East German themes included peace, ecology, and resistance to militarization. Lithuania had a long-standing group of activists chronicling the adversities of religious life in the country.

With the exception of Poland, the old-style dissident groups were always small and deliberately unstructured to avoid prosecution; they relied strongly on support from the intellectuals and largely refrained from advancing political programs. Rather than attempting to influence the establishment, they sought to protect their own members and to influence public opinion. Some groups centered on samizdat periodicals, such as the Polish underground publications during the martial law period, the Hungarian *Beszelő* and *Hírmondo*, or the *Chronicle of the Lithuanian Catholic Church*.

Many dissidents believed that with the defeat of the Prague Spring in 1968, the idea of "Reform Communism" was dead. In its place the notion of a polity that was parallel and simply indifferent to the official state structure gained currency; the objectives of "self-sufficiency" and of shielding the ruled from the misdeeds of the rulers gathered momentum. Before Gorbachev, then, the independent groups were largely defensive, protective, and given to the dissemination of noncommunist values; they did not participate politically, and reform and dissent remained largely separate concerns.

*The Revival of Contest and Participation.* Gorbachev's program in pursuit of efficiency became increasingly receptive to political change; as the policy of glasnost broadened, the Communist state's coercive practices were relaxed. This gave a new lease on life to the idea of interaction between dissidents and the establishment, an idea that many had thought discredited and inherently futile. Official reformism created a climate favorable to the public's aspirations to participate in politics. People were beginning to seek to influence public matters in association with others. Politics were returning to communism; but the process was uneven, differing from country to country.

In Poland, with its large and multifarious network of independent organizations which never ceased to operate, the pressure for labor union pluralism increased. Farmers' Solidarity and the banned students' union wished to restart legal activism. Freedom and Peace struck roots as an organization advocating the right to conscientious objection, a change in the conscripts' oath (to remove the pledge of loyalty to the USSR), and general demilitarization. The Polish Socialist party announced its reconstitution. Some progress was evidently made in negotiations to grant the Roman Catholic Church full legal status. Lech Wałęsa and several veteran Solidarity activists spoke approvingly of Gorbachev's reformism and of their own willingness to participate in domestic reform programs.

Hungary went the furthest in politicizing independent initiatives. The Democratic Forum, created in 1987, was joined by other groups, such as the Association of Young Democrats, the Network of Independent Initiatives, and the Democratic Union of Academic and Scientific Workers. Journalists asked for permission to create a Glasnost Club. A number of ad hoc groups (for example, of experts analyzing official economic and political platforms) were active. The recognition that the country's government was no longer capable of correcting itself had permeated parts of the establishment, such as the Patriotic People's Front, which had begun to pressure governing politicians into far-reaching change. The borderline between dissent and radical reformism had become blurred. The presentation of alternative political programs for the country from outside the top echelons of the one-party state had become commonplace, with a strong emphasis on the need for economic and political pluralism.

In Czechoslovakia, Charter 77 and other movements were joined by new groups, such as the Democratic Initiative and the Independent Peace Association. The police broke up a meeting at which Charter 77 activists and other dissidents pledged to support the setting up of "an open movement" with a plainly political "alternative program." Other new groups included a "Community of Friends of the USA" and a society to publicize the legacy of Thomas G. Masaryk, the country's first president. The solidarity among religious believers in Czechoslovakia and their awareness of their own strength received a tremendous boost from the more than half-a-million signatures that were collected on a 31-point petition demanding religious freedom; some non-Catholic activists also supported the move. Charter 77 spokesmen made an "official" call on Cardinal František Tomášek during which the two sides made clear that they had common interests. The Cardinal later announced that he would hold regular consultations with experts of his own choosing on matters of Church-state relations.

Peace, antimilitarism, the ecology, and emigration remained the main themes of the independent scene in East Germany; but the vigor with which they were taken up made them more political than before. The Initiative for Peace and Human Rights was seeking to give dissent a clearly political dimension. Domestic reform may not have been on the establishment's agenda, but it had become a topic of debate outside it. Shielding the activists from the state's repressive powers, the Evangelical Church enhanced its own independent role in society.

A number of independent ecological groups in Bulgaria, in the town of Ruse, for example, became so active that the régime repressed them, fearing that they might give rise to a more political dissident movement. Individuals and small groups expressing independent opinions became more numerous in Romania; they included Orthodox Christian activists, veterans and young recruits of pre-Communist political parties, advocates of technocratic reforms, literary dissidents, and defenders of the cultural rights of ethnic minorities (especially the Transylvanian Magyars). The level of organization in both Bulgaria and Romania was, however, so far lower than elsewhere in the bloc.

With regard to the Baltic states, in addition to the groups of dedicated Lithuanian Catholics that had been publishing the *Chronicle* and *Ausra* for many years, the Lithuanian Freedom League was reactivated. Groups in Latvia included Helsinki 86 (a human rights watch group that embraced pressure-group tactics by, for example, initiating demonstrations on national themes), the Ecological Club, the Renaissance and Renewal group of young Lutheran clergy, and a spate of groups among the resident Russians, such as the pro-perestroika Third Modernization, which also called for the publication of all the works of Aleksander Solzhenitsyn. Estonia was distinguishing itself not only by the creation of an Independence party but above all by the great extent to which ideas for change were being articulated within the intellectual establishment; a program of economic and political self-management for the republic was addressed to Moscow over the heads of the Estonian party leaders. A group of reform-minded communists founded the People's Front in Support of Perestroika, with a highly independent political platform.

*Political Culture Changing?* Given that independent but politically participating pressure groups were also proliferating in the Soviet Union, the transition of dissent from the defensive to the politically active could not be seen as an East European rebellion. Rather, it signaled nascent changes in the political culture of communist societies.

A political system can be seen as having two components: the structural (institutions and processes) and the cultural (attitudes and beliefs). Whether there is congruence or incongruence between them to a large extent determines the system's performance. The "ideal" communist system has a totalitarian or at least authoritarian structure and a "subject" or at least a "parochial" (that is submissive or indifferent) culture. In the past, when the political culture had aspired to rise to the "participant" level and people had sought to become involved in politics, as in Hungary in 1956, Czechoslovakia in 1968, and Poland in 1980-1981, an acute case of incongruence had arisen that was only resolved when the structural component of the system repressed the public's cultural aspirations. Gorbachev appeared to recognize that the conventional communist congruent mix of authoritarianism, subjection, and parochialism was a system that could not meet the challenges of the modern world. Having initiated institutional and procedural reforms, he was now faced with a growth of independence in the political culture of the societies that his predecessors and their satraps had incorporated into the Communist empire.

People wished to match the reformist intentions of the leaderships with independent action of their own and, indeed, to push their leaders into more substantial change. Reform was no longer just about power struggles within the Communist bloc's leaderships, it was also about popular participation. The question remained how much independence even a reformed communist system could sustain.

# 41
## COORDINATING COMMITTEE OF NON-RUSSIAN NATIONALITIES
Bohdan Nahaylo

Representatives of six non-Russian national movements met in the Western Ukrainian city of Lvov on June 11 and 12, 1988, and founded a "Coordinating Committee of Patriotic Movements of the Peoples of the USSR." According to documents issued by the participants, the new committee was supported by national rights campaigners from the Ukraine, Lithuania, Estonia, Latvia, Georgia, and Armenia. Coming just after the formation of an inter-nationality group to defend political prisoners, the establishment of the new body represented the most ambitious attempt in the post-Stalin period by non-Russian dissidents to form a common front against Moscow's rule.

Shortly after the Gorbachev leadership inaugurated the policy of glasnost and began freeing political prisoners, Ukrainian and Armenian dissidents formed their own committees in defense of political prisoners.[1] In September 1987, it was announced that the two groups had decided to join forces and found a joint Ukrainian-Armenian Committee for the Defense of Political Prisoners. The initial press statement issued by this body was signed by Viacheslav Chornovil for the Ukrainians and Pariur Airikian for the Armenians.[2] Not long afterwards, representatives of a new Georgian Committee for the Defense of Political Prisoners joined the Ukrainians and Armenians, and the name of their organization was changed to the Inter-National Committee in Defense of Political Prisoners.[3]

In December 1987, the authorities showed their unease about the new unofficial activity, which was was focusing attention on the nationalities question, by preventing Chornovil and Airikian from attending an unofficial human-rights seminar in Moscow at which the two were to have chaired a section dealing with this sensitive issue.[4]

Despite this setback, on January 12-14 the first meeting of the Inter-National Committee in Defense of Political Prisoners was held in Erevan. The meeting was attended by five Armenians, two Georgians, and two Ukrainians.[5] The participants called on representatives of other nationalities to join forces with their organization, and they issued a statement addressed to the Soviet leadership. In the statement they drew attention to the fact that non-Russians traditionally made up a disproportionately large number of the Soviet Union's political prisoners and linked the Soviet government's repressive policies to the country's "unresolved" national problems.

In the same document, the representatives of three national movements proposed a series of "minimal" measures to facilitate a solution of the nationalities question. These included: the introduction of constitutional provisions in all the non-Russian republics making the national language of a republic a state language; the safeguarding of cultural facilities for smaller nations without their own statehood, as well as for national minorities living within the borders of other republics; the repeal of clauses in the laws on education having the effect of promoting Russification; the review of national problems left over from the Stalin era; recognition of the right of peoples to be reunited with their compatriots living outside the Soviet Union; and greater say for non-Russians in the way that the USSR's resources were to be distributed and environmental questions handled.[6]

In February unrest in connection with the situation in the Nagorno-Karabakh region broke out, and within a few weeks Airikian was arrested for his role in the Armenian protests. Interestingly, he was arrested on March 25, only days after Ukrainian and Georgian dissenters had been in Erevan for a further meeting of their Inter-National Committee. The day after Airikian's arrest, the Ukrainian representative, Pavlo Skochok, issued a statement expressing the support of his Ukrainian colleagues for the Armenian activist.[7] On May 13, the Soviet Ukrainian daily *Radianska Ukraina* accused Skochok of having gone to Erevan to agitate the Armenians to continue their protests and of having "taken it upon himself to promise them 'the support of the Ukrainian people.'"[8]

Thereafter, the Inter-National Committee was joined by Baltic activists. At the meeting in Lvov in June, leading representatives of the national movements in Estonia, Latvia, and Lithuania, were also present. The meeting issued a new appeal from the Inter-National Committee to the Soviet government. Its authors demanded the release of all political prisoners and their full rehabilitation, as well as investigations into the circumstances of the deaths of a number of imprisoned dissidents. The existence of political prisoners, the signatories argued, placed in question the sincerity of the authorities' professed desire to build a society with the rule of law. It was still a case of "democracy with a gagged mouth."

The non-Russian activists also announced that they were forming a "Coordinating Committee of the Patriotic Movements of the Peoples of the USSR." Its objective, according to the inaugural declaration, was to provide a means of exchanging experience between the various non-Russian "national democratic movements," coordinating activity between meetings, and elaborating a common program.

In the same document, the founding members of the "Coordinating Committee" expressed their concern about the "inability" of the Soviet leadership to resolve the national question. They noted that the Kremlin's handling of the Nagorno-Karabakh dispute and the "Gromyko Commission's" response to the demands of the Crimean Tatars had not only disappointed but also served as a warning to non-Russians "who placed their hopes on the Soviet leadership's new course." The election as delegates to the party conference of persons who bore responsibility for many of the problems in the Union republics had had, they also noted, the same effect. Apart from endorsing the positions previously adopted by the "Inter-National Committee," the signatories stressed that, as far as they were concerned, change for the better in the Soviet Union "is inseparably linked with the complete political and economic decentralization of the USSR, which we envisage in the future as a confederation of separate sovereign states."

Another related document called on all other "democratic" national movements in the USSR to support the Coordinating Committee. It categorically opposed any attempt by what it called reactionary forces "to preserve the status quo and divide us, setting Azerbaijanis against Armenians, Russians and Ukrainians against Crimean Tatars, Christians against Muslims, Orthodox against Catholics, and inciting everyone against the Jews."

Concerning the Russians, the founders of the Coordinating Committee sounded a critical and suspicious note. Having emphasized that they considered themselves to be representatives of nations that had been "forcibly made part of the Soviet Union," the non-Russian dissenters expressed the view that just as in the past, so now

> many of the activists in the Russian democratic opposition have not yet grasped the primary axiom of democracy: nations cannot be genuinely free if they oppress other nations, or if they serve as instruments of such oppression.

# 42
# CONSCIENTIOUS OBJECTORS
Barbara Donovan

The Polish government announced on January 19, 1988, that it would propose the establishment of an alternative to military service.[1] Those objecting to military service, government spokesman Jerzy Urban said, could choose to work for a period twice as long as the regular service (two to three years) as hospital attendants, environmental protectionists or on other community projects. According to Urban, this alternative would be open to all conscientious objectors, including pacifists and Jehovah's Witnesses. Legislation allowing for alternative service was first introduced in Poland in 1979 and 1980 but appeared to be largely ignored by the authorities; alternative service was only rarely sanctioned, mostly in cases of poor health.[2]

The Polish plan envisaged the first alternative service in Eastern Europe, where compulsory military service that allowed few or no concessions for conscientious objectors was the practice. These policies met with increasing public opposition throughout the region. A growing number of young men were refusing service with arms or refusing the draft entirely, and their demands to be allowed to claim conscientious objection were supported by the dissident communities in Hungary, Czechoslovakia, the GDR, and Poland. There were also appeals for the authorities to establish an alternative civilian service.

*Most Noble Patriotic Mission.* In all the European Warsaw Pact countries military service was compulsory and lasted from 16 months to 3 years, depending on the country and the branch of the service. The Bulgarian constitution cited military service as the "highest duty;" for the East German authorities it was "a right and an honorable duty;" for the Poles the "holiest duty;" and for the Czechoslovak "the most noble patriotic mission" for young citizens. Penalties for noncompliance ranged from one to five years imprisonment, averaging two years. Those who "persistently" evaded military service could face prison terms of up to 10 years.

Exemptions from compulsory service were few. In Poland, the following categories of people were among the few exempted from the draft: those with health problems; the only family member able to earn an income; the only family member able to run a farm; coal miners and religious seminarians. In Bulgaria, people belonging to certain minority groups (assumed to be potential security threats) often spent their service working in construction crews; there was also an option for those drafted to spend 10 years working in a field where trained specialists were needed.

The Polish plan was the first of its kind in Eastern Europe. In Hungary since 1977, members of some small religious sects, such as the Nazarenes, the Seventh Day Adventists, and radical groups of Jehovah's Witnesses were permitted to serve in unarmed units. The state did not, however, extend this possibility to members of the Catholic Church, arguing that pacifism was not a fundamental article of its faith. In the GDR since 1964, draftees had the option of working in construction units rather than doing regular military service. An estimated 500 people a year chose this alternative. It nevertheless entailed working on military sites and taking the regular military oath.

*Changing the Terms of Military Service.* In preceding years there had been a considerable increase in the efforts of individuals and groups throughout the region to have the authorities grant the right to conscientious objection and to establish alternatives to military service that were open to religious and moral objectors and that remained completely separate from the military realm.[3]

Members of Hungary's "democratic opposition" and of the so-called basic communities associated with the dissident priest György Bulányi that emerged among Catholics, openly encouraged conscientious objection. (Bulányi's followers had thus come into conflict with the hierarchy of the Catholic Church, which had justified bearing arms in defense of the country.)[4] In the fall of 1987, Hungarian dissidents sent an appeal to the delegations to the CSCE Review

Conference in Vienna urging that the representatives of nations that were signatories to the Helsinki Final Act consider the plight of conscientious objectors in Eastern Europe.

The Czechoslovak human rights group Charter 77, in a statement released on January 2, 1988, expressed its full support for the Hungarian appeal.[5] Other Charter 77 documents called for a reduction of military service to one year, for conscientious objection to be recognized by the authorities, and for the establishment of an alternative civilian service.

The Evangelical Church in the GDR had long been engaged in supporting conscientious objectors, and its efforts contributed to the introduction in 1964 of construction units as an alternative form of service. Discrimination in jobs and other types of action against veterans of these units as well as the militarily-oriented activities of the units, however, made the demand for a "social peace service" one of the first issues raised by the peace and ecology groups that emerged in the late nineteen-seventies. By 1981 the Church had endorsed this demand and had been advocating it in its consultations with the state ever since.

In Poland, demands from the public that conscientious objection be recognized by the authorities led to the emergence of the Freedom and Peace movement in 1985. The group was formed by a group of people protesting the imprisonment of Marek Adamkiewicz, who had received a two-and-a-half-year prison sentence for refusing to take a military oath pledging Poland's fraternal alliance with the Soviet Union. Since its inception, Freedom and Peace had sought to win the authorities' acceptance of conscientious objection and the abolition of the obligation to take the military oath. In contrast, conscientious objection did not become a public issue in Bulgaria or Romania, although a small number of objectors were reportedly imprisoned.[6]

*The Political Motive.* Clearly, the emergence of conscientious objection as an explosive political issue was closely linked to the emergence of independent peace and ecology groups in the late nineteen-seventies and early nineteen-eighties. Their broad discussion of human rights and peace, and of the excessive militarization of society inevitably included the question of conscientious objection. Moreover, the groups provided an organizational framework through which the individuals affected could be helped and demands to change the system of military conscription could be formulated and articulated. The close link between these groups and conscientious objection also meant that what was initially a question of religious principle spilled over into the political sphere, and an increasing number of conscientious objectors were taking a stand on political and moral grounds.

The Polish Freedom and Peace movement arose, for example, as a protest against the army's role in Poland and against being forced to take an oath that referred to the fraternal alliance with the army of the Soviet Union.[7] In February 1987 the first political conscientious objector was arrested in Hungary: his reasons for refusing military service were similar to the objections raised in

Poland. Zsolt Keszethelyi, an editor of samizdat material, returned his draft papers to the recruitment center with a letter stating that he refused to serve in an army "that is not placed under the control of a government elected by universal suffrage.[8] The Hungarian dissident Miklós Haraszti, in an article that appeared in *The New York Times*, argued that objection to serving in armies responsible for the only armed conflicts in Europe for the past 40 years was not only a matter of religious principle but also "an indication of popular, nonviolent, democratic resistance and solidarity."[9]

Conscientious objection also became fused with criticism of the foreign policies of the Warsaw Pact states. In a Charter 77 document, the authors stated that "no durable détente can take place in a divided Europe as long as there are people who are being prosecuted for refusing to consider other peoples their enemies." Similar sentiments were expressed by groups advocating conscientious objection in the GDR.

*Official Reactions.* The authorities in Eastern Europe made very few concessions in response to these campaigns and instead warned against "dangerous pacifism." In all but the Polish case, they resisted appeals for the provision of an alternative service. It seems they feared that the number of young people refusing to do military service would grow to unmanageable proportions if civilian service were instituted. Moreover, such a move would be a concession to the political opposition in these countries.

Since the fall of 1985, however, the East German authorities had reportedly not imprisoned any of the young men who refused both military service and service in construction units: the 50 or so men arrested prior to that were soon released, after the Church appealed to the state. This unspoken concession could not, however, make up for the lack of a civilian service in the eyes of the independent human rights groups.[10]

Although, in announcing the Polish proposal the Polish government spokesman denied that it was tantamount to recognition of Freedom and Peace, which he described as "a political organization aiming itself against Polish defense alliances," the move did look like a major concession to the group's demands. Indeed, the move directly followed a crackdown on conscientious objectors: about 10 members of Freedom and Peace were sentenced to more than two years each in prison or were awaiting trial in jail.[11]

Spokesmen for Freedom and Peace welcomed the proposal as "slight progress" but criticized the length of the proposed service and its low pay.[12] Nevertheless, the Polish proposal was bound to give an impetus to the campaign for the acceptance of conscientious objection in other East European countries and was certain to make it that much harder for the other régimes to resist appeals for alternative service.

## 43
## THE GROWTH OF CIVIL SOCIETY IN HUNGARY
Alfred Reisch,* John Reed,** Judith Pataki,***
Edith Markos****

*Critique by Former Premier.* A lengthy interview with former Hungarian Prime Minister András Hegedüs was published in the literary weekly *Élet és Irodalom,* dated August 28, 1987, under the provocative title "Aren't You Trying to Square the Circle?" The poet András Mezei, a staff member of the weekly since 1960, conducted the interview.

Hegedüs, a former protege of Mátyás Rákosi, the Stalinist party leader of Hungary after World War II, served as Prime Minister from 1955 to 1956. He fled to the Soviet Union after signing the document that called for Soviet armed assistance to crush the October 1956 Uprising. Following his return to Hungary in 1958, Hegedüs underwent a remarkable metamorphosis and began searching for possible ways to renew and democratize "socialist society." He was found guilty of "traditional rightist-revisionism" and of having attitudes characteristic of the New Left, and was formally expelled from the HSWP in May 1973. In 1984 in Vienna he gave a series of interviews to Radio Free Europe. The interviews, which were in effect his memoirs, were published as a book.[1]

Asked in the interview to interpret the program of economic and social development adopted by the HSWP Central Committee in July 1987,[2] Hegedüs bluntly called on Hungary's social institutions to abandon their characteristic emphasis on formalism and the avoidance of criticism, which had once again been illustrated by the CC's claim that 27 agencies had given their approval to the program and this, Hegedüs said, without any discussion or criticism of it.

Nevertheless, Hegedüs said, although the Hungarian leadership had become "bureaucratized" at various levels, East European societies had never been turned into mere "marionettes." In Hungary social forces that were trying to break through the old, restraining framework had made a strong appearance in recent years, and the leaders of institutions such as the National Council of Trade Unions (SZOT), the Communist Youth League (KISZ), and the Patriotic People's Front (PPF) should release these forces. Society as a whole, not just the state or the party, should take part in the development of industry, agriculture, and trade; and the CC's resolution should serve merely as a framework.

---

*Author of sections 1 and 4.

** Author of section 2.

***Author of sections 3 and 7.

**** Author of sections 5 and 6.

If SZOT, KISZ, the PPF, and other social organizations were to become more independent, Hegedüs argued, this would be tantamount to the recognition of social pluralism.[3] When asked how he could have faith in such pluralism without advocating a multiparty system, Hegedüs said that the road to socialism in East European societies did not lead through a multiparty system but rather through a pluralism in which "the various institutions of civic society function autonomously and can exercise effective control over the party and the state, in other words over institutionalized power."[4]

Hegedüs said that both the economy and politics could be redeemed by enterprising individuals and groups. Without entrepreneurship, stagnation would result sooner or later. Hegedüs expected Hungary's development into "entrepreneurial socialism" to be achieved through both a market and a nonmarket economy. His comment spurred the interviewer to acknowledge that in its program of economic reform Hungary had discovered the art of squaring the circle and had shown the unbelieving world that while everything remained the same, something new and "Hungarian" was taking place.

*Democratic Opposition Posits Social Contract.* In June 1987 Hungary's democratic opposition offered one of the most detailed and sophisticated proposals for political reform ever to come out of Eastern Europe. The 60-page document, entitled "Social Contract," appeared in a special issue of the samizdat periodical *Beszélő.*

The document's basic premise was simple: for economic reform to be successful in Hungary, political reform was essential; and in order for political reform to succeed, the party would have to give up its monopoly on power and make society an equal partner in political life (hence the title). While agreeing with the ideas of the 1956 Revolution, the document's authors were realistic enough to acknowledge that the one-party system would remain in Hungary for the foreseeable future. At the same time, they said, a degree of pluralism was possible if the party were made accountable to the people through a series of controls and legal guarantees.

The program consisted of five points:

1. *The Party's Power and Government Accountability.* The document's authors began by saying that any meaningful political reform had to be based on decentralization and the limitation of the party's power through a series of legal measures. While the party could retain its "leading role" in Hungarian society, its status as a body that acted above the law would have to be ended. The program proposed limiting the Central Committee's decision-making powers to matters of foreign policy and making it subject to the law. The National Assembly's powers, meanwhile, should be extended significantly to include all matters relating to finance and citizens' rights. The National Assembly should be given the right to call for a vote of confidence in the government, appoint the heads of the radio and television services, and convene special subcommittees to consider major financial investment projects. Voting by secret ballot should be

introduced, and the electoral system should be reformed to include a broader range of candidates.

In addition to allowing the National Assembly more power, the government should be made accountable to society through new laws requiring it to inform the public regularly on matters of national interest such as the foreign debt. The political power of the populace should also be increased through a new legal framework allowing grassroots initiatives, including the distribution of leaflets, petitioning, and demonstrations. The government's power could be further decentralized by allowing genuine self-government in the regional councils.

2. *Legal Limits to Censorship*. Although the document's authors acknowledged that true freedom of the press was unattainable in contemporary Hungary, they said that censorship could be limited through a series of new laws. Organizations and individuals should be allowed to found periodicals and publishing houses. In addition, the party should be stopped from using the media as a direct propaganda tool; and only party and government publications should be required to espouse the official line. Party and government publications should not be censored before publication, and violations of the rules of censorship should be punishable only after publication and by a court of law. The criteria for censorship, including what could be classified as a "state secret," should be more clearly defined.

3. *Legal Protection for Workers*. The program's authors pointed out that throughout nearly 20 years of economic reforms in Hungary, the laws governing workers' rights had remained virtually unchanged. Work, they said, should be a "voluntary, private agreement between employer and employee;" and employers should have no say in what their employees did outside the work place. The law making work compulsory should be abolished. The state's control over large concerns should be reduced, and workers' self-government should be instituted.

The document's authors went on to call for a major reform and democratization of the Hungarian trade unions which, they said, had lost their purpose and consistently supported the government line rather than defending workers' interests. They proposed the creation of a federation of new, regionally organized trade unions and other interest groups to work alongside, and perhaps eventually instead of, the existing trade unions. Voting by secret ballot should be instituted, and leaders should be elected directly by union members. The parliament should pass a law giving workers the right to strike. Additional laws providing for the creation and protection of various interest groups, such as unskilled workers, religious believers, and environmentalists, should be passed.

4. *Fair Social Policies*. The idea that full employment and a universal benefit system made social welfare programs unnecessary had proved invalid in the course of 40 years of communism, the document said. The current economic slump had served to call attention to the inadequacy of Hungarian social policies, and radical changes were needed.

The proposal devoted considerable attention to the problem of unemployment, which had appeared in Hungary on a large scale only recently. The unemployment compensation system, it said, should be expanded to include trained workers who could not find jobs in addition to those who had been laid off. Retraining should be provided for workers who had to move into another field, and "public works" jobs should offer the same benefits as normal jobs. Additional reforms in the school system, family compensation, and the pension system should be passed to improve the lot of large families and old people. The document's authors came out in favor of the new personal income tax, but warned that it should be modified to favor the poor.

In order to finance increased spending on social welfare programs, several possible measures were suggested. Education and health care should only be free at the basic level. The ceiling on pensions should be lowered. Unemployment should be allowed to spread to the government, where, for example, the number of economic planners could be reduced. Lastly, organizations such as KISZ and the trade unions should be made self-financing.

5. *Legal Guarantees for Human Rights*. Although respect for human rights was guaranteed by the Hungarian Constitution, the document said, the legal structure to back it up was lacking. Too often, executive orders rather than written laws were used by the authorities to justify human rights violations; and although Hungary had approved international human rights treaties such as the Helsinki Final Act, none of them had the force of law. "The citizen is at the mercy of the authorities," the document's authors said.

To remedy this situation, legal guarantees should be created to back up existing human rights agreements. The law should take precedence over executive decrees, and the powers of the police should be curbed. At the same time, courts should play a greater role in human rights cases, and they should be reformed to make proceedings more open and jury selection more democratic. The state should be prevented from interfering in Church affairs, and social groups such as alcoholics and the mentally ill should be legally protected.

The document's authors said that conditions for reform had never been better, especially with Gorbachev in power in the Soviet Union. Political reform was an increasingly popular topic in all circles of Hungarian life, and some points of the program were in fact under discussion. At the same time, the leadership under Kádár continued to drag its feet. Without fundamental changes in the political system, the *Beszélő* document said, the government would be forced to stifle all dissent, recentralize the economy, or create a "Hungarian South Korea," that is, free enterprise accompanied by political repression.

*Democratic Forum.* 150 to 160 Hungarian intellectuals met on September 27 in the small town of Lakitelek, east of Kecskemét in southeastern Hungary, to discuss the nation's problems. The participants, who met in the back yard of the populist writer Sándor Lezsák, included populist authors, reformist economists and scientists, the so-called urban writer György Konrád, and General

Secretary of the Patriotic Peoples' Front (PPF) and HSWP CC member Imre Pozsgay.

Konrád was the only "urban" author invited to the meeting, indicating the split that existed between populist and "urban" writers, which the régime had sought to capitalize on in order to divide the opposition. The populist authors, most of whom came from Christian backgrounds, primarily represented a rural, small-town, and patriotic view, whereas the "urban" authors, many of whom came from Jewish backgrounds, were more cosmopolitan and city-oriented. Writers in both camps, however, expressed regret that more "urban" authors had not been invited to the meeting at Lakitelek; and some participants expressed the hope that this would change in the future.

The participants ended the meeting by adopting a resolution calling for the formation of a "Hungarian Democratic Forum," whose membership would be open to anyone interested in solving the numerous problems facing the nation. Participants also called for open and uncensored debates in periodicals.

Pozsgay was the main speaker at the meeting, which lasted more than seven hours. He said that Prime Minister Károly Grósz was willing to enter into a constructive dialogue with the participants in the spirit of the government's new program for economic reform. Pozsgay called on them to formulate their own alternative program for radical reform, saying that the government was ready and willing to consider it.[5] Pozsgay also said that the idea of reform needed to be broadened to apply to areas other than economics. Reform was not essentially economic but sociopolitical, and should be used to humanize politics and break down the barriers that obstructed growth and change, from the top to the bottom level of the bureaucracy.

The relationship between the Hungarian Socialist Workers' party and the government, he said, needed to be clarified, and the present bureaucratic "party-state" structure should be changed because it demeaned the party. If the one-party system were retained, the party's activities would need to be opened to public scrutiny.

The role of the National Assembly needed to be redefined, he said, so that it would operate on the principle of popular sovereignty and supervise the government. The National Assembly would thus become an open political forum, in effect the political school of the nation.

He also spoke of the need for dissident opinions to be heard, and said that all forces in society might be able to join in a coalition based on constitutional principles. This was the second time in a month that a high-level official had said that dissident views needed to be considered; the first such statement had been made by Grósz.[6]

According to Pozsgay, some legal obstacles had to be overcome, but he said that he hoped a referendum system to decide important national issues would be introduced. To remove some of the obstacles, a new constitution could be adopted to replace the Presidential Council with a "republican presidium." (The

21-member Presidential Council had been criticized, because it made laws when the National Assembly was not in session, thereby avoiding public debate.)

Most of the speakers who followed Pozsgay on September 27 depicted the country as being in crisis and attempted to explain how it had gotten there. The participants agreed that only a radical change or "reform" that would bring in a new leadership could help the country out of its situation.

The meeting at Lakitelek and the resolution to form the Hungarian Democratic Forum indicated that the populist authors were becoming more vocal and would take part, along with the more urban democratic opposition, in formulating programs to lead the country out of its crisis. The meeting also showed that the time was not yet right for cooperation between populist and "urban" authors. Relations between the two groups further deteriorated in the spring of 1988, when in April the cultural monthly *Mozgó Világ* printed a controversial poem by the "urban" author György Spiró in which he allegedly referred to the populists as "scum." Many populist authors felt insulted and asked the Hungarian Writers' Union to refer the poem to its Committee on Ethics.[7]

The speeches at Lakitelek indicated, however, that different segments of society agreed that the national crisis could only be resolved if the new government were willing to introduce more political reforms and remove those leaders responsible for the problems. Asked whether he viewed the meeting as having been a citizens' initiative, Pozsgay said that he did and that it was right that democracy should offer opportunities for such initiatives as well as movements initiated from the top. The main direction of the debate had been determined by "the need to harmonize socialism, democracy, and reform," he said; and although a variety of views had been expressed with no agreement being reached on numerous issues, the exchange of views about Hungary's possibilities had been responsible and based on the principle of a dialogue with the authorities. The forum had tried to handle these differences of view, Pozsgay concluded, in a spirit of peaceful coexistence and concern for the fate of the country.

*Statement of Democratic Forum Published.* Six weeks after the Lakitelek gathering, the group's founding statement was published in the November 14 issue of *Magyar Nemzet*, the daily of Hungary's Patriotic People's Front (PPF). It was contained within a page-long interview by Gábor Tóth with Pozsgay.

In the first part of the interview, Pozsgay made a strong stand in support of civic initiatives and associations, saying that for a consensus to be achieved within society,

> people need greater freedom, civic autonomy, and participation in decisions, that is, a situation in which government for the people is replaced by government by and through the consent of the people.

He called for a new law on associations to be drafted and said that the HSWP would be running a great risk if it failed to provide society with more maneuvering room within the framework of existing political institutions.

Broaching the problem of eliminating bad feelings within Hungarian society, Pozsgay said that dividing walls among the people had to be torn down and their opportunities for showing initiative increased. Individuals felt ill at ease, he said; and society as a whole felt that its room for maneuvering was too narrow. Consequently, a general agreement had to be reached on increasing that societal maneuvering room. For Pozsgay, such an agreement was still possible, since the majority of the people still accepted "socialism" as a common cause. Reaching a consensus nonetheless required that people have

> greater freedom, civic autonomy, and participate in decisions, that is, a situation in which government for the people is replaced by government by and through the consent of the people.

This kind of government, Pozsgay said, required that citizens take the initiative by setting up their own associations, building society from below. Indeed, the opportunity for doing so, he said, should be a right protected by greater guarantees than political good will alone. In Hungary's public and political life, the right of association went back to the liberal age of reform in the eighteen-thirties and eighteen-forties, Pozsgay said; and there always had been a great need for it. According to Pozsgay, self-administration and the direct pursuit of individual interest were also very much needed for the preservation of national unity.

The statement by the government's spokesman to the effect that "the government favored the creation of any correct, well-intentioned ... association" was an encouraging sign, Pozsgay said, because there was still much "bureaucratic resistance" to civic initiatives and associations, which the authorities tended to consider a threat. According to Pozsgay, there was no greater threat to society than when citizens became passive. Moreover, it was now very difficult for the state to scold its citizens for inactivity after such a long period of neglect; asking them to become more active required that their rights of association be redefined by law.

Asked whether the gathering at Lakitelek[8] had been an oppositional meeting, Pozsgay gave a clear no, saying that many governments around the world would be glad to have such partners with whom to discuss their countries' futures. He said that many views had been aired during the meeting, at which "so-called dissidents" and people who doubted that communism could solve human problems had participated. Such doubts existed elsewhere in Hungarian society on account of the country's difficulties, Pozsgay noted.

Pozsgay confirmed that the most radical, "hard-core" dissidents had been absent from Lakitelek but denied that differences between the so-called populists and urbanists—the "hard core" numbering mostly among the latter—were the real problem. For him, a place had to be found within "socialism" for all different views, including those of the opposition, because some of their proposals deserved consideration. The old populist-urbanist debate had caused problems at Lakitelek, he said, but one should no longer focus on that "cursed heritage"; the question now was who had the good of the nation at heart. Few people would opt for a policy of "the worse, the better"; the majority wanted a "dialogue" on the basis of a "wide national consensus." Although "Hungary's political life" (that is, the party) was perhaps not yet ready to accept some of the voices heard at Lakitelek in the spirit of glasnost, it would have to get used to them in the future.

Tóth asked Pozsgay whether he could tell the readers about the Democratic Forum's statement. Pozsgay first commented that although the statement was "legally unobjectionable," it contained many political elements that required "further debate." Then, by way of an answer to Tóth's question, the text of the statement was printed:

> More than 150 members of Hungary's intellectual circles gathered in Lakitelek on Sunday, September 27, 1987, for a friendly exchange of views. They invited to the meeting Imre Pozsgay, general secretary of the PPF.

> The Hungarian nation has drifted into a serious crisis in its history. Its national strength has been broken, its self-confidence and bearing have been shaken, the bonds of its cohesion have been tragically loosened, its self-knowledge is startlingly insufficient. It is anticipating possible economic collapse. Hungary as an ethnic entity is affected by an unprecedented division. Our nation does not possess a commonly acceptable vision of the future.

> In the course of the discussions, mention was made of the socio-economic crisis shaking the country, the lack of democracy, the inadequacies of the institutional political system, the worsening problems of public morality, the alarming symptoms in cultural life and public education, and the worries about our survival. Those who attended and spoke, surveying the prospects for the Hungarian nation, tried to find ways of getting out [of the crisis] through necessary renewal and truly effective reforms in a spirit of common sense and level-headedness.

> Filled with a feeling of responsibility for the fate of the country and of the Hungarian nation, those assembled felt it necessary and timely to establish a framework that would permit the members of society to participate as true partners in the creation of a social consensus. After

their discussions, the participants agreed that such a consensus could be achieved only if all progressive social forces joined hands. We are of the opinion that the crisis can be solved only through social participation, involving both society and the country's political leaders. The present system of political and social organization does not provide any guarantee for the expression of autonomous and independent views. This is why [we] propose the establishment of a Hungarian democratic forum as an arena for sustained public discussion. Such a forum would be suitable for discussing our serious worries, analyzing a given topic, and preparing alternative proposals. The participants see this forum as being open, with both a democratic and a national spirit. They count on people with different ideologies and party leanings to cooperate in its work. They consider it important that the country's public should become acquainted with the content of these discussions and analyses. This is why we feel it necessary to create independent press organs functioning within constitutional limits.

We believe that we can get out of the crisis through large-scale collaboration among the forces of renewal.

*Demonstrations for Democratic Reforms.* An estimated 10,000 people, according to Western news agencies, demonstrated in Budapest on March 15, 1988, to demand civil liberties and democratic pluralism. The mood of the demonstrators was festive and confident. Although the police arrested several of the organizers and confiscated samizdat literature just before the demonstration, they did not interfere in the demonstration itself.

According to Western correspondents, the demonstrators, many of whom were wearing cockades of the Hungarian colors and waving national flags, marched several kilometers down Budapest's main boulevards. They chanted slogans and carried written banners with such demands as "real reform," "freedom of assembly," "freedom of the press," and "free elections." They attracted large groups of passers-by, some of whom joined the march as it moved through downtown Budapest. The crowd stopped at the monuments of the heroes of the revolution of 1848—Sándor Petőfi, Lajos Kossuth, Lajos Batthyány, and József Bem—to lay wreaths and to hear speeches. Leaflets bearing greetings in Hungarian and Polish from the Polish free trade union Solidarity were handed out to the demonstrators on their way to the Batthyány monument. The leaflets drew cheers for Solidarity from the demonstrators.[9]

In one of the speeches, the philosopher and samizdat publisher János Kis told his audience that the democratic demands of 1848 had yet to be fulfilled in present-day Hungary. The Transylvanian-born philosopher Gáspár Miklos Tamás demanded "a new constitution," "free elections," and (probably alluding to HSWP Secretary-General János Kádár among other officials) the resignation of "leaders who have lost the confidence of the people." He also appealed to the Hungarian public to redouble its support for the Magyar ethnic minorities in neighboring countries. The wife of Gábor Demszky delivered a speech prepared by her husband, who was among those dissidents arrested on the morning of March 15, in which he blamed the Soviet political and economic model for leading Hungary into the present crisis. Demszky argued that democratic demands in Eastern Europe "can best be achieved not within a merely national framework" but through the efforts of Eastern Europe's "small nations working together in solidarity." Demszky hailed the growing cooperation among Poland's Solidarity, Czechoslovakia's Charter 77, the Hungarian democratic opposition, and "the forces striving for the democratic renewal of Romania;" and he called for friendship among the Danubian peoples. The demonstrators dispersed peacefully after three hours.

*Independent Labor Union.* Hungary's first independent labor union since the communist takeover was established on May 14. The Democratic Union of Scientific and Academic Workers (TDDSZ) was also the first independent union in Eastern Europe since Solidarity emerged in Poland in the summer of 1980.

The decision to set up an independent professional union was taken in December 1987 at a meeting of the research staff of the Historical Institute of the Hungarian Academy of Sciences. At that meeting some 50 researchers, protesting a 15 percent cut in the institute's budget, voted to leave the official Union of Public Employees and demanded the setting up of an independent union. The historians were soon joined by hundreds of scientific researchers from various institutes of the academy and faculty members from several universities in Budapest and the provinces. Their move reflected the view of many professionals that the official union had long failed to represent their interests. SZOT, which had been steadily loosing members in the preceding years, issued a statement rejecting in principle any organization separate from the existing trade unions.[10]

At the founding meeting in Budapest on May 14, it was said that the new union had 1,026 members; they included university professors, lecturers, teaching assistants, scientific researchers, laboratory assistants, and some unemployed scientists and scholars. Among them were some party members, one of whom, the historian György Kerekes of the Social Sciences Institute, emerged as an articulate spokesman for the union. The union's organizers had been granted permission by the Dean of Budapest's Loránd Eötvös University to hold its founding meeting there but had to change the location to the cultural Metro Club after the university's rector had withdrawn the authorization at the last minute. Nevertheless, the Hungarian media did not shy away from reporting on the meeting and, on the whole, did so objectively, in some cases even appearing to sympathize with the efforts to organize an independent union.[11]

According to Radio Budapest, the founding meeting was attended by more than 500 people, who elected a 59-member steering committee.[12] The founding meeting also elected a union chairman, Pál Forgách, the Hungarian representative at the World Federation of Trade Unions for many years and the former head of the official Chemical Workers' Union. Forgách hailed the establishment of the union as "unprecedented" in the past 40 years of Hungarian trade unions and told the assembled members that "only the elderly can remember what a truly democratic union meant." In an interview with Radio Budapest, Forgách said that the new union intended to "break with dogmas and with rigid hierarchical structures [and did] not have objectives that conflict with the defense of its members' interests." Historian Péter Hanák also addressed the meeting and seconded Forgách's criticism of the official labor unions as being antidemocratic and as failing to represent their members' interests.[13]

Kerekes, who was also a member of the steering committee, was quoted as having said that the new union would "take action to guarantee an increase in the real value of funds to be allocated to scientific and scholarly research, and to resist layoffs and the phasing out of personnel." He added that the independent union's leaders planned to calculate and publish cost-of-living indexes regularly and to arrange for unemployment insurance for its members. In further contrast to the official labor unions, Kerekes said that the independent union's budget from membership dues would be published annually. He also said that the union would seek to improve members' working conditions and to protect their professional rights and job security.[14]

The official labor union federation, SZOT, did not immediately act on its initial threat to move against the independent union and seemed instead to be preparing to co-opt it. Its president, Sándor Gáspár, an HSWP Politburo member, said that SZOT would not interfere with the new union's organizing effort. In the same breath, however, Gáspár suggested that representatives of the independent union consider the "conditions for cooperation" with SZOT in the future. In an apparent effort to draw away potential members from the independent union, the official Union of Public Employees announced plans to set up a new trade union within SZOT, the Union of Scientific Workers.[15]

The new union's representatives maintained that it was not a broadly based political movement like Solidarity in Poland but a social interest group aimed at representing its members' professional interests. At the same time, they made no secret of their hope of setting an example to other interest groups. In an interview with Radio Budapest, steering committee member Elemér Hankiss said that the main significance of the independent union lay in demonstrating that "every social group or segment can take action in behalf of its own interests." He expressed the hope that the union would serve as "a model for those who will perhaps be defending more important social interests than we [are]." Kerekes, in turn, predicted that within two years new unions organized according to trades would proliferate, in contrast to the old structure, which had been based on industrial branches.[16]

*Independent Political Groups Mushroom.* By the spring of 1988, loosely organized groups advocating political change had become increasingly active. Their claim that their activities were legal under the constitution caused considerable disturbance in the party and government. The groups did not apply for registration as associations in order to avoid party control over their activities. There seemed to be confusion and indecision within the party over how to deal with these groups.

Another new political development was the founding on March 30 of the Federation of Young Democrats (FIDESZ), a political organization for young people that aimed at ending the monopoly of the Communist Youth League (KISZ). Although KISZ supported the foundation of independent associations such as sports and dancing clubs, this was the first attempt to organize a politically oriented group for young people independent of the official youth league.

The 37 founders (mostly college and university students) issued a statement defining their major goals and the place they sought in Hungarian society. The federation, it said, was committed to "founding a new independent social alliance that would group together politically active, radically reform-minded youth groups and individuals." Although it wished to remain independent, it would cooperate with KISZ, probably in the hope that KISZ would then give it support.

The statement said that the organization would operate in accordance with the constitution and that its activities would be directed at "building a new Hungary" based on pluralistic democracy. Special attention would be paid to the problems of ethnic Hungarian minorities in other countries. The statement said that the young people were not responsible for Hungary's present crisis but had to bear the burden of past mistakes. Thus, the young had a responsibility for the future and had to mold it in the way they wanted. The statement appealed to all young people who agreed with the federation's aims to join it in formulating a program. It also called on the official Communist Youth League to support "every initiative that would enrich the political representation of young people." (The membership of the official youth league had dropped considerably in the previous few years and at that time comprised only about a third of all young Hungarians, many of whom were members on paper only.)

The authorities tried to disband the group without using force. On April 8 five members had to report to the Budapest police department, where they were given a warning for having organized an illegal association. Since the media covered the event, many people became aware of the existence of the organization.[17] Two of the five individuals came from the provinces, indicating that the organization was not concentrating its activities in Budapest alone.

Despite the police warning, the Federation of Young Democrats held a meeting on April 17 which was attended by some 200 people. A number of spokesmen were appointed. After the meeting, the five who had already received warnings were summoned by the state attorney responsible for antistate activities in the chief prosecutor's office. He first threatened them and then proposed as a compromise that the five discontinue their activities until the following fall when the National Assembly was to begin debating a new law on associations.

The five, who were either law students or had a doctorate in law, informed the authorities that they had not organized an association and that therefore neither the 1981 law regulating associations nor a future law on associations would apply to them. The federation, they said, based its activities on the right to assemble or form social organizations to further social, cultural, or economic activities—a right guaranteed by the Constitution.

Confusion was evident on several occasions when Prime Minister Károly Grósz answered questions about the activities of the new federation. In a briefing for journalists, Grósz said that his government would tolerate independent political and other groups that were being formed across the country almost daily but would refuse to deal with them directly until a new law on associations had been submitted to the National Assembly in December.[18] In another statement to journalists, Grósz said that the behavior of the group's leaders violated the existing law on associations.[19] It was therefore unclear which law, if any, applied to the Federation of Young Democrats and to similar groups.

Meanwhile, some 1,000 people had joined the group and it received several letters of support from leading intellectuals, writers, political scientists, and sociologists and from members of the Democratic Forum. Its greatest success came when the council of a local group of some 66,000 university and college students acknowledged at a meeting in Veszprém that there was a need for a new political organization such as the federation.[20] The student assembly council noted this in its final resolution as well.

An umbrella organization of diverse dissident, environmental, Church, and other organizations, the Network of Free Initiatives was formed on May 1 in the Hági Restaurant in Budapest. According to one of the organizers, the philosopher János Kis, the founding of the organization was the first step in building up a framework for a political opposition.[21]

The organization was started when 45 dissidents and intellectuals drew up a petition that was issued on March 17 and was signed by several hundred people. The appeal called on the Communist government to enter into discussions in good faith with the whole of Hungarian society in order to overcome the present crisis. It called for the formation of a multiparty democracy that would constitutionally guarantee the rights of individuals. The petition proposed a free enterprise system and called for good economic, political, and military relations with the Soviet Union, stating, however, that Hungary should be a sovereign and equal member of the European family of nations.

At its meeting on May 1 the Network of Free Initiatives elected a council of about 50 people that would designate spokesmen. It stressed that it wanted to achieve changes through constitutional means. In a position paper adopted a few days after its founding, it condemned the government's attempt to suppress the Democratic Forum, whose aims were often similar to those of the network. The resolution protested the expulsion of four party members for associating with the forum, the exclusion of independent groups from a government-sponsored environmental organization, and the death in jail of the Czechoslovak dissident Pavel Wonka.

Since the formation of the Democratic Forum in Lakitelek in the fall of 1987, other new groups had followed their example by claiming that their activities were protected by the constitution. The lack of adequate legislation on associations sowed confusion among party and government officials about how to deal with these mushrooming independent political organizations, which obviously threatened the one-party system. The régime was trying to assert its authority by disrupting or hindering their activities by, for example, confiscating their publications or expelling party members who participated in their activities. Yet there were voices even within party circles that continued to ask for political reforms that would permit the establishment of independent groups, although within the framework of the one-party system.

# XI. HUNGARY'S REFORM OF A REFORM

## 44
## ECONOMIC FAILURE ACKNOWLEDGED
### Károly Okolicsanyi

*Tough Stabilization Program.* By mid-1987, the Hungarian régime had publicly acknowledged the dismal state of the economy. After a meeting of the HSWP CC on July 2, 1987, which was devoted entirely to the economy, it was announced that it was impossible to postpone making a start on "eliminating the accumulated [economic] difficulties." The statement did not specify what those difficulties were; nor did it attribute the blame for them to the party or the government, beyond saying that "we have hesitated to adjust ourselves to the [world economic] situation, which has changed.[1]

The Hungarian economy was weak because of low productivity, technological backwardness, and above all the lack of private ownership and the profit incentive. These factors made Hungarian products uncompetitive on the world market, which resulted in a deficit in convertible currency. The failure to acknowledge and even the covering up of such structural inefficiency meant the granting of state support to industry, especially the steel, coal-mining, building, and meat industries, which in turn produced a record government deficit of 46,900 million forint (about $1,000 million) in 1986 alone.[2] (This was 7.6 percent of the total budget.) Only by resorting to foreign loans had it been possible to avoid taking economic action for the preceding 15 years; but Hungary was now facing a liquidity crisis, since foreign lenders—having observed the squandering of previous loans—were raising their interest rates on new loans. At the same time, the government was having difficulty in servicing the old ones.

The deputy head of the CC's Economic Policy Department, László Mohai, indicated that the "program of economic and social unfolding" would have two stages. The first would be the modernization or stabilization of the economy, which would last two to three years and was likened by *Magyar Hírlap* to a "diet" for getting the economy into better shape. The second stage would be a social and economic reform that would occur during the next five-year plan period (1990-1995). Mohai acknowledged that the first phase would cause a decline in the living standard.

A bitter commentary in the weekly *Ötlet* spoke of the gap between the leaders and the public as a glass wall that distorted communications. The commentary asked who had acquired all those foreign loans and built those prestigious factories (working at a loss), because no responsibility had been apportioned in the CC's statement. As the three major Hungarian samizdat publications pointed out in a joint declaration on July 10, there was no mention in the CC's statement of the party leadership's responsibility or any individual's responsibility for the setting up of unrealistic plans, for the halting of the reform movement in 1972-1974, or for the slowing down of 1983-1985. The declaration also pointed out the imbalance of the statement, which called for sacrifices without offering corresponding rights or guarantees.

*The Central Committee's Proposals.* The first part of the CC statement emphasized the need for a short period of stabilization, during which there had to be a "gradual halt to the process of increasing [foreign] debt and the deficit in the state budget must be eliminated." The reduction of state subsidies to unprofitable enterprises had to be "continued more forcefully" and "bankruptcy legislation must be strictly adhered to." The further exploitation of "opportunities within international cooperation" was also urged. The statement said that the reinforcement of long-term and direct relationships with companies from advanced capitalist countries was desirable. Economic cooperation with enterprises in the Soviet Union and other CMEA member countries was also urged in order to achieve a balance in trade and to increase the number of joint ventures.

The second part of the statement urged the "development of markets by observing [market] rules," but also spoke of the need for an "improvement in the planned control of the national economy." The CC proposed wage differentiation according to performance and stricter adherence to the forces of supply and demand.

The CC noted the need for enterprise managements to take more risks and to be held accountable for their actions. The statement endorsed the introduction of value-added tax, income tax, and wage reform, saying that "salaries and wages should be made proportional to the social usefulness of the work performed."

The document envisaged a new law to support a "variety of business forms" and said that "new, flexible, [and] profitably operating small and medium-sized [enterprises] must be encouraged." Moreover, "counterproductive, monopolistic organizations must be eliminated."

At a press conference on July 3, János Barabás, deputy head of the CC's Agitprop Department, denied that Hungary was in a state of crisis. He said, however, that the new economic measures would result in temporary unemployment and inflation and that more sacrifices would be required from the public.[3]

*Price Increases.* The call for sacrifices took concrete form on July 19 when Hungary announced major price increases. The new hikes affected four categories of products: bread and bakery product prices were boosted by an average of 19 percent; gasoline and diesel prices rose by 10 percent; cigarette prices increased by 20 percent; and household energy prices increased on average by about 20 percent.[4]

Although the increases were anticipated, the rise in energy and bread prices was greater than expected. The price increases drastically reduced the consumers' purchasing power and overshadowed the previous increases in 1987 in coffee, restaurants, meat, alcohol, furniture, and postal rates.[5]  Increases in pensions and welfare payments were announced at the same time to cushion the effect of the price hikes.  However, these measures did not offset the burden on the aged, especially those in rural areas, and the disadvantaged.

The continuing recession manifested itself in the country's highest planned government deficit: 43,800 million forint.[6]  Rising inflation and the continuing poor performance in industry and trade compelled the government to borrow again in 1987. The latest loan package, $400,000,000 over 8 years, was led by Morgan Guaranty Trust; compared with the previous loan, the interest rate and initial processing charges and underwriting fees had increased.[7]  Doubts about the government's solvency were reinforced by the fact that the IMF was considering a standby loan package.[8]  Hungary had the largest per capita foreign debt in Eastern Europe.[9]

The price increases were large but did not include any new regulations or proposals for expanding output and productivity. Measures had not yet materialized for reforming the deficit-ridden industrial sector, which stockpiled goods worth 731,000 million forint in 1986.[10]

*The Bank Reform.*  "The green light is on but the traffic is standing still." This is how *Heti Világgazdaság* (July 14, 1987) described the experimental period of the Hungarian bank reform that started on January 1, 1987, with the introduction of a two-tier banking system (consisting of a central bank and a series of commercial and specialized banks). The reform was intended to encourage business-like thinking among managers and to make the financial activities of enterprises responsive to interest rates. The experimental period ended in June. At that point enterprises became free to choose their own banking partners instead of having them assigned.

All five new commercial banks struggled with shortages of office space (in both their central and branch offices) and of trained personnel; their main problems, however, were the various unforseen policy questions that arose. They also had to face the gigantic task of creating a public image for themselves. After all, the Hungarian National Bank (HNB) had simply allocated customers in the past to branch offices, which were distributed arbitrarily about the country. Problems also arose from the fact that the new commercial banks began with greatly varying amounts of capital.

During the first six months of 1987, the newly established banks were burdened by the restrictive money supply policy of the HNB. Although short-term loans to enterprises were available in abundance, there was not enough money to grant many loans for long-term, large-scale investment projects. Thus, the new banks found themselves at a disadvantage vis-à-vis the state, which showed no sign of relinquishing its hold over this investment area.

The new banks tried to attract capital by issuing bonds. The Budapest Bank sold 500,000,000 forint worth of bonds in March,[12] as did the National Commercial and Credit Bank, which also sold another 1,000 million forint worth of stocks in July.[13] The Hungarian Credit Bank tried setting up a subsidiary called the Investment and Turnover Bank.[14] The new banks were not, however, allowed to establish connections with Western banks, which were still restricted to offshore banks. (A new offshore bank, Unicbank, was set up in January.) The oldest and most successful of the Hungary-based offshore banks was the Central-European International Bank Ltd. (CIB), whose assets reached $436,900,000 in 1986.[15] In only one major case did a bank (the Hungarian Credit Bank) initiated bankruptcy proceedings.

The new banks were stock companies themselves, although their shares were not traded, just as the stocks of numerous other large enterprises were not traded. The total value of stocks, mostly state-owned, in existence in Hungary reached 30,000 million forint ($666,000,000).[16]

To facilitate the trading of bonds and, in the future, of stocks as well, 22 banks and financial institutions signed an agreement in July 1987 about the opening of a financial market.[17] The signatories included insurance companies, the Hungarian Chamber of Commerce, the Ministry of Finance, and all the new commercial banks (including even Citibank Budapest Co., a subsidiary of Citibank US). The most active sponsor was, not surprisingly, Budapest Bank, which was instrumental in developing bonds in Hungary. In the first six months of 1987, bonds worth 7,743 million forint were issued, more than the total value of bonds issued in 1986. The main attraction of bonds was the state guaranty. Since 1982 bonds worth a total of 16,128 million forint (about $358,000,000) had been issued.[18] The bond-issuing boom was aided by uncertainty over how bond returns would be taxed in 1988.

There had been fear that, given the indirect bureaucratic controls on enterprises and the shortage of capital, the new banks would simply be specialized branches of the HNB. This did not happen, however, as the new banks learned their trade fast and were chipping away at the powers of the HNB. Despite the long period of administrative control, it did not take long for the new generation of bankers to learn the trade. Hungarian banking, however, would not be able to expand much more without a further reduction of the state's role in enterprise operations.

*Tax Legislation.* On September 19, after a lively debate, the Hungarian National Assembly approved laws introducing the first comprehensive personal income tax in a communist country as well as the first Western-style value-added tax. The income tax bill was passed with 10 negative votes and 21 abstentions; the bill on value-added tax (VAT) was passed with 1 vote against and 5 abstentions.[19] The media did not reveal the names of those voting against the measures.

On September 18, 1987, in a live broadcast on Hungarian Radio and Television, Finance Minister Péter Medgyessy presented the two bills to the National Assembly.[20] In presenting the government's program, Prime Minister Károly Grósz had said earlier that the government would to some extent be easing its regulation of enterprises' activities. Reinforcing this point, Medgyessy explained that the maximum level of enterprise tax would be reduced from 90 percent to 70 percent. This would be accomplished, he said, by eliminating the capital tax, the accumulation tax, the wage tax, and taxes levied by city and local authorities as well as by reducing the enterprise income tax significantly. These modifications would reduce enterprises' taxes by between 100,000 million and 110,000 million forint a year, a loss to the state coffers that would be offset by the introduction of the personal income and VAT taxes. Indeed, the main aim of the new laws was originally to introduce a system to replace the present, incomprehensible, inconsistent, and exemption-ridden tax system. What Medgyessy did not say, however, was that the tax bills in their final form failed to carry through the original intention of doing away with practically all the old taxes, many of which remain alongside the new ones. This failure was likely to cause considerable confusion.

Under the new laws, enterprises were required to ensure that workers' net incomes remained the same as before the introduction of a personal income tax. Maintaining most of the old taxes meant that enterprises would, however, not have enough funds to meet this legal obligation; so how this problem would be resolved was left unclear. As things now stood, the VAT and personal income tax were not replacement taxes, as intended, but an additional burden on enterprises and individuals. Behind this state of affairs lay the authorities' uncertainty about how much revenue would be collected in taxes under the new system.

Medgyessy also introduced a package of social benefits to help offset the price increases caused by the new tax laws. He admitted, however, that these measures would only partly counterbalance the planned, mammoth price increases.[21]

The introduction of a personal income tax was a departure from the socialist type of collective responsibility. Although the citizens ultimately paid the state's bills in every society, the way in which the burden was distributed was important. Individuals in Hungary would now be able to see for themselves, although not to the full extent, how much they had contributed to the wasteful state machinery, because deductions for taxes would be shown on their paychecks. This was likely to lead to increased questioning and pressure on the authorities, as citizens would have an even more solid justification for demanding the rights they had not been given before. They would also have "evidence" of the inefficient state bureaucracy's squandering of funds. Furthermore, the personal tax system would reward the individual initiative of those who, with extra effort and care, could find the exemptions and loopholes in the system.

45

MOUNTING PRESSURES FOR CHANGE

Alfred Reisch

The draft policy statement issued by the HSWP Central Committee on March 31, 1988, met with strong criticism from the party's rank-and-file. The draft was submitted to the basic party organizations for a three-week debate prior to its endorsement at the party's national conference scheduled for May 20-23.[1] More than half the party's members were reported to have expressed their views on the draft, strongly criticizing many of its aspects in an unprecedented display of dissatisfaction, anger, concern, and impatience with their leaders' proposed measures for extricating Hungary from its economic and social difficulties. The response from a number of Hungary's social and economic organizations was equally critical. In short, the party leadership was left no other choice but to sit down and rewrite the draft in time for the CC to approve it at a meeting on May 10, only 10 days before the start of the national conference.

*The Draft.* During the debates within the party organizations a great many party members said that the draft statement was too general, too formal, sketchy, and generally flawed. It had a cumbersome and complicated style, they said, so that workers had to read it several times before they could understand it. It contained little that was new, being filled with political commonplaces.

While approving of the self-critical tone in which the CC's draft had evaluated the situation in Hungary, party members said that the evaluation had not gone deep enough or been sufficiently thorough or sincere. In all, the party membership showed itself to be united in its strong criticism of the wording and style of the document. The rank-and-file placed the blame for past mistakes squarely on the party leadership and not the party membership as a whole.

Most members felt that not enough time had been allowed for discussion of the draft. Some said that the selection of delegates to the national party conference had not been democratic, having been done hurriedly at meetings of the regional party secretaries; it would have been more democratic and have enhanced the legitimacy of the conference if delegates had been elected by the membership at large. Doubts were also voiced as to whether the conference would pay heed to the party debates that had preceded it. Some members felt that the difference between a party congress and a party conference had not been made adequately clear; thus, they were not sure what the May gathering could achieve.

*The Issue of Responsibility.* The question of who was responsible for the mistakes that had led Hungary into its current difficulties was probably the most hotly debated issue at the meeting of the various party organizations; and in some cases it took up half of the time spent debating the CC's statement. Party members asked for a "scientific analysis" of the social and economic developments of the past 10 to 30 years and for the party conference to set a deadline for the completion of this analysis. The members wanted to know why mistakes had been made and by whom, and they complained that the draft had failed to examine the responsibility of the 13th HSWP Congress of 1985 and had ignored the issue of personal responsibility.

Critics said that, in addition to holding the CC responsible for Hungary's current situation, the statement should also have mentioned the Politburo. Many members felt that the party was too centralized, that the Politburo and its Secretariat had too much control over decisions, and that this should be remedied by granting the Central Committee more authority. Responsibility began at the decision-making level, they said, and should not have been limited by the draft document to those implementing decisions. Personal and not just collective responsibility had to be established for past mistakes and appropriate action taken, including the recall of party leaders. This was vital if confidence was to be restored between the party members and their leaders and between the party and society at large.

Closely related to the issue of responsibility was the party members' demand that the draft document have adequate guarantees for the successful implementation of the HSWP's reform program. This was needed, they considered, because many good resolutions in the past had been passed but not implemented. Party members also felt that a political movement could mobilize society only if its policies were credible and attractive.

*Shortcomings in the Party.* It emerged during the meetings of the party organizations that the members generally felt that democracy within the party was "too formal" and that the rank-and-file were excluded from the making of political decisions. Rather than "democratic centralism" and "socialist democracy," the members would have liked to have "democratic socialism," that is, more democracy within the party. They said that the party's leaders did not know the views of the rank-and-file, who should be allowed to express their views openly. One member squarely blamed past mistakes on the fact that doubts, criticism, and alternative views had been considered unjustified within the party. The members of party cells debated and criticized party policies among themselves but refrained from doing so in party forums for fear of being reprimanded. Some members said that while the differences between party and nonparty members had decreased, those between the party's rank-and-file and its leaders had increased. Others alluded to long-standing conflicts between party members and the party apparatus. Party members bemoaned the party's excessive bureaucracy and the diminished role played by elected bodies; they called for a "self-correcting mechanism" that would place the party leadership under greater supervision by party members as well as by social organizations.

The view was expressed that if the planned limit of two five-year terms for party officials were to be calculated from the 13th HSWP Congress in 1985, individuals who had already been in office for 15 years or more (Kádár being the obvious example) would remain in their posts for up to 10 more years, which was unacceptable. Members also said that they should have a say in the election of the Central Committee. Many wanted a clearer definition of the party's leading role, its place in society and in Hungary's political system, its policy of alliance with the masses, and its position in relation to the reform.

*Ideological Weakness.* Party members said that the party's ideology had become unclear; they no longer knew what kind of "socialism" they were building. They also complained that the views they had expressed earlier in 1988 during a debate on party ideology were missing from the draft statement. In their opinion, the success of the reform depended to a large extent on the ability of the masses to understand it in ideological terms. Its ideology had to be clarified, therefore, and debate was needed both within and outside the party so that people's views could become known. Most of all, ideology had to be adjusted to fit the changes that had taken place in the economy.

*Minority Views and Factions.* Considerable confusion seemed to persist about the party's relationship with Hungary's growing number of oppositionists. An official of the Budapest district party committee, Béla Katona, angered by the use of the term to describe the opposition, proclaimed that he, too, was a person "holding differing views." The usage implied that all party members thought alike, he said—an implication that he rejected. Correct decisions, he argued, could be arrived at only on the basis of a variety of opinions that had to be given a chance to clash in genuine debate. The Budapest Municipal Party Committee asked that the term "people holding differing views" be deleted from the draft document.[2]

Strong views were expressed on the issue of minority views within the party. Chairman of the Budapest Municipal Council Pál Iványi said, for example, that if the intention was to defend party unity, he could agree that party members should not be allowed to organize factions to support their own interests. Nevertheless, minority views were needed as a source of new ideas, Iványi said; the party should not recoil from such views. It should allow members to express their own views and even to propagate them within the party without being accused of factionalism. It was not only the leadership that could come up with good ideas, Iványi said, and if members were not allowed to express their views within the party, these views would soon find their way out of the party.[3]

*KISZ Strongly Critical.* For Hungary's Communist Youth League (KISZ), the draft document was not specific enough. KISZ objected to the proposed timetable for party elections and felt that the personnel and other changes being considered for the 14th HSWP Congress (in 1990) should be carried out right away. It called for a widening of open debate within the party and for clarification of the party's line on minority views. It also noted that accountability within the party was impossible so long as personal responsibility could not be established because of the desire to protect various interests. It was unclear who was responsible for what in society, the party, KISZ, and the state apparatus, at both the decision-making and executive levels. KISZ said that rigorous "collective self-criticism," which had been virtually nonexistent until now, was needed, as was a major political turnabout in both the party and Hungarian society. KISZ said that a comprehensive reform concept had to be worked out in time for the party congress in 1990 at the latest.[4]

*PPF Finds Document Inadequate.* The HSWP CC also sent its draft document to a number of social and economic bodies, including the Patriotic People's Front, led by Secretary General Imre Pozsgay, an HSWP CC member in the forefront of radical political reform in Hungary. In a major statement published on April 23 in the PPF daily *Magyar Nemzet* and in a considerably watered-down form in the party daily *Népszabadság*, the PPF Presidium said that while it supported the party's reform efforts, it felt that the draft document, particularly its "overgeneralized findings," failed to meet Hungary's new needs. The PPF considered that some of the resolutions of the 13th HSWP Congress (1985) had become obsolete and that there was no way out of the country's grave situation without a deep analysis of how and why it had got there. Without such an analysis, there would be no national support for the party and the desired turnabout could not achieved, the PPF said.

The people's confidence could be restored only if there were legal guarantees that they could oversee the exercise of power following the reform of the political system, the PPF said. It also stressed the importance of separating the responsibilities of the party and the state. Since all citizens should be allowed to express their opinions and to know how their views were being put to use, the PPF supported the proposal for legislation to institute referendums on both national legislation and local regulations. It also supported the drafting of a new constitution; new laws on elections, the councils, and associations; and the creation of two courts to handle administrative and constitutional matters, respectively. It said that more precise regulations on civic rights should be formulated, more information should be made available to the public and welfare policy should be clarified.

The PPF criticized the draft for failing to reflect the PPF's current and future roles. In this respect, it said, the draft had even taken a step backward compared with earlier party statements, because it expected the PPF merely to carry out the political will of the HSWP. If this were the role assigned to the PPF, it would lose society's support and subsequently its whole reason for being. The PPF reminded the party that the vast majority of Hungarians were not party members and did not want to be treated as second-class citizens in political matters. Thus, the PPF, as a political group embracing party members and an embodiment of the party's policy of alliance with the masses, needed autonomy and saw itself as performing an independent political role. While it hoped that the national HSWP conference would bring about a favorable political change, the PPF said that it would also carry out its own program for change. (The KISZ statement also noted that the draft document's comments about the PPF were "useless," especially if pluralism were to be taken seriously; and KISZ asked that the PPF's role be given "more substance.")

In a radio interview,[5] PPF Secretary Béla Molnár said that democracy could not develop in society if there was little democracy within the party. At present, Hungary had more civic democracy than party democracy, he said, as exemplified by the multiple candidacies at general elections. In his view, political pluralism could exist in a one-party system when various social bodies were able to submit alternative proposals on major issues through truly public debates reported in the media. To this end, legal guarantees were needed to protect responsible civic action against any possible retribution, Molnár said. He also said that the young should be represented by more organizations than just KISZ.

*Leadership's Reaction.* The April 23 meeting of the Budapest HSWP Committee was attended by János Kádár and was addressed by Ferenc Havasi, its first secretary since June 1987 and a member of the party's Politburo. In a strongly proreform speech, Havasi pointed to the collapse of the old Stalinist ideological system and to the need for the communist system to be cleansed of "harmful deposits." In his view, comprehensive economic changes were needed for Hungary to find a way out of its current crisis. The country's political institutions had to be modernized within a one-party system but with society guaranteed wide supervision over the party on the basis of a partnership, Havasi said; without this, the issue of a multiparty system would continue to be raised. In his view, the party had to practice self-control and have a "self-correcting mechanism"; but even that would be inadequate without a proper political environment in which the party would be monitored in an institutionalized manner. Only then could the party win the country's support and act as a national integrating force. Havasi said that the national party conference was competent to make the necessary personnel and organizational changes within the HSWP, to assess the implementation of the resolutions of the 13th HSWP Congress, and to set new political priorities and objectives.[6]

HSWP CC Secretary György Fejti and CC Agitprop Department Head Erno Lakatos were promptly interviewed by Radio Budapest. They acknowledged the validity of the party leadership's criticisms, especially in regard to personal responsibility, lack of clarity on ideology, and the anachronistic concept of party unity, as well as the problem of minority views and factions, views that differed from the party line, and alternative proposals. Fejti announced that the Politburo would review the redrafted position paper and submit it for discussion to the Central Committee on May 10 and that the party conference from May 20 to 22 would have the final say.[7]

During a tour of Zala County, Prime Minister and HSWP Politburo member Károly Grósz said that the membership's sharp criticism had been "natural and acceptable" and had shown both "anxiety and a readiness to help." In his view, a new national consensus was needed; but it could not be as broad as that of post-1957 because too much tension had built up in society. If the government tried to accomplish everything at once, immediate and lasting "chaos" and even economic collapse would result; thus, a compromise between the necessary and the possible had to be reached. Although a multiparty system was, historically speaking, a long-term possibility, Grósz said that in practice it could not develop under Hungary's current social and political conditions. His aim was to modernize the party's operations; he also wanted a single, unified trade union and a single, unified youth organization that would be in some ways be autonomous, but not be entirely independent of the party. The National Assembly should enact legislation and oversee the government, but Grósz said that parliamentary rule was infeasible in Hungary.

Grósz said that the nation needed leaders who were able and willing to solve conflicts and overcome resistance, who could win the support of the populace, and who would also withdraw (that is, resign). In an implied reference to Kádár and his old guard, he said that "biological laws" applied to everyone and that leaders could become tired and less able to bear burdens. Grósz also said that leaders could have different views about Hungary's situation, since it was so complicated, and that the surest way to get out of it had not yet been found.[8]

# 46
# THE FALL OF KÁDÁR
Alfred Reisch

János Kádár, Hungary's party leader for nearly 32 years, was replaced by Prime Minister Károly Grósz as general secretary on May 22, 1988, at the conclusion of the special three-day HSWP national conference. Kádár, 76, was made party chairman, a new position whose duties were not fully outlined. The conference ended on May 20 with a rambling, disjointed speech by a tearful Kádár that strongly resembled a farewell address; after 15 minutes Radio Budapest interrupted its live reporting of his speech and played music instead.[1] Kádár had led the party since October 25, 1956, when he took over a disintegrating Hungarian Workers' Party. On November 3, 1956, he set up, with armed Soviet assistance, a new government and became head of the renamed Hungarian Socialist Workers' Party (HSWP).

Grósz, 58, had been a member of the HSWP Politburo since 1985 and prime minister since June 1987. A typical party apparatchik, who had been labeled a dogmatist, he then set about with great energy and determination to revive Hungary's gravely ill economy, a seemingly impossible task. He earned a reputation as a hard worker, a pragmatist who stressed good organization and efficiency, and a no-nonsense man who always spoke his mind. In regard to reforms, his thinking and actions clearly resembled those of Gorbachev; and Grósz had obviously won the former's sympathy and support. According to Hungarian officials, however, this was the first time the Soviets did not play a direct role in the election of a Hungarian party leader.[2]

Next to the election of Grósz, the inclusion in the Politburo of the HSWP's two leading advocates of reform was the most significant development of the national conference.

The 65-year-old Rezső Nyers, who had already been a Politburo member from 1966 to 1975, was a former printer and Social Democrat who joined the Communist party after 1948. The main initiator of the Hungarian economic reforms launched in 1968, he was removed from both the Politburo and CC Secretariat when the brakes were applied to the reform. In later years, in a large number of articles and interviews, Nyers called for drastic, comprehensive economic and political reforms in Hungary.

The 55-year-old Imre Pozsgay was the HSWP's strongest and most sincere advocate of political reform; he joined the party at the age of 17 and in 1957 obtained a teaching degree in Marxism-Leninism from the party college. From 1971 to 1975 he served as deputy editor in chief of the party's theoretical and political monthly *Társadalmi Szemle*, writing a great many theoretical articles on social issues. As a steadfast, prominent supporter of the economic reform, Pozsgay helped shape some of its key principles. He was made minister of culture in 1976, acquiring the reputation of a liberal who had helped create a relatively tolerant atmosphere in Hungarian artistic and intellectual life. Pozsgay was removed as Minister of Culture in 1982, and was made general secretary of the Patriotic People's Front. His election to the Politburo symbolized the victory of the new over the old in the party.[3]

*Statements by Berecz and Grósz.* At an international press conference on May 22, CC Secretary János Berecz said that although an effort to rejuvenate the party was under way, it did not entail a systematic campaign to replace every leader at every level, which he said was unnecessary. Nonetheless, he encouraged the party's members to be less cautious in demanding the removal of those leaders with whom they were dissatisfied. Berecz revealed that Kádár himself had requested not to be nominated again as general secretary because of his age and the party's desire for "renewal," and that Grósz had proposed that Kádár be made party chairman to show its esteem for his achievements and to give him some kind of role in the party. As chairman, Berecz said, Kádár was no longer a Politburo member but could participate in its meetings as a CC member.

Berecz also noted that the Politburo had in part been rejuvenated and enhanced by people with political and economic experience. He said that its new composition also was in response to "the need for unity within the party." When asked how long Grósz would hold both his party and government jobs, Berecz said that Grósz still needed "a few months" before he could pass on the post of prime minister to a successor. The rejuvenation of the Politburo, Berecz said, would be followed by a similar process at the territorial and lower levels of the party.[4]

In a radio and television interview immediately after the party conference, Grósz said that the conference had approved a "new political concept" modifying the program adopted in 1985 at the 13th HSWP Congress. He said that the move to separate the party and the state was not incompatible with the top state and party posts being held by the same person but that this was not standard practice in Hungary. Thus, Grósz said, the two functions would have to be separated again "in the not-too-distant future."[5]

On May 23, in a lengthy interview published in the government daily *Magyar Hírlap*, Grósz said that it was primarily the decision-making mechanisms of the party and government that had to be separated, in that the CC and Politburo should no longer decide governmental issues. Moreover, the party apparatus should not interfere in the state's executive apparatus or "chaos" would result.

*Policy Statement Adopted.* The final policy statement adopted on May 22 by the 986 delegates to the Hungarian party's third national conference pointed the way for the development in Hungary of what the document termed "socialist pluralism." A CC work group headed by HSWP Politburo and CC Secretary János Berecz had spent three days in late April sorting thousands of suggestions from the party's rank-and-file in order to include the most "indispensable" recommendations in a new draft version, which the Central Committee adopted on May 10 and then submitted to the party conference.[6] The conference delegates amended the document further, so that the final version clearly reflected the membership's mounting demand for more than just cosmetic changes.

The final version retained the statement that Hungary could achieve lasting economic results only if the reforms were continued and that the implementation of economic reform had been hindered by the fact that fundamental changes had not been introduced in the rest of society. In the first such admission by the party, the final document said that economic difficulties were both the cause and the consequence of "functional disturbances in the system of political institutions." Another addition was the admission that, along with a decrease in the number of working-age people, the population's "unsatisfactory state of health has had an adverse effect on society's capability to perform."

*Need To Reform the Party.* Given the HSWP's leading role in a one-party system, the document said, any continuation of the reform had to start with the party itself. The final text said that the main task was to bring about greater democracy within the party. It said that regional party bodies, party organizations in work places, the basic party cells, and, indeed, every party member had to have the opportunity to participate in shaping policy and to have more independence and responsibility in organizing and monitoring the party's activities. In making decisions, the party's leading bodies should also consider the views expressed by public organizations and interest groups and at public forums, the final text said.

The final text said forcefully that although the principle of collective leadership prevailed in the party, those involved in the making and implementation of decisions had a "personal political responsibility." In order to make the party more democratic, a certain percentage of the members of the party's leading bodies would have to be elected directly by the basic organizations, who could also recall them if need be. At every level, party elections had to be secret and several candidates could be nominated if requested. This new system for party elections, the final text said, had to be gradually introduced, starting in 1988.

Dealing with the party's ideological and political unity, the draft version had said that views and doubts needed to be expressed within party forums but not outside them; statements not in accordance with resolutions were to be prohibited, as was the organizing of factions. To this, the final text added, however, that before a decision was made, party members could state their own viewpoints. The final document retained the draft version's limit of two five-year terms for party officials down to the level of county party secretary and included CC department heads.

*Goals for Political Reform Clarified.* The document included the novel statement that the exercise of power by the people had to be based on "socialist pluralism built around the leading role of the party." The document did not, however, clarify what was meant by socialist pluralism. The final text also said that Hungary's social and political development made it necessary to "review"—that is, revise—the constitution (rather than draft a new one, as some delegates had proposed). The National Assembly's main task should be to enact legislation, a function over which it had "exclusive jurisdiction." Moreover, bodies of popular representation should become "forums for open politicking."

In response to a barrage of criticism, the document was revised to say that "the autonomy of public organizations and movements must be increased" and that they should draft their own proposals on issues of importance to their members. Greater emphasis was to be placed both on a "partnership" between these organizations and the state bodies, based on the recognition of the party's leading role, and on the involvement of public organizations in political, social, and economic decision-making.

The Patriotic People's Front (PPF) was specifically mentioned as "an important institution of socialist pluralism," working to achieve a consensus (between the party and the people) and a lasting alliance between the various "forces" of society. It was to have some measure of autonomy but was also said to work under the theoretical direction of and in cooperation with the party. The party, the document said, should make greater use of the PPF's forums.

*Assessment.* Although no revolutionary revisions were made, the final policy statement of the conference echoed the party rank-and-file's vocal criticism of the leadership's past mistakes and its call for reforms within the HSWP to enable the basic party cells to play a growing role in the decision-making process. The call for collective and personal responsibility of party leaders was taken seriously in that the new CC removed with one sweep János Kádár and his entire old guard from the Politburo.

The need for both party and institutional reform was stated much more strongly than in the draft version, and the steps toward this goal, such as the creation of specific CC work committees and the setting of deadlines, were laid down more clearly. The stronger emphasis on political reforms undoubtedly bore the mark of Pozsgay,[7] as well as of Hungary's various oppositional and independent proreform groups that had mushroomed since the beginning of the year and whose ideas and suggestions had received increasing attention both within and outside the party.

*The End of the Kádár Era.* Although the authorities consistently denied that there was a Hungarian model for the "building of socialism," such a model—"Kádárism"—undoubtedly existed. Although unclear which specific aspects could be attributed to Kádár himself, all of them required his approval and bore the mark of his particular approach. Kádárism was essentially a working compromise between the party and society that arose out of the national trauma of 1956 and was reinforced by Kádár's own values. Although highly political in nature, it was based on the depoliticization of society, that is, the removal of ordinary citizens from political life, a process that involved the vast majority of Hungarians. Although Kádárism had a carefully constructed ideological rationale, it was highly pragmatic and flexible. The compromise was clearly aimed at providing undisputed party control over the state, the economy, and society. At least until the early nineteen-eighties, it brought significant benefits to Hungary's citizens, so long as they remained tacitly willing to accept an arrangement that they had had no part in formulating.

The slogan "He who is not against us is for us"—first used at a meeting of the Presidium of the Patriotic People's Front in December 1961—illustrated Kádár's policy of an alliance between the party and the people. Kádár had often said that Marxism-Leninism was the "best system of political ideas," yet he was clearly willing to coexist peacefully with people who were not Communists, provided that they forwent active opposition to the régime.

Kádár's best-known achievement was the gradual, cautious reform of Hungary's economic management system (the New Economic Mechanism, or NEM), launched in January 1968. The success of the NEM in the face of considerable internal and external difficulties earned him and his administration good marks at home and abroad for close to two decades. Although the process was halted throughout most of the nineteen-seventies it achieved success little by little primarily because of Kádár's well-known willingness to compromise when necessary. The NEM was also remarkable in that it deviated from the overall policy of other East European countries, which, until Gorbachev came to office, paid much more attention to ideology as determining economic and social policies. Even so, the economic reform was hesitatingly and inconsistently implemented, although from the early nineteen-eighties on, Hungary once more resolutely followed a reformist path. Rather than rushing into a process of "privatization" or of "counterfeit capitalism," Hungary sought to encourage its enterprises to show initiative; its reforms aroused keen interest in China but were merely tolerated by a distrustful Leonid Brezhnev, who applied them on a limited basis to agriculture in the Soviet Union.

Under Kádár, Hungary gained experience in implementing economic reforms by replacing the Stalinist system of a strictly centralized, planned economy with one based on planning according to economic indicators and on the stimulation of market forces. Attention was also paid to supply and demand, competition, initiative, profit-sharing and the basing of wages on productivity. Despite the ideological and political problems that emerged, the Kádár régime remained committed to developing the state planned economy and improving as well as speeding up the reform process. A series of sound decisions were not properly implemented, however, and thus the reform was largely flawed.

The second half of the nineteen-eighties marked the twilight of Kádár's long rule. The exceptionally perceptive and shrewd politician—who, after turning against the revolution in 1956, had become nationally accepted as the party's leader and even recognized as legitimate—began to see the undoing of some of his major achievements. Most important, the tacit support given the party was increasingly challenged, as well as the acceptance of his rule as the best possible under the circumstances. Moreover, the complete depoliticization of society—and the accompanying firm control by the party—gradually gave way to mounting social and political activism. At the same time, there was a limited measure of privatization and more opportunity for independent initiative in every field, except for political decision making.

Kádár's legitimacy was, however, based primarily on the régime's ability to maintain or improve the standard of living. Since the early nineteen-eighties a number of major economic and political problems emerged in Hungary, for which the party alone, given its perennially proclaimed leading role in society, had to take the blame.

At the economic level the régime was now paying the price for halting the reforms in the first half of the nineteen-seventies and for borrowing heavily from the West. It had to constantly struggle to maintain its financial solvency and its foreign trade equilibrium by trying to increase exports while limiting imports. The very openness of Hungary's economy made it all the more vulnerable to any international economic crisis; and the Soviet Union's increased efforts to coordinate Hungary's economy more closely with its own and that of the other CMEA countries had been far from beneficial, since this deprived Hungary of much-needed hard currency. Economic growth was replaced by stagnation, and living standards deteriorated for some people, such as those on pensions or fixed incomes, those with large families and those just starting their career. As the need to restructure industry and to streamline or eliminate unprofitable enterprises (another unimplemented aspect of the NEM) grew more pressing, the specter of unemployment and poverty arose in Hungary.

At the political level, the party was faced by a growing number of civic initiatives—for instance, in support of peace, charitable causes, and environmental protection. In order to retain its role as the sole controller of society, it sought to hinder or absorb these movements and at most allowed them very limited autonomy. For fear of going too far, however, the régime balked at genuine political reform and continued to place limits on open discussion by Hungarians at home and visiting abroad. Hence, the exact nature of the reform, which large segments of middle-level management and the party apparatus feared because it would cost them power and privileges, was never made quite clear to the populace. With the advent of Gorbachev's reformism in the USSR and the worsening of Hungary's economy, independent, spontaneous political activism—long limited to a few hundred Budapest intellectuals calling themselves the "democratic opposition"—increased, especially from the fall of 1987 onward. The new civic initiatives even challenged the monopoly of the official labor union and youth organizations, and they reflected the growing disarray and uncertainty in party ranks.

Adding to the problems was the rise of the nationality issue in the nineteen-eighties; this was fueled by the continued mistreatment of the Magyar minorities, especially in Romania, where a full-scale policy of assimilation prompted tens of thousands of ethnic Hungarians to leave the country and seek residence in Hungary. The Hungarian authorities, who had long remained silent on the issue for fear of being accused of intervening in neighboring allies' internal affairs, were finally forced to speak up for Magyars both at home and in international forums.

By the end of 1986 it had become obvious that Hungary was in the middle of a serious economic and sociopolitical crisis for which Kádár was being increasingly blamed both outside and inside the party. While for some 15 years he had been perceived as being the major guarantor of reform, he now looked more and more like an impediment to the radical and comprehensive changes urgently needed in Hungary. The vigorous reformist policies of Gorbachev and the declining energy of the aging and ailing Kádár helped reinforce this image. In June 1987, Grósz was appointed prime minister, with the unenviable mission of salvaging Hungary's economy by means of a three-year austerity and stabilization program and also of introducing a modicum of reforms within both the party and the country's political institutions.

Kádár created a stir when for the first time, in September 1987, he addressed the fall session of Hungary's National Assembly, which had been called together to debate and approve Grósz's tough economic stabilization program. In a halting and often slurred address, he went so far as to take the blame, as the oldest member of the party's top leadership, for the mistaken decisions that had led Hungary into its present economic and social predicament. After that, however, Kádár began steadfastly denying that there was an actual crisis in Hungary, speaking instead of a number of difficulties and contradictions that, in his view, were of a temporary nature and could thus be solved in the future. This evaluation, however, ran contrary to that of the vast majority of the Hungarian population and of many well-informed experts, including a number of leading party officials. In the end, the issue of his personal responsibility and the impression that his evaluation of Hungary's situation was no longer fully adequate made Kádár appear behind the times and out of touch with reality.

47
KÁDÁRISM WITHOUT KÁDÁR?
Bennett Kovrig

*The Middle Cadres Rebel.* Since 1986, the party's authority had been steadily eroded by the economy's near bankruptcy and austerity measures that imposed immediate sacrifice in exchange for the promise of distant recovery. Kádár's historic "alliance policy" was a tacit bargain offering material benefits and a liberal cultural policy and demanding no more than passive acceptance of communist rule. Economic stagnation and decline undermined this social contract, and the régime's competence came under open attack both from the dissident groups that proliferated and from within the party itself.

The party's middle-ranking officials, county first secretaries and the like, found themselves caught between two millstones. Popular discontent spilled over into the party's rank-and-file, raising questions to which the officials had no answers.

The disunited and disoriented central leadership could offer little guidance and even less assistance. Meanwhile, intellectuals within and outside the party engaged in open debate on the party's responsibility for past and present failures, the need to reconsider its leading role, and for more institutionalized pluralism and economic liberalism.

This crisis of authority and legitimacy had a deeply demoralizing effect on the party itself and on its dependent organizations. According to official sources, some 45,000 members left the party in 1987, although by 1988 the number was probably twice as high. Most basic units had simply ceased to function. The Communist Youth League's largely inactive membership had fallen from 900,000 in 1986 to 720,000, and its leadership in desperation jumped on the bandwagon of radical reform. Growing numbers of workers were deserting the official trade unions. Attempts were made to create a trade union of scientific and academic workers and a youth organization outside the official structures. The center was not holding.

Kádár made some last-minute attempts to restore order. He expelled from the party four reformist intellectuals and reprimanded the two most outspoken communist reformers, Imre Pozsgay and Rezső Nyers. These measures only aggravated the party's malaise, and the delegates to the conference, most of them middle-level cadres, were out for blood. At its last meeting before the conference, the Politburo worked out a plan for rejuvenation of the leadership. Kádár would be kicked upstairs to the presumably ceremonial post of party president but would retain a seat on the Politburo, while a few of the conservative "mummies" would be replaced by younger and more reform-minded leaders.

Even this radical scenario failed to satisfy the delegates. Kádár's self-serving opening address was followed by sharp criticism of the leadership's failures; and by early morning on the last day of the conference Kádár had to acknowledge that his days as an active leader were over and give up his Politburo membership. The delegates, voting secretly, administered a further rebuke to the conference's stage-managers by failing to elect to the Central Committee several veteran leaders who had been slated to serve on the new Politburo. Even that old master of cajolery and compromise, the former ideological and cultural tsar György Aczél, retained his Central Committee seat only by the slimmest margin of votes. These personnel changes were the most dramatic outcome of the middle cadres' revolt; but what did they signify for Kádárism and reform?

*Cosmetic Remedies for a Deep Crisis.* The newly-elected party leadership had yet to display its collective will, but Hungarians tended to regard it as more suited to continuity than radical change. Its members were mostly bureaucrats of modest competence, while the new secretary general, Károly Grósz, was widely perceived as a rather demagogic politician motivated more by personal ambition than by ideology or other constant values.

Of the two outright reformers elevated to the Politburo, Rezső Nyers was a former left-wing Social Democrat and the father of the original economic reform of 1968, an aging figure nearing the end of his political career. The other, Imre Pozsgay, head of the Patriotic People's Front, had become a favorite among Hungarian intellectuals and dissidents for espousing the cause of an ill-defined "socialist pluralism." Possessed of an undistinguished record as an administrator and lacking wide popular support, Pozsgay was reportedly considered by Grósz for the prime ministership, a trial balloon that was promptly shot down by the conservatives. Co-opted into the leadership, Pozsgay could well find that his freedom to promote political reform had been curtailed.

The policy statement approved at the party conference called for the democratization of party life (including the notion of limited terms of office, made fashionable by Gorbachev) and for a "socialist pluralism" that did not constrain the leading role of the party. Grósz was on record as having said that the single-party system and single trade union and youth organizations were here to stay and that Western-style parliamentary government was out of the question. The party's endorsement of constitutional reform, improvements to the electoral system, public referendums, and the better representation of interests was therefore the classic Kádárist tactic of squaring the circle, of creating the illusion of democracy without altering the substance of party supremacy.

The Grósz leadership faced a society and economy in deep crisis. Insolvency could be postponed for several years with Western help; and the economy's performance could benefit marginally from the proposed law on economic associations, which should legitimize more varied forms of ownership and entrepreneurship; but an uncompetitive industrial sector and an agricultural sector whose relatively high output was only to be achieved with uneconomically high inputs demanded bolder and more painful reforms than the régime was likely to attempt. Meanwhile, the glitter of central Budapest hid a creaking and decaying infrastructure of public and social services.

The political opposition was marked by a certain cleavage between those (clustered around the Network of Free Initiatives) who saw no real promise of democracy and reform in rejuvenated Kádárism and others (the more populist, nationalist adherents of the Hungarian Democratic Forum) who were readier to anticipate and seek incremental improvements and rest their hopes in Pozsgay. Active dissent was largely limited to the intelligentsia and students, who had no link with the workers. It remained to be seen whether the promised law on public associations would give legal legitimacy to the rapidly growing number of unofficial groups and clubs; but it was unlikely that it would sanction independent organizations that pursued political objectives. Political reform in Eastern Europe essentially aimed at a centrally-controlled, hierarchical structure for the representation of people's interests. This "socialist pluralism" was undoubtedly an improvement on the Stalinist totalitarian model, but it stopped far short of authentic, participatory democracy.

The demoralization and exasperation displayed by party activists at the conference did not reflect a disposition to alter radically the leading role of the party. Their wish was that a forceful and rejuvenated leadership under Grósz would restore the party's authority and self-respect, improve the economy's performance, and maintain public order. Cautious economic reform, tolerance for ineffectual dissent, and a managerial rather than ideological style of government had been the hallmarks of Kádárism at its best; and the new leadership was likely follow the same path.

Although Gorbachev and Grósz praised each other, the similarity between their roles was deceptive. The former was facing an uphill battle to sell major reforms to a reluctant party, bureaucracy, and public. Hungary was well ahead of the Soviet Union in most aspects of reform, with mixed results. Grósz's task was to demonstrate that the Hungarian experiment with perestroika and glasnost could work and that the party could remain in control even in the midst of social pluralism. The outcome of the upcoming CPSU conference was awaited with some anxiety in Hungary, for the scope of its own further reforms would inevitably be affected by Gorbachev's success or failure. Kádárism was essentially a formula for marginal adaptation and compromise, and its spirit promised to survive its inventor.

# XII. YUGOSLAVIA AND THE FUTURE OF SOCIALISM

## 48
## THE AGROKOMERC SCANDAL
### Milan Andrejevich

A major financial scandal surrounding the Agrokomerc enterprise in Bosnia, which broke in August 1987, was dubbed "Agrogate" by the Zagreb daily *Večernji List*.[1] Agrokomerc was accused of issuing promissory notes without collateral to 63 Yugoslav banks for a sum equal to between $290,000,000 and $500,000,000. The size of the sum was all the more scandalous coming, as it did, at a time when Yugoslavia was unable to pay back even an installment of $240,000,000 in principal and interest on its foreign debt of over $20,000 million.

This scandal was but one of thousands since "workers' self-management" went into effect in June 1950, though none approached the enormity of the Agrokomerc affair. In Yugoslavia, as in other Communist-ruled countries, corruption and dishonest management were more or less acceptable ways of attaining goals that could not be achieved through legitimate means.

*The Scope of the Scandal.* The deteriorating economy was one part of a struggle that was being waged by various groups trying to serve the interests of the regional party or government. The Agrokomerc affair revealed that for 40 years individual republics (in this case, Bosnia-Herzegovina) had, with impunity, made use of funds from other republics, thereby posing a serious threat to Yugoslavia's already fragile economic and political balance.

Agrokomerc was established in the town of Velika Kladuša, in northwestern Bosnia-Herzegovina in 1963. From an initial work force of some 30 workers, it grew to become one of the major agroindustrial enterprises in Yugoslavia, with a work force of 11,691 employees. It produced over 14,485 tons of goods in 1986; and concluded agreements valued at $173,000,000 with 22 foreign countries.

Fikret Abdić, a Bosnian Moslem, who in 1967 at the age of 28 became the head of the Executive Board, spending  much of the year at his mansion in Vološko, near Opatija on the coast, was a member of the Bosnian CC since 1982 and of the Federal Chamber of the Yugoslav National Assembly since 1986. He was closely associated with the two Pozderac brothers, Hakija, who had been a member of the Council of the Federation since 1982, and Hamdija, the vice-president of the Yugoslav State Presidency when the scandal broke.

Abdić, who enjoyed immunity from arrest because of his position as a Federal Chamber member, had the privilege legally taken away from him by a commission of the chamber. By September 8, 1987, numerous Agrokomerc officials, including Abdić, had been arrested and charged with having "committed the criminal act of threatening the social order in a counter-revolutionary manner with the aim of undermining the country's economic system."

The revelation that banks commonly accepted bills of exchange without actually examining the collateral exacerbated the chaotic situation in Yugoslavia's banking system. The practice, according to some economists, had already contributed greatly to the country's triple-digit inflation rate.

Jozo Smole, president of the Socialist Alliance of Slovenia, stated at a press conference in Ljubljana before foreign journalists on September 5, that the affair had "shown that the link between politicians and businessmen must be severed in Yugoslavia" and that the Agrokomerc scandal was "a chance to sort out matters in the country."[2] Janko Smole, however, (Jozo's elder brother), who served under Tito as finance minister and governor of the National Bank of Yugoslavia and was a ranking official of the World Bank, said that the affair was symptomatic of a state in the midst of "civil war,"[3] meaning that everyone was at odds with everyone else, and law and order had broken down.

Agrokomerc could be seen as a microcosm of Yugoslavia, which for decades had been living beyond its means on foreign credits that could not be repaid. Agrokomerc came to symbolize Yugoslavia's general economic decay.

*The Party as Culprit.* The Agrokomerc scandal claimed the vice-president of the nine-member State Presidency, the country's collective leadership, as one of its victims. Hamdija Pozderac's resignation was unprecedented in that this was the first time since the institution of the State Presidency after Tito's death in May 1980 that a major political leader had resigned under pressure; this was not the case even in the wake of the Kosovo riots in 1981.

The Belgrade daily *Večernje Novosti* said that the resignation was "encouraging" and that it showed that "no one in the country can evade [taking] responsibility" for his actions.[4] Although individuals had indeed been criticized and replaced for various reasons over the years, they had been, however, no more than scapegoats; the system itself was to blame for the serious economic climate that had led to malpractice.

The fall of Pozderac was the direct result of allegations that he had supported the development programs of Agrokomerc. Pozderac, in his first public statement on the Agrokomerc affair, said in an interview carried by the Belgrade weekly *NIN* that he, "like everyone else in the leadership of the republic of Bosnia-Herzegovina, did not know of the illegal criminal acts in that organization."[5] He added, however, that he and members of the Presidium of the CC of Bosnia-Herzegovina had known of Agrokomerc's uncovered promissory notes since April 1987, when general information had been provided to them by the Ministry of Internal Affairs of Bosnia-Herzegovina.

Prime Minister Branko Mikulić, a Croat party leader from Bosnia-Herzegovina, was also involved in the scandal. A Belgrade tabloid, quoting *Kladuške Novosti*, alleged that Mikulić had spoken to Abdić about Agrokomerc at the beginning of 1987, and had "expressed satisfaction at what he had been told and supported all [Abdić's] ideas and projects for increasing the firm's exports."[6] According to this version, Abdić did not inform Mikulić about the firm's financial speculation.

Although a number of people were mentioned, criticized, and dismissed as a result of the Agrokomerc affair, the real culprit was a system that applied political criteria and power not accountable to the public, in order to control and manipulate the economy, despite the trappings of "self-management." The economist Dragan Veselinov, from Belgrade, explained why affairs like the one involving Agrokomerc were possible in Yugoslavia. Veselinov argued that in the party, loyalty was a more important prerequisite than expertise and that this had "primitivized economic life," resulting in a lack of professionalism in managing the economy.[7]

> For this reason, the party must involve itself in various arbitrary acts daily, more than any other political party. In this way it has dangerously undermined the legitimacy of state agencies ... Such a decay of the state apparatus has led to the spread of criminal offenses, which cannot be stopped by any romantic confidence communist ideology cherishes in the morality of the working people.

According to Veselinov, the Communist party "does not usually try to analyze ... its own arbitrary behavior as the real cause of such affairs but rather blames criminals and chauvinists." Veselinov believed that "corruption and degeneration" was the result of a "lack of democratic control and a weak parliamentary system."

The echoes of such discontent were heard throughout the country. In the Slovenian Socialist Youth magazine *Mladina*, a reader said that "for 40 years we have been listening to how 'socialist democracy' has been .... This is why we are now up to our necks in filth."[8]

*A Product of the System.* As more details were revealed about the scandal, the country continued to move toward economic collapse. Party and government officials tended to see the scandal as a blessing in disguise, however, because it exposed weaknesses in Yugoslavia's whole economy. Indeed, an economist in Ljubljana described the affair as a product of Yugoslavia's "feudal economic system."

The scandal added to the multitude of problems bedeviling the federal government of President Branko Mikulić. Criticism of his proposals to combat inflation had been intense. On November 4, the Ljubljana branch of the Confederation of Yugoslav Trade Unions said that the federal government "could no longer function" and demanded its resignation.[9] The press called on Mikulić to explain his knowledge of Agrokomerc's "criminal activities" but Mikulić only said that it had been brought to his attention in April 1987. The Presidency's report indicated an intense conflict within the party. In fact, Tanjug reported that when Pozderac was informed on April 13 of the initial findings by Bosnia's Ministry of Internal Affairs, he had allegedly responded "very sharply" and said that he would go to Bosanska Krajina (a region in where Agrokomerc's headquarters were located) to "conduct a political battle against the RSUP" (the Bosnian Ministry of Internal Affairs). In fact, Pozderac was repeating a vow made by his brother, Hakija, in March. According to the Presidency's report, Hakija, who was also involved in the scandal, had launched "an all-out campaign against the internal security forces" to hamper its investigation of Agrokomerc.

In an interview published in the Belgrade biweekly *Duga*,[10] Bogomir Kovač, an Assistant Professor of Economics at the University of Ljubljana, said that the Agrokomerc affair was "a product of the system," which was "nothing unusual" under the present conditions. Kovač said that the Agrokomerc case "may be small in comparison with what has happened within the framework of the National Bank of Yugoslavia in terms of some of its enormously unsuccessful investments." He warned that the greatest danger of the Agrokomerc affair was the fact that it was not an isolated case: although the enterprise had conducted "its business affairs in an irrational way," it had actually behaved "rationally within the framework of an irrational system." Kovač said that Yugoslavia had more of "a feudal system" than a real market economy with mobility and free movement of products.

A fundamental solution, Kovač said, would be to establish a market economy in which enterprises were encouraged to be more efficient by being allowed to decide how to use profits (after normal taxes) generated by so-called socially owned capital. (In theory, "social ownership" in Yugoslavia was a middle ground between the Western-style private ownership, or capitalism, and Soviet-style state ownership, or communism.) Kovač said that the Yugoslav system was supposed to be managed by the workers, but that in practice they had little say. The implementation of any market-oriented reforms was complicated, Kovač continued, by the fact that the economics of the republics of Macedonia and Montenegro and of the autonomous province of Kosovo were not compatible with the rest of the federation; in other words, their problems were so severe they would be the least able to institute such reforms; the two republics and the autonomous province had already declared themselves bankrupt. Kovač said that Bosnia-Herzegovina would soon join this list.

*Bosnian Workers' New Union and Party?* On November 20, 1987, the controversial weekly *Mladina* printed a letter claiming that an independent trade union and "new communist party" had been established at the Zenica Mining and Metallurgical Works in central Bosnia. The letter said that the independent union and party had been created primarily in response to the Agrokomerc scandal and that the union was "fed up with the state-managed trade unions."[11]

*Večernje Novosti* subsequently reported on the letter and quoted excerpts from it. The paper, while investigating whether a new union actually existed, discovered both resentment and confusion among local officials and workers. Local party and trade union officials responded sharply to the reports of the new organizations in Zenica. On December 3, the local party cell released a statement accusing *Mladina* of "deception" and claiming that the weekly had published the letter without verifying the facts. Zenica officials accused *Mladina* of "crude political provocation" that "was an attempt to undermine the political system of socialist self-management." The statement also attacked *Večernje Novosti* for giving "publicity to the letter in *Mladina*." Zenica's public prosecutor came to the assessment that the articles in both publications were "not well-intentioned" and added that there was a possibility of filing criminal charges against them for "spreading false news."[12]

Meanwhile, *Mladina* stuck to its story that something was happening in Zenica and that the independent trade union and party did, indeed, exist, despite the denials by Zenica officials. It stated, however, in its December 25 issue that it was Radio Belgrade and *Večernje Novosti* that had spread the news about the Zenica organizations.

Details about the new organizations were not known until December 26, when a retired Zenica metallurgical engineer, Branko Tuco, was arrested on suspicion of having written anonymous hostile letters signed "The Independent Trade Unions of Yugoslavia" and "The New Communist Party of Yugoslavia." In a search of his apartment, investigators discovered 182 letters signed with 30 different pseudonyms; among the letters were two copies of the document sent to Mladina.[13]

On December 29 Tuco was sentenced to 60 days in jail for publishing "false reports and upsetting the population." Tuco, who had been expelled from the party in 1974 for singing Ustasha (Croatian nationalist) songs, admitted to the judge that he was the "founder and sole member" of the independent union and party and that he had decided to write the letter to *Mladina* in late September after reading the extensive reports in the Yugoslav media about the Agrokomerc affair (he said he had mailed copies of the letter to seven Yugoslav dailies and three weeklies). Tuco said in his defense that he had "tried to awaken the conscience of the people and prevent affairs such as Agrokomerc." The Yugoslav media reported Tuco's sentencing on December 30.

There were some striking similarities between Tuco's actions and those of a Zenica iron worker, Anto Simić, who spoke out at the Sixth Congress of the Bosnian Trade Unions in October 1982 against the political and economic abuses committed by Bosnian and Yugoslav party and trade union officials. Simić called for the nationalization of the property of those officials who had become millionaires at the expense of the workers. Hamdija Pozderac, who was then head of the Bosnian party, was apparently annoyed by Simić's remarks; and within a few months the party pronounced Simić "an enemy of the people." In the wake of Pozderac's downfall in the Agrokomerc scandal, the iron workers sought to have Simić rehabilitated. According to the Socialist Alliance daily *Borba*, more than 30 delegates at the trade union congress spoke even more sharply against social inequalities than Simić but no action was ever taken against them.[14]

Both cases reflected the volatile political situation that had existed in the town of Zenica for some time, and both seem to have been used successfully as political scapegoats.[15]

## 49
## WHAT WENT WRONG WITH SELF-MANAGEMENT?
### Vlad Sobell and Ljubo Sirc

The roots of the economic crisis in the countries of Eastern Europe lay in the inability of the Soviet-type economic systems to stimulate efficiency and technological change and hence to compete with the rest of the industrialized world. By the late nineteen-eighties, change in the system had come to be recognized as the only viable remedy; most communist régimes began to prepare reform programs with this objective in mind. But what went wrong in Yugoslavia, the country that had abandoned the Soviet model as early as the nineteen-fifties in favor of its own model of "self-managed, market socialism" and that was now on the verge of economic collapse? Should the roots of the crisis be sought in specifically Yugoslav characteristics and conditions, or was there something wrong with the self-management model itself? Did it prove socialism fundamentally unviable, whether it was "self-managed" or centrally-commanded?

The case for identifying the roots of the crisis in uniquely Yugoslav features rested on three arguments. The first argument, usually put forward by the Yugoslavs themselves, was that the less developed republics did not get enough aid from the more developed ones; while the latter complained that they were held back because of their obligation to support the poorer ones. Secondly, the crisis was said to be caused by the federal government's lack of authority; this tended to be the view of Western experts and creditors. Finally, it was argued, notably by reformist Communists elsewhere, that the Yugoslav working class was not mature enough to make the self-management system function as it should, because the workers did not understand what was in their real interest. It was said that if a "real" working class, such as that in Czechoslovakia or the

GDR, were given the opportunity to manage their enterprises, things would be radically different.

*Was Self-Management Tried?* Many commentators in Yugoslavia and elsewhere maintained that the crisis did not stem from the self-management system, because for a variety of reasons—mainly the authorities' persistent intervention in economic affairs—genuine workers' self-management had never been given a fair chance to show its worth. These observers forgot, however, that indeed, there had been an attempt to introduce genuine self-management in the nineteen-sixties and that the Communist authorities had been prepared to disengage themselves from economic management had the self-management system shown itself capable of taking over.

The initial self-management measures introduced in 1952 consisted of giving the enterprises authority over their day-to-day operations while keeping most investment decisions in the hands of the central authorities. This arrangement proved a failure, because of the center's predilection for setting up factories with an irrational production structure and a wasteful production process. In an attempt to remedy this tendency, the party opted for a more radical version of self-management: all decisions, including investment decisions, were transferred to the enterprises. As a result, in the Yugoslav (as in the capitalist) system, enterprises enjoyed complete autonomy but nevertheless remained socialist, because the means of production formally remained in "social ownership" and the state gave the workers extensive rights in the management process through workers' councils.

It soon became clear, however, that this arrangement had serious flaws. The principal difficulty was that the workers failed to show sufficient concern for the long-term well-being of "their" enterprises and were not prepared to sacrifice wage raises for the sake of investment in the enterprise. It was unlikely that this fundamental flaw in the self-management system could be cured by more radical measures, such as formally handing over the means of production to the workers' councils instead of simply "entrusting" them with decision-making powers, because collective self-management, whatever its form, seemed to conflict with innate, noncollectivist human instincts. When it came to a choice, the workers preferred to use their right of self-management to secure the maximum wages (regardless of the enterprises' ability to pay for them), because private savings accounts continued to be regarded as more important than those of the collective.[1]

The enterprises' lack of sufficient savings to sustain the high level of investment eventually forced the party to step in and introduce "social compacts," which stipulated how much the enterprises should set aside for investment, and eventually to draw up legislation regulating this matter. At this point a virtue was made out of necessity, and the market and legislation were eventually replaced by what the Yugoslav theorists referred to as an "agreement economy," under which "self-managers" would restrain each other's selfish behavior by means of agreements or compacts. Since the efficacy of these compacts fell well short of the economic criteria effective in a well functioning market system, however, the Yugoslav economy went to pieces and the party had to attempt to restore order by ad hoc administrative measures. This disorder of the system was the background against which the current economic crisis was unfolding.

*Confusion Between Earnings from Labor and Capital.* Excessive wages and insufficient enterprise investment funds were only one aspect of the problem. Another was the considerable differences in wages from one enterprise to another, even among enterprises with comparable labor structures. These discrepancies were largely due to variations in enterprises' fixed capital, for (regardless of what Marx said) workers using more equipment were more productive than workers with less equipment. As a result, workers in less well equipped enterprises began demanding the same wages as workers in better equipped factories received, regardless of the consequences for their enterprise.[2]

The authorities attempted to resolve the problem of lack of investment funds by printing more money and financing investment through banks loans. The enterprises were required to pay interest on what they borrowed, but since interest rates constantly lagged behind the rate of inflation (which was also fueled by the printing of money), real interest rates were negative and the real value of loans could never be recouped. Such a climate encouraged reckless investment and irresponsibility.

The Yugoslav experience also showed that the self-managing workers were not interested in maximizing yields on capital (as a capitalist would be) but in maximizing their own productivity and hence their wages, even if this meant that their less established fellow workers, or newcomers to the labor market, remained unemployed.[3] Under the self-management system there seemed to be no reliable mechanism for achieving the optimum mixture of labor and capital. It was unlikely that making the workers formal owners of the enterprises would solve the problem, because such a measure would not eliminate the direct dependence of the workers' living standard on their wages; workers would still not be motivated to use their enterprises' capital in an optimum manner.

*"Managing" in One's Spare Time?* The art of capitalist-style entrepreneurship does not lie merely in pocketing the yield from investment on the stockmarket, as the detractors of capitalism would have it, but in personal talent, a long accumulation of information and experience, and exacting managerial work. Even granted that some workers did have the necessary managerial qualities, they could still not act as competent managers because they had their own work to do. The notion that workers could somehow competently collectively manage in their spare time was nothing if not utopian.

The inescapable need for the division of functions meant that it was the enterprise managers and technicians (and not the theoretically self-managing workers) who made most of the key decisions, although the workers did have the right to approve them.[4] Yet the formal rights of the workers in a self-managed system fatally weakened the managerial command structure: since the managers ultimately owed their positions to the workers' councils, they were ill-placed to do anything but cooperate with the latter's pressure for excessive wage increases.

*Continuity of Responsibility Lacking.* Finally, a well functioning economy requires that economic decisions has consequences for those who make them. It is ultimately the certainty that there will be either profits or losses that encourages responsible management. For this to be achieved, there must be continuity in management, which cannot be maintained under the conditions of self-management.

In the first place, the workers' collective was not usually yet existent when the authorities decided to establish a new plant. If this decision was misconceived, the workers were saddled with its consequences while its initiator was relieved of all responsibility. The same applied to day-to-day managerial decisions. Individuals in an enterprise came and went, so that the composition of the managing collective was never exactly the same over a period of time. This is one reason why workers in Yugoslavia tended to refuse to accept responsibility for the consequences of decisions taken earlier.

Circumstances of this kind made it difficult for managers to resist the workers' demands for higher wages, and this was another flaw of the system. There were also other reasons for this, however. For example, since wages were low, any reduction would lead to genuine hardship. One could only cut wages with good conscience for those who earned more than minimum needs warranted; and most workers in Yugoslavia did not fall into this category.


## 50
## THE PARTY CONFERENCE: TIME RUNNING OUT
Milan Andrejevich


The First Conference of the League of Communists of Yugoslavia was held from May 29 through 31, 1988. A 38-page report issued for the conference stated that "the party is capable of seeking and finding a way out of the economic and political crisis" and that economic reform measures would be in place by the end of the year.[1] In closing the conference, Boško Krunić, the president of the Central Committee Presidium, urged the party to implement the "necessary changes without delay"; he added that the discussion at the conference had shown that the party was prepared to make those changes and that it had completed its work in accordance with the guidelines drawn up beforehand. What all this would mean in practice, however, was another matter.

*Background.* The idea for the conference originated with local and republican party organizations, which considered that the decisions reached at numerous party plenums and at the last party congress in June 1986 had not been properly implemented. Proposals for an extraordinary congress of the LCY were repeatedly rejected, however, by leading party officials as being too expensive and difficult to organize. It was also claimed that it would come too soon after the last, 13th LCY congress in June 1986 and provide an implicit challenge to the party program laid down then, when solemn pledges had been made that the political and economic crisis would be resolved and that the working class would be given more political power and a better standard of living.

What changed the economic and political scene was the uncovering in mid-August 1987 of the $1 billion financial scandal involving the Bosnian agroindustrial conglomerate Agrokomerc. The Agrokomerc scandal shook Yugoslavia's financial and political systems; it led to the resignation of the Yugoslav State Vice President, Hamdija Pozderac, in early September; and by the end of the year it had prompted the resignation of hundreds of party, government, banking, and industrial officials. It became apparent to most party officials that, if not an extraordinary congress, then at least some sort of a conference was in order. The conference was intended to be largely advisory in nature, and did not have the broad powers to make personnel and party rule changes as did the congress. The conference had 809 participants—785 delegates, and 24 guests of officials of the government.

*The Party's "Last Chance."* The Yugoslav press counted on the conference to bring about radical changes in the country's economic and political system. Some editorials warned, however, that the party must now assert itself if it really wished to remain in control of the reforms that were being openly advocated by both the public and party and state leaders.

The Belgrade weekly *Novosti 8* commented in early March 1988 that the party conference would be "the last chance for the party to restore its prestige" and for the party leadership to "secure its legitimacy." The weekly predicted that the conference would either "mark a definitive split between the leadership and the base or restore confidence in the LCY and its leaders." Referring to the growing demands for radical changes to the system, the commentary said that "the genie has been let out of the bottle and cannot be returned to it until it has completed its job." [2]

*Stream of Criticism.* The conference produced a stream of accusations and complaints, and numerous remedies for the country's problems were proposed. Party leaders and many of the delegates spoke frankly about the party's shortcomings and of corruption in the party; the possibility of leadership changes; the party's relinquishment of the monopoly on power; and the need for different opinions to be recognized and for minority as well as majority views to be respected. In practice this meant respecting the progressive minority, concentrated mainly in Slovenia and Croatia, as well as the old-line, dogmatic majority of officials and party organizations from the south of the country. In fact, however, the conference could do no more than resort to self-criticism and finger-pointing, since it had neither the power to enact measures nor to change top party leaders.

*A Divided Party.* From what was said by the participants in the conference, in the party report, and by Krunić in his closing speech, it seemed that the party had remained deeply divided over the pressing issue of what practical measures were needed to pull the country out of its worst economic, political, and ideological crisis of the postwar era. Moreover, many of the issues raised by some of the party's leaders and many of the delegates had already been discussed at numerous central committee plenums, both at the national and regional levels. This raised doubts as to whether the conference had achieved any more than simply repeating what had been said many times before.

Paradox and confusion proved to be the order of the day. Recognizing their lack of any real power, delegates repeatedly recommended the convening of an extraordinary party congress in order to institute a reform package and make changes in the party's leadership. This recommendation was made despite the party's view that an extraordinary congress would only divide the party further. It was eventually announced at the conference that there would, indeed, be no extraordinary congress because, it was claimed by Ivan Brigić—a Bosnian representative in the CC Presidium—the convening of a congress would cast doubt on the achievements of the conference. Krunić said that the conference had been a success.[3]

*Assailing Party Leaders.* The most striking feature of the conference was that for the first time in communist Yugoslavia several party and government officials were criticized by name for leading the country into its crisis. The party leadership in general was criticized for its ineptitude, toleration of corruption, and abuse of privileges; these were accusations frequently made and printed in the state-run media. The senior officials named were Krunić; Milanko Renovica, who was president of the party in 1986-87; and Federal Secretary for Internal Affairs Dobroslav Ćulafić.[4]

Krunić suggested that there should be a radical purge of party members; he added that "indifference to thievery, immorality, and dishonesty is not permissible" in the LCY. Many delegates, however, called for a complete overhaul of the party, beginning with the party's Presidium.[5]

Zvonimir Hrabar, then President of the Confederation of Trade Unions, demanded that an official investigation be conducted to determine whether Renovica had indeed misappropriated funds by ordering the construction of seaside villas for himself and other party officials at the resort of Neum on the Bosnian-Herzegovinian coast. Press reports linked Renovica, the wife of Prime

Minister Branko Mikulić, and several other leading Bosnian party and state leaders with similar shady dealings.[6]

Slobodan Milosević, the President of the Presidium of the Serbian CC, suggested that if the party had not implemented a complete social reform program by the autumn of 1988, "then an extraordinary congress of the party should be called." He went on to say that "either the leadership will fulfill the will of the people or the people will replace it."[7]

*Assessment.* The old differences within the party continued, as the LCY proved unable to produce anything more than vague formulations and empty phrases to deal with a situation rapidly deteriorating, despite the leadership's attempts to give the impression that they supported reform and their expressed recognition that things could not go on unchanged

The real problem was that economic reforms could not be implemented without political reforms and the LCY's support for ideologically unpalatable measures, such as the development of a real market economy. In the words of the Slovenian party President Milan Kučan, "economic measures are not enough without political reform." In turn, one of the major obstacles to all reform was the strange combination of the dominant role of the party combined with the extreme regional autonomy that had existed in Yugoslavia since the constitution of 1974, which attempted to strengthen both centripetal and centrifugal forces at the same time. This led to political paralysis and to the de facto existence of eight parties, one for each of the six republics and two autonomous provinces.

Given this lack of unity at the top, it was futile to expect the party to set down a coherent policy, purge its ranks, and provide the firm leadership that was Tito's hallmark. The document produced by the conference was long-winded, vague, and full of jargon and tired expressions such as "we must" and "it must be that." Once again, as at the earlier CC plenum on Kosovo, important and even vital issues were discussed at length; because of the political paralysis, however, hopes that the gathering would produce anything more than phrase-mongering were disappointed. Moreover, the situation was unlikely to change so long as the system as a whole remained in its current state, and popular opinion, although it could be expressed in print and in official bodies, could not exercise control over the centers of power.

51
# ATTEMPTED ARMY COUP IN SLOVENIA?
Milan Andrejevich

During the June 27, 1988, session of the Presidium of the Slovenian Central Committee, its president, Milan Kučan, spoke about the general political situation in Slovenia. He stressed the need to continue with the economic, constitutional, and political reforms that were adopted at the party conference in May and said that Slovenia's role in bringing about these changes would correspond to its economic power and "level of development and civilization."[1]

Kučan defended the republic's role in the latest efforts to institute reforms in economic, government, and party affairs and denied claims that Slovenia's actions had been counterrevolutionary or aimed at seceding from the Yugoslav federation. He said that the Slovenian party would not abandon the introduction of democratization, economic reform, and a rejuvenation of the LCY, because "to do so would mean to continue living in a society that is in a crisis without prospects," which would "ultimately lead to military communism."

Fear of military intervention had caused consternation in Slovenia in the previous four weeks. Two journalists and a noncommissioned officer were arrested and accused by the military authorities of being in possession of military secrets after the publication in the spring of articles critical of the minister of defense and the army. The arrests led to mass public protests as well as verbal and physical attacks on soldiers and their families stationed in the republic (19 such attacks had been registered by the police since March). Kučan condemned the attacks, which also included assaults on several civilians of non-Slovenian origin, and described them as "excesses" that could result in the loss of "true allies and sympathizers in Slovenia and in other parts of Yugoslavia." He added that the attacks were not typical of "everyday life in Slovenia," however, and cautioned some of the media in Yugoslavia against "manipulating public opinion" by presenting an unobjective view of events in Slovenia.

*Criticism of the Military.* Slovenia, Yugoslavia's most economically developed and politically liberal republic, became a target of criticism from party conservatives elsewhere in the country and from the military for allowing youth periodicals to publish articles strongly criticizing the army, an institution not accustomed to the scrutiny of the press. The attacks on the army escalated in February, when the officially sanctioned publication of the Slovenian Socialist Youth Alliance, *Mladina*, published a story describing Minister of Defense Admiral Branko Mamula as a "merchant of death" because of his involvement in arms sales to Ethiopia. On May 15 Mamula left office; the reason he gave was his retirement from active military service. The article also accused Mamula of exploiting army conscripts and of using "slavery" to build his seaside villa at the state's expense. In another article, *Mladina* denounced the army as "an undemocratic institution, always ready to stage a military coup." Articles criticizing the army appeared frequently in several youth publications (*Katedra* and *Tribuna*) and in the Ljubljana weekly *Teleks*.[2]

Several Slovenian party officials, numerous veterans' associations, and government officials throughout the country protested the publications, describing them as "counterrevolutionary mouthpieces." Some high-ranking government and army officials said that the criticism in the media was part of a "special war" supported by émigré groups in the West. In response to these allegations, *Mladina* published an editorial entitled "Defenders of the Revolution." It said that the country's leaders had a political monopoly and that the party was morally corrupt. The editorial made 14 demands, including "the public control of the Yugoslav Peoples' Army and of foreign and domestic policy." The editorial was signed by "the counterrevolutionary Editorial Staff." A temporary ban was slapped on the magazine, which coincided with Gorbachev's visit to Ljubljana on March 16 and 17.[3]

*Rumors of an Army Coup.* Criticism of the army in the press escalated, however, after *Mladina* reported that there was a plan for the army to move against reformist elements in Slovenia. Slovenian government, party, and security officials denied that there was such a plan. The Slovenian government's official response was that military intervention had been discussed in early March but that it had eventually been decided by the top party and state leadership that such a move "would have a detrimental effect on the political situation in Slovenia." Kučan's response to the allegations was that they were an attempt "in someone's interest to stir everything up again ... [at a time when] every effort is being made to introduce economic and political reform."[4]

*Mladina* and numerous grassroots organizations in the republic were not dissuaded from seeking the truth about the alleged contingency plans for the quelling of liberal dissent. The Belgrade daily *Politika Ekspres* criticized the Slovenian statement, saying that it was "highly unconvincing" and only fueled speculation that the army had indeed been planning to intervene in Slovenian affairs.[5]

The arrest on May 31 of the journalist Ivan "Janez" Janša and of Sergeant Major Ivan Borstner and the arrest of the journalist David Tasić on June 4, all on the grounds that they were allegedly in possession of military secrets, led to mass protests involving a total of 40,000 people in the capital, Ljubljana, and in Slovenia's second largest city, Maribor. Some 35,000 people gathered at a benefit concert in Ljubljana on June 21 that was described by *Mladina*, referring to the imprisoned South African anti-apartheid leader, as a concert for Slovenia's "three Mandelas."[6]

Janša, a regular contributor to *Mladina*, was one of four candidates for President of the Slovenian Socialist Youth Alliance and author of the many critical articles on Mamula and the army that had appeared in the paper. Tasić, an editor for *Mladina*, had written a provocative study about Yugoslavia's best known prison, Goli Otok. The arrests triggered a wave of support for the three men and demands for their release from individuals and organizations throughout Yugoslavia, as well as from human rights groups in the West and intellectuals in the East bloc. A petition bearing more than 20,000 signatures and the names of more than 200 organizations in Yugoslavia called for the release of the three men. In another petition, six prominent physicians and medical professors demanded that they be allowed to examine the prisoners, who had reportedly been tortured by military guards.[7] Moreover, *Mladina* said that it had received letters protesting the arrests from 15 dissident intellectuals in the East bloc, namely, Larisa Bogorazova, Sergei Kovalev, and Lev Timofeev in the Soviet Union; Petr Pospíchal, Petr Uhl, and Jan Urban in Czechoslovakia; Peter Grimm, Gerd Poppe, and Reinhard Weisshuhn in the GDR; Miklós Haraszti, Ferenc Kőszeg, and Ferenc Miszlivecz in Hungary; and Andrzej Celiński, Jacek Kuroń, and Henryk Wójec in Poland.[8]

*Mladina*'s Editor in Chief, Robert Botteri, and its managing editor, Franci Zavrl, who was arrested and released by the police in early March for having insulted Mamula and slandered the army, were both questioned by military investigators on June 15. *Mladina* said that this constituted an attempt to "halt democratic trends in Slovenia" and "to turn free thought into a crime." The magazine also claimed that the alleged secret documents in their possession had been planted by the state security forces and that more journalists and some political leaders, including President of the Slovenian Socialist Alliance Joze Smole and Kučan, were on the army's list of those to be arrested in an emergency.[9] Slovenian officials denied that there was such a list; but they did not exclude the possibility that the military would try to bring charges against other nonconformist journalists and intellectuals.

The secretary of the Slovenian Ministry for Internal Affairs, Tomaz Ertl, said that the discovery of documents in the apartments of the arrested men related "to measures concerning the army's combat readiness in Slovenia." In early May there was a second phase of military maneuvers in Slovenia, completing an earlier operation conducted in mid-October 1987. The military maneuvers were planned long before the attacks on the army in the media, but the military build-up might have been construed by some as an excuse to crush extremists in Slovenia. Meanwhile, the Slovenian National Assembly determined that the police and military authorities had acted within their legal and constitutional powers and that there were "no grounds for linking the arrests with rumors about an alleged military coup." It also warned that the authorities were "not obliged to inform any other organizations about the measures they undertake within their powers." Moreover, the Slovenian Assembly rejected charges that the situation in the republic threatened the country's security and called on the Slovenian public to maintain good relations with the army.[10]

The editorial board of *Mladina* announced that the magazine would be published on a weekly rather than a monthly basis throughout the summer, because of the serious political situation in Slovenia. Explaining the move, the editors said that "enemies never sleep, that is what they taught us."[11]    The editors also promised that for the first time since it began publication in September 1943 the magazine planned prompt deliveries to seaside resorts on the Adriatic coast. The journal's circulation had increased considerably since late 1987, from 50,000 to 75,000. The latest plans for the journal were approved by the Slovenian Socialist Youth Alliance.

*Communist Legitimacy Questioned.* In an unprecedented move, even for relatively liberal Slovenia, the Slovenian Socialist Alliance daily *Delo* published a reader's letter attacking the Communist system and accusing the media of misinterpreting the cause of Slovenian discontent. The writer of the letter, Mate Dolenc, from Ljubljana, said that Slovenes were protesting because they "no longer believe in the legitimacy of the Communists." He justified his assessment by claiming that the history of "communist legitimacy" had a record of "bloodletting in the removal of other legal parties." He cited as examples the Kronstadt mutiny in 1921, Stalin's Terror in the Soviet Union, the issue of the "legitimacy of the occupation of Czechoslovakia in 1968 and before that in Hungary in 1956, and the military dictatorship in present-day Poland."[12]

Dolenc went on to say that in Yugoslavia "our Communists own [lack of] legitimacy was proved by Goli Otok and Starà Gradisa (at one time political prisons); and we cannot forget our 1,000 political prisoners today, which is more than in Poland, Czechoslovakia, and Hungary combined." He mentioned the trial in 1984 and 1985 of six dissidents in Belgrade and the arrest of Janša, Tasić, and Borstner in connection with the allegations in *Mladina*. Dolenc concluded by saying that "we cannot believe in Communists because of what they did [in the past] ... and that is why we do not believe in them now and it will be hard for us to believe in them in the future."

*Conclusion.* Slovenian officials and independent activists appeared to be divided on many issues. What they did agree on, however, was that the arrests in connection with *Mladina*'s charges dealt a blow to the process of democratization. Many Slovenes considered that they were paying a high price for 40 years of failed federal economic programs. The economic reform program had been adopted by the LCY on paper; but the Slovenes had long been experimenting with modified versions of market-oriented economic models, along with a fair degree of political tolerance, and had a relative degree of success. Although more than 8 percent of Yugoslavia's 23,500,000 people were Slovenian, the republic generated 27 percent of the country's exports and almost 33 percent of the gross national product.

## 52
## "YUGOSLAVIZATION" OF EASTERN EUROPE?
Vladimir V. Kusin

Although Gorbachev talked in liberal terms about the independence of all "fraternal parties," he did not renounce explicitly the Brezhnev Doctrine and thereby the Soviet option of intervening militarily in the bloc. The joint Soviet-Yugoslav Declaration issued on March 18, 1988, affirmed the content of earlier pronouncements about the allegedly sovereign rights of all countries and all parties; but it stopped short of issuing an irreversible guarantee of these rights. It did grant the bloc states a considerable amount of freedom for reformist action and lessen the threat of intervention that had been hanging over them.

*Still Equivocal.* When speaking of the inviolability of the bloc states' rights, the Soviet leader tended to place the matter within a larger context that included not only communist countries outside the bloc, such as Yugoslavia and China, but often all countries and the rights of a wide assortment of parties in the world at large. Thus, the Soviet-Yugoslav Declaration underlined "the significance of democratic principles" among all "Communist, Workers', Socialist, Social democratic, National liberation, and other progressive parties and movements, based on their inalienable right to decide independently their own roads of social development."

Where Gorbachev addressed directly the countries of "really existing socialism" (a term he used in his book on perestroika), he took for granted that all changes would have to be subordinated to the retention of the system and never queried the leading role of the party. The "international responsibility" of each and every member of the bloc, which Leonid Brezhnev invoked as an important justification for his doctrine, was not rescinded by the new Soviet leader. In his book *Perestroika: New Thinking for Our Country and the World*, Gorbachev said that "the ruling parties of the socialist countries are aware of the great extent of their responsibility, nationally and internationally."

While edging toward admitting that its invasion of Afghanistan was an error; Moscow still prevaricated over the invasion of Czechoslovakia, and no sign of a new attitude to the Prague Spring found its way into the Yugoslav document.

*Greater Leeway for Domestic Initiative.* However, the Gorbachev leadership was retreating from the unbending position associated with Brezhnev's rule over Eastern Europe. In his book Gorbachev said that "the entire framework of political relations between the socialist countries must be strictly based on absolute independence," and he added that each party's "sovereign right to decide the issues facing its country" was "an unquestionable principle."

The Soviet-Yugoslav Declaration restated the notion that every party was accountable "to the working class and people of its own country" and that there had to be "mutual respect for different paths in building socialism." It also repeated Gorbachev's earlier statements to the effect that "no one has a monopoly on the truth" and that neither the Soviet nor the Yugoslav party intended "to impose [its] concepts of social development on anyone."

The declaration also rephrased a provision from the Document of the Stockholm Conference on Confidence and Security Building Measures and Disarmament of September 1986 in which "the threat or use of force" was condemned with regard to all countries regardless of their political systems and "irrespective of whether or not they maintain with that state an alliance." The relevant passage in the Soviet-Yugoslav Declaration accorded all countries independence and equal rights "regardless of their ... sociopolitical system, the convictions they are guided by, the forms and nature of their international alliances, or their geographic position." Precepts were no longer imposed, it was claimed; instead, coordination was achieved through consultation and the pooling of experience.

Some earlier statements by Soviet politicians had gone further and been more specific about the Brezhnev Doctrine than the Soviet-Yugoslav Declaration. In December 1987, Gorbachev's chief foreign affairs spokesman, Gennadii Gerasimov, was asked by a television interviewer for the British Broadcasting Corporation: "Has the time now passed when it would be possible for the Soviet Union to intervene militarily in the name of socialism in Eastern Europe? Is that time now gone?" He replied: "Yes, it is." At about the same time, CPSU Politburo member and CC Secretary Egor Ligachev was in Paris responding to a newsman's question about possible Soviet intervention in Romania along the lines of the previous intervention in Hungary and in Czechoslovakia. Ligachev ruled out any such intervention. The Romanians, he hoped, would overcome their difficulties themselves. "Should it be otherwise—and that is anyway just hypothetical—we have no intention of intervening." Leonid Iagodovsky of the Soviet Academy's institute for socialist countries told a Japanese interviewer in February 1988 that he "totally denied the thesis" that the sovereignty of an individual country could be restricted in the common interest of the entire socialist community.

*"Yugoslavization"?* While not categorically excluding the possibility of Soviet intervention, Gorbachev's statements on relations in the bloc seem to have had the cumulative effect of opening up the way for client states to pursue internal changes of the magnitude carried out by Yugoslavia. Since Nikita Khrushchev revoked Stalin's "excommunication" edict, Yugoslavia had been regarded as a communist country in a category of its own with which more or less friendly relations could be maintained but whose reformist policies had a breadth and depth not be emulated.

In five areas in particular Yugoslavia had gone far beyond anything the bloc countries would have been allowed to do: the lessening of the League of Communists of Yugoslavia's leading role in economic and ideological control; the self-management system, which assigned what Moscow saw as excessive rights to workers' teams in individual enterprises; the scope of "marketization" in the economy; the extent of freedom of expression in the country; and the extent of economic and political cooperation with the West. In all five of these areas, the Kremlin now appeared to have lifted the restrictions on the bloc countries. The only differences that remained between the room for change allowed the bloc countries and Yugoslavia's position were the former's continued membership of the Warsaw Pact (and of the CMEA, of which Yugoslavia is an "observer") and their related acceptance of whatever was left of the Brezhnev Doctrine.

None of this meant that Gorbachev encouraged actual imitation of Yugoslav policies, which he well knew had not worked satisfactorily. He had, however, cleared the way for innovation in areas that were previously closed for all except the Yugoslavs.

# XIII. WEST GERMANY'S GROWING PRESENCE

## 53
## NEW DIPLOMATIC ACTIVISM

Stephen Ashley,* Louis Zanga,** Jan B. de Weydenthal,***
Jan Obrman,**** Peter Martin*****

*Bulgaria.* From June 2 to 5, 1987, President and BCP Secretary-General
Todor Zhivkov paid a four-day visit to the FRG, where he discussed East-West
relations, disarmament, and bilateral economic cooperation with President
Richard von Weizsaecker, Chancellor Helmut Kohl, Foreign Minister Hans-
Dietrich Genscher and other leading German politicians.

Four subjects dominated Zhivkov's discussions. The state of East-West
relations was inevitably a major concern in view of the circumstances that led to
the cancellation of the planned visit in 1984. Zhivkov arrived in Bonn almost
directly after the meeting in East Berlin of the Warsaw Pact's Political
Consultative Committee, which ended on May 29. In his talks with von
Weizsäcker, Kohl, Genscher, and various German party delegations, Zhivkov
focused on the progress of disarmament negotiations and the contents of the
communiqué issued after the Warsaw Pact meeting in the GDR. The work of the
Vienna CSCE Conference on Human Rights was also discussed, even though
Bulgaria's record on human rights, particularly with regard to its Turkish
minority, was among the worst in Europe. Indeed, on June 2, two
Turkish organizations in the FRG issued a joint public statement calling for an
end to Bulgaria's campaign of forced assimilation of ethnic Turks.[1]

---

*Author of the section on Bulgaria.

** Author of the section on Albania.

***Author of the section on Poland.

****Author of the section on Czechoslovakia (except for the last six
paragraphs).

*****Author of the last six paragraphs on Czechoslovakia.

Zhivkov also spoke about Bulgaria's program of restructuring, claiming that the BCP had embarked on reform even before Mikhail Gorbachev's accession to power. He insisted that the current policies in Bulgaria had been designed to meet specific national needs and were not "a mechanical copy or an automatic transfer ... of foreign experience."

A third subject that was discussed extensively at each of Zhivkov's high-level meetings was the future of Bulgarian-German trade and economic and technical cooperation. For many years the FRG had been Bulgaria's leading partner in the West, and Sofia evidently had strong hopes of increasing the scope and benefits of the relationship. Although the volume of bilateral trade had increased by 17.9 percent in 1985, it still accounted for only 0.2 percent of West Germany's foreign trade. The FRG, however, provided 3 percent of Bulgaria's foreign trade and 42 percent of its trade with the EEC.[2]

In April 1986 Ognyan Doynov, the Chairman of the Bulgarian Economic Council, visited the FRG to tour the Hannover International Trade Fair, where Bulgarian manufactures featured prominently, and signed a Treaty for the Mutual Promotion and Protection of Investments. The purpose of the treaty was to facilitate the establishment of cooperative ventures and joint enterprises. In November 1986, the Bayerische Vereinsbank and the Bulgarian Foreign Trade Bank founded a Bavarian-Bulgarian trade bank, which started business on May 4, 1987.

Another issue that arose was West Germany's application to open a branch of the Goethe Institute in Sofia but the issue had sensitive ideological ramifications that made Zhivkov reluctant to accede to the request. In an interview with the second West German television channel on May 31, Zhivkov appeared to link the extension and institutionalization of cultural contacts between the two countries to West German economic concessions.

German government spokesman Friedhelm Ost told the press on June 2 that Zhivkov and Kohl had agreed in principle on the reciprocal establishment of cultural institutes; but Zhivkov made no mention of this in any of his toasts or speeches, so that a degree of ambiguity persisted on the subject. During their discussions on June 2 the two foreign ministers, Petar Mladenov and Genscher, agreed that a bilateral scientific and cultural agreement should be concluded as soon as possible. The subject of cultural cooperation was also raised by Lower Saxony Prime Minister Ernst Albrecht, who told Zhivkov that universities in his state were "prepared to accept Bulgarian students."[3]

Zhivkov had been keen to make his visit to West Germany. When Bundestag President Philipp Jenninger asked him in August what the prospects for the visit were, Zhivkov reportedly answered, "My suitcase is packed!" In 1984, the Bulgarian government had been reluctant to cancel Zhivkov's visit to West Germany and did so only under Soviet duress. On September 6, 1984, three days before Bonn announced that it had received notice of the postponement, an article by Bulgarian Foreign Minister Petar Mladenov in the party daily

*Rabotnichesko Delo* emphasized "Bulgaria's good relations with the West," saying that "We are convinced that they will survive the current cold winds, especially as they are in the interest of both the socialist and the Western states."

West German-Bulgarian relations were not seriously harmed by the 1984 postponement of Zhivkov's visit. Bonn undoubtedly appreciated the relative independence that Sofia showed in refusing to mimic strident Soviet denunciations of West German "revanchism." In March 1985, Genscher went to Sofia on a whirlwind tour of Eastern Europe that seemed designed to improve relations with the states in the area. In a commentary on his visit on March 7, *Rabotnichesko Delo* wrote that it had demonstrated that both countries were ready to "promote cooperation" and "contribute to an improved international climate."

Visits to Bonn were made by Milko Balev, a BCP Politburo member and close confidant of Todor Zhivkov's, in May 1985 and by a National Assembly delegation headed by Politburo member Stanko Todorov in September of the same year. Then in May 1986 Foreign Minister Petar Mladenov visited the FRG for talks with Genscher and Kohl in which various subjects were discussed, including nuclear disarmament, the CSCE process, and bilateral political and economic contacts. This series of visits showed that the restrictions on high-level Bulgarian-West German contacts had been lifted as East-West tension eased. In December 1986 Genscher returned Mladenov's visit and while he was in Sofia commented on the "excellent" and "problem-free" relations between the two countries.

*Albania.* Steady, if gradual, progress toward the establishment of diplomatic relations between the FRG and Albania had been taking place for the best part of the decade preceding 1987. The establishment of formal relations in that year was another major political and diplomatic advance for Albania and a highly important step in Tirana's emergence from its long period of self-imposed isolation. Indeed, the normalization of relations with a state of West Germany's economic, political, and cultural weight in Europe could not fail to have an impact on Albania's economic development.

For Bonn, the development marked the completion of a process that it had initiated during the late nineteen-sixties to establish diplomatic relations with all European communist states. After Albania's break with China, it was thought that this small, isolationist, and semideveloped but strategically placed country offered an opportunity for Bonn to play a stabilizing role and limit Soviet influence in the Balkans.

The first offer to establish diplomatic relations was made by the Brandt-Scheel administration in 1969. The prospect evidently held little appeal at that time for the late Albanian leader Enver Hoxha, who replied that Bonn would first have to pay "billions in reparations," a precondition that he knew would be unacceptable.

Tirana at that time criticized Bonn's diplomatic progress in Eastern Europe, and as late as 1976 Hoxha alleged that the "Schmidts and Strausses" of the FRG were trying to avoid taking full responsibility for their country's past. In 1975 the West German Embassy in Belgrade was given the exact amount that Tirana demanded in reparations: "Two billion dollars in addition to interest at the rate of the 1938 dollar value." The West Germans refused to negotiate on these terms, citing the London Reparations Agreement of 1953, which stipulated that only after a peace treaty could there be any talk of reparations.

The Sino-Albanian break in 1978 saw a radical change in Albania's foreign policy and the advent of a much friendlier approach toward Bonn. The Albanian leaders began to praise Bonn for its "positive attitude" toward Albania. In 1981, preliminary talks about the establishment of relations opened at the diplomatic level, first in Belgrade, then in Vienna and Paris. Little progress was made, however, mainly because Albania remained inflexible in its demands for reparations.

In late 1982 the Albanian government described relations with West Germany as "satisfactory" and said that "old disputes" could be solved with good will. In early 1983 Albania's national folklore ensemble toured the FRG. Then, in the spring of 1984, an Albanian representative visited Bonn, and Albanian government officials issued a positive account of contacts between the two sides. Another two years passed and a new round of talks started, at Tirana's initiative, at the West German Embassy in Vienna; it was said that "things were moving." Finally, in June 1987 Albanian leader Ramiz Alia, in a departure from the normal practice for making such an important announcement, told the 10th Congress of Trade Unions that diplomatic relations between the two countries would soon be made formal.

On September 15 the preliminary signing of the documents on the establishment of diplomatic relations was completed in Tirana,[4] and the agreement was subsequently ratified by the Albanian and West German governments. After Albania dropped its demands for reparations, diplomatic relations were established on October 2. The FRG was the 18th state to set up an embassy in Tirana.

Albanian-German relations had traditionally been decidedly good; even the brief occupation of Albania during World War II was not characterized by the kind of brutality experienced in other occupied countries. There was considerable evidence of strong admiration for West Germany in Albania later.

The lack of diplomatic relations had not prevented other forms of positive contact between the two countries. After Italy, the FRG was Albania's second largest trading partner in the West; annual trade between them amounted to approximately DM 100,000,000. West Germany bought minerals, mainly chrome and oil, from Albania and exported industrial machinery. It was the quality of West German machinery that apparently impressed Tirana. Workers in plants with a mixture of machines from China, the GDR, and the FRG reportedly favored the West German machines and had a poor opinion of the others.

There were a number of significant visits to Albania by West German officials, particularly from Bavaria, a West German state that cultivated its role, based on historical as well as geographical reasons, as the FRG's gate to southeastern Europe. The Bavarian Prime Minister and Chairman of the Christian Social Party, Franz Josef Strauss, made trips to Albania in 1984 and 1986. It was generally assumed that these "private" trips had a political significance and helped to advance the establishment of diplomatic relations. Albanian officials praised the "historic awareness, the political wisdom, clarity, and the independent thinking" of Strauss. During his visit in 1986 Strauss declared that he was interested only in strengthening the "threads" between the two countries and in setting things in motion; when asked whether he had succeeded in this aim, he answered, "I think so."

In 1985 an economic delegation from Bavaria, headed by State Secretary Georg von Waldenfels traveled to Tirana, followed by a delegation of West German businessmen, to discuss the expansion of economic cooperation between the two countries. The delegates said that they had broached the possibility of increasing trade and discussed the "difficulties" of the Albanian 1986-1990 five-year plan.

Albanian academics had been attending a number of events in West Germany; and in September 1987, Albania's leading author, Ismail Kadare, came to Munich and Frankfurt to launch a translation of one of his works. Articles were published on the impressions of an increasing number of Albanian visitors to West Germany; on June 1 the two countries signed their first agreement on economic, industrial, and technical cooperation, including such areas as agriculture, energy, transportation, construction, and trade. The agreement was unusual in terms of protocol in that it was signed on the West German side by Genscher and on the Albanian by Farudin Hoxha, who had a lower ministerial rank. The two held a "friendly" meeting to discuss the development of bilateral relations.[5] The development of West German-Albanian relations and the remarkable warmth between them seemed to hold the greatest promise for Tirana's entry into the economic mainstream in Europe and the world, although Albania continued to reject any direct contacts with the USA or the USSR.

Tirana's establishment of diplomatic relations with Bonn fitted into Albania's overall expansion of links with the outside world. Indeed, the move was Alia's second major foreign policy achievement in two weeks. Earlier in the month a milestone in Greek-Albanian relations had been passed when the technical state of war between the two countries was formally lifted. Other, less spectacular diplomatic steps were the establishment of diplomatic relations with Spain, Australia, the Philippinnes, Jordan, Canada, Burundi, and Bolivia. There remained only two West European countries with which Albania lacked formal relations: Ireland and the United Kingdom. The absence of formal relations with

Ireland might have something to do with Ireland's intensely Catholic heritage in the face of Albania's proud claim to be an atheist country. Anglo-Albanian relations had been bogged down by the controversy over gold kept in London since the end of World War II to which the Albanians layed claim.

Albania's major diplomatic developments concerning the FRG and Greece did not mean that Alia was abandoning the foreign policy line of his predecessor and mentor Enver Hoxha. After all, toward the end of his rule Hoxha had already instigated a shift in this direction and launched the policy of rapprochement with both Greece and West Germany. Ramiz Alia, for his part, had shown skill in executing that policy.

*Poland.* Hans-Dietrich Genscher's four-day official visit to Poland from January 10 to 13, 1988, was aimed at giving a "strong impulse" to expanding and strengthening Polish-West German relations. The visit certainly contributed to the improvement of relations between the two governments but it also served to underscore the fragmented character of Polish politics.

Relations between the two governments had been strained as a result of the Polish authorities' imposition of martial law in December 1981 and the consequent restrictions on human and civil rights. The lifting of martial law in 1983 and the repeated release of political prisoners created conditions for improving Warsaw's relations with Bonn, but actual movement in that direction was slow and erratic. Genscher's visit had been repeatedly delayed owing to political differences between the two governments.

Originally set for November 1984, the visit was called off by the West German authorities when the Polish government imposed "unacceptable conditions" on the West German officials by refusing to grant a visa to a West German journalist, rejecting Genscher's request to lay a wreath at the grave of a German soldier killed in World War II, and publicly demanding that Genscher abandon his plans to visit the grave of Father Jerzy Popiełuszko, the Warsaw priest murdered by government security agents. In 1987, the West German foreign minister was again reported to have postponed a visit to Poland because the Polish authorities had raised the issue of reparations for Polish citizens forced to work in Germany during the war; West Germany formally rejected the reparation demands, arguing that Poland had renounced such reparations in 1953 and that the renunciation was confirmed in negotiations over the 1970 treaty between the two countries.

During this period, however, unofficial and semiofficial contacts between the two countries proliferated. Perhaps most significant was the increase in personal contacts and aid: hundreds of thousands of Poles visited the FRG, while the West German public provided massive and sustained private aid to Poland, sending food as well as clothing and medicine. At the same time, numerous politicians, journalists, and officials from both countries visited each other's country to attend seminars, symposiums, and meetings of all sorts. In addition, the two governments conducted regular talks, particularly on economic problems and financial relations.

In April 1987, Poland's foreign minister, Marian Orzechowski, visited Bonn to discuss such issues as the problems of the German ethnic minority in Poland (Bonn wanted Poland to facilitate the resettlement of ethnic Germans to the FRG), the expansion of cultural exchanges and contacts (Bonn wanted to open a cultural institute in Warsaw), and bilateral economic relations (Poland wanted new credits). Orzechowski's visit improved the general atmosphere between the two governments but brought few tangible results. Genscher's visit provided another opportunity for further discussions; each government obviously had major expectations of the other.

For the FRG, the visit offered not only a promise of improved relations with Poland but also the prospect of relaunching its *Ostpolitik*. For several years, Bonn's hopes of improving relations with the East by expanding direct economic and political cooperation with local governments had been dampened considerably by its growing disagreement with the Soviet Union over the deployment of Euromissiles; but now the *Ostpolitik* was entering a new era, in which Moscow and Bonn appeared to develop mutual political and economic interests.[6]

For the Polish government, Genscher's visit was a demonstration of international respect and recognition. The authorities clearly hoped that the visit would lend them an aura of permanence and stability.

According to the Polish government's spokesman, Genscher's talks with officials in Warsaw centered on economic issues, such as the possibility of extending new West German credits for Poland and the broadening of scientific and technological cooperation between the two countries, as well as on problems of environmental protection. The two sides were also said to have discussed the prospects for opening a West German consulate in Cracow and a Polish consulate in Hamburg.

The discussions were said to have improved the atmosphere between the two governments, but the wider differences between the two sides remained great.

This was particularly true in financial matters. Poland was heavily indebted to West Germany but had long been trying to obtain new West German credits, arguing that new credits would enable Poland to improve its industrial and trade capabilities and, thus, to pay off its old debts. West Germany agreed in 1986 to provide DM 100,000,000 in guaranteed credits after Poland had signed a series of rescheduling agreements with its Western creditors. These credits were stopped after only a few months, however, because Poland had failed to meet its commitments under the rescheduling accords; the decision was prompted by West German budgetary laws that barred the government from providing credit guarantees to countries in arrears.

The volume of bilateral trade declined in the years prior to 1988, largely owing to Poland's inability to pay for West German goods in hard currency and its difficulty in supplying products of a suitable quality.

The immediate significance of Genscher's visit was mainly political in that it reaffirmed the political diversity in Poland. During his four days in Warsaw, Genscher met members of the political establishment, such as the party's first secretary, General Wojciech Jaruzelski, and PUWP Politburo members Józef Czyrek, Marian Orzechowski, and Mieczysław F. Rakowski. He also met with Poland's primate, Cardinal Józef Glemp, and other officials of the Church. Finally, Genscher met with Solidarity's leader, Lech Wałęsa, and his advisors; he also received several Catholic intellectuals as well as representatives of the ethnic German minority in Poland.

Wałęsa said after his meeting with the West German foreign minister that the occasion had provided Solidarity with political visibility. "Solidarity must have the opportunity to present its views," Wałęsa was reported to have said—"even if we are not always right."[7] As for Genscher, he said that he wanted "to meet all Poles."

His activities included visits to a German war cemetery near Warsaw; a Catholic monastery that had once been the home of St. Maksymilian Kolbe, a priest killed in the Auschwitz concentration camp; and the grave of Father Popiełuszko. On each occasion Genscher saw and was seen by hundreds of ordinary people, who greeted him with applause and also sporadic political chants. The Polish media ignored these aspects of Genscher's visit; they were officially regarded as "private."

For Genscher it was a successful visit. It strengthened the favorable view of many Poles toward West Germany. An officially released public opinion poll said that about 26 percent of its respondents regarded West German-Polish relations as good and only about 12 percent saw them as bad.[8] The generally positive attitude among Poles toward West Germany emerged soon after the West German-Polish treaty of December 1970 and was gradually reinforced during the nineteen-seventies. It was further strengthened as a result of the popular support in West Germany for Solidarity and then, after the imposition of martial law in December 1981, the large amount of private aid sent by West Germans to the Poles.

*Czechoslovakia.* With the exception of President Gustáv Husák's previous official visit to Bonn in April 1978, Chancellor Helmut Kohl's visit to Czechoslovakia on January 26 and 27, 1988, was the highest-level meeting between representatives of the FRG and Czechoslovakia since Chancellor Willy Brandt went to Prague for the signing of the treaty on mutual relations between the two countries on December 11, 1973—not a very impressive record for 15 years of neighborliness. There were, however, many contacts at lower levels, which suggested that relations had begun to improve. "The new thinking" in Soviet foreign policy, Moscow's increasing interest in West Germany, and

Czechoslovakia's own effort to project a less rigid image made for an auspicious background to Kohl's visit.

High-level visits between Czechoslovakia and the FRG had been quite rare: since 1981 the Czechoslovak Foreign Minister had visited Bonn only twice (in 1984 and 1987); his West German counterpart had been to Czechoslovakia four times since 1981 (1983, 1984, 1986 and 1987); and the President of the Bundestag, Philipp Jenninger, had paid an official visit to Czechoslovakia in June 1987.

The West German Social Democrats (SPD) established quite close contacts with the Czechoslovak Communist party. In 1985 Chairman of the SPD Willy Brandt went to Prague and CPCS CC Presidium Member Vasil Bil'ak visited Bonn. Other contacts included several visits by leading officials from both parties, among them SPD Presidium Member Peter Glotz, arms expert Egon Bahr for the SPD, and CPCS Presidium Member (later General Secretary) Miloš Jakeš, who headed a CPCS delegation to West Germany in October 1986 at the invitation of the SPD. Moreover, representatives of the two parties met several times to discuss cooperation in arms reduction and other spheres. The same topics were discussed on a number of occasions by the Young Socialists of the SPD and members of the West German peace movement, and the Czechoslovak Socialist Youth Union. The most publicized result of these contacts was the declaration in May 1986 of the so-called working group of the CPCS, the Socialist Unity Party of Germany (GDR), and the SPD on the need for the creation of a chemical weapons-free zone in central Europe, which came under fierce attack in the West. Leading officials of the SPD also strongly supported a renewed offer by the Czechoslovak and East German governments to create a nuclear weapons-free zone in Europe, which was again proposed by Czechoslovak Prime Minister Lubomír Štrougal in April 1987. The CPCS and SPD also formed task groups of experts on environmental protection and issued several documents stressing the importance of cooperation in this field and the interdependence between peace and environmental protection. The other major West German political parties also sent delegations to Czechoslovakia, but less frequently than the SPD and with virtually no practical outcome.

North Rhine-Westphalia and Bavaria maintained quite close contacts with the Czech Republic on ecological matters. Bavaria was the German state most affected by pollution from Czechoslovakia. As far as North Rhine-Westphalia was concerned, its Social Democratic government was again the driving force in establishing fairly close links with the Czech authorities on environmental issues. These lower level contacts eventually led to the signing of an environmental protection agreement between the two federal governments in October 1987. West German cooperation with Czechoslovakia and the GDR in this field was, in fact, closer than among the members of the CMEA.

The FRG was Czechoslovakia's most important trading partner in the West. Czechoslovakia was the FRG's fourth most important Eastern trading partner.

By 1988, trade between the 2 countries amounted to more than DM 4,000 million annually, but it had been stagnating for the previous 5 years and even declined in 1987. Czechoslovak officials increasingly complained that it was almost impossible to export machinery to the West. Although Czechoslovak industry traditionally concentrated on the production of machinery, it only accounted for 10 percent of the country's exports to the FRG. The main reasons for this were its low quality, the industry's poor service, and unreliable delivery dates. As a result, the majority of Czechoslovakia's exports to the FRG consisted of raw material, semifinished products, chemical products, and food. In an attempt to rectify this pattern, Czechoslovakia had signed 81 production cooperation agreements with West German companies since 1980. This cooperation was considered by the Czechoslovaks to have been "very successful."

Czechoslovakia was rated by Western bankers as one of the most creditworthy members of the CMEA. It had the lowest net debt of all European Communist countries and the least problems in repaying it. The Czechoslovak government had been a very cautious borrower and had imported little Western technology. Moreover, in order to modernize Czechoslovakia's industry, there had been several hints that the government was looking for Western loans, on the condition that foreign currency earnings from specific exports would cover the new debts. Several delegations representing West German banks traveled to Prague. Czechoslovakia was also poised to set up more joint ventures with Western companies, and a number of West German companies seemed to be interested. On his visit to Prague in October 1987, West German Economics Minister Martin Bangemann said that "in the future the conventional exchange of goods and services will not be enough" and indicated his interest in joint ventures and "other modern forms of cooperation."

Another potential generator of Western currency that had not been developed in the ČSSR was tourism. It accounted for only 2 percent of its hard-currency income. Of the 19,000,000 or so tourists visiting the ČSSR, only about 1,000,000 came from Western countries in 1987 and well over 50 percent of them were from West Germany. Officials repeatedly indicated that major efforts would be made to attract more West Germans. These were to include the opening of a Czechoslovak tourist office in Frankfurt, more advertising, and the issuance of visas on the West German-Czechoslovak border instead of through the embassy in Bonn.

Soviet Foreign Minister Eduard Shevardnadze's visit to Bonn and the favorable development of Soviet-West German relations played a key role in providing Prague with more scope for action in its own relations with the FRG. Czechoslovakia's reputation as one of the Soviet Union's closest allies, particularly as far as foreign policy was concerned, had prevented closer cooperation with the FRG for a long time; the ups-and-downs of the two countries' relations depended very much on the climate in Moscow. Now, however, since the Kremlin was showing increasing interest in improving its relations with Bonn, the way seemed to be open for Prague as well.

Czechoslovak and Soviet motives for improving relations with the FRG differed considerably, however. While the Soviet Union was certainly interested in closer economic cooperation, the acquisition of technology, and more trade with the FRG (which was the USSR's largest trading partner in the West), its basic motivation appeared to be based on foreign policy objectives. As President Ronald Reagan put it in his annual report on national security, "the Soviet Union's campaign to separate Western Europe from the United States remains ... the main threat to America's global interests."9 West Germany was, without doubt, one of the main targets of this campaign. For the Soviet Union, economic cooperation with the FRG served more as a means of mediation than it did for Czechoslovakia, whose interest in better relations was largely economically motivated.

At a press conference for West German reporters on January 21, Prime Minister Lubomír Štrougal made it clear that his government was basically interested in increasing economic and ecological cooperation and expected these two issues to dominate the talks. He also announced that the relaxation of travel restrictions between the two countries was now more a technical question than the political one it had been before. He failed to say, however, whether this easing of travel would concern only German tourists or whether it would mean more freedom for Czechoslovaks to visit West Germany.

A subject that was much discussed during Helmut Kohl's visit to Czechoslovakia in January was future economic and technical cooperation between the two countries. Štrougal referred to the Czechoslovak leadership's proposed economic reforms and said that Czechoslovakia wanted to democratize its society further and to pursue an open policy "not only at home but also toward neighbors." Kohl expressed interest in and support for the Czechoslovak steps to "modernize, reform, and restructure" the country's economy. He said that economic ties were a solid pillar of cooperation between the two countries and that the West Germans were willing to cooperate in various forms, ranging from cooperation between companies to joint ventures. Kohl said that he knew Štrougal to be particularly active in encouraging economic cooperation of this sort.

An inland shipping accord was signed that opened the German section of the Danube to Czechoslovak ships (an important gain for Czechoslovakia) and enabled West German and West Berlin ships to fly the West German flag in Czechoslovakia.10 The conclusion of this pact represented a victory for the FRG. Štrougal told Kohl that his country needed West German cooperation if it was to implement its plans for environmental protection. He expressed interest in linking the two countries' power systems; in building a freeway link; in collaboration to improve the safety of nuclear power plants; in facilitating youth, cultural, and scientific and technological exchanges; and in greater cooperation on third markets. Kohl and Štrougal discussed a cooperation project under which the Volkswagen company would set up a plant in Czechoslovakia to produce engines for Škoda cars.[11]

On humanitarian issues, Kohl said that "pragmatic solutions to humanitarian questions are the cornerstone of good relations between neighbors." He welcomed the Czechoslovak government's assurance that it would continue to approve applications for exit visas for ethnic Germans in accordance with the two governments' exchange of letters on humanitarian questions; but he added that divided families not covered by the letters should also be speedily reunited.

Kohl called for more cultural exchanges and for the establishment of cultural institutes in each other's country. For a long time Czechoslovakia had refused even to discuss the subject; but in 1987 the Czechoslovaks said that they would be prepared to talk about it. Kohl urged that additional border crossing points be opened and the processing of border traffic eased; he also called for more youth exchanges, sister city arrangements, and unrestricted parliamentary contacts. Kohl said that he "wanted his visit to be a milestone on the path to good neighborliness" and that he firmly intended "to contribute to the construction of the Europe of tomorrow, guaranteeing people a peaceful future and human rights."

On January 27, Kohl met for one hour with the Czech primate, Cardinal František Tomášek, to discuss the situation of the Roman Catholic Church in Czechoslovakia. Kohl described their talk as "the heart of his visit." After the meeting he said that he had told the Czechoslovak leaders that the way the Roman Catholic Church was being treated was of decisive importance for those who wanted Prague to win confidence in the West. Noting that important negotiations were under way between Czechoslovakia and the Vatican, Kohl said that he hoped his visit would influence the talks favorably.[12]

Members of Kohl's delegation met in Prague with supporters of Charter 77 and discussed the country's political, economic, and social situation. The Charter 77 supporters expressed cautious optimism about the state of the country and said that they hoped that Kohl's visit would contribute to an improvement in conditions there.[13]

54
## CREDITS TO HUNGARY
Alfred Reisch

Károly Grósz, HSWP Politburo member and prime minister since June 1987, paid an official visit to the FRG from October 7 to 10, 1987, at the invitation of Chancellor Helmut Kohl, thus returning the latter's visit to Hungary in June 1983. The last visit by a Hungarian Prime Minister to the FRG had been made by Grósz's predecessor, György Lázár, in October 1981.

*Political Background.* Both sides described their political relations as "exemplary" for two states that belonged to different political and military alliance systems.[1] In the previous decade or so, diplomatic contacts and political dialogue had been frequent, even when the overall East-West climate took a chilly turn. On September 30, the official Hungarian news agency MTI stated that the aim of Grósz's visit was "to strengthen the well-developing cooperation between Hungary and the FRG over recent years." According to Grósz, bilateral contacts were "problem-free" and political dialogue had remained "continuous and intensive."

*Very Successful Talks in Bonn.* After private talks in "a cordial atmosphere" between Kohl and Grósz which lasted an hour, two delegations met in a plenary session to review international and bilateral issues. They praised the pending Soviet-American agreement over nuclear missiles and stressed their interest in the continuation of the Helsinki process. Grósz spoke about the social and economic situation in Hungary and of the most important tasks ahead for economic stabilization. He thanked the FRG for supporting Hungary in its negotiations with the European Economic Community and said that Hungary could only accept an accord with the EEC that would be in harmony with its rights as a GATT member.

Kohl and the German delegation said that they were following with "sympathy and great interest" Hungary's reform process and its efforts at economic stabilization—efforts that the FRG was interested in seeing succeed. They also lauded Hungary's foreign policy, saying that its constancy had contributed to the preservation of East-West dialogue. The previously announced easing of foreign travel opportunities for Hungarians was also praised, and Kohl accepted an invitation from Grósz to make an official visit to Hungary.[2]

Five different agreements were then concluded in the presence of the two heads of government, the most important being a government-guaranteed credit for Hungary of DM 1,000 million signed between the Deutsche Bank and the Hungarian National Bank, which came as somewhat of a surprise. The other documents signed were a five-year agreement on technical and scientific cooperation; an accord on expanding cultural relations by setting up cultural and information centers in each other's country; an agreement under which the FRG would give financial and other support to help meet the cultural (mainly linguistic) needs of Hungary's ethnic German minority; and, as a first step toward dropping all West German visa requirements for Hungarians visiting the FRG, an easing of the West German regulations in this area. In addition, ratification documents were exchanged for an investment protection agreement signed by the two countries in April 1986.

*Mutual Praise and Understanding.* In his speech at a gala dinner in Grósz's honor, Kohl praised Hungary's "courageous, forward-looking" reform process and the Hungarian leadership's resolve to pursue this course regardless of the economic difficulties." Kohl promised that, so far as it could, the FRG would "actively help you on your difficult road"; and he noted that Hungary's reform policy had always sought to improve economic cooperation with the West. Kohl also praised Hungary's treatment of its German and other national minorities and expressed full support for its policy in this area.

In his reply, Grósz said that ever since it had settled in Europe in the ninth century, the Hungarian nation had been able to survive and develop only by remaining open to European scientific development and cultural values; it had been German science and culture in particular, he continued, that had helped it to keep pace with the rest of the world. He thanked the FRG for its interest and understanding of Hungary's situation and objectives, and expressed satisfaction at the desire of both sides to expand bilateral relations in all fields. He reaffirmed Hungary's intention of relying even more on international economic relations and on opening its doors even wider to all foreign partners, including West German firms willing to take part in modernizing its economy on the basis of mutual benefit.[3]

On the second day of his stay in Bonn, Grósz held talks with a host of top West German officials, starting with Vice Chancellor and Foreign Minister Hans-Dietrich Genscher, with whom he discussed international issues and the opening of a Hungarian consulate in Munich, primarily because of the expected increase in travel between the two countries. (West Germany was interested in opening a consulate in Pécs, where many ethnic Germans lived.) He also held discussions with Bundestag Chairman Philipp Jenninger; the prime minister of the State of Lower Saxony, Ernst Albrecht; the chairman of the Social Democratic Party, Hans-Jochen Vogel, whom Grósz thanked for his party's "pioneering role" in developing Hungarian-West German relations; Free Democratic Party parliamentary group leader Wolfgang Mischnick; and two representatives of the Greens, Waltraud Schoppe and Otto Schily, who asked several pointed questions about ecological issues in Hungary and suggested to Grósz that military service should be a decision left to the individual. Grósz was also received by West German President Richard von Weizsäcker, who had much praise for Hungary's policy toward national minorities and expressed the wish to see Hungary's own minorities living abroad treated in the same way.

On the same day, at a joint press conference in Bonn, the West German government spokesman Friedhelm Ost and Deputy Foreign Minister László Kovács made it clear that both sides were very pleased with the progress of Grósz's visit. According to Ost, Kohl had called the visit an "unlimited success" and had said that high-level political relations had been strengthened and the path cleared for more economic as well as cultural cooperation. Kovács said that Grósz was also very satisfied with the visit, saying that it had resulted in concrete agreements and not just words, thus opening a new chapter in bilateral relations. The DM 1,000 million in West German bank credits would be used to help modernize the Hungarian economy and industry and to increase its export capability, Kovács said; it would also help to provide West German firms with good business opportunities. He also thanked West Germany for supporting Hungary's negotiations for a comprehensive trade agreement with the European Economic Community, saying that Budapest would continue to count on this support and on other forms of international cooperation, particularly with West German firms, in implementing its program for economic recovery.[4]

*Talks in Munich and Stuttgart.* On October 9 Grósz flew to Munich for a meeting with Bavarian Prime Minister Franz Josef Strauss, who outdid the politicians in Bonn in telling his guest how interested Bavaria was in Hungary's economic policies. Strauss said that he was convinced these policies would succeed and spoke positively about the easing of travel regulations and the setting up of a Hungarian cultural institute in Munich. Strauss mentioned his own role in helping to secure the West German bank credit for Hungary and in promoting the successful outcome of Budapest's negotiations with the EEC, and also referred to the bridge-building role played by the German ethnic minority in Hungary. Economic relations between Bavaria and Hungary, already very significant (a third of Hungary's exports to the FRG went to Bavaria and close to 20 percent of West Germany's exports to Hungary originated there), should continue to expand, Strauss said.

Grósz then visited Munich's BMW automobile factory, where he met with 400 Hungarian guest workers employed there (out of a total of 1,400 working on contract in the FRG) and was presented with a BMW car by the management.[5] On October 10 Grósz concluded his crowded schedule by discussing economic issues in Stuttgart with Baden-Wuerttemberg State Prime Minister Lothar Späth; both sides agreed on an exchange of experts in technology and investment. Baden-Württemberg laid claim to 14 percent of Hungarian-West German trade, and companies located there had cooperation agreements with over 60 Hungarian enterprises. Grósz's final visit was to the computer center of the University of Stuttgart.

*Cultural Institutes To Be Set Up.* At the end of their talks in July 1987, which set the stage for Grósz's visit to Bonn, Genscher and his Hungarian counterpart Péter Várkonyi announced that a scientific and technical cooperation accord would be signed during the Grósz's visit and that it had also been agreed to set up cultural institutes in each other's country.[6] In August the West German Foreign Ministry confirmed the proposal to establish cultural institutes and announced that the first would be a West German institute in Budapest.[7] This had been a long-standing West German request on which the Hungarians had been dragging their feet because of East German opposition. (Romania was the only other Warsaw Pact country to allow a West German cultural institute on its territory. It opened in 1979.)

According to the bilateral agreement signed during Grósz's visit, the German institute in Budapest was to be set up under the auspices of the Goethe Institute in Munich; it was to provide information about German cultural and scientific achievements and also promote the teaching of the German language. As for Budapest, it requested that its cultural center be set up in Munich.

*Ethnic German Minority To Benefit.* The marked improvement in cultural relations was bound to benefit the ethnic German minority in Hungary, which numbered about 200,000 and which had long had its German cultural contacts limited to the GDR. With travel to the West becoming easier for Hungarians, contacts between the so-called Donauschwaben and the FRG increased. In October 1986 West German President Richard von Weizsäcker became the first leading West German politician to visit Hungary's ethnic German community, which gave him a very warm reception.[8] Hungary subsequently drew repeated praise from the FRG for the way it treated its ethnic Germans, who on the whole appeared to be satisfied with their lot. The number of ethnic German immigrants to the FRG from Eastern Europe rose during the first half of 1987 by 47 percent compared with the same period in 1988, from 16,246 to 23,930; they included 13,209 from Poland, 6,225 from Romania, 3,840 from the USSR, and only 237 from Hungary. (By the end of September, the total number of ethnic German resettlers from Eastern Europe had reached 51,363.)

Under the terms of the accord signed during Grósz's visit and tied to the 1977 cultural cooperation agreement between the two countries, Hungary and the FRG were to undertake further joint measures to help preserve the cultural traditions and mother tongue of ethnic Germans in Hungary. This would mean primarily West German financial contributions to the education of ethnic German children from nursery school to university and to the establishment of a German-language theater and cultural center, probably in the city of Pécs.[9] There were wider implications to this development, however; for there were close to 300,000 ethnic Germans living in Romania as well as ethnic Germans in Poland and the Soviet Union, and Bonn could now hope that these countries would follow Hungary's lead in their treatment of ethnic minorities. Any improvement in the lot of ethnic Germans in Romania, however, was unlikely to benefit the 2,000,000 to 2,500,000 Magyars living in Romania under very difficult conditions.

Cultural contacts between Hungary and the FRG were also increasing and a number of artistic events, art exhibits, concerts, and student exchanges took place between the two countries. Some of them were major events, such as the Hungarian cultural week in Dortmund in May 1987. More than 20 universities signed direct cooperation agreements, and 12 departments of Hungarian studies were set up at West German universities.

*Tourists Yes, Refugees No.* Tourism between the two countries continued to grow rapidly. In 1986 some 860,000 West Germans visited Hungary, bringing with them much-needed hard currency. In 1987, this figure leaped to 1,097,000, a 27.3 percent increase compared to 1986. On October 8 the 1,000,000th West German visitor to Hungary, a 43-year-old secretary from Frankfurt, disembarked from the plane in Budapest and was promptly presented with a four-year-old Hungarian mare worth 60,000 forint. Some 250,000 Hungarians visited the FRG in 1987; this number was likely to increase, however, with the removal on January 1, 1988 of Hungarian restrictions on the frequency of travel to the West. On the other hand, Hungarian travelers would remain unable to obtain any more hard currency, which would mean that only Hungarians with helpful relatives living in the West would be able to take full advantage of this change. Hungary suggested that visa requirements between the two countries be abolished, as in the case of Austria and a few other Western countries. In response, West German officials said that Bonn was willing to ease visa procedures as a first step toward abolishing visa requirements altogether. The accord would introduce such changes as the easing of visa procedures for certain groups (businessmen, for example) and granting multiple-entry visas of several years' duration for others. An immediate abolition of visa requirements was not in the cards owing to objections from West Germany's EEC neighbors, primarily France, who were concerned about security. In his press conference in Bonn on October 8, the West German government spokesman, Friedhelm Ost, mentioned the resistance from other West European states and within Bonn's own Interior Ministry. Hungary was expected not to spoil the deal by flooding the FRG with spies.

Meanwhile, in September 1987, Hungary's National Office of Tourism opened a tourist office in Frankfurt, its first office abroad, to strengthen ties between West German and Hungarian tourist companies and increase tourism from the FRG to Hungary.[10] The 100-room, 4-star Hotel Budapest in Munich was also opened in September.

The FRG was anxious that any increase in the number of visiting Hungarians should not result in a rise in the number of asylum seekers. Minister of the Interior Friedrich Zimmermann was determined to stem the flow through stricter approval procedures of asylum seekers, whose overall number was expected to reach 60,000 in 1987. Some 45.2 percent of all applicants for political asylum in the FRG in September 1987 came from Eastern Europe: 1,851 from Poland, 327 from Czechoslovakia, 249 from Romania, and 200 from Hungary. From the summer of 1987 onwards, Hungarians and Poles seeking asylum—who, according to the West German authorities, usually faced no risk of reprisals if forced to return home—could face deportation.[11]

*Conclusion.* It was a very satisfied Grósz who sipped wine during his plane flight home after four days of hard work. He was delighted with the great sympathy for Hungary that he had found among his hosts as well as their willingness to support Hungary in its negotiations with the EEC. Grósz said that he had expected West Germany to provide business and financial support for Hungary but was nevertheless surprised by its size. For someone who had told a West German journalist before his trip that he was not going to the FRG to bring back money,[12] he had done extremely well indeed.

Extremely positive editorials appeared in the Hungarian media on the outcome of Grósz's visit, which was said to have opened a new chapter in Hungarian-West German relations and to have brought about many tangible results. The editorials welcomed the FRG's interest in the continuation and success of Hungary's reforms and the opportunity that West German support offered for Hungarian industry to modernize using the most modern equipment and technology; the fact that a "civilized dialogue" was possible in spite of ideological differences was also welcomed, as were the similarities between the two countries' views on many international issues.[13]

As for the West German press, it made clear that Bonn had its own interests in not allowing the Hungarian reform to flounder. The continuation of the Hungarian reform was of prime importance to similar reforms elsewhere in the Communist bloc, all of which contributed to stability in Europe, which was the FRG's ultimate goal. In this way, the political significance of the latest package of measures to help Hungary out of its economic difficulties went beyond demonstrating to the CMEA countries that technological salvation came from the West and not the East. As well as widening the range of economic options open to Grósz and enhancing his personal standing, the visit was another example of Hungarian and West German *realpolitik* in which the FRG made clever use of its opportunities in Central and Eastern Europe.

## 55
## BENEFITS TO THE GDR FROM THE FRG
### Barbara Donovan

During East German state and party leader Erich Honecker's visit to the FRG in September 1987, the East Germans showed a keen interest in expanding economic relations. At what Honecker described as an "exceptionally important" meeting between representatives of East and West German industry, the East

German delegation showed considerable enthusiasm and confidence about the future of economic relations with the FRG.[1]

The East Germans had long profited from their special economic relationship with the FRG. Because the GDR was not considered a foreign country by West Germany, it received preferential treatment in trade. Moreover, it was estimated that the GDR received DM 2,500 million in hard currency a year, aside from trade, from public and private sources in the FRG. Although it was almost impossible to measure all the benefits this economic relationship had given the GDR, the West Germans had undoubtedly helped the GDR gain access to Western markets and maintain financial liquidity and a relatively high standard of living. Later, the expansion of economic relations, particularly the possibility of new forms of cooperation, became more significant because of the GDR's need to acquire Western technology in order to modernize its industry and sustain economic growth at an adequate level.

*Trade.* By 1987, East and West Germany exchanged approximately DM 16,000 million in goods and services a year, which accounted for about 4 percent of all trade between the East bloc and capitalist countries.[2] Inter-German trade expanded fairly steadily over the years, having more than doubled since 1974. It later began to stagnate, however, dropping 5 percent in the first half of 1987 compared with the same period in 1986.[3]

Inter-German trade was important to the two countries for different reasons. For the FRG, the relationship was of less significance economically than as a means to influence the GDR politically.[4] In the GDR, however, the economic gains from the relationship were foremost. Trade with the FRG, East Germany's most important trading partner after the Soviet Union, accounted for about 30 percent of the GDR's trade with the West and 8 percent of all its trade. For the FRG, however, trade with East Germany constituted 20 percent of its trade with the East bloc and only 1.5 percent of all its trade.[5]

*Special Benefits.* Because the GDR was not considered a foreign country, its goods entered the FRG duty-free; agricultural exports were not subject to EEC levies and importers and exporters in the FRG received preferential tax treatment in trading with the GDR. Furthermore, the GDR enjoyed benefits from the "swing," an interest-free credit that was designed to prevent interruptions in trade caused by temporary account imbalances. In 1987, the "swing" was set at DM 850,000,000, but the GDR had been drawing less than 30 percent of this amount annually. In addition, the GDR did not have to purchase goods from the FRG in hard currency but rather on the basis of a clearing unit of account equal in value to the West German mark.

A study by the West German Institute for Economic Research[6] concluded that the GDR purchased from the FRG goods essential for its own production that it did not produce itself and could not obtain from CMEA countries. Capital goods, however, made up only a relatively small share of inter-German trade (20 percent of the GDR's imports from the FRG). In the early nineteen-eighties, the

GDR's policies of austerity and rationalization brought the large-scale importing of machinery and technological equipment to a virtual halt, although later figures showed that this trend was being reversed.[7] Imports of crude oil, chemical products, iron, and steel were apparently more important to the GDR. Indeed, over 50 percent of inter-German trade consisted of primary and intermediate goods.

Inter-German trade was also important to the GDR for securing materials or spare parts needed on short notice because of unforeseen circumstances or failures in planning. During an unusually cold winter in 1987, a last-minute delivery of 300,000 metric tons of hard coal from the FRG temporarily relieved a severe energy shortage in the GDR. Deliveries from the FRG could be organized and transported quickly.[8]

Consumer goods, such as electric appliances, textiles, and clothing, accounted for 27 percent of the GDR's exports to the FRG[9] but for only 11 percent of the GDR's imports in 1986. The freedom from tariffs allowed the GDR to earn hard currency easily by exporting goods to West Germany. Moreover, the FRG was the most receptive Western market for East German exports, especially in textiles and clothing, chemicals, and agricultural and refined petroleum products, which could not reach other Western markets because of protectionist restrictions.

*Hard-Currency Transfers.* The two governments concluded a number of financial agreements on matters other than trade that brought the GDR an estimated DM 1,000 million a year. The largest expenditure was the lump sum of DM 525,000,000 that Bonn paid each year in transit and maintenance fees for the highways, railways, and canals between the FRG and West Berlin. West Germany also paid for major improvements for roadways to Berlin and for postal and communication fees. Since 1962 East Germany had gained additional money from the FRG's purchase of freedom for political prisoners. The prices were not disclosed but were estimated to range between DM 20,000 and 100,000 per prisoner.

These amounts were supplemented by private sources of hard currency, such as mandatory currency exchanges for visitors to the GDR, visa and transit fees, and the revenue from foreign currency shops. The mandatory exchange of DM 25 per day, for example, was estimated to bring in almost DM 500,000,000 a year.[10]

Such public and private transfers to the GDR were estimated to total between DM 2,000 million and 2,500 million yearly and to allow the GDR to build up substantial hard-currency reserves. Indeed, according to one study, the GDR's hard-currency income from these transfers alone was enough to service its Western debt, even in 1981 and 1982 when growth was slow in the GDR and its debt problem was severe.[11] In addition, private gifts, estimated at between DM 1,000 million and 2,000 million per annum, did much to maintain and improve living standards in the GDR and thus contributed to social stability.

*Helping the GDR Weather Storms.* During times of domestic economic strain and external pressure, the special status of inter-German trade assumed additional significance. Indeed, the economic relationship with the FRG enabled the GDR to cope more effectively than its CMEA partners with economic problems, such as the liquidity crisis in the early nineteen-eighties. In 1982 and 1983 the GDR sharply reduced imports from other Western countries in order to control its indebtedness but increased imports from the FRG,[12] indicating that the GDR used trade with West Germany as a substitute for that with other hard-currency countries. Two unprecedented government-guaranteed bank loans of DM 1,000 million and DM 950,000,000, granted by the FRG in July 1983 and July 1984, respectively, also helped ease the GDR out of the crisis by reestablishing its creditworthiness with its Western trading partners.

Relations with the FRG also promised to help the GDR overcome a lack of capital and a low level of technological development (problems that plagued other CMEA countries), so that it could carry out modernization and maintain its position in international markets. A thorough modernization of the GDR's economy (a project previously postponed because of the austerity policies of the early nineteen-eighties) was essential if the SED was to sustain economic growth in the long run and thus remain able to argue that it had no need for Soviet-style reforms. The West Germans indicated that they were willing to share their technology, especially in environmental protection, and possibly to grant the GDR more credit.

*New Forms.* A number of obstacles stood in the way of a major expansion of trade between East and West Germany (East German goods were increasingly less competitive on the FRG market), and the GDR had begun looking for new forms of economic cooperation. The accords signed during Honecker's visit on scientific and technological cooperation, nuclear safety, and the environment gave the GDR opportunities to receive technology and investments from the FRG.[13] Cooperation between industrial firms had thus far remained low, apparently because the GDR was reluctant to allow contacts between its citizens and West Germans. During Honecker's visit, however, the East Germans said that in future, industrial combines would enjoy more flexibility in cooperating with the FRG, possibly indicating that the GDR was considering the viability of joint ventures.

*How Important Were Relations with the FRG?* Despite the obvious economic gains, it would be inaccurate to assume that its relationship with the FRG was the only reason that the GDR had done so well economically compared with the other CMEA states. Other factors such as greater economic efficiency, the restructuring of the industrial sector, and the policies of austerity and rationalization, to name just a few, all contributed to the GDR's relative economic success.[14]

Moreover, although eager to use the opportunities offered by the FRG, the GDR feared that the FRG would use trade to extract political concessions and so took care to limit its dependence on the FRG by diversifying its trade with "nonsocialist" states. Thus, since the early nineteen-seventies, the GDR's trade with West Germany had been declining in comparison with its trade with other Western countries.[15]

Inter-German trade and the additional benefits from the two nations' economic relationship were instrumental in securing economic stability and the relatively high standard of living in the GDR. The special trading status made it easier for the GDR to withstand economic pressures. The East German authorities appeared less cautious than before about developing economic links. This was partly a result of the stabilization of the political relationship. Moreover, the GDR's keen interest in expanding economic relations and Honecker's political concessions in such areas as travel indicated that the East German leadership considered economic cooperation with the FRG a prerequisite to modernization and continued economic development. The GDR also wanted to secure a source of hard currency income in the long run. These considerations were the key factors prompting Honecker to continue his efforts to improve political relations with Bonn.

## 56
## CHANGING RELATIONS WITH MOSCOW?
### E. Kautsky

*Dobrynin in Bonn.* The six-day visit to West Germany October 8-14, 1987, by Anatolii Dobrynin, the CPSU CC secretary for international affairs, drew attention to Moscow's new interest in improving relations with the Federal Republic. Dobrynin, the highest-ranking Soviet official to go to Bonn since 1983, went to the FRG at the invitation of the West German Social Democratic Party and met with Chancellor Helmut Kohl, to whom he delivered a letter from Gorbachev. According to press reports, Gorbachev thanked Kohl for his willingness to eliminate Germany's 72 Pershing 1A missiles in conjunction with a US-Soviet arms control agreement on intermediate-range nuclear forces in Europe. Officials in Bonn said that the Soviet leader had declared his willingness to meet with Kohl in "the not too distant future."[1]

Dobrynin's visit came after several indications of renewed Soviet interest in improving relations with West Germany and amid growing speculation in the West over a possible shift in Soviet policy on the German question. West German President Richard von Weizsäcker's visit to the USSR in the spring and a steady increase in contacts between the two countries' ministries indicated that

Soviet-West German relations were again improving. Furthermore, Moscow's approval of SED leader Erich Honecker's trip to Bonn was also proof of a more relaxed Soviet attitude toward inter-German ties and evidence that Moscow was no longer trying to isolate the FRG diplomatically.

*Philosophical Speculation*? There was speculation about far-reaching Soviet initiatives toward both German states. In early October, for example, State Secretary Ottfried Hennig of the West German Ministry for Inter-German Affairs claimed that Gorbachev had commissioned four foreign policy experts to come up with an alternative means of dealing with the German question.[2] The Bonn official warned that the Soviet leadership might propose a demilitarized inter-German confederation in an attempt to lure Bonn out of NATO.[3]

Hennig's remarks were followed by those of Valentin Falin, the former Soviet Ambassador to the FRG and head of the Novosti press agency. Speaking on West German television, Falin said that he could envision "more interesting models" for managing relations between Bonn and East Berlin, including the removal of all foreign troops from German soil and greater contacts between the two German states; Falin added that the Four-Power Agreement on Berlin was not necessarily "the final word" on the fate of the divided city.[4] The Western press also reported the remarks of a Soviet diplomat in Geneva, Stanislav Cherniavskii, who had told a group of West European army chaplains that he believed the Berlin Wall was nearing "its final days."[5]

The significance of such remarks was later played down by all sides. At a Bonn press conference, Dobrynin, emphasizing that he was speaking for the Soviet Central Committee, claimed that Moscow's position on Berlin and on the German question was clear and unchanged and that speculation and "fantasies" should be stopped.[6] In Moscow, Foreign Ministry Spokesman Gennadii Gerasimov confirmed Moscow's traditional position on Berlin.[7] Falin, reportedly a member of the Moscow group commissioned by Gorbachev to reconsider the German question, denied that a group existed.[8]

In Bonn, the government spokesman Friedhelm Ost said that Bonn had no hard evidence that Moscow was planning any major moves on the German question.[9] In East Berlin, Honecker replied to Falin's remarks by noting that the Four-Power Agreement was working fine and that in a future common "European house" one could certainly imagine greater movement "between different rooms," including the two German states, suggesting that this was what Falin had really meant.[10] *Neues Deutschland* covered a press conference in East Berlin with Igor Maksimychev, the second ranking man at the Soviet Embassy, who suggested that the remarks of Falin and Cherniavskii be interpreted in a "philosophical sense" and over a period of 100 to 150 years.[11]

*Bonn and Moscow: Abiding Interests.* For the Soviet Union, the FRG was the second most important capitalist country in the Western world following the United States. West Germany's significance for the Soviet Union resulted from Bonn's geopolitical position in the heart of Europe, its influence within NATO councils on arms control and security issues, and the fact that the Federal Republic was Moscow's leading trading partner in the West. For these reasons West Germany inevitably held a central position in Soviet policy toward the West, especially toward Western Europe. At the same time, the division of Germany, Bonn's interest in tempering the costs of partition by improving inter-German relations and reducing arms, and Moscow's obvious influence on how relations in Central Europe were run all combined to make the Soviet-West German relationship of crucial importance to any West German government regardless of its political complexion.

Both countries, despite their obvious differences, had abiding interests that tied them into a complex bilateral relationship containing elements of confrontation, competition, and cooperation. There were a number of ups and downs in relations between Bonn and Moscow over the years. In the nineteen-seventies Bonn became Moscow's leading partner on the continent in promoting the Soviet policy of détente. In the early nineteen-eighties, on the other hand, West Germany's role in the NATO dual-track decision made Bonn the prime target in a Soviet campaign aimed at preventing Western deployment plans by exploiting domestic opposition in West Germany and differences within NATO.

Following the start of Euromissile deployment, Moscow launched a campaign against West German "revanchism" in order to "punish" Bonn for its "complicity" in the NATO deployment. As a result, Soviet-West German relations stagnated. Given the nature of both Soviet and West German interests, however, it was inevitable that this phase of chill or confrontation would eventually be overcome. The question was when, why, and with what implications.

*A Soviet Reassessment?* Observers agreed that a major reassessment of domestic and foreign policy was in progress in Moscow. In particular, relations with Western Europe were being reexamined as witnessed, for instance, by Gorbachev's visit to France in 1985 and Soviet interest in recognizing the European Community. However, despite a steady flow of statements by Gorbachev and other Soviet officials proclaiming an interest in constructing a new, common "European house," such statements sounded hollow so long as it was apparent that Moscow did not have a coherent policy toward the key country in Western Europe, the FRG.

For nearly a year Bonn and Moscow seemed to be on the verge of reestablishing bilateral discussions. After West German Foreign Minister Hans-Dietrich Genscher went to Moscow in the summer of 1986, both sides spoke of turning a new page in their bilateral relations; but Chancellor Kohl's controversial interview with *Newsweek* later in the fall, in which he compared Gorbachev to the Nazi propaganda minister Joseph Goebbels, and Bonn's position in the "double-zero-option" controversy, put a temporary halt to previous signs of progress. Von Weizsäcker's visit to the USSR, Soviet support of Honecker's visit to Bonn, Kohl's declaration on the Pershing-1A dispute,

Dobrynin's trip to the FRG, and the prospect of a meeting between Gorbachev and Kohl, however, seemed to indicate that Moscow had abandoned its attempts to isolate Bonn.

There were two apparent reasons why the Soviets had decided to improve relations with Bonn. If arms control agreements and economic assistance were the two key items that Gorbachev hoped to obtain from the West to assist him in his own reform plans, Bonn was crucial in his obtaining either or both. While the USA remained Moscow's prime negotiating partner in arms control discussions, especially on strategic and space weapons, Bonn would be very influential in any future talks on arms reductions in Europe. This was particularly true with regard to conventional forces, since the West German army was the backbone of NATO's ground forces. Second, Bonn's influence was also crucial for obtaining increased trade with the West, financial credits, or access to technology. In addition to being Moscow's leading Western trading partner and having provided significant commercial credits in the past, the FRG was one of the few countries to have expressed serious interest in bilateral joint-venture projects.[12] It was also perhaps the only country in the West both financially able and sufficiently committed in political terms to give the Soviet Union any serious assistance in its modernization plans.

Gorbachev's reforms and "new thinking" elicited considerable interest in the FRG and in public opinion polls in the FRG the Soviet leader received high marks for diplomacy, indeed higher than US President Ronald Reagan. Bonn's strong interest in the outcome of Gorbachev's reforms was stressed by West German government officials, especially Genscher. The West, according to Genscher, could not afford to sit idly by and await the outcome of Gorbachev's reforms but would have to try to encourage and thereby influence this process so that it would develop in accordance with Western interests. Bonn, too, emphasized its interest in arms control, expanded East-West economic cooperation, and the construction a "European peace structure," its version of a "European house."[13]

*On the Threshold of a New Era?* Following his return from Moscow and his conversations with Gorbachev, Bavaria's prime minister and the head of the Christian Social Union (CSU) Franz Josef Strauss said that West German-Soviet relations were "at the threshold of a new era."[14]

It was not only the FRG that held an important position in future Soviet policy toward the West, but the West German right-of-center parties as well. This was obviously tied to the fact that a CDU-led coalition was in power in Bonn and would remain there at least until 1991. Moreover, the influence of West German conservative circles on defense and security policies and questions of East-West finance was obvious.

In their conversations with Western visitors, Soviet officials emphasized one aspect of Gorbachev's "new thinking": Moscow had ostensibly comprehended the fact that attempts to drive wedges between NATO members or between political parties within NATO countries could be counterproductive and that real and durable progress in East-West relations could only be achieved by agreement. In the West German political context, this meant that Moscow had understood, at least in theory, that while it may have more in common with the SPD, it could not base a long-term policy of rapprochement with Bonn on the SPD alone, nor could it hope to achieve progress on security issues if there was a divisive and sustained debate within the FRG over how to deal with Moscow.

*West German Interests.* Bonn, too, had its own special reasons for wanting to improve relations with Moscow. First, one of the key changes introduced by Bonn's "new" *Ostpolitik* in the early nineteen-seventies was its clear orientation toward Moscow. As the French Ambassador to the USSR Roger Seydoux de Clausonne told Egon Bahr when the latter arrived in the Soviet capital in December 1969 to head the negotiations that led to the Moscow treaty of August 1970, the fact that Bonn was showing itself capable of dealing autonomously with the USSR for the first time since the war had permanently changed the political landscape in Europe. At that time Bonn had been interested in exploiting Moscow's interest in improving Soviet-West German relations to pressure a recalcitrant GDR into a more flexible position toward inter-German relations. The GDR later became a much more cooperative partner for Bonn. Nonetheless, the cultivation of a proper relationship with Moscow was still widely seen in Bonn as a requirement for progress in inter-German relations.

Second, the FRG was the NATO country most directly exposed to Soviet military power in Central Europe and also the country with the greatest concentration of Western military forces on its soil. It was therefore apparent that Bonn, too, had great interest in improving West German security through balanced arms control agreements on conventional and chemical weapons. This was seen increasingly in the West German debate over *Ostpolitik* as well. Whereas in the nineteen-seventies security issues had been deliberately kept out of West German policy toward the East, in the nineteen-eighties they had gradually become a central component of *Ostpolitik* and were widely viewed as the key to improving relations not only with the Soviet Union but with Eastern Europe as well.

Third, West German *Ostpolitik* had always been based on the notion that Western policy should support efforts in the Soviet bloc to reform communism. Change from above was widely seen in the FRG as the best and perhaps the only way of achieving the type of change in Eastern Europe that would alleviate the problems of a divided European continent and of a divided German nation. West German spokesmen, especially Genscher, were the most outspoken of leading Western politicians both in underscoring the advantages to the West if Gorbachev's reforms succeed and in saying that the West should help them as much as it could.

*Conclusion.* Despite both Bonn's and Moscow's apparent interest in improving bilateral relations, several major factors in the Soviet-West German relationship remained. First, while West German officials insisted that the German Question was not on the agenda of on-going East-West discussions, it was clear that the real motive behind West Germany's *Ostpolitik* was its dissatisfaction with the status quo between the two German states. Moscow, to be sure, did not necessarily share Bonn's aspirations for long-term change in the GDR or for Bonn's efforts to maintain the identity of a single German nation. Gorbachev made it quite clear that he viewed the continuing existence of two German states as the basis for any bilateral dialogue.[15] At the same time, he realized that progress in the areas he deemed important would be difficult if not impossible with West German resistance; and was therefore taking steps to try to reassure important political figures in West Germany that Moscow harbored no hostile intentions against Bonn.

Second, the USSR's claims that it was truly interested in a cooperation with the West based on consensus, had to be tested in practice. One can assume that Moscow and its allies were well aware of the differences within the Western alliance as NATO struggled to come up with a new concept for the next round of negotiations with the Warsaw Pact. Moscow would have to decide whether it would try to exploit differences within NATO to weaken the alliance's cohesion or whether it was really interested trying to find a common denominator and a possible compromise in what promised to be difficult and sensitive negotiations. Erich Honecker's letter to Kohl and his offer to renounce modernization of short-range nuclear weapons in the GDR if Bonn promised to do the same in the FRG, showed that the Warsaw Pact would continue to try to influence the debate within West Germany.[16]

It was nevertheless clear that Bonn had a pronounced interest in exploring the possibilities offered by Gorbachev's "new thinking" and that Moscow, too, was testing the waters to see just how interested Bonn was in improving East-West relations in Europe and what it was willing to do to foster this goal. The relationship between the FRG and the USSR was becoming an crucial factor in East-West relations.

# XIV. FOR A DIFFERENT SOVIET UNION: THE PARTY CONFERENCE

## 57
## A REFORMER'S MANIFESTO
### Richard W. Judy

On May 2, 1988, *Pravda* published a letter some 6,000 words long under the title "On the Strength and Authority of the Party." Written by V. Selivanov, the letter started on the front page, where it was conspicuously adorned with a border to draw readers' attention, and continued on page three, where it occupied two full, page-length columns. The letter was replete with trenchant criticism of the CPSU and its leadership. Given the authoritative nature of *Pravda* and the incisiveness and scope of the letter's criticism, it seems hardly likely that the letter could have been featured so prominently without approval—and maybe even connivance—at the highest level. What follows is a paraphrase of Selivanov's main points that attempts to preserve some of the flavor of his sharply critical remarks.

According to Selivanov, Soviet society had, sorrowfully, degenerated. Many workers took no pride in their jobs, skills, or qualifications. Enterprises took no pride in what they produced or in its quality. Poor workmanship was not thought to be shameful. Neither was ill-gotten gain; indeed, that was rather admired. Young people were alienated; they aped Western values. Lawlessness and dissolution were widespread. Honesty and conscientiousness too often evoked hostility; they engendered retribution from corrupt and entrenched timeservers.

— The cause of this degeneration was the Soviet political and economic system that had arisen since the nineteen-twenties. Its overcentralized and authoritarian nature was immensely corruptive and destructive. It had bred selfishness, careerism, servility, cowardice, and dishonesty in the party and society. It had greatly retarded economic development. Genuine workers had become ever fewer while the number of bosses, coordinators, and functionaries had grown ever larger. Attempts of the nineteen-sixties to reform this system had been stillborn and accomplished nothing except to reinforce the notion that the system was immutable.

— The Communist party had ruled the country since 1917. It and its leadership, therefore, were responsible for the debasement of Soviet society. Corruption and charlatanism were common in its apparatus. Too many party leaders sought only to maximize their power, influence, awards, and special privileges. They and their families made membership in the power and patronage elites their only goal. They cynically continued to spout memorized lies from party podiums while ignoring the realities of life around them. The gap between word and deed had widened.

— Lack of democracy in the party and society had brought both to the brink of ruin. Intra-party democracy had been abolished by Stalin and his ilk. The party had become an army in which every member was a soldier subservient to higher authority and, ultimately, to the general secretary. The successors to Stalin, Nikita Khrushchev and Leonid Brezhnev, had chosen to retain his system because they relished the unchecked power it concentrated in their hands. Indeed, they strengthened and consolidated the system. Party leaders at every level had become obsequious before their superiors and contemptuous of their subordinates. Members of the Central Committee and the Politburo had become indifferent to the concerns of ordinary party members.

— The party's ranks were adulterated by mediocre and careerist riffraff. Because party membership had become a prerequisite for a successful career, vast numbers of unworthy opportunists had sought and achieved it. Membership standards declined, while honest individuals abjured party work. Many felt that intelligence and honor were incompatible with party membership. Nevertheless, the party's ranks grew, reaching 19 million members.

— Perestroika was imperative for economic progress. The democratization of society was a prerequisite for perestroika, but that was impossible without first democratizing the party, a huge task. The usual method of selecting delegates to party meetings was a mockery of democracy. The meetings themselves, with their official reports, unanimous votes, proclamations and decrees, were the same. Subsequent trumpetings about "party" decisions, announcements, and solemn pronouncements were but shams. All of this had to change.

Selivanov's signature indicated merely that he was a deputy director of a department in the Ministry of Aviation Industry and that he had been a member of the Communist party since 1972. From the text, it is may be inferred that he was once a pilot in the Soviet Air Force, perhaps a career military officer.

He almost certainly spoke for the most radical reformers in Gorbachev's entourage. Surely Iakovlev and possibly even Gorbachev himself must have seen the letter before its publication. There seems little doubt that the letter was a manifesto of the democratizers within the party leadership, a direct challenge to all who would arrest or reverse glasnost, perestroika, and *demokratizatsia* in the party and society.

The letter represented an attempt to influence the deliberations and decisions of the Nineteenth Party Conference due to convene in late June. Such influence was aimed both at the selection of delegates before, and at the voting behavior of delegates during the conference. Selivanov made eleven specific proposals:

1. Purge the party membership of misfits and miscreants. The suitability of every Communist for continued membership should be attested by a secret vote in his work group after examining how well he had upheld the party's program and rules. If this were to lead to drastic cuts in party membership, so much the better. The revolution of 1917, Selivanov grumbled, was accomplished by a mere 300,000 Bolsheviks. A few million, said he, should suffice for perestroika.

2. Accelerate the purge in party organizations that had put obstacles in the way of perestroika.

3. Rewrite the Criminal Code to require party members to submit to a legal standard higher than that expected of ordinary citizens. Party membership should be regarded as an aggravating rather than a mitigating circumstance in judging a defendant's misbehavior.

4. Include in the Central Committee at least 200 top professionals and workers who could credibly demonstrate distinction in their work. This move would dilute the influence of professional party apparatchiks in the Central Committee and thereby remove impediments to perestroika and the consolidation of Gorbachev's power.

5. Mandate distribution of all relevant materials, reports, etc. to participants in party meetings sufficiently in advance to allow proper study and consideration of leadership proposals.

6. Introduce direct, secret balloting for all party offices at the level of raions, cities, and oblasts. Establish definite terms of office for each post.

7. Mandate the election of editors of all party newspapers and journals.

8. Establish a minimum number of the signatories needed on appeals and letters from party members to require the publication of official responses to them. Abolish all restrictions on criticism from below.

9. Disseminate complete accounts of the proceedings of all party meetings to the entire membership even if they contained classified portions. Any secret information so disseminated should bear the date after which it would be declassified.

10. Allocate a portion of membership dues collected to primary party organizations to defray local expenses.

11. Increase the apparat of the general secretary to facilitate investigation of complaints contained in members' letters. In those cases where such investigation substantiated members' complaints, the publication of punishment administered as well as all other follow-up action should be mandatory.

## 58
## CONTESTED PREPARATIONS
### Elizabeth Teague

Gorbachev first suggested convening a party conference in January 1987. His object was to consolidate his hold on power and obtain a mandate for his reform program. At the time of the Twenty-Seventh Party Congress in 1986, he had lacked the authority to sweep out many of the holdovers from the Brezhnev era in the Central Committee; he had also been unable to introduce the kind of party reforms he thought desirable. These included a compulsory retirement age for party officials and a limit on the number of terms they might hold a particular post. By calling for a party conference, the general secretary was seeking a second opportunity to "restructure" the party and redefine its functions in relation to those of state and government bodies. His purpose was to transfer responsibility for day-to-day management of the economy from the party to the soviets (local government councils). In this endeavor, Gorbachev faced stiff opposition from middle-ranking members of the party bureaucracy, whose jobs and privileges were threatened by the reforms he wished to make.

Gorbachev's strategy had been to form an alliance with the grass-roots party membership in order to put pressure—"from above and from below," as he said—on these middle-ranking functionaries, thereby making the party both more obedient to directions from Moscow and more responsive to local needs. In return, he offered rank-and-file members of the party a greater say in decision making and better career openings. Ordinary members of society were promised a more influential voice in the way they were governed.

Since Gorbachev's election as party leader in 1985, his candid admission that the Soviet Union was heading for a crisis and his policies of glasnost and perestroika spurred members of the Soviet public to express an amazing range of opinions on how the USSR should resolve its problems. The approach of the party conference, at which at least some of these options were to be debated, caused a polarization of public opinion and unmistakable signs of strain in the party leadership.

Under the party rules, the powers of a party conference were extremely vaguely formulated. It was therefore clear from an early stage that what Gorbachev would be able to do at the Nineteenth Party Conference depended more or less entirely on how powerful he was at the time the conference convened. Interviewed by *The Financial Times* on July 28, 1987, Gorbachev's economic adviser Abel Aganbegian stated confidently that, while there would not be "completely new" elections to the Central Committee, "we shall 'renew' some of it." The head of the Propaganda Department of the CPSU Central Committee, Iurii Skliarov, confirmed on Soviet television on June 20, 1988, that a party conference could indeed change the composition of the leading party organs.

Gorbachev had a clear motive for wanting to inject fresh blood into the Central Committee. At the Twenty-Seventh Party Congress in 1986, he had succeeded in replacing only 41 percent of the full members of the Central Committee. Holdovers from the Brezhnev era remained a powerful force within the body. Between March 1986, and June 1988, however, 20 percent of the members of the Central Committee had died, retired, or were removed from posts carrying ex-officio membership of the Central Committee. On the eve of the conference, therefore, those members whose status remained unchanged were almost equally divided between Brezhnev and Gorbachev appointees, and it was not hard to see why Gorbachev wished to tip the balance in his favor by introducing a fresh contingent of his own men. (In the event, Gorbachev did not prove able to renew the composition of the Central Committee at the party conference.)

*Conflict Over Selection of Delegates.* Preparations for the conference were stormy. The election of delegates was delayed for six weeks as arguments raged over how they should be chosen. Once the election got under way, charges of ballot-rigging abounded. Supporters of reform called for the conference to be postponed to allow delegates to be chosen in a more democratic way; they complained that the wishes of rank-and-file party members had been ignored by middle-level party bodies and that bureaucrats hostile to change made up the majority of the delegates eventually elected. This was possible because of loopholes in the election procedures. Candidates were, for the first time, nominated not from above but at grass-roots level by primary party organizations and work collectives; non-party members could even participate. The hitch was that the nominations then had to be approved by party organizations at various levels (raion and city) before finally being voted on at republican and oblast level; in the process, there was ample opportunity for party officials to remove the names of energetic rank-and-file activists and substitute candidates more acceptable to the bureaucracy. Only last-minute intervention by Gorbachev himself secured the election in Moscow of a handful of popular reformers who had been nominated at grass-roots level but were subsequently eliminated by middle-level party officials. Even then, such well-known figures as sociologist Tatiana Zaslavskaia, playwright Aleksandr Gelman, and economist Gavriil Popov, all of whom were nominated by grass-roots party groups, failed to win election.

*Popular Protests Over Electoral Abuse.* In allowing the elections to be conducted in a way so open to abuse, Gorbachev made a serious error. But it was an error that, by using the weapon of glasnost, he turned at least in part to his advantage. As the election campaign drew to a close, the official press was flooded with accounts of electoral skulduggery. This publicity aroused enormous anger among the general population. On the Far Eastern island of Sakhalin, some 4,800 people gathered in a stadium to voice their disgust at the undemocratic way conference delegates had been selected; their protests led to the sacking of the oblast party first secretary. In the Siberian city of Omsk, enraged citizens filled an 8,000-seat football stadium to castigate local party leaders for pushing though their list of candidates without consulting the public. In Moscow, 200 student activists and members of informal political action groups marched through the city center chanting "Honest elections!" In the Volga city of Iaroslavl, popular protests resulted in the withdrawal of delegate status from the oblast's former party leader, Fedor Loshchenkov—a close associate of Kremlin leader Egor Ligachev.

The demonstration in Iaroslavl was officially authorized, and the wide press coverage given to the protests led some observers to suspect that they might have had Moscow's blessing and represented a deliberate attempt by Gorbachev and his colleagues to set off a witch hunt against "conservatives," "bureaucrats," and "dogmatists." This did not, of course, mean that the protest meetings were fraudulent. The resentment of the population was real enough. But it would have been well within the power of a politician of Gorbachev's acumen to turn popular feelings against his own enemies.

*Preparing the Conference Agenda.* The row over the elections was accompanied by a month of behind-the-scenes wrangling over the conference agenda, known as "The Theses of the Central Committee." These were eventually published for general discussion in an emasculated form, which, according to reformist Soviet intellectuals, indicated that the proposals had been watered down to make them more acceptable to conservative opinion.

Even so, the Theses contained a number of proposals that were, in the Soviet context, extremely radical. Gorbachev's record had shown him to be a skillful politician who compromised when he had to, but pressed his advantage whenever he could—often at times when his adversaries least expected it. He knew the right moment to take one step back in order to be able to take two steps forward at a later date. The Theses gave official sanction to a number of formulations close to Gorbachev's heart but highly distasteful to party conservatives. These included the concepts of "Socialist pluralism" and "a Socialist state in which the rule of law prevails."

*Reforming the Party.* The most detailed proposals in the Theses dealt with reform of the Communist party. Gorbachev made it clear that he perceived the party in its present form to be part of the problem, not part of the solution. He enumerated the party's failings at a landmark plenum of the CPSU Central Committee in January, 1987. "The problems that have accumulated in society," Gorbachev said, "are to a considerable extent linked with shortcomings in the work of the party itself." The greatest problem, he went on, was that party bodies at enterprise and ministry level tended to identify with the interests of the organizations whose work they were supposed to be monitoring. Party officials—whose responsibilities were in theory confined to the political and ideological sphere, with particular reference to the selection of efficient managerial staff—got caught up in purely economic activities. As a result, they neglected their supervisory functions and put local and organizational interests above the "public" interest. (This problem dated back to the very early days of the Soviet state.)

Other critics were even blunter. A reader's letter quoted in *Izvestiia* on March 22, 1988, spoke of "a crisis of confidence" in the party. Writing in *Sotsialisticheskaia industriia* on May 22, 1988, Professor S. Dzarasov complained that the party had been "transformed from a political vanguard into an organizer of all spheres of activity" and that it had become "merged with the state." The party and state bureaucracy, Dzarasov went on, had turned into "a special administrative class." Interviewed on September 30, 1987, by the Belgrade newspaper *Borba*, another Moscow academic blamed Stalin for this. Under Stalin, said Anatolii Butenko, "the party was destroyed ... and a party of another kind was created." This idea was taken up in the course of a phone-in program shown on June 15, 1988, on Soviet television. "If the party was destroyed by Stalin," one viewer asked the panel, "do we have the right today to describe it as Lenin's party?"

Gorbachev identified the lack of democracy in the party as the main problem and promised that the party conference would see the CPSU removed once and for all from day-to-day management of the economy; it would confine itself to "guiding" instead of "directing" Soviet society and the economy. Gorbachev's aim was a leaner party with a considerably reduced bureaucracy. Officials would lose the lifetime job security and special privileges they had come to enjoy under the leadership of Leonid Brezhnev, and they would be required to account for their actions both to Moscow and to the rank-and-file. As one viewer put it during the phone-in on June 15: "What right does a party of 20 million members have to command a population of 280 million Soviet citizens?"

*Transferring Power To Local Government.* The aim was to transfer the party's administrative functions in such areas as agriculture, light industry, and consumer services to the organs of local government (the soviets) and to non-state organizations, including citizens' initiative groups. Fedor Burlatskii, known to be Gorbachev's close associate, told a press conference in Vienna on May 7, 1988, that this would inevitably entail some transfer of power away from the party and in the direction of the "civil society" that must, Burlatskii said, gradually be built in the USSR. The soviets must be given greater independence; their deputies should become full-time, paid officials instead of expending their energies on holding down jobs as dairymaids and boilermakers; and the soviets should have their own budgets to spend as they saw fit.

*Electoral Reform.* Electoral reform was assigned a key role in Gorbachev's plans for restoring the credibility of the soviets in the eyes of the general public. It was promised that multiple candidacies and secret voting would be introduced both for local elections and in the party. Burlatskii was only one of the prominent reformers who would have liked to see the Soviet Union's rubber-stamp Supreme Soviet transformed into a real parliament that would meet on a permanent basis and subject legislation to genuine debate. On June 14, 1988, the writer Ales Adamovich told a television audience that the Supreme Soviet was "a joke and a laughing stock."

*Building A "Lawful State."* The long-term aim of these reforms, according to the Theses, was the creation in the USSR of "a Socialist legal state" (*sotsialisticheskoe pravovoe gosudarstvo*)—a concept reminiscent of that of the *"Rechtsstaat"* or "lawful state." Gorbachev's policy of glasnost had already inspired an upsurge of popular interest totally new in a Soviet public generally dismissed as "apathetic" and "apolitical." The first delicate shoots of the "civil society" of which Burlatskii spoke could be detected. At the same time, opposition to change ran deep and had its supporters at all levels. Much was at stake. No less a person than the chief editor of *Pravda* expressed concern lest the reforms being discussed cause the party to be "dissolved" in the population. Gorbachev's strategy was clear. It was to mobilize support for his policies among the general public, to spark discussion, interest, and enthusiasm among ordinary people, and to turn the force of this popular emotion against the bloated ranks of Soviet officialdom. The intense popular interest aroused by the preparations for the Nineteenth Party Conference suggested that, to some extent at least, Gorbachev's gamble was already beginning to pay off.

## 59
## PRESIDENTIAL SYSTEM PROPOSED
### Dawn Mann

In his opening speech to the conference, Gorbachev created a complete surprise by his suggestion that a Congress of People's Deputies be created. The 2,250 members, to be elected once every five years, would convene yearly to discuss constitutional, political, social, and economic issues. Their real tasks, however, would be the election of 400-450 deputies to serve in a standing Supreme Soviet, the election of members to a new body—the Constitutional Review Committee—and the election of the Chairman of the Supreme Soviet.

Fifteen hundred members of the Congress of People's Deputies would be chosen on the basis of territorial and national criteria; the other 750 would represent party, trade-union, cooperative, youth, women's, veterans', scientific, and other, unspecified, organizations. CPSU Central Committee Secretary Aleksandr Iakovlev, speaking at a press conference some hours after Gorbachev delivered his address, said that non-party members would also be able to run for election as deputies.[1]

The Supreme Soviet of the Congress of People's Deputies would be in permanent session, would be accountable to the Congress of People's Deputies, and would handle questions of a legal, administrative, or monitoring nature. It would be divided into two houses. As was the practice in the Supreme Soviet, draft laws and decisions on key issues would continue to be discussed by both houses. The Supreme Soviet would also have the right to review appointments to the USSR Council of Ministers. In addition, the Council of Nationalities would handle all nationalities-related questions, while the Council of the Union would deal with all-Union questions such as citizens' rights and the ratification of international treaties. In a one-sentence aside, Gorbachev remarked that a good deal of thought had been given to the question of a periodic renewal of part of the Supreme Soviet, but he did not make clear how this might be achieved.

*The Chairman of the Supreme Soviet.* Apparently there had been some debate within the Central Committee on the question as to which office should be the top office in the Soviet Union. Gorbachev said that a number of proposals, among them the creation of the post of president of the USSR or the simultaneous holding of the offices of general secretary and chairman of the Council of Ministers by one individual, had been rejected in favor of naming the chairman of the Supreme Soviet as the USSR's chief executive domestically and on the world stage.

The chairman of the Supreme Soviet would be elected by a secret ballot of the members of the Congress of People's Deputies and would be subject to recall by the deputies. He would act as head of the Defense Council, a job held by the general secretary, and would have "sufficiently broad state powers," as well as the right to nominate the candidate to the post of head of the government (i.e., the chairman of the Council of Ministers).

Furthermore, working under him would be the Presidium of the Supreme Soviet, to consist of two first deputy chairmen (one of whom would be the chairman of the People's Control Committee), one representative from each of the fifteen Union republics, and the chairmen of each of the two houses, of their standing commissions, and of their committees.

*Elections and Terms of Office.* In keeping with the ideas advanced in the Theses, Gorbachev called for changes in the electoral system, including an expansion of the electoral experiment carried out earlier in the year. He also called upon the delegates to discuss the wisdom of a third term of service, but said that the introduction of a mandatory retirement age was not necessary. As democratization proceeded, he said, this question would be decided by the voters themselves. Finally, democratization of the election process would not, according to Gorbachev, endanger proportional representation, inasmuch as qualified delegates were to be found among "the working class, the peasantry, and the intelligentsia."

*Conclusion.* Many crucial questions remained open. For example, would the general secretary stand for election as the chairman of the Supreme Soviet? If he were not elected, would the Central Committee draw "the appropriate conclusions"? And what would be the role of the *ispolkom*?

Although Gorbachev said that he would like to see the necessary legislation submitted to the Supreme Soviet by the autumn of 1988, (*i.e.*, in time for adoption at the December convocation), this seemed an overly optimistic timetable. Many changes in the USSR Constitution would be required. According to Vladimir Kudriavtsev, director of the Institute of State and Law, discussions about constitutional amendments were still "very theoretical."[2]

## 60
## POWER TO THE SOVIETS
### Viktor Yasmann

The centerpiece of the new political system proposed by Gorbachev and approved by the conference entailed the redistribution of power from the Communist party to the soviets. It appeared that the old Bolshevik slogan "All Power to the Soviets" had been revived, but this time with a new meaning. In March 1917, Lenin was calling on his party comrades to win political power through the soviets; now, in order to retain power, Gorbachev was calling on the Communist party to share its monopoly of power with elected bodies, the soviets.

*Why Change?* Gorbachev's scheme to separate party and state involved a sharing not so much of power as of the burden of government and daily responsibilities. A local party committee had the final say on what was built in its area, be it a stadium or a kindergarten. Neither the local community, which was usually not informed of such matters at all, nor the local soviet, which was supposed to represent the community, had any voice in choosing priorities. But the local party committee's power to make decisions on every petty problem also entailed responsibility for all failures, miscalculations, and abuses in the exercise of that power that might ensue. When people were dissatisfied with the state of affairs, they blamed the party, and not just local party functionaries but the system in general.

At the same time, keeping all economic and social life under its own strict control involved a local party committee dealing with problems that were far beyond its competence and did not further its ultimate interest, which was to maintain political power. In his speech to the conference, the chief editor of

*Izvestiia*, Ivan Laptev, described a typical secretary of a local party committee struggling to fulfill an impossible task:

> He is at once supplier and financial expert, agronomist and purchaser, specialist in psychology and building contractor, bureaucrat and fighter against bureaucracy .... The party can no longer fulfill this universal, limitless role, [it could] not be performed by any organization at all.[1]

*A New Model.* The resolution endorsed by the conference included organizational, functional, legislative, and financial changes, of which the principal ones proposed:

—empowering the soviets with full authority over the executive organ, the executive committee (*ispolkom*). In mid-1988, the relationship was, as yet, reversed.

—creating a standing presidium of all soviets, excluding rural ones. (These, however, predominated, numbering 46,462.)[2]

—broadening the range of issues on which soviets could decide without external reference. This effectively meant that the standing commissions of a soviet would assume the responsibilities looked after by branch departments of the local party committee.

The proposals were accompanied by the suggestion that deputies be released from other duties to work full time for the soviets. Both at the conference and before, a great deal was said in favor of making work in soviets at all levels—local, republican, and the Supreme Soviet—a full-time, salaried job. If this were the case, it would give the lie to the Marxist-Leninist nostrum that professional politicians, employed by the ruling class, were an attribute of capitalist, not socialist society.

It was further proposed that:

—more than one candidate be offered for election by secret vote.

—as a rule, the first secretary of the local party committee be "recommended" for the position of chairman of the corresponding soviet.

—the range of sources of budgetary income be broadened gradually. At that time, soviets received their income from local taxes and a levy on local enterprises. According to the draft reform, soviets would in future levy taxes on all enterprises in their area, including large industrial enterprises subordinated to republican and all-Union ministries. In addition, soviets would themselves have the right to engage in economic activities such as cooperatives, advertising agencies, and equity-based enterprises.

The two last proposals were innovations of crucial importance. The issue of appointing first secretaries to the chairmanship of soviets was hotly debated at the conference and elsewhere. Opponents of the proposal were divided by two different considerations. The more conservative were apparently frightened by the threat of competition posed, first, by the multicandidate system within the party committee, and, second, by secret balloting within the local soviet. Partisans of the democratization process, however, appealed to logic: if, they said, the party were no longer to substitute for state organs, and clear demarcation was sought between the functions of government and party, why were party first secretaries to chair soviets? Gorbachev twice came back to this point,[3] saying: "We are a ruling party and in every country it is the prerogative of the ruling party to form governmental bodies. We have nothing to be ashamed of."[4]

Understandably, Gorbachev was not prepared go into greater detail. He was in a delicate position because, as party general secretary, the principle of appointing first secretaries to the chairmanship of soviets would by inference entail his appointment to the post of chairman of the Supreme Soviet. The modesty so assiduously cultivated by Gorbachev forbad such personal ambition. His associates and dedicated campaigners for restructuring were more open about details of the general design.

*"Power to the Constructors of Perestroika."* In commenting on the outcome of the conference, Boris Kurashvili of the USSR Academy of Sciences' Institute of State and Law admitted that if one person were to hold the positions of general secretary and chief of state, it would encourage authoritarian tendencies. Kurashvili, however, supported the proposal because of "the necessity to overcome the resistance of conservative elements. That requires the concentration of power in the hands of the leader of the country."[5]

Victor Mironenko, the first secretary of the Central Committee of the Komsomol, advanced another argument in a heated debate on Soviet television with leaders of informal groups.[6] Confronted with the question: "Why is the party, while talking about democratization, trying to force its first secretary [on us] as the leader of the area?" Mironenko replied:

Let us be realists. Now, the party first secretary is the [most important] person and the real boss in an oblast or raion. If we drop the proposed rule for his chairmanship of the soviet, and at the same time empower the soviet with full authority, can we expect him to tolerate another leader on his territory? The party secretary would spare no effort to overpower the other leader ... and he has and will have the real power to do so.

Drawn by the question, "What would happen if the party secretary did not win election in the soviet?" Mironenko replied that he would be sent home and replaced.

In this context, the aim of Gorbachev's political reform was becoming more clear. It was to create a system of competition carefully judged to ensure the election of an able candidate suited to the party and satisfactory to the people. In no case, however, would a first secretary have to face an electorate of ordinary voters. True, within his party organization he would have to be elected in a secret vote against other candidates, but only party members would take part in the voting.

Then, as confirmation of his competence and popularity, a first secretary would have to win election as chairman of the local soviet. And here there was consolation for those afraid that Gorbachev might willfully destroy the political power of the party: the chairman of the soviet was to be elected, not by ordinary voters, but by the members of the soviet. This procedure was not amended during the conference, and so it stood in the resolution.[7] (The practice of a small circle selecting a leader appeared to remain the rule in political life. When several delegates to the conference proposed that the congress rather than the plenum of the Central Committee elect the general secretary, the proposal met with outright defeat: 145 votes for, 4,773 votes against.)[8]

What was new, however, was that the party was to seek approval of its candidate within the soviet, because it was concerned to be more in touch with public opinion. The fact that Gorbachev himself called the mechanism nothing more than a" subsidiary control system"[9] suggests that it was a gesture toward democracy lacking in substance.

The soviet was a place where a first secretary might, however, be challenged, not for his party membership, but for his qualities as a leader. As the composition of the soviets was to be substantially broadened in the course of the planned election reform—with the inclusion of more representatives of the public and of cultural, youth, and, theoretically, informal organizations in the newly constituted soviets—were these community leaders to blackball the first secretary, it would signal to the central party apparatus that something was wrong with the local party.

The party might recall a "compromised" first secretary and "recommend" an alternative candidate. It might happen, of course, that there was no appropriate candidate in the district or that the first secretary was recalled in the middle of his term. In such cases the party might support a local candidate, even if he was not a party member, and meanwhile prepare its best candidate for the next election. In any case, it would not look like a defeat for the party as a whole but would be regarded rather as a failure of the local party organization.

But what of the "leading role of the Communist party?" In the conference Theses, in Gorbachev's speech, and in the resolution, the party was called on to concentrate on three key areas: political strategy, ideology, and cadre policy. Cadre policy was apparently becoming a key element in how the party was to dominate society. The new cadre policy was much broader in vision than the old notion of selection of functionaries from the party ranks. The new policy embraced all of society and its main principle was that the party should pursue its policies not through institutions but through people. This sprang from the conviction that it was more important, and ultimately more efficient, to have devoted and determined people in public office than to keep all institutions under total, rigid control.

This principle conformed with the Gorbachev-Iakovlev doctrine of "the mobilization of the intellectual potential of the country." Now that the Soviet leadership had the intelligentsia on its side, and with no real political competitors, it had a choice of the best people and ideas. Glasnost would also be instrumental—as the chief editor of *Pravda* put it: "Glasnost helps us fish about for the brightest ideas in society."[10]

*Conclusion.* Even a cursory reading of the draft for political reform in the USSR showed a clear intention to concentrate real political power in the party's hands. To this end, Gorbachev wanted to relieve the party of some superfluous responsibilities and make the apparatus more compact and flexible. He wanted to preserve the leading role of the Communist party through people rather than institutionally. The new political system was far from democratic, as understood in the West: if implemented, it would maintain a single-party system, but at the same time give the people of the Soviet Union more say, at least in local affairs.

## 61
## REACTIONS IN EASTERN EUROPE AND CHINA
### Michael Shafir

Reactions to the CPSU conference in Eastern Europe and elsewhere in the communist world proved to be a faithful mirror of the ruling parties' attitude toward reform. In Bulgaria, Czechoslovakia, Hungary and Poland the deliberations of the CPSU conference were deemed to be of immediate relevance to the country's political life and/or to the "socialist community" as a whole. This raises the question of the extent to which the efforts to free the "internationalist essence" of socialist relations from "the consequences of the past," as Gorbachev put it in his main address to the conference, had been successful. Despite this similarity in the four countries' praise of the conference, there were some important differences in their approach.

*Bulgaria.* At a ceremony to award medals to the second Soviet-Bulgarian space crew, Bulgarian leader Todor Zhivkov said that "the 19th Conference of the CPSU will give a powerful impetus to the process of renewal in socialist countries." Zhivkov did not, however, specifically mention Bulgaria among the countries bound to be influenced by the outcome of the conference and only mentioned its "exceptional importance for the Soviet Union." Similarly, an editorial in the party daily *Rabotnichesko Delo* of July 4, spoke of the conference as "confirming categorically and unequivocally that the only correct road for Soviet society is the road of revolutionary reconstruction," but it did not mention this in connection with Bulgaria itself. The paper thus seemed to contradict itself, since on June 30 it had written about Gorbachev's report at the conference: "We expected it, our thoughts and hopes were related to it." The views expressed in the editorial of July 4 were reminiscent of those of the GDR on reform.[1]

Unlike the SED, however, the BCP appeared to be divided over its attitude toward the reform process induced by Moscow.[2] At a rally in Sofia at which the cosmonauts were welcomed, Politburo member and CC Secretary Yordan Yotov was less reluctant than Zhivkov to associate his country's course with that of the Soviet Union. "Side by side with the Soviet Union," Yotov said, the Bulgarian Communists "are following the common goal" that envisaged a "new pattern of socialism." Apparently inspired by the space crew's presence, Yotov said that "restructuring" was "a revolution within the revolution, which is the only possible way to a new orbit, adequate [for] the principles of Marxism-Leninism." (The phrase a "revolution within the revolution" was apparently borrowed from the Poles, who used it twice in one week.) In Western eyes, however, Yotov was not usually associated with the reformists. Prime Minister Georgi Atanasov, who, unlike Yotov, was considered a reformist, hailed the Soviet gathering as one of "historic optimism and confidence in the creative forces of socialism and the entire people" in an interview in *Pravda* on July 3.[3]

*Poland.* In its editorial of June 30 the Bulgarian paper *Rabotnichesko Delo* had called Soviet "restructuring" an "irreversible process." This view was shared in Poland, where PUWP CC Secretary Józef Czyrek said in an interview to the official news agency PAP that he had "no doubts" that perestroika was "irreversible." Like Yotov in Bulgaria, Czyrek saw the conference that had just ended as having provided "a tremendous amount of rich material to ponder on, and not only for Soviet Communists, but also for us, [the] other Communist parties in power." In an attempt to capitalize on Soviet developments and draw a parallel between Polish party and state leader Wojciech Jaruzelski's policy of "renewal" and Gorbachev's perestroika, Czyrek made comments that seemed out of touch with the spirit of the times. In a statement reminiscent of the kowtowing of the Stalinist period, the Polish CC Secretary said: "We will refer many times to Mikhail Gorbachev's address, to the resolutions of the conference ... especially as our party is intensively preparing for its [own] conference."

Striving to build legitimacy on foreign "credit," Czyrek added that

Many solutions which will be put into effect in the Soviet Union, in the CPSU itself, are convergent with the concepts adopted at the Ninth PUPW Congress and developed at the Tenth Congress.

Moreover,

The triumph of the innovative policy that Mikhail Gorbachev personifies will contribute to a strengthening of proreformative mainstreams in our country and our party as well. The success of Mikhail Gorbachev is ... therefore also the success of all the proreformative forces of renewal in our country.

Earlier, Polish CC Secretary Stanislaw Ciosek had told the daily *Życie Warszawy* that, as a result of the Soviet conference, Poles wanting change would "now take on more self-confidence, conviction and faith"; as if to confirm his words, PAP said that "In Poland, in our party, we are deeply satisfied with the course of the CPSU conference." Similar official statements increased on the eve of Gorbachev's third visit to Poland, which began on July 11. While Czyrek described the Moscow conference as the "four days that shook the world," for Jaruzelski, the conference's significance could only be compared to the October Revolution itself. Poland and the Soviet Union, he added, were now going along a similar path. In the same vein, Politburo member Mieczysław Rakowski spoke of "the full concordance of goals and the unanimity" of the two countries and parties.[4]

*Hungary.* Meanwhile, however, the first East European leader to meet with Gorbachev after the conference was Károly Grósz, who arrived in Moscow on July 4. Like the Polish party's leaders, Hungary's leaders emphasized the similarity of their reform process to that in the Soviet Union, but certainly with more justification than the Poles. Addressing a meeting of leading Hungarian company managers on July 2, Grósz said that he felt confident before the visit, because "the process taking place in the Soviet Union is in many respects identical with what [has happened] in Hungary." The tasks facing the two parties were "similar," he added, as was their appraisal of "socialist renewal, reforms, [and] the development of democracy." The Soviet perestroika, Grósz said, "creates favorable historical conditions for us too." The new Minister of State in charge of political reforms, Imre Pozsgay, said that he was "happy" about the conference in Moscow, because what had so far been only "a hope" had now become "a certainty."[5]

In an interview with Soviet television on July 3, Grósz said that the conference had shown the way for the "renewal" of socialism. There was more to this than similar appraisals made elsewhere in Eastern Europe. In an aside undoubtedly directed at the Romanians, who were involved in a confrontation with Hungary that was likely to have been discussed in Moscow, Grósz said that the Soviet example "should be followed in every socialist country." Even more revealing was HSWP CC Secretary Mátyás Szűrös's interview in the party daily *Népszabadság* of July 2. Emphasizing that "what happens in the Soviet Union has an influence on world policy and is of world political significance," Szűrös quoted Gorbachev's remark that "priority should be given to general human values;" this was undoubtedly a reference to Bucharest's plan to destroy

Romanian as well as ethnic Hungarian and German villages, against which Budapest had protested precisely on humanitarian grounds. The results of the Moscow conference, he added,

> may encourage, also in the other socialist countries, the renewal of political and ideological concepts, the reform of the economic and political system, and the extension of democracy, including the enforcement of human and minority rights.[6]

*Czechoslovakia.* The Czechoslovak party daily *Rudé právo* also hailed the Soviet conference as an event that "will be an inspiration and a source of practical enlightenment for us"; but this was not entirely convincing, since, according to *Rudé právo*, the ideas of the conference were merely "worth thinking about."

The Czech and Slovak party's conservative faction must have been horrified to hear such phrases as "the human image of socialism" and "action program" in Gorbachev's closing address to the conference, because of their association with the Prague Spring. The party's proreform faction, on the other hand, seemed to have been encouraged by the outcome of the Moscow conference. A senior adviser to Prime Minister Lubomír Štrougal, Jaromír Sedlák, was quoted as having said that the situation in Czechoslovakia could not continue any longer and having added that his ideal was "lively debate in Moscow." As if to confirm conservative suspicions, a group of Czechoslovak dissidents—including Jiří Hájek, the Minister of Foreign Affairs in 1968—sent a letter to Moscow saluting the fact that the forces supporting "restructuring" had grown stronger and asking the conference to act in order to reveal the truth about the 1968 invasion. Moreover, in an interview with Austrian television, Alexander Dubček himself said that he was "happy" to see Gorbachev's line triumph at the conference, adding that what had happened in the USSR was well suited to Czechoslovakia's conditions also. Czechoslovakia's leaders, according to Dubček, used to insist on emulating the Soviet Union; but now "the same people are very selective when it comes to deciding what suits Czechoslovakia and what not." In a letter addressed to a conference in Bologna, Dubček also called on the Warsaw Pact states to acknowledge that their invasion of Czechoslovakia had been a mistake. Such an acknowledgment was, however, unlikely to be made in the near future. At a news conference in Prague on July 8, Soviet Prime Minister Nikolai Ryzhkov said that Moscow still agreed with the assessment of the 1968 events issued by the Czech and Slovak party in 1970.[7]

*The GDR.* Faithful to the standard line, the East German media reported factually on the conference but refrained from any comment. On July 2 the SED party newspaper *Neues Deutschland* devoted two pages to the discussions of the conference's last day, including almost a whole page to Gorbachev's closing speech. There was even a reference to the heated exchange between Boris Eltsin and Egor Ligachev, though this was considerably shorter than the TASS dispatch that *Neues Deutschland* drew from. Readers in the GDR were thus able to learn from Eltsin's own comments that the leadership of the CPSU was divided by "constant differences of opinion." It was only on July 8 that the SED party organ printed a commentary on the conference. Reiterating the line of the party ideologist and Politburo member Kurt Hager, who had addressed a forum of the East German Academy of Arts the day before using similar arguments, *Neues Deutschland* emphasized that while it welcomed the Soviet conference, the SED was persuaded that every party "must find those solutions that best do justice to specific national conditions and requirements." The CPSU conference itself, the paper said, had expressed the view that no party was "in possession of a prescription appropriate for all." In conclusion, it was stated that the SED was determined to continue to act in accordance with the decisions it had adopted as long ago as 1971, at its 11th congress. In other words, reform was not on the party's agenda.[8]

*Romania.* The East German position insisting on specific solutions befitting the country's conditions had long been advocated by the RCP as well. However, the Romanian coverage of the conference was much less detailed than the East German coverage. According to a short dispatch in the party daily *Scînteia* of July 2, the conference had focused "on the process of socialist renewal." The paper emphasized that in his speech Gorbachev had shown that the meaning of "democratization" should not be interpreted as weakening the party's leading role. His proposal to elect party first secretaries as chairmen of local soviets was actually aimed at strengthening the party's role, *Scînteia* stressed. In other words, Gorbachev was merely emulating Ceauşescu, who had "unified" party and state positions a long time ago. Earlier, *Scînteia* had selected precisely those parts of Gorbachev's speech that once again appeared to justify Bucharest's line. Gorbachev, *Scînteia* indicated, had admitted that in the past "important decisions had been taken without proper consultation with friends." This had caused an "inadequate reaction" in Soviet evaluations of "other states' policies."[9] In other words, Moscow had now admitted that the RCP had been right in the past, when it had occasionally refused to follow the Kremlin. More important, however, it had admitted that it might be wrong even now, for, after all, nobody in the Kremlin consulted Bucharest before launching perestroika, which Ceauşescu refused to emulate.

*Yugoslavia and China.* The Yugoslavs and the Chinese, on the other hand, were obviously pleased with the conference in Moscow. A Tanjug dispatch in English from the Soviet capital, dated July 2, appreciated that the conference had "struck a strong blow against the hypertrophied and almighty apparatus." At the same time, Tanjug pointed to the contradiction inherent in the decision to separate party and state functions, on the one hand, and let party first secretaries become chairmen of the local soviets, on the other. Tanjug also reported that it was assumed that the general secretary of the party would become the country's next president in the system proposed by Gorbachev at the conference, emphasizing that "as president of the Supreme Soviet, he would have great power in his hands, similar to that held by the president of France." The Hungarians were apparently also unhappy about this development, but not as willing to air their misgivings openly. Discussing this issue at the meeting in Budapest with economic managers, Grósz said only that Gorbachev's call for a reform of the political structure, including the adoption of a presidential system of government, had been qualified by the "crucial" requirement that party and state functions be divided.[10]

Finally, a Xinhua dispatch from Moscow said that the 19th Soviet party conference had dealt "a serious blow to the old political structure," and had helped "deepen the process and ensure that the reforms are irreversible." While providing a detailed description of the procedures, including the heated debates about personnel questions and questions of principle, Xinhua emphasized that "many delegates expressed strong disapproval of allowing the establishment of any 'opposition' party." It also said that the conference had decided to limit tenure of office to two consecutive terms at most, "thus abolishing the system of 'tenure for life.'" In short, one could actually conclude that the 19th CPSU All-Union Conference had followed Deng's policies and practice.[11]

## 62
## HOW DEEP A CHANGE?
Vladimir V. Kusin

Although the CPSU conference did not meet some of the expectations raised by Gorbachev, it exceeded others; the event was bound to go down in history as a momentous occasion. Its importance was liable to become even greater if the course and pace that it set were maintained. Conversely, its importance was certain to wane if the Soviet system's unfriendliness to change were to render its reformist provisions inoperable.

The conference gave the campaign for far-reaching reforms a boost not only because of Gorbachev's vigorous handling of the proceedings but also because his Politburo and Secretariat evidently cooperated with him in promulgating the program. If there was a conservative opposition, even a backlash, it was not allowed to show; it was, however, much spoken about.

Besides its general endorsement of reformism, the conference decided on a mixed bag of provisions, some of them probably valuable, others difficult to evaluate, yet others seeming recipes for confusion or even prone to backfire. 10 tentative conclusions could be made.

(1) The conference conveyed the message of change to the Soviet populace more persuasively than Gorbachev and the intellectuals on his side had previously succeeded in doing. The sheer novelty of the exercise, the stage it created, and the unusually disputatious character of the proceedings combined to break down the communications barrier between the center and the provinces. The reform campaign became public property.

(2) The conference marked the beginning of a transition from glasnost to freedom of expression. The controlled release of information and encouragement of criticism expanded into an open debate of issues and policy. Openness in the media was explicitly endorsed, and the public was emboldened to speak up. This did not guarantee the success of the process, however.

(3) The conference declared war on the traditional immobilism of the party, state, and other bureaucracies. In identifying bureaucracy as the main enemy (a cornerstone of Leon Trotskii's critique of the decadence of Stalin's state), the conference opened the door to broader popular participation in the affairs of state at all levels. The response of the agitated bureaucrats to the onslaught remained to be seen.

(4) The conference declared itself a harbinger of further change—not a mere guardian of consolidation of what had already been attained. While enunciating constraints implicit in the preservation of the leading role of the party, it left Gorbachev's reformism very much an open-ended undertaking.

(5) The conference prompted no personnel changes in the party's top leadership. Not even the "dead souls" in the Central Committee—those demoted, deceased, or no longer eligible for membership because of their offices—were replaced. The CC remained a more conservative body than the conference, thus hampering the implementation of its decisions.

(6) Important parts of the reform package, such as the role of the military and "new thinking" in foreign policy, were mentioned only in passing. This foreshadowed strife in areas for which the conference provided no guidelines. Also, the handling of the potentially explosive Soviet-East European relations, was left to the discretion of the leadership, without any provision for public participation in the shaping of policy. The conference was not consulted on the military's role in society or the formulation of foreign policy, nor did it address the military burden on the country's economy.

(7) The conference failed to explicitly support either independent political activity or national autonomy. As a result, conflicts between the rank-and-file and officialdom in those areas of momentous importance for the cohesion of the Soviet state and Soviet society were bound to continue.

(8) The institutional reforms propounded by the conference tended to be confusing, irrelevant, inadequate, and potentially counterproductive. It was not clarified how universally and corporately elected deputies could fruitfully coexist

in the proposed super-parliament or how purposeful two sets of legislative agencies could possibly be. The significance of the proposed presidential system in view of the CPSU chief's traditional paramountcy in the Soviet party-state remained likewise unclear. Local party bosses doubling up as chairmen of soviets could not only invigorate local government but also tighten the party's stranglehold over nonparty offices. Above all, the provisions on free multicandidate elections were not clear enough. Who was allowed to contest whom? How were group interests to be translated into electoral platforms? Who would vet the candidates?

(9) The claim that democracy was at work during the conference should be taken with a good grain of salt. While a disputatious exchange between Eltsin, Ligachev, and Gorbachev stunned the audience which included Western correspondents, behind-the-scenes commissions passed all but unchanged the numerous resolutions presumably drafted by the CC Secretariat. All major themes of Gorbachev's opening speech were incorporated into the resolutions without any apparent influence by the conference.

(10) Despite the progress of glasnost, Soviet policy-making remained in need of dispassionate analysis which the party leadership alone could not provide. Despite the admirable Soviet and Western reporting, the significance of the conference's dazzle was not automatically translated into a greater amount of substantive information. Just as the Soviet media and most Soviet scholars once extolled the tenets of Stalin and Brezhnev, so they now nodded their approval of those of Gorbachev. *Plus ça change...?*

# NOTES

## PAPER 1:

1. Central Television, TASS, November 2, 1987.
2. Reuters, October 14, 1987.
3. See the entry on Stalin in *Velikaia Oktiabrskaia Sotsialisticheskaia Revoliutsiia* (Moscow: "Entsiklopediia," 1987).
4. See, for example, the historical discussion in *Kommunist*, No. 12, 1987, pp. 66-79. See also RL 189/87, "Glasnost and the Rewriting of Soviet History," May 18, 1987.
5. *Pravda*, March 24, 1987.
6. *Sovetskaia Rossiia*, April 19, 1987.
7. Ibid.
8. *Literaturnaia gazeta*, July 22, 1987
9. Reuters, October 9, 1987.
10. See RL 169/87, "Conflicting Views on Stalin's Collectivization Expressed by Soviet Writers and Scholars," April 29, 1987.

## PAPER 2:

1. *The New York Times*, October 30, 1987; *The Financial Times*, October 30, 1987; *The Guardian*, October 30, 1987; *Los Angeles Times*, October 30, 1987.
2. UPI, October 31, 1987.
3. *Pravda*, February 27, 1986.
4. *Le Monde*, July 16, 1986; *Moskovskaia pravda*, July 20, 1986.
5. *Die Zeit*, May 7, 1986.
6. *Stern*, May 7, 1986.
7. Tanjug, October 23, 1986.
8. See RL 474/87, "Signs of a Conservative Backlash," November 18, 1987.
9. See RL 325/87, "Ligachev Versus Gorbachev?," August 12, 1987.
10. Radio Moscow, August 5, 1987.
11. *Pravda*, September 11, 1987.
12. *El País*, September 24, 1987.
13. *Pravda*, February 27, 1986.
14. See the account of the plenum of the Moscow City Party Committee published in *Pravda*, November 13, 1987.
15. Ibid.
16. Ibid.
17. See RL 277/86, "Partial Transcript of Eltsin's Speech Appears in Samizdat," July 17, 1986.
18. *Moskovskaia pravda*, April 14, 1987.
19. *Pravda*, November 3, 1987.
20. *The Washington Post*, November 12, 1987.
21. *Pravda*, November 13, 1987.

22. *Sovetskaia Rossiia*, November 24, 1987.
23. *Pravda*, November 13, 1987. In a rare telephone interview with CBS News on October 31, Eltsin categorically denied that he had criticized Gorbachev.
24. TASS, October 31, 1987.
25. *Süddeutsche Zeitung*, November 2, 1987; *The Christian Science Monitor*, October 29, 1987.
26. *The Los Angeles Times*, November 1, 1987.
27. *Sovetskaia Rossiia*, November 24, 1987. Eltsin and Chief Editor of *Moscow News* Egor Iakovlev were not the only officials to threaten resignation in 1987; Gorbachev himself reportedly told journalists in February that he might have to step down if resistance blocked his reform program (see Reuters, February 19, 1987).
28. *The Los Angeles Times*, November 13, 1987.
29. *Pravda*, December 13, 1987.
30. *Sovetskaia Rossiia*, November 24, 1987.
31. *The Washington Post*, November 12, 1987.
32. *The Los Angeles Times*, November 12, 1987.
33. *Stuttgarter Zeitung*, October 31, 1987.
34. *The New York Times*, November 19, 1987.
35. *Sovetskaia Rossiia*, November 24, 1987.
36. See RL 474/87, "Signs of a Conservative Backlash," November 18, 1987.
37. *Pravda*, November 16, 1987.

PAPER 3:

1. The speech was broadcast on Central Television on April 9, 1988.
2. *Izvestiia*, March 26, 1988.
3. Because of its wide range of recondite references, observers speculated that the letter was not all Andreeva's own work and had been helped into print by influential patrons; the name of Egor Ligachev was mentioned most frequently.
4. TASS, April 5, 1988.
5. See, for example, the letter published in *Sotsialisticheskaia industriia* on March 20, 1988, (and quoted with disapproval by *Pravda* on April 5) denouncing the Soviet Union's path as leading to"petit-bourgeois socialism founded on commodity-money relations."
6. Interview in *Borba* (Belgrade), November 3, 1987.
7. *Voprosy filosofii*, No. 6, 1984, pp. 23-29; *Novyi mir*, No. 2, 1988, pp. 205-228
8. Letter from Professor V. Dashichev published in *Izvestiia*, April 13, 1988.
9. Popov on Central Television, April 1, 1988; Kurashvili as reported by APN on the same day.
10. Stephen F. Cohen, *Bukharin and the Bolshevik Revolution* (New York: Oxford University Press, 1980), p. 276.
11. Egor Iakovlev in *Moscow News*, January 17, 1988; Dmitrii Kazutin in *Moscow News*, February 7, 1988; Evgenii Ambartsumov in *Otechestven Front* (Sofia), February 26, 1988.

12. *Izvestiia*, March 3, 1988.
13. Andrei Nuikin, "Idealy ili interesy?" Part 2, *Novyi mir*, No. 2, 1988, pp. 205-228.
14. Ibid.
15. Radio Budapest, March 19, 1988.
16. Nuikin (op. cit.), for example, attacked the Marxist fundamentalist journalist Elena Losoto as a leader of "the ideological attack on perestroika." In her reply, Losoto denounced Nuikin's arguments as "an anti-perestroika position" aimed at "discrediting those who ... are trying to ensure that the processes now under way are not deflected from the Socialist path" (*Komsomolskaia pravda*, April 3, 1988).


PAPER 4:


1. Soviet Television, April 22, 1988.
2. See in particular Michel Tatu, *Gorbatchev: l'URSS va-t-elle changer?* (Paris: Editions du Centurion, 1987).
3. See, for example, the letter published in *Pravda* on January 18, 1988. "Like many others," wrote a thirty-year-old mother of three, "our generation was brought up under socialism and without belief in God. One might say that socialism and its ideals were our God.... As a result of the policy of glasnost and unrestrained criticism ... the idea of socialism, under which we have lived for seventy years and which determines our aims and the purpose of our existence, has to some extent been discredited. I cannot speak for everyone, but my own faith has been shaken."
4. See paper 3 above.
5. During Gorbachev's absence in Yugoslavia, Ligachev's name began to appear in press reports at the head of those of his Politburo colleagues—that is, it was listed first and out of alphabetical order (TASS and Radio Moscow, March 18, 1988).
6. See paper 23, *SEES 1986-87* pp. 135-138.
7. *Sovetskaia kultura*, April 9, 1988.
8. RL 154/88, "Ownership and Economic Reform," April 6, 1988.
9. See, in particular, Andrei Nuikin, "Idealy ili interesy?" Part 1, *Novy mir*, No. 1, 1988; Anatolii Butenko, "What Kind of Socialism Are They Mourning?" *New Times*, No. 15, 1988; Fedor Burlatskii, "Kakoi sotsializm narodu nuzhen," *Literaturnaia gazeta*, April 20, 1988.
10. Burlatskii, op. cit. This was the first time the term "civil society" was known to have been employed in a positive sense in the official Soviet media, though the concept had acquired wide currency in unofficial circles in Hungary, Poland, and Czechoslovakia. The concept envisaged a system in which society was capable of autonomous political action independent of the state.
11. See RL 78/87, "Gorbachev Talks to Representatives of Soviet Mass Media," February 16, 1987; RL 280/87, "Gorbachev Answers His Critics," July 15, 1987.
12. Radio Moscow, April 22, 1988.

13. *Argumenty i fakty*, No. 18, 1988.
14. TASS, April 20, 1988.
15. For a selection of the proposals, see RL 59/88, "Party Report and Election Campaign Winds Down," January 27, 1988.
16. See RL 66/86, "The Minority Should Be Heard," February 10, 1986; RL 79/86, "Lifestyle of Elite Called Into Question," February 14, 1986.
17. As cited in *The Daily Telegraph*, May 5, 1988.
18. *Sovetskaia kultura*, April 30, 1988.


PAPER 5:

1. Reuters (East Berlin), January 23, 1987.
2. Ibid.


PAPER 6:
1. General Dmitrii Iazov, "Warsaw Treaty Military Doctrine—for Defence of Peace and Socialism," *International Affairs*, October 1987, p. 6.
2. V. G. Kulikov, "The Guard of Peace and Socialism," *Krasnaia zvezda*, February 21, 1988, p. 2.
3. "Conventional Arms Control: The Way Ahead." Statement issued under the authority of the heads of state and government participating in the meeting of the North Atlantic Council in Brussels (March 2-3, 1988).
4. Quoted in Iurii Tepliakov, "Reliable Defence First and Foremost," *Moscow News*, February 21, 1988, p. 12.
5. A. Kokoshin, "The Development of Military Affairs and Reduction of Armed Forces and Conventional Arms," *Mirovaia Ekonomika Mezhdunarodnye Otnosheniia*, January 1988, pp. 20-32.
6. V. V. Zhurkin, S. A. Karaganov, and A. V. Kortunov, "On Reasonable Sufficiency," *SSA: Ekonomika, Politika, Ideologiia*, December 1987, pp. 11-21.
7. *The Washington Post*, November 12, 1987.
8. Charles Thomas, Deputy Assistant Secretary of State for European and Canadian Affairs, quoted in *USIS* (Washington), November 3, 1987.
9. At his press conference following the summit in Washington in December 1987 Gorbachev said that it was time to "put our cards on the table" and exchange data on the military forces in Europe. A similar exchange had been suggested by Soviet Defense Minister Iazov when he met U.S. Secretary of Defense Frank Carlucci in Bern, Switzerland, on March 16 and 17, 1988 and by Soviet Foreign Minister Eduard Shevardnadze the following week during his talks in Washington with Secretary of State George Shultz. The Sofia appeal's reference to such an exchange of data marked the first time an alliance to alliance exchange has been formally broached by all the members of the Warsaw Pact.
10. A statement by Bulgarian Deputy Foreign Minister Ivan Ganev, as reported by TASS (Sofia), March 30, 1988.
11. *The Military Balance 1987-1988* (London: The International Institute

for Strategic Studies, 1988), pp. 41-42.

## PAPER 7:

1. *The Guardian*, Reuters, AFP, and AP (all from Vienna),  May 20, and June 7, 8, and 9, 1988, respectively; RFE Correspondent's Reports (Vienna), May 28, and June 3, 7, and 14, 1988.
2. Radio Bucharest, June 2, 1988, 8:00 P.M.
3. RFE Correspondent's Reports (Vienna), June  7 and 14, 1988; AP and AFP (Vienna),  June 9 and 10, 1988. See also Romanian Situation Report/2, *RFER* March 6, 1987, item 5, for earlier Romanian proposals in Vienna to set up specialized CSCE forums to "work out measures" in some of those areas.
4. Vladimir Socor, "The Budapest Cultural Forum Ends Without Agreement", RAD Background Report/14 (East-West Relations), *RFER*,  January 22, 1986; and Romanian SR/7, *RFER*,  July 2, 1986, item 8.
5. BBC World Service,  May 19, 1988; RFE Correspondent's Reports (Vienna), October 30, 1987, June  7 and 14, 1988; *Financial Times* (correspondent's  reports from Vienna), June 7 and 14, 1988; AP (Vienna), June 9, 1988; AFP (Vienna), June 8 and 10, 1988.

## PAPER 8:

1. It was rumored but never confirmed that Czechoslovakia led the revolt (see, for example, Peter Wiles, ed., *The New Communist Third World* (London and Canberra: Croom Helm, 1982), p. 30.
2. The following developing countries participated as observers at the CMEA Council sessions: Ethiopia, Angola, Afghanistan, the People's Democratic Republic of Yemen, Mozambique, Laos, and Nicaragua.
3. *The Economist*, June 26, 1987.
4. See UPI (Bangkok),  October 22, 1986. Also see UPI (Bangkok),  November 3, 1986, on an editorial in the party daily *Nhan Dan*. Truong Chinh visited Moscow in August 1986.
5. For example, UPI (Bangkok),  May 21, 1987.
6. See V. Sobell, "Reconciliation Between China and Eastern Europe," *The Washington Quarterly*, Spring 1987.
7. See, for example, *Financial Times*,  April 14, 1986; or *The New York Times*, March 2, 1987. Press reports on CMEA aid to Cuba cited unspecified "diplomatic sources." The figure of $1,000 million probably referred only to Soviet economic aid, while the upper range of the estimate probably represented total CMEA aid, including military aid.
8. The intra-CMEA pricing system (by which oil prices were based on a five-year moving average of the world-market prices) meant that up to 1985 the price of Soviet oil within the CMEA was nominally below the world-market price. Since

the collapse of world-market prices in early 1986, however, the CMEA countries were paying more than the world-market price. Nevertheless, since the bulk of Soviet oil was imported on barter terms, its importation amounted to Soviet subsidization regardless of the nominal price. That is to say, the CMEA countries would always find Soviet oil a better deal, simply because they did not need to use their scarce hard-currency earnings to buy it. Moreover, Cuba and the other CMEA countries re-exported "surplus" Soviet oil (in the form of oil products) to the West for hard currency. In 1985 this activity secured Cuba, for example, about $600,000,000, or over 50 percent of its hard-currency proceeds.

9. *The Economist*, June 26, 1987.

10. See, for example, *The Washington Post*, April 12, 1986.

11. On June 24, 1987, the Soviet government paper *Izvestiia* featured a pessimistic report from Nicaragua implying that Nicaragua's economic crisis was exacerbated by bad management. Western analysts believe that the Soviets may have advised Nicaragua to diversify its sources of aid to include Western countries (see, for example, Dmitri Simes, "Are the Sandinistas Collapsing?," *Philadelphia Inquirer*, August 5, 1987.)

12. See, for example, A. N. Iakovlev, "The Attainment of a Qualitatively New State of Soviet Society and Social Sciences," *Kommunist*, no. 8, 1987, pp. 3-22; and Jerry Hough, *The Struggle for the Third World* (Washington D.C.: The Brookings Institution, 1986), pp. 283-286.

13. See, for example, Bill Keller, "Soviets in Foreign Policy Shift," *The New York Times*, May 25, 1987.


PAPER 9:

1. AR 4-88, "The Soviet Public and the War in Afghanistan: Discontent Reaches Critical Levels," May 1988. For data on previous years, see AR 4-85, "The Soviet Public and the War in Afghanistan: Perceptions, Prognoses, Information Sources," June 1985 and AR 1-87, "The Soviet Public and the War in Afghanistan: A Trend Toward Polarization," March 1987.

2. It was announced, for instance, that Academician Tatiana Zaslavskaia was to head an All-Union Center for the Study of Public Opinion on Social and Economic Questions (*Literaturnaia gazeta*, March 9, 1988).

3. See, for example, Radio Liberty Research Reports RL 188/87, "Ukrainian Mother's Protest Attracts Numerous Letters on the Afghanistan Theme," May 18, 1987 and RL 483/87, "Popular Discontent with the War in Afghanistan," November 30, 1987.

4. See, for example, the remarkably candid articles by Aleksandr Prokhanov in *Literaturnaia gazeta* of February 17, 1988, and Oleg Bogomolov in *Literaturnaia gazeta* of March 16, 1988, both of which implied that the Soviet intervention in Afghanistan was a mistake. These articles are analyzed in RL 65/88, "Soviet Admission of Failure in Afghanistan," February 18, 1988 and RL 116/88, "Bogomolov Reveals Opposition to Afghan Invasion," March 17, 1988.

## PAPER 10:

1. *The New York Times*, August 23, 1987.
2. Boulder, Colorado: Westview Press, 1987.
3. Ibid., pp. 39-42.
4. Ibid., p. 217.
5. Ibid., pp. 162-179.
6. Patrick Moore, "Vietnam's Moment of Truth?" RAD Background Report/ 165 (Asia), *RFER*, November 18, 1986, and Leif Rosenberger, "The Soviet-Vietnamese Alliance and Kampuchea," *Survey*, autumn-winter 1984.
7. Patrick Moore, "The Sixth Congress of the Vietnamese Communist Party," RAD BR/22 (Vietnam), *RFER*, February 12, 1987.
8. M. Trigubenko, "Cooperation Between CMEA and Vietnam: Checking the Slowdown," *Far Eastern Affairs* (Moscow), No. 4 1988, pp. 23-33.
9. *Far Eastern Economic Review* (Hong Kong), June 8, 1988.

## PAPER 11:

1. RFE Correspondent's Report (Belgrade), February 26, 1988.
2. Louis Zanga, "Albanian Foreign Minister Sets Forth Albania's New-Look Diplomacy," *RFER,* RAD Background Report/36, March 4, 1988
3. *Rabotnichesko Delo*, January 30, 1988.
4. Full text published in *Rabotnichesko Delo*, February 25, 1988.
5. RFE Correspondent's Report (Ankara), October 28, 1987.
6. Ibid., February 27, 1988.
7. *Zeri i Popullit*, February 25, 1988.
8. ATA, March 1, 1988.
9. *Rilindja,* February 27, 1988.
10. Tanjug, February 24, 1988.
11. *Rilindja*, February 27, 1988.

## PAPER 12:

1. See RL 200/86, "Former Outcast Elected Head of Cinema Workers' Union," May 21, 1986; and RL 211/86, "Whirlwind of Change in Soviet Cinema," May 30, 1986.

## PAPER 13:

1. *Znamia*, No. 9, 1987, p. 210.
2. *Novyi mir*, No. 12, 1953, pp. 218-45.
3. *Ogonek*, No. 30, 1969. pp. 26-8.
4. *Novyi mir*, No. 6, 1987, pp. 222-38.
5. RL 143/87 "Who's Afraid of Restructuring in Literature?" April 15, 1987.

6. *Molodaia gvardiia*, No. 7, 1987, pp. 220-47.

7. *Iunost*, No. 6, 1987, pp. 68-73.

8. *Literaturnaia gazeta*, August 5, 1987.

9. *Voprosy literatury*, No. 7, 1987, pp. 39-79.

10. Published both in *Znamia*, No. 2, 1987, and in *Novyi mir*, No. 3, 1987.

11. Published both in *Oktiabr*, No. 3, 1987, and in *Neva*, No. 6, 1987.

12. *Literaturnii Azerbaidzhan*, Nos. 9 and 10, 1987.

13. *Druzhba narodov*, No. 1, 1987.

14. *Znamia*, Nos. 3 and 4, 1987.

15. See RL 228/86, "Khrushchev's Son-in-Law Writes about Soviet Science under Stalin," June 11, 1986.

16. *Neva*, Nos. 1-4, 1987.

17. *Novyi mir*, Nos. 8-10, 1956.

18. *Znamia*, No. 12, 1986.

19. *Druzhba narodov*, No. 10, 1986;

20. *Oktiabr*, No. 4, 1987; *Znamia*, No. 7, 1987.

21. *Znamia*, Nos. 10 and 11, 1986.

22. *Novyi mir*, No. 7, 1987.

23. *Don*, Nos. 1-3, 1987.

24. *Novyi mir*, No. 8, 1987.

25. *Pravda*, August 9, 1987.

26. *Molodaia gvardiia*, No. 7, 1987, pp. 227-28.

27. Ibid., p. 225.

28. Ibid., p. 227.

29. A. Ovcharenko, "Knigi dlia naroda," *Molodaia gvardiia*, No. 7, 1987, pp. 248-62.

30. *Molodaia gvardiia*, No, 9, 1987, p. 254.

31. Ibid., No. 3, 1987, p. 269; No. 9, 1987, pp. 281 and 284.

32. Ibid., No. 9, 1987, p. 234.

33. Ibid., No. 7, 1987, p. 242; No. 9, 1987, pp. 268-69.

34. Ibid., No. 9, 1987, p. 235.

35. Arkadii Lisenkov and Iurii Sergeev, "Kolovert bespamiatstva," ibid., No. 10, 1987, pp. 257-70.

36. Ibid., No. 9, 1987, p. 228.

37. Ibid., No. 8, 1987, pp. 225-26.

38. Viacheslav Gorbachev, "Chto vperedi?" ibid., No. 3, 1987, pp. 250-77. See also RL 342/87, "The Emergence of 'Pamiat' and 'Otechestvo'," August 26, 1987.

39. Ibid., No. 9, 1987, pp. 227-28.

40. Sergei Perevezentsev, "Stranichka istorii," ibid., No. 10, pp. 279-82.

41. See, for example, RL 4/88, "Materials Defending Stalin in the Soviet Press," December 21, 1987.

42. For the proceedings of the plenum, see *Literaturnaia gazeta*, No. 10, 1988, pp. 2-10.

43. See RL 264/86, "The Eighth Congress of Soviet Writers: An Appraisal," July 15, 1986.

44. The more interesting of these are summarized in RL 387/87, "A Survey of Russian Literature Published in the Past Year," September 30, 1987.

45. Regarding the ties between *Nash sovremennik* and "Pamiat," see RL 463/87, "A Second 'Pamiat' Emerges," November 16, 1987.
46. For details of articles by Losoto and Gutionov, see RL 100/88, "A Little More Glasnost for Soviet Jews," March 14, 1988.
47. *Znamia*, No. 1, 1988, pp. 188-203.
48. See RL 40/88, "*Ogonek* Exposes Corruption in Literature," February 2, 1988.
49. *Ogonek*, No. 50, 1987, pp. 17-18.


## PAPER 14:

1. *Komsomolskaia pravda*, February 21, 1988; *Literaturnaia gazeta*, February 24, 1988; *Nedelia*, No. 8, 1988.
2. For an analysis of the earlier Soviet treatment of Beriia's end, see RS 2/84, "Smert i vtoraia zhizn Lavrentiia Beriia," January 4, 1984.
3. *Znamia*, No. 1, 1988.
4. For details of the creation of the one-party dictatorship by Lenin, see, for example, Richard Pipes, "Sozdanie odnopartiinogo gosudarstva v Sovetskoi Rossii (1917-18)," *Minuvshee. Istoricheskii almanakh*, Paris Athenaeum, Nos. 3 and 4, 1987.
5. Cited in Mikhail Heller and Aleksandr Nekrich, *Utopiia u vlasti. Istoriia Sovetskogo Soiuza s 1917 goda do nashikh dnei*, Vol. 1 (London: Overseas Publications Interchange Ltd., 1982), p. 147
6. *Novyi mir*, No. 1 and 2, 1987.
7. See *Odinnadtsatyi sezd RKP (b), mart-aprel 1922. Stenograficheskii otchet* (Moscow: Politizdat, 1961).
8. See, for instance, *Izvestiia*, August 11, 1987, and RL 348/87, "Socialist Legality and the Falsification of History," August 20, 1987.
9. Lenin, Collected Works, Vol. 45 (Moscow: Politizdat, 1964), pp. 190-91. Lenin's justification of terror is discussed in detail in Aleksandr Solzhenitsyn's *The Gulag Archipelago*, Vol. 1, Part 1, chapters, 2 and 8.
10. See RL 401/ 87, "Soviet Historian Calls for Clarification of Katyn Massacre," October 7, 1987.
11. On March 8, 1988, AP carried the text of the letter.
12. *Argumenty i fakty*, No. 10, 1987, reprinted in *Molodezh Estonii*, April 7, 1987. On Vlasov, see Catherine Andreyev, *Vlasov and the Russian Liberation Movement* (Cambridge: Cambridge University Press, 1987).
13. *Komsomolskaia pravda*, March 3, 1988
14. Hints at disapproval of the Soviet suppression of the 1956 Hungarian revolution were made in Ilia Erenburg's recollections, published in *Ogonek*, Nos 23-25, 1987.
15. On Khrushchev, see Fedor Burlatskii, "Khrushchev: "Shtrikhi k politicheskomu portretu," in *Literaturnaia gazeta*, February 24, 1988. See also *Literaturnaia gazeta*, February 11, 1987, *Moscow News*, No. 9, 1988, which deals in passing with Khrushchev's fall; and *Ogonek*, No. 6, 1986.
16. For instance, at a press conference in Moscow in 1987, playwright Mikhail Shatrov called for the publication of the speech in the USSR, see *Argumenty i*

*fakty*, No. 44, 1987. For the text of the speech, see *SSSR: Vnutrennie protivorechiia* (New York: Chalidze Publications, No. 6, 1982).

17. Seliunin was the author of other forthright pieces in the Soviet press. In an article in *Novyi mir* in August, 1985, he lampooned Soviet labor policy, saying that "we have forgotten what [unemployment] means,... [but what good is that] if we only half-work?" He collaborated with economist Grigorii Khanin on *"Lukavaia tsifra"* (Tricky Figures), a devastating attack on the USSR Central Statistical Adminstration that appeared in *Novyi mir* in February, 1987. He was also one of the first to point out the flaws in the Law on State Enterprise; and he argued that the Soviet welfare state had turned Soviet citizens into "social dependents" unable or unwilling to manage their own lives (*Literaturnaia gazeta*, No. 44, 1987).

18. *Sovetskaia kultura*, April 26, 1988.

19. *Nash sovremennik*, No. 4, 1988, pp. 160-75.

20. See Dmitrii Kazutin in *Moscow News*, No. 19, May 8, 1988; Beniamin Sarnov in *Ogonek*, No. 19, 1988; and, Nikolai Erofeev in *Sovetskaia Rossiia*, May 5, 1988. The article by Kozhinov was also the focus of two pieces published on June 12 in *Moscow News* under the title "Stalin and Stalinism: Two Points of view." One piece was written by mathematician Igor Shafarevich, the author of numerous samizdat articles in the nineteen-seventies and a former close associate of Solzhenitsyn, and another by maverick Marxist historian Roy Medvedev. Shafarevich praised Kozhinov's article as the most profound attempt to analyze the roots of Stalinism yet to have appeared in the Soviet press. Medvedev, by contrast, was very critical of Kozhinov's approach.

21. Iurii Afanasev made comments on Peter the Great that came close to Seliunin's in a public speech at a gathering in January 1988 at the Union of Writers building in Moscow. The text of the speech was not published in the Soviet press. Regarding his speech, see *Frankfurter Rundschau*, January, 1988. See also Nikolai Popov in *Sovetskaia kultura*, April 26,1988.


## PAPER 15:


1. V. I. Lenin, *Left-Wing Communism: An Infantile Disorder*.

2. See RL 242/84, "Reformers Keep Up the Pressure," June 18, 1984. Since Gorbachev came to power, the public advocates of NEP had multiplied.

3. Alexander Erlich, *The Soviet Industrialization Debate, 1924-1928* (Cambridge, Massachusetts: Harvard University Press, 1960).

4. S. Shatalin, "Nashe—znachit niche?" *Sobesednik*, No. 25, 1987, p. 10.

5. N. Shmelev, "Avansy i dolgi," *Novyi mir*, No. 6, 1987, pp. 142-58.

6. For example, A. McAuley, *Economic Welfare in the Soviet Union* (London: Weidenfeld and Nicholson, 1979); and M. Matthews, *Privilege in the Soviet Union* (London: Allen and Unwin, 1978).

7. For example, P. Wiles, *The Political Economy of Communism* (Oxford: Blackwell, 1962).

8. M. Bornstein and D. R. Fusfeld (eds.), *The Soviet Economy: A Book of Readings*, 1st ed. (Homewood, Illinois: Irwin, 1962), p. 2.

9. P. Gregory and R. C. Stuart, *Soviet Economic Structure and Performance*, 1st ed., New York: Harper and Row, 1974, p. 381.
10. *Narodnoe khoziaistvo SSSR v 1974 g.*, p. 103.
11. *Narodnoe khoziaistvo SSSR v 1985 g.*, p. 381.
12. *CIA, Handbook of Economic Statistics 1986*, p. 38.
13. P. Hanson and K. Pavitt, *The Comparative Economics of Research Development and Innovation in East and West: A Survey* (New York: Harwood Academic Publishers, 1987).
14. Combining estimates by Abram Bergson and Stanley Cohn, as cited by Gregory and Stuart, loc. cit., and extended by them through 1972, linked with CIA estimates of Soviet GNP since 1972 at 1982 ruble factor cost. For 1913-86, it is assumed that the level of GNP in 1913 was approximately the same as in 1928.
15. Simon Kuznets, *Economic Growth of Nations* (Cambridge, Massachusetts: Harvard University Press, 1971).
16. Alexander Eckstein, "The Background of Soviet Economic Performance," in Bornstein and Fusfeld, op. cit., at p. 4, for 1928; *CIA, Handbook of Economic Statistics 1986*, p. 38 (geometric mean of alternative estimates of relative GNP) and p. 54 (population) for 1985.

## PAPER 16:

1. *Ekonomicheskaia gazeta*, No. 29, 1987, p. 3.
2. *Literaturnaia gazeta*, No. 29, 1987, p. 1.
3. *Komsomolskaia pravda*, August 21, 1982.
4. *Istoriia SSSR*, No. 6, 1975, p. 22.
5. *Sovetskaia Rossiia*, August 2, 1987.
6. *Literaturnaia gazeta*, No. 21, 1987.
7. *Trud*, August 1, 1987.
8. *Izvestiia*, July 26, 1987.
9. *Selskaia zhizn*, July 24, 1987.
10. *Trud*, July 29, 1987.
11. *Narkhoz 85*, p. 182.
12. *Novyi mir*, No.6, 1987, p.147.
13. *Sovetskaia Rossiia*, August 8, 1987.
14. *Sovetskaia Rossiia*, January 10, 1988.
15. *Pravda*, August 7, 1987.
16. *Oktiabr*, No. 12, 1987, p. 13.
17. *Literaturnaia gazeta*, No. 36, 1987, p. 10.
18. *Selskoe khoziaistvo*, No. 1, 1986, pp. 52-3.
19. *Novyi mir*, No.6, 1987, p.146.

PAPER 17:

1. The communist governments maintained that socialism was superior in the provision of the basic socioeconomic rights, such as the right to work, the right to basic education, and the right to a health service, and that these rights were ultimately more important than those where their record was very poor such as the freedom of movement or the right to information.
2. See, for example, Walter Connor, "Generations and Politics," *Problems of Communism*, May 1975, pp. 20-32; Seweryn Bialer, *Stalin's Successors* (Cambridge: Cambridge University Press, 1980); and Alex Pravda, "East-West Interdependence and the Social Compact in Eastern Europe," in Morris Bornstein, Zvi Gitelman, and William Zimmerman, eds., *East-West Relations and the Future of Eastern Europe* (London: Allen and Unwin, 1981).
3. Peter Hauslohner, "Gorbachev's Social Contract," *Soviet Economy*, vol. 3, no. 1 (January-March), 1987, pp. 54-89. See also "Gorbachev and the Soviet Social Contract," RL 361/87, September 7, 1987.
4. *Izvestiia*, August 24, 1987; Gostev repeated Ryzhkov's statement in *Pravda*, August 19, 1987.
5. *Sovetskaia kultura*, January 4, 1986; in a later issue of *Sovetskaia kultura*, Kostakov modified his views by writing that these redundancies might not be necessary if certain conditions (such as earlier retirement, more leisure, and more full-time students) were met (see *Financial Times*, February 24, 1986). Another Soviet economist, Nikolai Shmelev argued in the June 1987 issue of the monthly *Novyi Mir* that the frictional unemployment rate in the Soviet economy was 2 percent. However, he said, the figure would rise to 3 percent if vagrants (who were not registered) were included. This would put Soviet frictional unemployment at about 4,500,000.
6. Addressing a Central Committee session (Reuters [Warsaw], December 16, 1987).
7. UPI (Stockholm), April 6, 1987.
8. AP (Warsaw), March 16, 1987 (Kaleta was said to have made these statements to an unspecified student periodical).
9. Complaints about slack labor discipline were commonplace in all communist countries. In the open atmosphere of Czechoslovakia of 1968 it was estimated that hidden unemployment amounted to between 300,000 and 500,000 (in a total work force of 6,500,000) (see *The Economist*, July 5, 1968). According to Ota Šik, the man responsible for the planned Czechoslovak reforms of 1968, the reform would eventually result in about 800,000 unemployed (dpa [Prague], January 19, 1968).
10. MTI in English, 4 September 1987; Radio Budapest, August 25, 1987, 6:30 P.M.; and Hungarian Situation Report/6, *RFER*, June 30, 1987, item 4.
11. Gorbachev's replies appeared in *Pravda*, February 8, 1986.
12. BTA (Sofia), August 15, 1987.
13. MTI in English, August 29, 1987.
14. Perhaps the most comprehensive theoretical exposition of the link between Soviet-type central planning and full employment is in János Kornai, *Economics of Shortage*, 2 vol. (Amsterdam: North Holland, 1980), especially chapters

11 and 12. Kornai concluded that full employment under communism was not so much a result of morally superior policies (as East European officials liked to claim) but rather an inevitable outcome of the centrally planned system, in which everything, including labor, was in short supply (on this point, see also Bartlomiej Kaminski, "Pathologies of Central Planning," *Problems of Communism*, March/April 1987, p. 90).

15. See Hungarian SR/6, *RFER*, June 30, 1987, item 4. On the other hand, layoffs were clearly highly unpopular among the individuals concerned. Workers in a Bulgarian factory reportedly struck in protest against the decision to close it (Bulgarian SR/5, *RFER*, July 8, 1987, item 1) and some Hungarian Communists reportedly returned their party cards in protest against the policy of unemployment (Hungarian SR/6, op. cit.).

## PAPER 18:

1. Whereas cooperatives contributed some 13 percent of total Soviet industrial production in 1928, by 1960 they contributed about 5 percent. See Alec Nove, *The Soviet Economy* (New York: Praeger, 1961), Chapter 1.
2. *Pravda*, June 27, 1987.
3. "V politburo KPSS," *Pravda*, February 6, 1987, p. 1.
4. *Sobranie postanovlenii Pravitelstva SSSR*, No. 10, 1987, pp. 195-222.
5. See RL 343/87, "Obstacles in the Way of the Cooperative Movement," August 28, 1987.
6. According to an interview with Gelii Shmelev, sector chief at the Institute of Economics of the World Socialist System, in *Trud*, April 24, 1988, p. 1. These figures were subsequently confirmed by Nikolai Ryzhkov in his opening address to the Supreme Soviet. *Sotsialisticheskaia industriia*, May 25, 1988, pp. 1-3.
7. Ryzhkov's speech to Supreme Soviet, op. cit.
8. *Izvestiia*, March 6, 1988, pp. 2-5. The title of the document is "O kooperatsii v SSSR." Literally, this is translated as "On Cooperation in the USSR," not "On Cooperatives in the USSR," This is no doubt because Lenin referred to the concept "*kooperatsiia*," and wrote an article entitled "O kooperatsii."
9. *Argumenty i fakty*, No. 18, 1988, p. 8.
10. AP, May 27, 1988.
11. See "Proekt odobren," *Izvestiia*, May 24, 1988, p. 3.
12. Ibid.
13. Ryzhkov's speech to Supreme Soviet, op. cit.
14. Ibid.
15. *Argumenty i fakty*, No. 21, May 1988, p. 8.
16. Speech to the Supreme Soviet by Alexei Ponomarev, *Izvestiia*, May 27, 1988, p. 4.
17. Reuters, May 26, 1988.
18. *Pravda*, June 8, 1988.
19. "Progressivnyi nalog kooperatorov budet izmenen," *Izvestiia*, May 31, 1988, p. 2.

## PAPER 19:

1. N. Shmelev, "Novye trevogi," *Novyi mir*, No. 4, 1988, pp. 160-75.
2. N. Shmelev, "Avansy i dolgi," *Novyi mir*, No. 6, 1987, pp. 142-58.
3. This is a biased sample. *Novyi mir* was read primarily by the intelligentsia. Public opinion in general would no doubt have been less positive about some of Shmelev's proposals—such as the use of unemployment to weed out unproductive labor.
4. *Novyi mir*, No. 4, 1988, pp. 161-62.
5. Ibid.
6. See the interview with Zbigniew Brzezinski in *Moskovskie novosti*, No. 19, 1988, p. 7.

## PAPER 20:

1. Alexander Zinoviev, *Kommunizm kak realnost* (Lausanne, L'Age d'Homme, 1981); English edition published by Gollancz, 1984.
2. E.g., Oleg Bogomolov, "Mir sotsializma na puti perestroiki," *Kommunist*, No. 16, 1987, pp. 92-103. Stanislav Shatalin may have been the first Soviet author to use this phrase in print.
3. RL 237/87, "The Reform Debate: What Are the Limits?" June 23, 1987.
4. *Izvestiia*, March 6, 1988, pp. 2-5. See RL 111/88, "The Draft Law on Cooperatives: An Assessment," March 15, 1988.
5. Bogomolov was described by Anders Aslund (see "Gorbachev's Economic Advisors," *Soviet Economy*, Vol. 3, No. 3, 1987, pp. 246-69) as one of Gorbachev's kitchen cabinet of four close but informal economic advisers, along with Abel Aganbegian, Leonid Abalkin and Tatiana Zaslavskaia.
6. Tamás Bauer, "Economic Reforms Within vs. Beyond the State Sector," Györ Conference Paper, March 1988. See also János Kornai, "The Hungarian Economic Reform Process: Visions, Hopes and Reality," *Journal of Economic Literature*, Vol. 24, December, 1986.
7. Quotation on China from Wolfgang Quaisser, "The New Agricultural Reform in China: From the People's Communes to Peasant Agriculture," in Peter Gey, Jiri Kosta, and Wolfgang Quaisser (eds.), *Crisis and Reform in Socialist Economies* (Boulder: Westview Press, 1987), pp. 173-97. Polish legislation reported by Radio Warsaw, April 1, 1988.
8. D. M. Nuti, "Financial Innovation under Market Socialism," European University Institute Working Paper, No. 87/285, 1987. Similar criticism of Hungarian arrangements was voiced by Peter Medgyessey, a Hungarian deputy prime minister (Radio Budapest, Domestic, March 4, 1988).
9. "Perestroika i uroki khoziaistvennykh reform," *Voprosy ekonomiki*, No. 2, 1988, pp. 55-80.
10. *Izvestiia*, May 14, 1987.
11. Bogomolov, op. cit.

PAPER 21:

1. *Sovetskaia Rossiia*, November 30, 1986.
2. See *Pravda*, January 4, 8, and 30, and February 15, 1987. See also RL 48/87, "Kiev's Response to the Berkhin Affair: Too Little, Too Late," January 28, 1987. Although Dichenko's rank was never mentioned in the press, his police counterpart, G. Vetrov, head of the Voroshilovgrad Oblast Administration of Internal Affairs, was reported to hold the rank of general (see *Pravda*, January 4, 1987). Furthermore, since the oblast had a population of over 3 million, it was unlikely that the local KGB would be headed by an officer with a rank lower than that of general.
3. *Meditsinskaia gazeta*, October 16, 1987, and February 5, 1988. See also RL 160/88, "Video versus the KGB," April 11, 1988.
4. *Meditsinskaia gazeta*, October 16, 1987.
5. *Literaturnaia gazeta*, No. 49, 1987; No. 4, 1988; and No. 5, 1988.
6. It was an unwritten rule that all KGB officers and staff must be either party or Komsomol members; expulsion from the party therefore automatically entailed dismissal from the KGB.
7. *Pravda*, January 20, 1988.
8. *Izvestiia*, November 10, 1987.
9. *Literaturnaia gazeta*, No. 6, 1988; see also RL 160/88.
10. *Izvestiia*, March 13, 1988.
11. *Krokodil*, No. 11, 1988, p. 13.
12. *Krokodil*, No. 1, 1988, p. 14.
13. *Krokodil*, No. 7, 1988, p. 13.
14. *Moscow News*, No. 14, 1988, p. 13.
15. *Nedelia*, No. 5, 1988, p. 11. This official slant on the history of the security organs—i.e., the careful differentiation between "good" and "bad" Chekists—gained credibility for many people when it became generally known that Nikolai Bukharin had made just such a distinction in his letter "To a Future Generation of Party Leaders." In that letter, which was composed before Bukharin's arrest but did not receive broad publicity until its publication in the Soviet press toward the end of 1987, he spoke of "the remarkable traditions of the Cheka" under Dzerzhinskii and went on to castigate the "degenerate" NKVD agents who became Stalin's henchmen. (The letter was reprinted in *Ogonek*, No. 17, 1988, p. 31.) Roy Medvedev made a similar distinction in an article in *Sobesednik*, No. 18, 1988, pp. 12-13.

PAPER 23:

1. Peter Hauslohner, "Gorbachev's Social Contract," *Soviet Economy*, Vol. 3, No. 1 (January-March), 1987, p.54.
2. See especially "Raspredelenie i spravedlivost," *Ekonomicheskaia gazeta*, No. 40, 1986, pp. 6-7; and "Uravnilovka: korni i posledstviia," *Argumenty i fakty*, Nos. 27 and 28, 1987. These articles were written by Nataliia Mikhailovna

Rimashevskaia, head of a department at the Central Mathematical-Economics Institute of the USSR Academy of Sciences.

3. "Ne za stepen, a za trud," *Literaturnaia gazeta*, January 15, 1986, p. 12.
4. *Sobranie postanovlenii Pravitelstva SSSR*, No. 43, 1986, pp. 603-622.
5. "Perestroika zaplaty," *Trud*, June 20, 1987.
6. TASS, July 29, 1987.
7. See RL 382/86, "'Social Justice' and Economic Progress," October 7, 1986.
8. *Pravda*, June 26, 1987, p. 1.
9. *SSSR v tsifrakh v 1986*, p. 219.
10. Ibid.
11. "Zhilishchnaia problema: kak ona reshaetsia v stranakh SEV," *Argumenty i fakty*, No. 44, 1985, p. 2; "Chelovek i ekonomika," *Ogonek*, No. 29, 1987, p. 4.
12. *Pravda*, June 26, 1987, p. 4.
13. Aganbegian said that he would like to remove subsidies on basic foodstuffs "as soon as next year" (Radio Moscow, in Hungarian, 2200, August 4, 1987).
14. "Perestroika i tsenoobrazovanie," *Izvestiia*, August 30, 1987; "Radikalnaia reforma tsenoobrazovaniia," *Pravda*, August 25, 1987.
15. "Skolko platit za produkty?," *Literaturnaia gazeta*, August 12, 1987, p. 12. There were more than 70 million families in the USSR ("Tsifry i fakty. TsSU SSSR soobshchaet," *Kommunist*, No. 1 [January], 1987, p. 127).
16. "Chego ia boius," *Literaturnaia gazeta*, August 12, 1987, p. 12.
17. "Sotsialnoe razvitie i ekonomicheskii rost," *Kommunist*, No. 14 (September), 1986, p. 63.
18. "Voprosy truda i zaplaty v promyshlennosti: Rech na I Vsesoiuznom sezde otdelov ekonomiki truda i tarifno-normirovochnykh biuro, 7 iiulia 1926 g.," in F. E. Dzerzhinskii, *Izbrannye proizvedeniia*, Moscow, Vol. 2, 1957, p. 322.
19. "Avansy i dolgi," *Novyi mir*, No. 6 (June), 1987, p. 149.
20. "Vstrecha na izbiratelnom uchastke," *Izvestiia*, June 22, 1987.
21. "Zaniatost: defitsit ili izbytok?," *Kommunist*, No. 2 (January), 1987, p. 85.
22. "Chelovecheskii faktor razvitiia ekonomiki i sotsialnaia spravedlivost," *Kommunist*, No. 13 (September), 1986, p. 70.
23. "Znaet koshka...," *Literaturnaia gazeta*, No. 12, 1988, p. 13.
24. "Novye trevogi," *Novyi mir*, No. 4 (April), 1988, pp. 163-175.

PAPER 24:

1. "Kto tam, za chertoi bednosti?," *Sotsialisticheskaia industriia*, June 1, 1988.
2. *Chislennost i sostav naseleniia SSSR*, Moscow, 1984, p. 252.
3. *Narkhoz SSSR za 70 let*, Moscow, 1987, p. 439.
4. *Sobranie postanovlenii Pravitelstva SSSR*, No. 17, 1985, Article 80.
5. "Papa, mama, i mal mala menshe," *Semia*, No. 11, 1988, p. 4.
6. Radio Moscow, June 7, 1988.
7. "Miloserdie po subbotam?," *Sobesednik*, No. 33, 1987, p. 10.
8. See, for example, "Byvshii intelligentnyi chelovek...," *Literaturnaia gazeta*, May 30, 1979.

9. "Bezhal brodiaga...," *Literaturnaia gazeta*, May 28, 1986.
10. "Pridonnyi sloi," *Ogonek*, No. 8, 1987, pp. 12-13.
11. "Pisma ... ne dlia pechati," *Izvestiia*, February 10, 1988.
12. "Bomzh," *Izvestiia*, February 13, 1988.
13. "Pozdniaia doroga k domu," *Izvestiia*, March 1, 1988.
14. "Ne otvodite vzgliad!," *Moskovskie novosti*, March 13, 1988, p. 11.
15. "Nastupat na alkogol," *Pravda*, November 15, 1987. Professor Vladimir Treml of Duke University estimated that there were between 20 million and 22 million alcoholics in the Soviet Union, registered or not (RL 317/87, "An Interview with Vladimir Treml on Alcoholism in the USSR," August 3, 1987).
16. Derived from "Otkrovenno o vazhnom," *Argumenty i fakty*, No. 10, 1987, p. 5. At a press conference in Moscow in February 1988, Dr. Aleksandr Churkin, the chief psychiatrist of the USSR Ministry of Health , announced that 2 million names were to be removed from "the psychiatric register"—i.e., the official list of mentally ill people—in the near future (AFP [Moscow], February 11, 1988).
17. "Cinq cent mille 'parasites'," *Le Monde*, October 20, 1984, p. 6.
18. *The Times*, April 19, 1988.

PAPER 25:

1. *Trybuna Ludu*, January 14, 1988.
2. Marek Henzler, "How To Count and on What?" *Polityka*, January 23, 1988.
3. Leon Podkaminer, "Prices," September 20, 1987.
4. Radio Warsaw I, January 25, 1988, 6:55 P.M.
5. Ernest Skalski, "Under the Guise of Reform" and "Fatal illness," *Tygodnik Powszechny*, September 6, and November 1, 1987.
6. K.H., "Why We Are Eating This Frog," January 20, 1988.
7. Reuters, April 25, 1988; and John Tagliabue, "Polish Transport Workers Strike and Win a Wage Increase," *The New York Times*, April 26, 1988.
8. UPI, April 27, 1988.
9. AP, April 26, 1988.
10. Roman Przeciszewski, "Shoving on the Railway Siding," *Polityka*, March 12, 1988.
11. For details, see Polish Situation Report/4, *RFER*, March 17, 1988, item 3.
12. Jackson Diehl, "Polish Workers' Unrest, Strikes, Raises Specter of Labor Uprising," *The New York Times*, April 27, 1988.
13. *Trybuna Ludu*, April 28, 1988.
14. PAP, April 1988; and Radio Warsaw, April 30, 1988, 7:00 P.M.
15. PAP, April 29, 1988.
16. AP, May 2, 1988.
17. Quoted by Jackson Diehl, "Security Forces Break Up Shipyard Strike," *The Washington Post*, May 6, 1988.
18. Janusz Korwin-Mikke, "Moth-eaten Paper," *Ład*, March 27, 1988; Adam Michnik, "More Dreams!" *Tygodnik Powszechny*, April 24 and May 1, 1988.
19. Ernest Skalski, "We Still Do Not Understand Each Other," *Tygodnik Powszechny*, April 17, 1988.

20. Figures cited in Skalski, loc cit.; and Witold Gadomski, "Stagflation," *Ład*, April 3-10, 1988.
21. Jerzy Baczynski, "The Decline Before the Increase," *Polityka*, January 9, 1988.
22. Mirosława Marody, "Advance and Collapse," *Polityka*, April 30, 1988.
23. Radio Warsaw, April 19, 1988, 6:30 A.M., and April 30, 1988, 8:30 A.M.
24. PAP, May 5, 1988.
25. Quoted in *Tygodnik Mazowsze*, May 4, 1988.
26. AP, May 25, 1988.
27. "The Majority of Polish Society, Critical and Impatient, Wants to Solve Its Problems in Peace," *Trybuna Ludu*, May 19, 1988.
28. Radio Warsaw, May 11, 1988, 3:55 P.M. Wojna developed this idea in "Will an Anti-Crisis Pact Materialize?" *Odrodzenie*, May 21, 1988.
29. "There Will Be No Retreat From Reforms and Democratization," *Trybuna Ludu*, May 16, 1988.
30. For an account of this discussion, see Polish Situation Report/5 *RFER*, April 11, 1988, item 3.
31. PAP, May 31, 1988.
32. "Walk-Out in Warsaw," *The Spectator*, May 21, 1988.
33. For more on the August strikes, see Polish Situation Report/13 and 14, *RFER*, August 26, and September 2, 1988.
34. For an analysis of this meeting, see Polish Situation Report/14, *RFER*, September 2, item 1.
35. Quoted by Reuters, August 30, 1988.
36. For an account if these meetings, see Jan B. de Weydenthal, "The Challenge of Solidarity," RAD Background Report/187, *RFER*, September 13, 1988.

## PAPER 26:

1. The formation by the Moscow Oblast Komsomol Committee of "Pamiat's" forerunner, the club "Rodina," was announced by journalist Vasilii Peskov in *Komsomolskaia pravda*, June 4, 1965.
2. See John B. Dunlop, *The Faces of Contemporary Russian Nationalism* (Princeton: Princeton University 1983).
3. See RL 357/85, "Gorbachev's New Propaganda Chief a Critic of Russian Nationalists," October 31, 1985; and RL 233/87, "Personnel Changes in the Politburo," June 26, 1987.
4. See RL 342/87, "The Emergence of 'Pamiat' and 'Otechestvo'," August 26, 1987.
5. See, for example, *Literaturnaia Rossiia*, No. 42, 1987, pp. 2-7, for the text of a speech eulogizing "Pamiat" delivered at a meeting of the Secretariat held in Vladivostok in September.
6. These are: *Nash sovremennik* (220,000), *Molodaia gvardiia* (640,000), and *Moskva* (430,000). Total circulation: 1,290,000.
7. *Sovetskaia kultura*, October 29, 1987.
8. *Nash sovremennik*, No. 9, 1987, pp. 188-89.
9. *Sovetskaia kultura*, November 24, 1987.

10. A talk by Strelianyi is translated in RL 321/87, "'Whom Does Silence Benefit?' A Member of *Novyi mir*'s Editorial Board Speaks Out," August 4, 1987. For an account of a controversial article by Shmelev, see RL 237/87, "The Reform Debate: What Are the Limits?," June 23, 1987.

11. *Literaturnaia Rossiia*, No. 31, 1987, pp. 2-3; *Oktiabr*, No. 8, 1987, pp. 3-65; *Molodaia gvardiia*, No. 10, pp. 271-76.

12. Cited in Peter Reddaway (ed.), *Uncensored Russia* (New York: American Heritage Press, 1972), p. 431.

13. *Russkaia mysl*, March 27, 1987. See also RL 191/87, "Eltsin Meets with Members of 'Pamiat',"" May 19, 1987.

14. See, for example, *Nash sovremennik*, No. 7, 1987, pp. 150-57; and *Sovetskaia molodezh*, August 11, 1987.

15. *Vecherniaia Moskva*, May 18 and June 1, 1987. The struggle against kefir may have aroused a certain amount of skepticism in a country where an entire workers' collective has been hospitalized for drinking a pesticide (see *Nedelia*, No. 46, 1987, p. 5).

PAPER 27:

1. In Estonia public commemorations were held on February 2, 1988, the day of the signing in 1920 of a treaty by which the Soviet government renounced in perpetuity any territorial claims on Estonia; on February 24, the 70th anniversary of the independent Estonian republic; on March 25, the day of mass deportations in 1949; and on June 14, the day of mass deportations in 1941. Latvians commemorated their independence day on November 18 and the anniversaries of the deportations on March 25 and June 14. Lithuanians held public commemorations on February 16, Lithuania's National Day of Independence; on May 22, the day of mass deportations in 1948; and on June 14.

PAPER 28:

1. *Pravda*, June 9, 1988.
2. AFP, from Moscow, June 9, 1988.
3. See RL 305/87, "Crimean Tatars Demonstrate for Restoration of Autonomous Republic in Crimea," July 27, 1987.
4. Ibid., and RL 405/87, "Crimean Tatar Commission Works against Background of Continuing Protests," October 13, 1987.
5. AFP, from Moscow, May 2, 1988.
6. *Pravda*, October 16, 1987. Also RL 459/87, "Commission Makes Cultural Concessions to Crimean Tatars," October 23, 1987.
7. *Pravda*, February 5, 1988.
8. *Pravda Vostoka*, March 6, 1988.
9. See *Pravda Vostoka*, March 11, 1988, for more details of the cultural concessions.
10. AS 6204.
11. *Pravda Ukrainy*, May 8, 1988.

PAPER 29:

1. *Vestnik statistiki*, 1980, No.10, p. 70.
2. See Firuz Kazemzadeh, *The Struggle for Transcaucasia, 1917-1921* (New York: Oxford University Press), pp. 291-292.
3. The 1926 Soviet census gave the Armenian share of the population of Nakhichevan as 14.9 percent (and 81.4 percent for the Azeri share). The latest census, of 1979, showed that Armenians made up only 1.4 percent of the total.
4. *Süddeutsche Zeitung*, March 1, 1988.
5. *Izvestiia*, February 24, evening edition, as quoted by UPI, Moscow, February 23, 1988.
6. See RL 79/88, "More Demonstrations in Armenia," February 22, 1988.
7. *Kommunist* (Armenia), February 25, 1988.
8. Reuters and UPI, Moscow, February 23, 1988.
9. *Kommunist* (Armenia), February 23, 1988.
10. AP, Moscow, February 23, 1988.
11. AP, Moscow, February 25, and *The Guardian*, February 25, 1988.
12. Radio Erevan, in Russian, February 26, 1988.
13. "Hope's Name Is Gorbachev," *La Repubblica*, March 7, 1988.
14. Dpa, Moscow, February 27, 1988; *The New York Times*, February 27, 1988.
15. Dpa, Moscow, February 27, 1988.
16. Dpa, Moscow, February 29, 1988.
17. TASS, March 4, 1988.
18. TASS, February 29, 1988.
19. AP, Moscow, February 29, 1988.
20. Reuters, Moscow, March 3, 1988.
21. Reuters, Moscow, March 7, 1988.
22. AFP, Moscow, March 7, 1988.
23. For a chronology of criticisms of the Armenian party organization in general and of Demirchian in particular, see RL 335/87, "Armenia's Demirchian: Reforming Indifferently?" August 13, 1987; and RL 24/88 "For Whom the Bell Tolls, or Gorbachev, Armenia, and Perestroika, January 19, 1988.
24. *Bakinskii rabochii*, March 3, 1988.
25. *Bakinskii rabochii*, March 8, 1988.
26. Reuters and AFP, Moscow, March 18, 1988; AP, Moscow, March 19, 1988.
27. *Il Messagero*, March 18, 1988; AFP, Moscow, March 1988.
28. See the issue for March 17.
29. AP, Moscow, March 21 and 22, 1988.
30. TASS, March 23, 1988.
31. Reuters and AP, from Moscow, March 24, 1988.
32. AFP, Moscow, March 24, 1988.
33. See RL 121/88, "Attitudes Harden as Gorbachev's Nagorno-Karabakh Deadline Approaches," March 22, 1988.
34. *The New York Times*, March 25, 1988.
35. TASS, March 24, 1988.
36. *Kommunist* (Armenia) March 24, 1988; *The Los Angeles Times*, March 25, 1988.

37. *The New York Times*, Reuters, Moscow, March 25, 1988.
38. Reuters, Moscow, March 26, 1988.
39. Reuters, Moscow, March 27, 1988; and *The New York Times*, March 27, 1988.
40. AP, UPI, Moscow, March 27; Reuters, Moscow, March 28, 1988.
41. Reuters, Moscow, March 30, citing *Trud* and Sovetskaia Rossiia.
42. Reuters and AP, from Moscow, May 19, 1988; *The New York Times*, May 19, 1988.
43. AFP and UPI, from Moscow, May 13, 1988.
44. Reuters and UPI, May 16, 1988.
45. AFP, from Moscow, May 9, 1988; AFP, from Moscow, May 13, 1988.
46. Reuters and UPI, Moscow, May 13, 1988.
47. Reuters, from Moscow, May 19, 1988.
48. AFP, from Moscow, May 18, 1988.
49. AFP, from Moscow, May 19, 1988; see also *The Washington Post*, May 20, 1988.
50. *Izvestiia*, March 25, 1988; for the text of Kaputikian's response, see AS 6192.
51. TASS, in English and Russian, May 21, 1988; and *Pravda*, May 22, 1988.
52. Austrian Television, March 13, 1988.
53. *The Baltimore Sun*, February 25, 1988, and AP, Moscow, February 25, 1988.
54. *The Los Angeles Times*, May 24, 1988.
55. *The Sun* (Baltimore), July 7, 1988.
56. Reuters, Moscow, July 8, 1988; *Frankfurter Rundschau*, July 9, 1988.
57. Reuters, UPI, Moscow, July 8, 1988.
58. Reuters, AP, Moscow, July 7, 1988.
59. Dpa, Moscow, July 8, 1988.
60. *Los Angeles Times*, July 7, 1988.
61. *The New York Times*, July 11, 1988.
62. AFP, Moscow, July 7, 1988; *Frankfurter Allgemeine Zeitung*, July 9, 1988.
63. Dpa, Moscow, July 9, 1988.
64. Reuters, Moscow, July 11, 1988.
65. AFP, Moscow, July 9, 1988.

PAPER 30:

1. *Aktualnye voprosy ateisticheskogo vospitaniia na sovremennom etape* (Moscow: Znanie, Scientific Atheism series, No. 12, 1986), p. 8.
2. *Vvedenie khristianstva na Rusi* (Moscow: Znanie, Scientific Atheism series, No. 2, 1987), p. 16.
3. *Izvestiia*, July 30, 1986, p. 4.
4. *Deutsche Tagespost*, May 29, 1987; *Ostkirchliche Information*, June 1987, p. 6.
5. TASS, in English, March 23, 1987.
6. *Zhurnal Moskovskoi Patriarkhii*, No. 1, 1987.
7. *The Washington Times*, May 22, 1987.
8. *Moskovskie novosti*, (*Moscow News*) No. 4, 1987, p. 12.
9. *Literaturnaia gazeta*, No. 29, 1987, p. 12.
10. *Literaturnaia gazeta*, No. 34, August 19, 1987.

11. *Moskovskie novosti*, No. 37, 1987, p. 3.
12. *Sovetskaia Litva*, August 27, 1987.
13. *Sovetskaia Litva*, June 2, 1987.
14. *Molodezh Estonii*, April 30, 1987.
15. APN, September 7, 1987.
16. *Frankfurter Allgemeine Zeitung*, September 9, 1987.
17. *Pravda*, December 21, 1987.
18. Radio Moscow-2, December 20, 1987.
19. RL 258/83, "Orthodox Monastery Returned to the Church," July 6, 1983.
20. *Moskovskie novosti*, No. 51, 1987.
21. *Sovetskaia Rossiia*, January 9, 1988.
22. TASS, August 29, 1988.
23. *Baptist Times*, December 10, 1987.
24. Ibid., January 7, 1988.
25. *Moskovskie novosti*, No. 2, 1988, p. 2.
26. Ibid., p. 13.
27. RL 472/87, "New Concession to Soviet Believers," November 25, 1987.
28. Reuters, February 27, 1988, AP March 3 and 8, 1988.
29. AS No. 6054, "Obrashchenie k Materi Terese Kalkutskoi."
30. TASS, August 21, 1987; TASS, in English, August 25, 1987; *Komsomolskaia pravda*, August 27, 1987; and, *Literaturnaia gazeta*, September 2, 1987.
31. TASS, August 21, 1987.
32. Ibid.
33. *Literaturnaia gazeta*, September 2, 1987.
34. *Moskovskie novosti*, No. 2, January 10, 1988.
35. *Literaturnaia gazeta*, December 9, 1987, p. 11.
36. *Vesti iz SSSR/USSR News Brief*, No. 9-2, May 15, 1987; No. 14-2, July 31, 1987.
37. *Pravda Vostoka*, March 25, 1987.
38. *Bild-Zeitung*, January 7, 1988.
39. RL 16/88, "No Respite for Pentecostals in Chuguevka," January 16, 1987.
40. AFP, February 28, 1988; International Society for Human Rights (IGFM) Press Release, Frankfurt-am-Main, February 19, 1988.
41. RL 450/87, "What Changes in Religious Legislation Are Being Proposed by Soviet Citizens," November 11, 1987.
42. AFP, September 30, 1987.
43. AFP, February 2, 1988; Reuters, February 3, 1988.
44. Keston News Service, No. 287, November 5, 1987, p. 7.
45. *Kommunist*, No. 4, 1988, pp. 115-123.
46. See RL 450/87,
47. See RS 107/87, "Dva interviu mitropolita Aleksiia," November 2, 1987.
48. *Sovetskaia Rossiia*, December 27, 1987.
49. *Meditsinskaia gazeta*, March 30, 1988.
50. *Moskovskie novosti*, No. 14., April 3, 1988, p. 11.
51. *Moskovskie novosti*, No. 2, January 10, 1988.
52. *Moskovskie novosti*, No. 15, April 10, 1988, p. 14.
53. See RL 258/83, "Orthodox Monastery Returned to the Church," July 6, 1983.

54. *Moskovskie novosti*, No. 15, 1988, p. 14.
55. Radio Moscow-1, July 7, 1986, 9:15 A.M.
56. "Raziasnenie OKVK po tsirkuliaru NKZ No. 90-33 ot 13/III, 1982. Po voprosu o zemlepolzovanii sluzhitelei kultov," *Zakon o religioznykh obedineniiakh RSFSR* (Moscow: Bezbozhnik, 1930).
57. *Pravda*, April 30, 1988; *Izvestiia*, May 1, 1988; *Sovetskaia Rossiia*, May 1, 1988; *Moskovskie novosti*, No. 19, 1988.
58. *Zhurnal Moskovskoi Patriarkhii*, No. 11, 1984, p. 19.
59. *Pravda*, April 30, 1988.
60. See, for example, *Sobesednik*, No. 20, May, 1988, pp. 10-11; *Ogonek*, No. 22, May, 1988, p.15; and, *Izvestiia* and TASS, May 27, 1988.
61. *Izvestiia*, December 13, 1987. The area described by the chronicler Nestor would comprise the park.
62. Dpa, March 11, 1988.
63. TASS, May 7, 1988; *Literaturna Ukraina*, No. 18, May 5, 1988, p. 2; and TASS, May 25, 1988.
64. *Literaturna Ukraina*, No. 18, May 5, 1988, p. 2.
65. *Izvestiia*, January 1, 1988.
66. *Literaturna Ukraina*, No. 18, May 5, 1988, p. 2.
67. *Visti z Ukrainy*, No. 8, March, 1988, p. 7; and *Radianska Ukraina*, March 27, 1988, p. 3.
68. *Golos rodiny*, No. 20, 1988, p. 12.
69. *The New York Times*, June 5, 1988, and *Los Angeles Times*, June 5, 1988.
70. See RL 230/88, "Ukrainian Catholic Issue Overshadows Start of Moscow Patriarchate's Millennial Celebrations," June 6, 1988.
71. TASS, June 10, 1988; and, Radio Moscow-2, June 10, 1988.
72. TASS, in English, June 11, 1988; and, *Izvestiia*, June 12, 1988.
73. *Sovetskaia kultura*, May 28, 1988, p. 8.
74. Radio Moscow-1, May 12, 1988; and *Literaturnaia gazeta* No. 19. May 1988, p. 4.
75. AP, May 11, 1988.
76. *Trud*, June 5, 1988.
77. *Moskovskie novosti*, No. 8, February 21, 1988.
78. *Moskovskaia pravda*, June 5, 1988, p. 8.
79. *Sovetskaia kultura*, June 7, 1988, p. 8.
80. Mefodii, Metropolitan of Voronezh and Lipetsk, was chairman of the finance directorate of Moscow Patriarchate and member of the board of Lenin Memorial Children's Foundation of the Soviet Union.
81. *Semia*, No. 23, 1988, p. 14.
82. AFP, February 2, 1988; Reuters, February 3, 1988; see also RL 138/88, "Policy toward Unofficial Religious Groups under Gorbachev," March 13, 1988.
83. *The Baltimore Sun*, June 12, 1988.
84. AP, June 7, 1988.

**PAPER 31:**

1. *Literaturnaia gazeta*, May 13 and June 10, 1987.

2. *Kommunist Tadzhikistana*, No. 3, 1988.
3. Ibid., September 3, 1986.
4. Ibid., January 31, 1987.
5. Ibid.
6. See *Kommunist Tadzhikistana*, January 31 and February 12, 1987, and Makhkamov's report to the Central Committee plenum, *Kommunist Tadzhikistana*, April 8, 1987. See also RL 101/87, "Protest against Arrest of Mullah in Tajikistan," March 11, 1987.
7. See Makhkamov's remarks in *Kommunist Tadzhikistana*, September 3, 1986.
8. *Agitator*, No. 5, 1988.
9. *Pravda*, November 16, 1985.
10. *Kommunist Tadzhikistana*, July 17, 1987.
11. Ibid., July 4, 1987.
12. *Literaturnaia gazeta*, January 13, 1988, p. 14.
13. AFP, December 8, 1987.
14. *Literaturnaia gazeta*, May 13, 1987, p. 13. The second part of the article appeared in the issue for May 20, 1987, p. 12.
15. In a speech published in *Kyrgyzstan madaniyaty*, December 17, 1987, p. 4, the renowned Kirgiz writer Chingiz Aitmatov obliquely referred to Belaiev's article, appearing to consider Beliaev's approach to "the struggle with nationalism" as extreme. He said: *"Literaturnaia gazeta* even alluded one day to an alleged Islamic column existing in Central Asia—this must be understood as a fifth column, which is only waiting for the arrival of Khomeini. But let us assume that this is extreme."
16. *Literaturnaia gazeta*, May 18, 1988, p. 10.

PAPER 32:

1. *Rudé právo* and *Pravda* (Bratislava), February 20, 1988; and AP, February 20, 1988.
2. *Informace o Církvi*, No. 1, 1988, pp. 16-17.
3. RFE Correspondent's Report (Rome), March 2, 1988.
4. See Czechoslovak Situation Report/16, *RFER*, November 3, 1987, item 6.
5. AP, March 5, 1988.
6. Reuters, March 5, 1988.
7. UPI, March 5, 1988.
8. Reuters and AP, March 6, 1988.
9. Pope John Paul read out the message at his weekly audience in the Vatican on March 2, 1988, the feast day of Blessed Agnes.
10. March 25 is the liturgical feast day of the Annunciation, marking the day that the Virgin Mary was first told of Christ's approaching birth.
11. On June 11 and 12, 1988, the Catholic Church in Czechoslovakia consecrated its first two auxiliary bishops for Prague and a bishop-apostolic administrator for

Trnava (Western Slovakia). The consecrations were seen as symbolizing the partial success of the Vatican's year-long efforts to have all the Church's 13 bishoprics filled with bishops who were not members of the prorégime association of clergy *Pacem in Terris*. (Reuters, AP, AFP, dpa, Ceteka, June 11 and 12, 1988.

12. The letter is now available in the West.
13. František Mikloško's letter dated March 21, 1988 is available in the West.
14. Czechoslovak Television, March 23, 1988, 9:35 P.M.
15. *Smena*, March 24, 1988, p. 4.
16. Kathpress, March 23, 1988.
17. AP, March 25, 1988.
18. Reuters, dpa, March 26, 1988.
19. RFE Correspondent's Report (Prague), March 26, 1988; Reuters, March 26, 1988.
20. Radio Prague, April 8, 1988, 6:30 P.M.
21. Ibid., April 12, 1988, 6:30 P.M
22. Erika Kadlecová, "Signatures for Catholics a Light of Hope from Czechoslovakia," *l'Unità*, March 30, 1988.
23. Literally: lightning-flash (*lampa*).

## PAPER 33:

1. *Evangelischer Pressedienst-Dokumentation*, 4a/1987.
2. The petition was originally presented for consideration at the Berlin Brandenburg regional synod in April. See *Evangelischer Pressedienst-Dokumentation*, 28/1987, pp. 30-33.
3. Süddeutsche Zeitung, April 26, 1988; ibid., April 21, 1988; *Evangelischer Pressedienst*, April 6, 1988.
4. Ibid., April 23, 1988.
5. See Barbara Donovan, "East German Police Raid Offices of Church-Based Dissidents," RAD Background Report/239 (German Democratic Republic), *RFER*, 15 December 1987.
6. Dpa, April 15 and 29, 1988. The West German Ministry for Inter-German Relations said that it knew of 639 East German citizens arrested for political reasons since the beginning of December 1987 after a general amnesty had emptied the jails.
7. Bishop Christoph Stier in *Evangelischer Pressedienst-Dokumentation*, no. 17, 1988, pp. 13-21. This was the same speech that was heavily censored when excerpts of it appeared in *Die Mecklenburger Kirche* in April.
8. Dpa, April 12, 1988; see also the interview with Bishop Gottfried Forck in *Frankfurter Allgemeine Zeitung*, April 23, 1988. Government officials in both Bonn and East Berlin denied that quotas were set on emigration.
9. See *Evangelischer Pressedienst-Dokumentation*, no. 17, 1988.
10. See the speech by Bishop Christian Demke at the synod of the Church of Saxony, ibid., p. 8.

## PAPER 34:

1. For some of the more comprehensive and cautious accounts, see Reuters (Vienna), November 20, 1987; AP (Vienna), November 21 and 23, 1987; *Le Monde*, November 24, 1987; *Frankfurter Allgemeine Zeitung*, November 25, 1987; *Die Welt*, November 26, 1987; and UPI (Bucharest), November 27, 1987; and *Index on Censorship* and *East European Reporter*, both of April 1988, pp. 3-4 and 61-63, respectively.

2. Israeli tourists returning from Braşov, interviewed by *Maariv* (Tel Aviv), November 24, 1987.

3. RFE Romanian Service correspondent's report (Milan), November 25, 1987; *Le Point*, November 30, 1987; *Libération*, November 26, 1987.

4. See Romanian Situation Report/13, *RFER*, November 25, 1987, item 4.

5. Agerpres in English, January 16, and April 17, 1986; *Karpaten-Rundschau*, November 13, 1987, p. 3; *Komsomolskaia Pravda*, October 13, 1984.

6. AFP and UPI, January 9, 1984; *Frankfurter Allgemeine Zeitung*, January 11, 1984.

7. UPI (Bucharest), Reuters (Vienna), and BBC World Service News, November 27, 1987; AFP (Vienna) and *The Independent* (Bucharest correspondent's report), November 28, 1987; AP (Vienna), November 30, 1987; *Time*, December 7, 1987.

8. UPI (Bucharest), November 27, 1987; *The Independent* (correspondent's report from Bucharest and Bras∞ov), November 28, 1987; AFP (Vienna), November 28 and 29, 1987.

9. Radio Bucharest, December 2, 1987, 7:00 P.M.; *Scînteia*, December 3, 1987.

10. *Scînteia*, November 20 and 21, 1987.

11. Ibid., November 26, 1987.

12. See Vladimir Socor, "The Workers' Protest in Braşov: Assessment and Aftermath," *RFER*, Background Report/231 (Romania), December 4, 1987.

13. *Erdély i Magyar Hirűgynökseg/Hungarian Press of Transylvania* (Timişoara), December 7, 1987; *Politika* (Belgrade) and Tanjug (in English), December 18, 1987; *Magyar Szo* (Novi Sad), December 20, 1987; *Die Presse* (correspondent's report from Belgrade and Bucharest), December 15, 1987; AP, AFP, and dpa (all from Bucharest), December 14, 16, and 17, 1987, respectively.

14. AP and AFP (Bucharest), December 16 and 17, 1987, respectively; AP and AFP (Vienna), both on December 25 and 28, 1987; *Magyar Szo* (Novi Sad), December 20, 1987 (a correspondent's report from Transylvania).

15. *Die Presse*, 24 December 1987; Austrian television's main evening news (Bucharest correspondent's report), 26 December 1987; AFP (Bucharest), 28 December 1987; Frankfurter Allgemeine Zeitung, 29 December 1987, AFP and Reuters, December 3, 1987, and AP, December 4, 1987 (all from Vienna); BBC World Service, December 4, 1987; *Die Presse*, December 5/6,

1987; *The Independent*, December 5 and 21, 1987; and *The New York Times*, January 5, 1988 (all reports from Budapest correspondents). For profiles of these groups see Vladimir Socor, "Romanian Democratic Action" and "Romanian and Hungarian Dissidents Find Common Ground," *RFER*, Background Reports/34 and 51 respectively.

16. Vladimir Socor, "The Workers' Protest in Braşov: Assessment and Aftermath," *RFER*, Background Report/231 (Romania), December 4, 1987; *Le Matin*, December 10, 1987; *Magyar Szo* (Novi Sad), December 17, 1987 (correspondents' report from Braşov); Reuters (Braşov), December 17, 1987.

17. *Le Matin*, December 10, 1987. This committee was also reported on in Solidarity's underground press in Poland (see *Przegląd Wiadomości Agencyjnych*, no. 45, 23 December 1987).

18. BBC World Service (Bucharest correspondent's report), December 16, 1987; AP (Bucharest), December 16, 1987; AFP (Bucharest), December 17, 1987.

19. *Newsweek*, January 4, 1988 correspondents' report from Braşov and Bucharest).

20. AP, AFP, and RFE Correspondent's Report (Vienna), December 18, 1987.

## PAPER 35:

1. Reuters and dpa, November 26, 1987; *Frankfurter Allgemeine Zeitung*, November 27, 1987; *Süddeutsche Zeitung*, November 28, 1987.

2. *Die Tageszeitung*, November 27, 1987.

3. See Stolpe's interview in *Die Welt*, November 27, 1987

## PAPER 36:

1. *Vjesnik* (Zagreb), June 19, 1988.

2. *Večernje* Novosti (Belgrade), June 18, 1988.

3. *Vjesnik*, June 18 and 19, 1988.

4. *Večernje Novosti*, June 18, 1988.

5. Radio Belgrade, in Serbo-Croatian, June 16, 1988, 12:00 noon.

## PAPER 37:

1. AFP, AP, dpa, Reuters, and UPI (Budapest), June 27, 1988.

2. A growing number of Romanian citizens, most of them from the estimated 2,000,000, ethnic Magyars in Transylvania, fled to Hungary to escape deepening economic hardships and what they considered to be forcible assimilation by the Ceauşescu régime. The share of ethnic Romanians among the refugees to Hungary equally increased. Authorities  estimated that there were 10,000 to 15,000 Romanian citizens living in Hungary as émigrés or refugees. Less than half of them registered officially with the state authorities and applied to settle in

Hungary; but the number of those doing so grew from 1,709 in 1985 to 6,499 in 1987. In the first three months of 1988 alone the Hungarian authorities granted 1,800 residence permits to refugees from Romania. The majority of refugees were young skilled workers; but they included professionals, mostly engineers and doctors. A large share of the refugees found semilegal or illegal work with Hungarian firms in the private sector.

3. Ibid, UPI.
4. *Magyar Nemzet*, June 27, 1988, and *Magyar Ifjúság*, June 24, 1988.
5. UPI (Budapest), June 27, 1988
6. Radio Budapest, June 28, 1988, 7:00 A.M.
7. Ibid., June 28, 1988, 9:00 P.M.
8. Dpa, June 30, 1988.
9. AP (Vienna), June 28, 1988.
10. Radio Budapest, June 30, 1988, 6:30 P.M.
11 *Magyar Nemzet*, June 29, 1988.


PAPER 38:


1. See paper 32 above


PAPER 39:


1. *Ogonek*, No. 36, 1987; *Moscow News*, No. 37, 1987. A report on the conference was also carried by the periodical *20 vek i mir*, which was not available at the time of writing.
2. *The Guardian*, September 12, 1987.
3. AS 6015.
4. *Vecherniaia Moskva*, August 7, 1987, and September 15, 1987; see also the attack on *Glasnost* and *Ekspress-khronika* in *Argumenty i fakty*, No. 1, 1988.
5. *Komsomolskaia pravda*, September 16, 1987.
6. See reference in *The New York Times*, January 12, 1988.
7. AS 6127 and 6132.
8. See the article by Mark d'Anastasio in *The Wall Street Journal*, September 9, 1987.
9. *Pravda*, December 27, 1987.
10. UPI, May 7, AP, May 8, *The Washington Post*, May 8, UPI, May 8, AP, May 9, 1988.
11. Martin Walker in *The Guardian*, May 9, 1988, listed the main unofficial groups that participated in setting up the Democratic Union.
12. For the criticism of the seminar "Democracy and Humanism," see, for instance, *Sobesednik*, No. 44, October, 1987. Although the Group for the Establishment of Trust between East and West was regularly criticized in the Soviet press, in December 1987 members of the group were allowed to express their views on Soviet television (see RL 498/87, "Moscow TV Airs Views of Independent Peace Group," December 8, 1987.

13. Reuters, May 9, 1988.
14. From April 1988 on, Soviet newspapers carried a good many letters by readers who proposed significant changes in the Soviet political system. See, for instance, *Sovetskaia kultura*, April 9 and April 30, 1988; and *Pravda*, May 2 and May 8, 1988.

PAPER 41:

1. AS 6171, pp. 8-9.
2. *Russkaia mysl*, September 18, 1987, p. 2.
3. AS 6089; Ukrainian Press Agency, News Release, No. 6 (October 8), 1987, and No. 9 (October 15), 1987.
4. Reuters, December 8, 1987.
5. AS 6172, p.5.
6. AS 6172, pp. 7-10. The proposals were also published in the samizdat journal *Referendum* edited by Lev Timofeev. See "Reshenie etikh problem otkladyvat nekuda," *Russkaia mysl*, March 11, 1988, p. 4.
7. Pavlo Skochok, "Ukrainskaia sleza na armianskuiu ranu," *Russkaia mysl*, April 15, 1988, p. 5.
8. I. Dmytrenko, "Choho prahnete 'panove'?" *Radianska Ukraina*, May 13, 1988, p. 3.

PAPER 42:

1. UPI and AP, both January 19, 1988.
2. See Polish Situation Report/2, *RFER*, February 10, 1987, item 5.
3. For a comprehensive overview see *From Below: Independent Peace and Human Rights Movements in Eastern Europe and the USSR. A Helsinki Watch Report,* (New York: US Helsinki Watch Committee, 1987).
4. See "Hungarian Catholics and Conscientious Objection," *Religion in Communist Lands*, Keston College, Spring 1987, pp. 96-99.
5. AP, January 14, 1988.
6. See Bulgarian SR/10, *RFER*, November 4, 1987, item 1.
7. See Polish Independent Press Review/3, *RFER*, April 13, 1987, items 1, 2, and 3.
8. Quoted in *From Below: Independent Peace...*, op. cit., p. 57.
9. *The New York Times*, August 15, 1987.
10. See Evangelischer Pressedienst (epd), September 21, 1987.
11. UPI, January 19, 1988.
12. AP, January 19, 1988.

PAPER 43:

1. *Élet Egy Eszme Árnyékában* [Life in the Shadow of an Idea], (Vienna: Zoltán Zsille, 1985), also published as *Im Schatten Einer Idee* (Zürich: Amman Verlag, 1986).
2. On what was, in effect, a drastic economic austerity program, see Hungarian Situation Report/7, *RFER*, July 22, 1987, item 3. On the Hegedüs interview, see AP (Budapest), August 29, 1987.
3. See Hungarian SR/3, *RFER*, April 3, 1987, item 2.
4. In 1984 Hegedüs said that a pluralistic society in Eastern Europe was inevitable, even if it was slow in coming; see his interview in *Corriere della Sera*, July 26, 1984. At the same time, he knew only too well that the maintenance of the one-party system remained an unshakable dogma of the HSWP. In a later interview (ibid., November 4, 1986), he noted a deepening gap between Hungary's pluralistic aspirations and the monolithic communist political system.
5. Reports of the Lakitelek meeting have reached the West. Since the texts of the speeches were not available at the time of writing, however, no direct quotations have been used in this text.
6. See Hungarian Situation Report/11, *RFER*, October 3, 1987, item 4.
7. "Walking Around a 14-line Poem," *Kritika*, October 1987, pp. 13-16.
8. Pozsgay had already briefly but favorably mentioned the meeting in an interview in the October 24, 1987, issue of the economic weekly *Heti Világgazdaság*. In the words of *Magyar Nemzet* interviewer Tóth, "Western radio [stations] have spoken about it as the Hungarian Democratic Forum."
9. AFP (Budapest), March 15 and 16, 1988; AP (Budapest), March 15 and 16, 1988; *Die Welt*, March 17, 1988; and *Die Presse*, March 17, 1988.
10. For additional details, see Hungarian Situation Report/4, *RFER*, March 30, 1988, item 7.
11. *Figyelő*, May 12, 1988; *Heti Világgazdaság*, May 14, 1988; Radio Budapest, May 14, 1988, 6:00 P.M.; *The New York Times*, May 16, 1988.
12. Radio Budapest, May 14, 1988, 6:00 P.M.; *Heti Világgazdaság*, May 14, 1988.
13. Radio Budapest, May 14, 1988, 6:00 P.M.; Reuters (Budapest), May 14, 1988.
14. *Heti Világgazdaság*, May 14, 1988.
15. Radio Budapest, May 14, 1988, 6:00 P.M., and May 18, 1988, 6:30 P.M.
16. Ibid.; Reuters (Budapest), May 14, 1988; *The Independent*, May 16, 1988.
17. *Magyar Hírlap*, April 9, 1988.
18. Reuters (Vienna), May 7, 1988.
19. Radio Budapest, May 7, 1988, 4:00 P.M.
20. *Magyar Nemzet*, April 26, 1988.
21. Reuters (Budapest), May 2, 1988.

PAPER 44:

1. Radio Budapest, July 3, 1987, 11:00 P.M.; and MTI (in English), July 4, 1987.

The party daily *Népszabadság* and all other Hungarian papers published the statement on July 4.
2. *Heti Világgazdaság*, June 27, 1987.
3. Reuters, July 3, 1987.
4. Radio Budapest, July 19, 1987, 6:30 P.M.
5. Hungarian Situation Report/5, *RFER*, June 15, 1987, item 4.
6. Radio Budapest, June 10, 1987, 6:30 P.M.
7. *Business Eastern Europe*, June 15, 1987.
8. *East European Markets*, a supplement to the *Financial Times*, May 29, 1987.
9. *International Herald Tribune*, June 1, 1987.
10. *Figyelő*, June 18, 1987.
11. See Hungarian Situation Report/11, *RFER*, October 31, 1986, item 9.
12. Radio Budapest, March 12, 1987, noon.
13. *Esti Hírlap*, July 21, 1987.
14. Radio Budapest, May 8, 1987, 18:30 P.M.
15. *Népszabadság*, April 14, 1987.
16. *Heti Világgazdaság*, July 25, 1987.
17. *Heti Világgazdaság*, July 25, 1987.
18. Ibid.
19. *Népszabadság*, September 21, 1987.
20. Radio Budapest, September 18, 1987, 9:00 A.M; *Magyar Hírlap*, September 19, 1987.
21. Radio Budapest, September 18, 1987, 4:00 P.M. *Magyar Nemzet* published the full text of the two tax laws in a special edition on September 24, 1987.

## PAPER 45:

1. For an overall review of the party debates, see *Népszabadság* and *Magyar Hírlap*, April 25, 1988, and MTI in English, April 24, 1988; also dpa (Budapest), April 26, 1988. On April 25 all county dailies published detailed accounts of the various county party committee meetings of April 23. For details of the draft document itself, see Hungarian Situation Report/5, *RFER*, May 2, 1988, item 1.
2. Radio Budapest, April 23, 1988, noon and 6:30 P.M. The program also reported on the county party committee meetings in Baranya, Komárom, Borsod, and Szabolcs-Szatmár counties.
3. Ibid.
4. Ibid., "168 Hours," April 23, 1988, 4:00 P.M. For interviews with KISZ First Secretary and HSWP Politburo member Csaba Hámori, see ibid., "168 Hours," April 30, 1988, 4:00 P.M.
5. Ibid., "168 Hours," April 30, 1988, 4:00 P.M.For an interview with Pozsgay, see ibid., April 22, 1988, 6:30 P.M.
6. Ibid., April 23, 1988, noon and 4:00 P.M; also *Heti Világgazdaság*, April 30, 1988.
7. Ibid., April 25, 1988, 5:15 P.M.
8. Ibid., April 27, 1988, 6:30 P.M.; and *Magyar Hírlap*, April 28, 1988. One journalist watching Grósz in Zala County observed that the Prime Minister acted like

a man who had "a revolver pointed at his head." See also the interview with György Fejti in *Magyar Hírlap*, April 30, 1988.

### PAPER 46:

1. For the text of Kádár's speech of May 22, see *Népszabadság*, May 23, 1988.
2. For a detailed study of Grósz's career, see Alfred Reisch, "An HSWP Politburo Member Wanted To Leave the Party in 1955-1956," RAD Background Report/158 (Hungary), *RFER*, November 5, 1986.
3. For two detailed reports on Pozsgay's career and views on reform, see Hungarian Situation Report/13, *RFER*, November 28, 1987, items 4 and 5, and Hungarian SR/5, May 2, 1988, item 2.
4. Radio Budapest, May 22, 1988, 10:00 P.M.; also *Népszabadság*, May 23, 1988.
5. Radio Budapest, May 22, 1988, 8:45 P.M.; also *Népszabadság*, May 22, 1988.
6. For an examination of the draft HSWP policy statement and the debate that preceded the conference, see Hungarian Situation Reports/5 and 6, *RFER*, May 2, 1988, and May 19, 1988, item 1 and 1, respectively.
7. For Pozsgay's reaction to the draft document, see ibid., item 2. See also the interview with Pozsgay on the need for an open dialogue between society's autonomous organizations and the holders of power on Radio Budapest, May 29, 1988, 8:05 A.M. (The interview was on May 21, before Pozsgay was elected to the HSWP Politburo).

### PAPER 48:

1. *Večernji List* (Zagreb), August 29, 1987.
2. *Politika*, September 6, 1987.
3. Ibid., August 25, 1987.
4. *Večernje Novosti* (Belgrade), September 13, 1987.
5. *NIN* (Belgrade), September 6, 1987.
6. *Večernje Novosti*, September 12, 1987.
7. *Ekonomska Politika* (Belgrade), September 7, 1987.
8. *Mladina* (Ljubljana), September 11, 1987.
9. *Delo* (Ljubljana), November 5, 1987.
10. *Duga* (Belgrade), October 17-31, 1987.
11. See Yugoslav Situation Report/12, *RFER*, December 18, 1987, items 6 and 7.
12. *Borba* (Belgrade), December 5-6, 1987.
13. Tanjug, December 26, 1987; *Večernje Novosti* (Belgrade), December 27, 1987.
14. *Borba*, January 5, 1988.
15. Hamdija Pozderac died of a stroke on April 6, 1988. Abdić, Hakija Pozderac and 25 codefendants implicated in the scandal were being tried from May 5, 1988. Verdicts were expected for late October 1988.

## PAPER 49:

1. There were, of course, some private savings on which the authorities could draw; but they were not sufficient to finance the high rate of Yugoslav investment, which was about 30 percent of the gross material product.
2. A charge on capital would be an obvious solution to this problem, but that would require a fully fledged capital market complete with a "capitalist" in some form to whom the charges would accrue. This would have been too much to accept, even for the relatively unorthodox Yugoslav Communists.
3. Yugoslavia was the only communist country that had tolerated open unemployment since the early nineteen-fifties (after it abandoned the orthodox, Soviet-type economic model).
4. Although such an outcome was inevitable, the accusation that managers and technicians had arrogated to themselves the function of management had, nevertheless, been rife in Yugoslavia.

## PAPER 50:

1. Radio Zagreb, May 31, 1988; Tanjug, June 1, 1988.
2. *Novosti 8* (Belgrade), March 10, 1988.
3. Politika (Belgrade), June 1, 1988.
4. *Renovica* denied the reported allegations, saying that "They were obviously trying to discredit me politically." *Borba* (Belgrade), June 2, 1988.
5. *Vjesnik* (Zagreb), May 30, 1988.
6. *Borba*, June 1, 1988. Hrabar's term as President of the Confederation of Trade Unions expired, and Marjan Orozen, a Slovene, was elected his successor on June 2.
7. *Večernje Novosti* (Belgrade), May 31, 1988.

## PAPER 51:

1. *Delo* (Ljubljana), June 28, 1988; *Vjesnik* (Zagreb), June 28, 1988. Several independent associations, such as a farmers' federation and the noncommunist Association of Slovene Intellectuals, were formed as affiliates within the Slovenian Socialist Alliance, the party's umbrella organization.
2. See Yugoslav Situation Report/3, *RFER*, May 2, 1988, item 4; and Yugoslav Situation Report/5, June 7, 1988, item 5.
3. *Mladina* (Ljubljana), March 18, 1988, no. 11.
4. *Vjesnik*, May 21, 1988.
5. *Politika Ekspres* (Belgrade), May 23, 1988.
6. *Mladina*, June 24, 1988, no. 25.
7. Ibid., June 17, 1988, no. 24, and June 24, 1988, no. 25.
8. Ibid., June 24, 1988, no. 25, p. 25.
9. Ibid., June 27, 1988, no. 24.
10. *Vjesnik*, June 17 and 23, 1988.

11. *Mladina*, June 24, 1988, no. 25.
12. *Delo*, June 18, 1988.

## PAPER 53:

1. RFE Correspondent's Report (Bonn), June 2, 1987.
2. BTA (Sofia), June 2, 1987.
3. *Rabotnichesko Delo,* June 4, 1987.
4. ATA, September 16, 1987; and various news agencies, September 15, 1987.
5. ATA, June 1, 1988.
6. See E. Kautsky, *Bonn and Moscow: At The Threshold of a New Era?*, RAD Background Report/1 (East-West Relations), *RFER*, January 8, 1988.
7. AP and UPI, January 12, 1988.
8. Radio Warsaw, January 12, 1988, 11:00 P.M.
9. RFE Correspondent's Report (Washington), January 21, 1988.
10. RFE Correspondent's Report (Prague), January 26, 1988. The completion of the Main-Danube canal in the early nineteen-nineties would give this waterway considerable economic importance and provide the first water link between the North and Black Seas.
11. AP, January 26, 1988.
12. RFE Correspondent's Report (Prague), January 27, 1988.
13. Ibid.

## PAPER 54:

1. See West German government spokesman Friedhelm Ost's press conference of October 2 as reported in *Népszabadság*, October 3, 1987, and AFP (Bonn), October 5, 1987; also see *Frankfurter Allgemeine Zeitung*, October 6, 1987, and *Magyar Nemzet*, October 7, 1987.
2. *Népszabadság*, October 8, 1987.
3. *Magyar Hírlap*, October 8, 1987.
4. RFE correspondent's report (Bonn), October 8, 1987; and *Népszabadság*, October 9, 1987.
5. Radio Budapest, October 9, 1987, 6:30 P.M.; and *Népszabadság, Népszava*, and *Magyar Hírlap*, October 10, 1987.
6. Dpa, July 22, 1987; *Népszabadság* and *Magyar Hírlap*, July 23, 1987. On Hungarian-West German relations in general, see *Magyarország*, October 2, 1987, p. 4, and *Tolna Megyei Népújság*, October 1, 1987.
7. Dpa, August 12, 1987; *Financial Times*, August 14, 1987. At the time of writing, Bonn's only cultural institute in Eastern Europe was in Bucharest; it was still trying to open institutes in Warsaw and Prague, while Bulgaria had agreed to allow one in Sofia.
8. See *Neue Zürcher Zeitung* and *Süddeutsche Zeitung*, October 18, 1986.

9. Radio Budapest, October 7, 1987, 6:30 P.M.
10. On this and West German tourism in general to Hungary, see *Heti Világgazdaság*, October 10, 1987.
11. See *Die Welt* and *Süddeutsche Zeitung*, July 3, 1987; *Die Welt* and *Münchner Merkur*, July 31, 1987; *Frankfurter Allgemeine Zeitung*, July 22, 1987.
12. *Frankfurter Rundschau*, October 7, 1987.
13. See Deputy Foreign Minister Lászlo Kovács's statement in *Magyar Hírlap*, October 10, 1987; *Magyar Hírlap*, *Népszabadság*, and *Népszava*, October 12, 1987.

## PAPER 55:

1. *Süddeutsche Zeitung*, September 10, 1987.
2. *Materialien zum Bericht über die Lage der Nation* (Bonn: Bundesministerium für Inner-deutsche Beziehungen, 1987), p. 630.
3. *Bulletin* (Presse- und Infomationsamt der Bundesregierung), August 27, 1987. Trade turnover first dropped by 9 percent in 1986, from DM 16,700 million to DM 15,200 million (*Bulletin*, March 5, 1987). The fall could largely be attributed to the drop in world oil prices.
4. See Josef Joffe, "The View from Bonn: The Tacit Alliance" in Lincoln Gordon, ed., *Eroding Empire: Western Relations with Eastern Europe* (Washington, D.C: Brookings Institute, 1987) pp. 153-159.
5. *Materialien*, p. 630.
6. Ibid., p. 631.
7. In 1986 East German purchases of capital goods from the GDR increased by 28 percent (*DIW Wochenbericht*, [Deutsches Institut für Wirtschaftsforschung], no. 11, 1987).
8. Reuters, January 22, 1987.
9. *DIW Wochenbericht*, no. 11, 1987.
10. See John Garland, "FRG-GDR Economic Relations," *East European Economies: Slow Growth in the 1980s* (Selected Papers Submitted to the Joint Economic Committee,Congress of the USA, 1986); Jeffrey Michel, "Economic Exchanges Specific to the Two German States," *Studies in Comparative Communism*, Spring 1987; *Frankfurter Allgemeine Zeitung*, July 8, 1987.
11. *Materialien*, p. 633.
12. From the middle of 1982 to the middle of 1983, imports from the OECD countries fell by $520 million while imports from the FRG rose by DM 1,700 million. Both developments were temporary. See Karl-Heinz Gross, "Inter-German Economic Relations," in "The GDR's Economy at the End of the Five-Year Plan; Part Two," *FS Analysen*, (Forschungstelle für Gesamtdeutsche Wirtschaftliche und Soziale Fragen), no 5, 1985.
13. See Horst Lambrecht, Cord Schwartau, "Stimulating Inter-German Trade through Special Programs," *Deutschland-Archiv*, no. 5, 1987; For the texts of the three accords signed, see *Bulletin*, September 10, 1987.
14. See Jan Vanous, "The GDR Within the CMEA," *Comparative Economic Studies*, Summer 1987; also John Garland, ed., "The GDR's Quest for Growth and Modern-

ization Through 'Intensification,'" *Studies in Comparative Communism*, Spring 1987.

15. See Peter Ploetz, "The GDR's Economic Relations with the Western Industrial Countries," in *FS Analysen*, no. 5, 1985, p. 88; In 1978 the GDR's trade with the FRG accounted for 36.2 percent of its trade with the West and in 1985 for 28.3 percent (*Statistisches Jahrbuch der DDR 1986* [East Berlin: Staatsverlag, 1986], pp. 240-241).

## PAPER 56:

1. See *Frankfurter Allgemeine Zeitung*, October 9 and 13, 1987.
2. The group was reported to have consisted of Georgii Arbatov, Valentin Falin, Nikolai Portugalov, and Daniil Melnikov.
3. *Frankfurter Allgemeine Zeitung*, October 24, 1987.
4. Falin was interviewed on the West German television program "Kennzeichen D." See *Frankfurter Allgemeine Zeitung* and *Süddeutsche Zeitung*, October 1, 1987.
5. AP, October 5, 1987.
6. *Frankfurter Allgemeine Zeitung*, October 10, 1987.
7. TASS, October 14, 1987.
8. *Frankfurter Allgemeine Zeitung*, October 1, 1987.
9. AP, October 25, 1987.
10. See his interview in *Neues Deutschland*, September 29, 1987.
11. Ibid., October 9, 1987.
12. See the interview with Friedrich Wilhelm Christians in *Der Spiegel*, February 23, 1987.
13. See Genscher's speech in Davos in February 1987 (*Bulletin*, no. 13, February 4, 1987), as well as his speech in Minneapolis, Minnesota, as summarized in *Frankfurter Allgemeine Zeitung*, October 10, 1987.
14. *Frankfurter Allgemeine Zeitung*, December 30, 1987.
15. See Mikhail Gorbachev, *Perestroika* (New York: Harper & Row, 1987), pp. 199-201.
16. For the text of Honecker's see letter *Frankfurter Rundschau*, January 6, 1987.

## PAPER 59:

1. AP, June 28, 1988.
2. *The Wall Street Journal*, June 27, 1988.

## PAPER 60:

1. *Pravda*, July 1, 1988.
2. *Narkhoz za 70 let*, 1987, p. 382.
3. First, in the course of the discussion on July 1; second, in his closing statement.

4. APN, July 2, 1988; see also *Argumenty i fakty*, No 26, 1988.
5. *Argumenty i fakty*, No. 26, 1988.
6. Central Television, July 5, 1988.
7. *Pravda*, July 5, 1988.
8. Radio Moscow-1, July 2, 1988.
9. *Pravda*, July 1, 1988.
10. Central Television, June 26, 1988.

### PAPER 61:

1. BTA (in English), June 30, and July 1, 1988; and *Rabotnichesko Delo*, July 4, 1988.
2. See "Can Todor Zhivkov Survive?" in the Bulgarian Situation Report/6, *RFER*; and Michael Shafir, "East European Leaders' Stance on Reforms as the CPSU Conference Opens," RAD Background Report/121 (Eastern Europe), *RFER*, June 29, 1988.
3. BTA (in English) July 1, 1988; TASS (in English), July 3, 1988; PAP (in English) June 28, 1988, quoting government spokesman Jerzy Urban; PAP (in English), July 3, 1988, quoting PUPW Politburo member and CC Secretary Józef Czyrek.
4. PAP (in English), July 3, 1988; Reuters, July 2, 1988; AP, July 1, 1988; TASS, July 7, 1988 and Tanjug (in English), July 9, 1988; PAP (in English), July 7, 1988.
5. AP, July 3, 1988; and Reuters, July 1, 1988.
6. Soviet Television, July 3, 1988, 7:00 P.M.; MTI (in English), July 2, 1988.
7. AP, Radio Moscow 1 and *The New York Times*, July 1, 1988; Reuters, UPI, AP, and DPA, July 7, 1988; Radio Prague, July 8, 1988.
8. *Neues Deutschland*, July 2, 1988; Dpa, July 7, 1988; ADN, July 8, 1988.
9. *Scînteia*, July 2, 1988 and June 30, 1988, respectively.
10. Tanjug (in English), July 2, 1988; and AP, July 3, 1988.
11. Xinhua (in English), July 2, 1988.

# INDEX

Abdić, Fikret, former head of Executive Board of Agrokomerc enterprise and member of Federal Chamber of Yugoslav National Assembly, 281-283

Abdulov, Aleksandr, actor in Lenin Komsomol Theater, 73

Ablaeva, Elvira, Crimean Tatar spokeswoman, 158, 160

Academy of Sciences of the USSR (AS USSR): civilian defense intellectuals, 46; United States and Canada Institute, 46; Institute for World Economy and International Relations, 46; Institute of the Economics of the World Socialist System, 112, 115; TsEMI, 115; Institute of Russian Literature (Pushkin House), 150

Aczél, György, Hungarian CC member, 277

Adamkiewicz, Marek, Pole imprisoned for refusal to take military oath, 242

Adamovich, Ales, Soviet writer, 79, 336

Afanasev, Iurii, director of Moscow Institute of Historical Archives, 80, 83-84, 360(n21)

Afghanistan, Democratic Republic of: and withdrawal of Soviet troops, 3, 26, 60, 64; number of Soviet troops in, 3; Islam in USSR and war, 8, 180; Soviet public opinion toward war, 60-64; military aspects of war, 60-61; mujahiddin, 61; Soviet media and war, 61-62; Soviet historical debates and war, 84

Aganbegian, Abel, Soviet economist, 98, 103, 123-126, 332, 364(n5)

Airikian, Paruir, Armenian dissident, 169-170, 238

Akhmadulina, Bella, Soviet poet, 74

Akhmatova, Anna, Soviet poet, 77

Akhromeev, Marshal Sergei, chief of Soviet General Staff, 39

Aksenov, Vasilii, Soviet émigré writer, 118

Albania, People's Socialist Republic of: and Kosovo issue, 11, 72, 226; and FRG, 12, 303- 306; and Balkan foreign ministers' conference, 69, 71-72; and Romania, 69, 71; and United Nations, 71; and Greece, 71, 305-306; and Yugoslavia, 71-72; and Committees of Balkan Understanding, 71-72; and USSR, 116, 305; and PRC, 303-304; Albanian-West German agreement on economic, industrial, and technical cooperation, 305; and USSR, 305; and Spain, Australia, Philippines, Jordan, Canada, Burundi, and Bolivia, 305; and Ireland, 305- 306; and United Kingdom, 305-306

Albrecht, Ernst, prime minister of Lower Saxony, 302, 314

Alekseev, Mikhail, Soviet writer, 76

Aleksii, former Patriarch of Russian Orthodox Church, 189

Aleksii, Metropolitan of Leningrad and Novgorod, 183, 185

Alia, Ramiz, general secretary of Albanian Communist party, 304-306

Aliev, Geidar, former first secretary of Azerbaijani Communist party, 21, 171

Alexander II, Russian tsar, 87

Ambartsumian, Viktor, president of Armenian Academy of Sciences, 166

Ananev, author of article published in *Oktiabr*, 96

Andreeva, Nina, Leningrad school teacher and author of conservative "manifesto" published in *Sovetskaia Rossiia*, 26-27, 30-31, 352(n3)

Andropov, Iurii, former Soviet general secretary, 30